G000254931

AROUND THE WORLD WITH
YEOVIL TOWN

IT'S SUMMIT I CAN'T MISS

EVEREST
Going up . . Mike on Everest

YEOVIL TOWN
Going nowhere . . at Yeovil

By JOHN COLES

SOCCER-mad explorer Michael Bromfield made a six-day trek home from Mount Everest for a game — only to see his beloved Yeovil Town LOSE.

Michael, 55, was 17,460ft up the world's highest mountain when he decided he couldn't miss Yeovil's bid to get into the play-offs.

So he left his expedition party and began the 4,700-mile trip home by hiking for three days alone through blizzards to a remote mountain airstrip.

There he managed to bag a seat on a plane which flew him to Kathmandu, capital of Nepal.

Determined Michael then stumped up a £350 surcharge to get on a fully-booked flight to London. It landed at Heathrow at 7am on the day of the game

Fan quits Everest to see Yeovil

and his wife Sharron then drove him to Yeovil's Huish Park ground. He arrived in Somerset just in time for the Division 3 game — then saw Yeovil lose 2-1 to Hull, dashing their hopes of getting into the promotion frame.

Dad-of-three Michael said yesterday: "The result was disappointing — but I have no regrets

and would do it all again tomorrow if I had to. My friends and colleagues who I left up the mountain thought I was mad but I knew I had to be there."

Michael — who is a Yeovil season-ticket holder — runs his own specialist travel firm in Sherborne, Dorset.

He had organised a three-week trip for clients who wanted to climb to the base camp of 29,029ft Everest.

His party had just arrived at the camp when he decided he had to go home.

Michael — who is now leading another expedition in Switzerland — said: "I had been following Yeovil's results on the internet and the satellite phone.

"When I realised the Hull game was the crunch match I knew I couldn't miss it.

"Football fans will understand my reasoning and motivation."

A Yeovil Town spokesman said: "He must have been gutted to see us lose out — but it shows a wonderful commitment."

YEOVIL, ENGLAND		MT EVEREST, NEPAL
HEIGHT: 220h	Michael sets out on Monday and hikes for three days through blizzards. He reaches tiny airstrip at Kukla on Thursday. Bags a seat on plane to fly him 90 miles south west to Kathmandu on Friday.	**HEIGHT:** 29,029h
POPULATION: 38,000.		**POPULATION:** No residents, only climbers possibly the odd yeti.
WEATHER: Mild winters, 17°C yesterday but cloudy.		**WEATHER:** Winds up to 150mph can send temperature to −40°C.
ATTRACTIONS: Pleasant market town. Highlights include the Fleet Air Arm Museum and the Yeovil Alpine Village for locals who can't get to Everest.	Eight hour 4,700-mile trip home. Wife picks him up from Heathrow and drives him to Somerset.	**ATTRACTIONS:** Greatest peak on earth, dubbed the 'Roof of the World' and the ultimate challenge for climbers.

4,700 miles

MAD IDEA: Mike at Yeovil FC and, right, at Everest base camp

FOOL ON THE HILL

He ditches Everest bid to watch Yeovil ... LOSE

CLIMBER Michael Bromfield quit Mount Everest to trek 4,700-mile to watch his beloved Yeovil Town in a crucial game — and they lost.

The adventurer was 17,460ft up the world's tallest mountain when he realised his team had to win their last home game of the season to have a chance of promotion.

So he set off on a six-day journey from Everest base camp to see the Division Three game with Hull City.

Storms

Dad-of-three Michael, 55, spent nearly three days hiking through Himalayan passes in blizzards and snow storms.

He reached a mountain airstrip at Kukla where he managed to bag a place on a 16-seater plane.

The 90-mile flight took him to Kathmandu in Nepal where he paid a £350 surcharge to get on a fully-booked plane to London.

After an eight-hour flight he touched down in the UK at 7am on the morning of the game.

His wife Sharron drove Michael from Heathrow to Somerset.

He arrived at Yeovil's Huish Park just in time to watch the Glovers lose 2-1.

■ by MATT JOHN

Michael said afterwards: "The result was disappointing.

"Hull's second goal cost us the play-off place.

"My friends and colleagues who I left up the mountain thought I was mad but I had to be there.

"I've got no regrets and would do it all over again

COMEDOWN: Mike saw his Yeovil blow it

tomorrow if I had to."

Michael, who runs holiday firm Casterbridge Tours based in Sherborne, Dorset, had travelled to Kathmandu with clients three weeks before.

A spokesman for Yeovil Town FC said: "Michael has shown wonderful support for the club to come such a long way."

Press cuttings from *The Sun* (left) and the *Daily Star* reporting on author Michael Bromfield's trip back from Everest to Huish Park in spring 2004.

AROUND THE WORLD WITH
YEOVIL TOWN

MICHAEL BROMFIELD

TEMPUS

First published 2005

Tempus Publishing Limited
The Mill, Brimscombe Port,
Stroud, Gloucestershire, GL5 2QG
www.tempus-publishing.com

© Michael Bromfield, 2005

The right of Michael Bromfield to be identified as the Author
of this work has been asserted in accordance with the
Copyrights, Designs and Patents Act 1988.

All rights reserved. No part of this book may be reprinted
or reproduced or utilised in any form or by any electronic,
mechanical or other means, now known or hereafter invented,
including photocopying and recording, or in any information
storage or retrieval system, without the permission in writing
from the Publishers.

British Library Cataloguing in Publication Data.
A catalogue record for this book is available from the British Library.

ISBN 0 7524 3735 6

Typesetting and origination by Tempus Publishing Limited.
Printed in Great Britain.

*This book is dedicated to four women – only the eldest of whom
has much interest in football!*

*First and foremost to my wife Sharron, who has had to put up
with so much.*

To my friend Ampai, who fleetingly appears in these pages.

*To my former P.A. for nine years Wendy, without whose assistance
this book would never have been completed but who could not
survive the demands of this book nor my personal life.*

*To my mother, who encouraged me in my youth and
consequently enabled my dreams of travel to turn into reality.*

*Also to John Fry, Gary Johnson, Steve Thompson, the players and
everyone at Yeovil Town, with congratulations and gratitude for
everything you have achieved and delivered to both Yeovil fans
and the local community in recent years.*

Michael Bromfield

Michael Bromfield was born and grew up in Bournemouth and after failing his eleven-plus went on to obtain degrees in Geography from University College London and Soviet Foreign Policy from the School of Slavonic Studies. He subsequently spent six years travelling in Asia and the Pacific and teaching in Australia.

After returning to England in 1979 Michael and his wife Sharron turned their enthusiasm and love of travel into a business and founded Casterbridge Tours, a special interest and educational travel company and now one of Britain's leading tour operators. Michael is currently the chairman of Casterbridge Tours, one of only a handful of travel companies to be awarded the Queen's Award for Enterprise.

Michael has an abiding love of the high mountains and each year leads a number of treks for Great Walks of the World, a division of Casterbridge Tours. He has a passion for and is a keen spectator of most sports. He has completed a 'Sprint' Triathlon in 2 hours and the London Marathon in 3 hours 36 minutes, still occasionally plays six-a-side football and describes playing tennis as one of the loves of his life.

His many interests include rock music, opera and the cinema, collecting art deco sculpture, graphic design and photography. Michael undertakes a number of travel lectures and rock and roll quizzes each year.

Michael and his Canadian wife Sharron have lived on the Somerset-Dorset border for twenty-six years and have three children, Sarah (twenty-one), Lisa (nineteen) and David (seventeen). As this book will testify, Michael is a compulsive traveller who has travelled extensively through six continents. Michael currently divides his time between travelling for business and pleasure and his homes in Somerset, the Swiss Alps and Canada.

He is an avid reader of all genres with a particular interest in biographies, mountaineering and sports literature. Michael, who is fifty-six, has been writing throughout his life but this is his first book.

Michael can always be contacted on mibct49@hotmail.com

Contents

Foreword by Gary Johnson

Whatever the future holds, my time with Yeovil is destined to be one of the highlights of my career in football – it could be no other way.

I spent over four years with Yeovil and it was a great time for all of us – management, players and fans as we journeyed from the Conference to League One. The community, fans, players and management all came together in a way that is rarely seen in football and I was proud to be given the opportunity to participate in the success that we shared.

I know there was disappointment when I decided that it was time to move on to a new challenge but I hope the fans will appreciate I was never less than 100 per cent devoted to the tasks I set myself at Yeovil and I feel I delivered and played my part in the success that we all enjoyed.

I will always treasure and look back on my tenure at Yeovil with fond memories of my time with the club. There were many highlights but, above all, I will always remember the commitment of my backroom staff and players and the tremendous loyalty and support we got from the Yeovil fans.

When I came to Yeovil the support was outstanding for a non-League club and it continued throughout my stay as we took tremendous support to venues such as Villa Park for the FA Trophy and also our first Football League game at Rochdale. It was the same during our momentous championship-winning season when we enjoyed fantastic support that was a very real 'extra man' for the club when we won away at championship rivals Swansea and Southend.

Yeovil has always been blessed with tremendous supporters and I feel privileged to have enjoyed a special relationship with them through my stay at Yeovil. Football by its nature is full of many characters and the opportunity to meet so many fascinating individuals has always been an important ingredient of my love and passion for the beautiful game. This book is written by an individual who is both a tremendous supporter of Yeovil Town and also a real character. His account of both his passion and our season make an entertaining read and there are plenty of amusing tales along the way!

We all have our own memories of last season and I saw it from one viewpoint just as every fan will remember it from their own perspective. However, even by the standards of the many eccentric and enthusiastic characters who are involved in football, Michael Bromfield's story will take some beating as there are not too many who come back from Everest to follow their team and Michael has done this not once but twice, as well as returning from a wide variety of destinations and interesting situations to watch Yeovil play. His passion and enthusiasm for Yeovil comes through on every page and his escapades as he balances his business, personal life and passion for Yeovil make for both a fascinating and amusing read.

This book has reminded me that just as the fortunes of a football team will dominate the life of every manager it can also dominate the life of so many fans day-in day-out throughout the year.

I am also reminded there that there are thousands who follow Yeovil's progress from 'around the world' and with no less commitment than those inside the ground so I guess that is a bit more responsibility on the manager's shoulders!

Around the World with Yeovil Town provides a complete record of our championship season but observed from a unique vantage. It is because of characters like Michael and supporters like those that follow Yeovil that football is such a unique game.

Just as it is so for Michael and thousands of others who support Yeovil, from both near and afar, Yeovil will always hold a special place in my heart and I will always follow the club and its progress with the greatest of interest and affection.

Meanwhile, enjoy the read!

Gary Johnson

Introduction

Although I did not realise it at the time, the idea for this book was conceived at Everest Base Camp, about 11,000 feet below the summit of the world's highest peak.

It was Sunday 25 April 2004 and about ten of us were huddled up in the mess tent of the Irish expedition that was attempting to climb Everest. I should hasten to add that I was very definitely not attempting Everest! I had not even been planning to stay overnight at the base camp area and had only spent three hours or so walking up four miles of the Khumbu glacier between the towering peaks of Nuptse and Pumori to make a brief visit. I had made slow but steady progress towards the magnificent amphitheatre that dominates the head of the Khumbu valley. Indeed, the West Shoulder of Everest, Khumbutse and Lingtren, together with the beautiful summit of Changtse a few miles further away in Tibet form one of the most spectacular mountain vistas in the world and drew me ever onwards.

I had been staying at the nearest 'settlement' of Gorak Shep where two shelters provide rudimentary accommodation for trekkers who aspire to walk to the foot of Everest as well as a last staging post for climbers before they set up their base camp on the glacier at the foot of the Khumbu icefall. This was my second visit to this area and I had decided to walk up to the base camp because Pemba, one of my Nepalese friends, was the *sirdar* (climbing leader) of the Sherpa support team assisting the Irish expedition, led by Pat Falvey, attempting to climb Everest. As the owner of one of Britain's leading trekking companies, I also knew a few other people who were either attempting or assisting with attempts on Everest itself. Although we had not met previously, Pat Falvey, with typical Irish exuberance and hospitality, insisted I stayed overnight as his guest. Pemba organised the erecting of a spare tent and a mattress and sleeping bag quickly appeared so clearly I had no choice but to stay!

It was cold, indeed very cold, probably at least fifteen degrees below freezing. Incongruously, thanks to solar power, ten of us were watching a Billy Connolly DVD on a laptop! Although the Sherpas were laughing, it wasn't one of the Big Yin's better performances and my mind was wandering... about 5,000 miles eastwards to Yeovil Town Football Club.

At Gorak Shep I had called home on my satellite phone to learn that Yeovil had beaten Southend 2-0 at Roots Hall courtesy of two Dani Rodrigues goals. We were still seventh in the table, which meant that, despite our faltering form since Christmas, we were on course to secure the final play-off spot in the first Football League season for a club that had for so long rejoiced in the description of 'England's best-known non-league club'. That was a title we had been pleased to jettison after finally securing promotion to the Football League in April 2003!

Former Conference rivals Doncaster Rovers may have outperformed us in our first Football League season but we could still secure promotion via the play-offs. I was planning to be back in England for the final game of the season, away at Lincoln, but it was beginning to look as if we might secure a play-off spot by winning our penultimate game at home to high-flying Hull City.

Billy Connolly isn't as funny as usual when you are sitting on a hundred feet of frozen ice, and my mind was calculating. It was already Sunday evening. Could I get back to England by next Saturday morning? It would mean getting a Friday evening flight out of Kathmandu and flights were always solidly booked in the trekking season. That meant I would need to get to Lukla by Thursday evening to get a Friday morning flight to Kathmandu and Lukla was about thirty-nine miles away. Furthermore the airstrip at Lukla, quite literally carved out of the hillside by Sir Edmund Hillary, is notoriously susceptible to being closed for days on end in the fickle mountain weather.

'I think I'm going to try and get to the game at Yeovil next Saturday,' I announced to a bemused collection of Irish and Nepali climbers and the decision was made. The following day, after looking around base camp and bidding my farewells to a few familiar faces, including one of our trekking guides Sue Todd, who subsequently became the sixth British woman to climb Everest, I made my way past the wrecked Russian helicopter (misjudgements can be costly when flying helicopters at 5,400 metres!) and made my way back to Gorak Shep through miserable weather and snow squalls.

The following morning, Tuesday, was beautiful. I felt good so I walked up the near-by hill of Kala Pattar, an outlying spur of Pumori, for what is one of the classic views of Everest and probably the best-known viewpoint in the Himalaya. I had hiked up Kala Pattar (5,600m/18,360ft) eighteen months earlier but you cannot be so close to one of the finest mountain panoramas in the world with a clear view of the South Col and the summit of Everest and not walk up again. This was not a case of been there, done that and don't want to do it again!

I walked up without any problems, in contrast to the army training group who were finding the altitude hard going, and immersed myself in the magnificent views of Everest and dozens of spectacular peaks for an hour or so. That left me about two and a half days to walk the remaining thirty-five miles to Lukla if I was going to have a chance of watching Yeovil v. Hull City!

I walked as far as Dugla with well-known Chamonix-based mountain guide and award-winning author Victor Saunders, his twenty-two-year-old client, Oliver, and well-known outdoor writer Paul Deegan, who were all attempting Everest. 'We're glad you're with us, Michael. It's nice to have someone along who can outtalk Victor for a while,' said Paul.

Most people thought I was crazy trying to get from Kala Pattar in the remote Himalaya to Yeovil in four days but Paul was an avid Fulham supporter who also remembered Yeovil upsetting Fulham in bygone years: 'It's an important game; of course you should go home to see it.'

Three cheers for the mountain man who understood and did not think I was crazy! Victor, Paul and Oliver were descending to enjoy the thicker air and strengthen their bodies before their final attempt on Everest and I bade farewell to them at the Dugla Tea House with its unsurpassed views of Ama Dablam, for many the most beautiful peak in the Himalaya.

After three long days of walking through unsurpassed scenery, past the monastery at Thyangboche and through a vicious thunder-and-lightning storm, I eventually arrived at Lukla and indeed caught up a Great Walks trekking group and was able to share their farewell 'end of trek' celebration in their hotel at Lukla.

On Friday 30 April 2004 the weather was good and we hurtled down towards the end of the runway, shot off the end above the valley below, thankfully climbed rather

Everest Base Camp and the Khumbu Ice Fall.

than plummeted and, after another hour, were back in Kathmandu to be met by my agent's representative, who advised me that both the overnight flights to London were full! After $300 changed hands a seat materialised and on Saturday morning I was met at Heathrow by my long-suffering Canadian wife, Sharron, who had me home in Stowell by 11 a.m. This left time to have a shower, lunch and get to the game, which was compelling to watch but with the wrong result! Hugo Rodrigues scored his first and only goal for Yeovil but Hull City, with a 2-1 victory on our turf, secured promotion from Division Three and Yeovil's destiny was taken out of our hands to rest on the result of Yeovil's final fixture at Lincoln and the results of our play-off rivals. It was a long way to come for a home defeat! However, at half-time I commented to some of the fans seated around me, 'I bet I've come further for this match than anyone else in the ground.'

'Where've you come from then mate?'

'I was on the slopes of a mountain next to Everest on Tuesday and in Kathmandu yesterday.'

'Cor, bugger me. You're joking? You want to ring up the *Gazette*, they'll be interested in that story.'

Would they? I rang the *Western Gazette* and *Western Daily Press* the following Monday and both expressed interest in it being a colourful local story. I wrote a short press release, cut half a dozen images onto a disc and sent it off, thinking no more about it.

Ten days later, despite a glorious win at Lincoln, we were excluded from the play-offs on goal difference and I was driving across Germany en route to Switzerland when my personal assistant Wendy called me and asked if I had sent the press release to the *Daily Mirror*. 'Of course not,' I replied. 'Why?'

'Because there is a full-page article in today's *Daily Mirror* about your return to Yeovil from Everest!'

Ten minutes later and my mobile rang again as I was driving along the banks of the river Rhine. 'BBC Five Live have just rung up and want to know if you can do a telephone interview about the story that was in today's *Sun*?'

The Sun? BBC Five Live? What was going on? It turned out that some enterprising reporter thought that the story might be of national interest and had marketed it to the national press, and it appeared as a full-page story in *The Sun*, *Daily Mirror*, *Daily Star*, *Daily Express* and *Western Morning News*! The headlines were quite amusing and included: 'Fool on the Hill – He ditches Everest bid to watch Yeovil… Lose' (*Daily Star*); 'It's summit I can't miss' (*The Sun*); 'Soccer nut struggles 4,700 miles home from Everest… to watch his team lose' (*Daily Mirror*); 'Forget Everest, I'm off to the football' (*Western Morning News*).

In truth I felt a bit of a fraud because I was getting more publicity in a day than all those brave souls who put their lives on the line and had climbed Everest that season! It sounded as if I had been actually climbing the mountain not messing around at the bottom!

However, it did not end there as, over the next twenty-four hours, I received requests to be interviewed by BBC Five Live, Talksport Radio, Sky Sports, BBC Leeds and BBC Scotland. I thought BBC Leeds were the most imaginative: 'Michael Bromfield? We've heard about your journey and we wondered if we could interview you on our end-of-season round-up next week. It's all doom and gloom up here. Leeds have been relegated, Huddersfield have missed out on automatic promotion and Bradford are facing receivership. We need a feel-good football story and you're it!'

Ironically, when my company Casterbridge Tours had won Britain's highest commercial honour, The Queen's Award for Enterprise, I had sent out dozens of press releases to little avail but, on this occasion, two brief press releases had resulted in extensive coverage in the national press and six radio and television interviews! And all because of a relatively straightforward, if brisk, hike through the Himalaya and a couple of 'iffy' flights to watch a football match! But the story had obviously caught the media's attention. And the germ of an idea was born. If a simple journey from Everest had aroused so much interest, could the concept be extended to an entire season?

I was planning to spend an eighteen-month period from April 2004 working and travelling overseas and I knew that I was likely to visit some colourful and interesting destinations and would be returning to watch Yeovil whenever possible and, if I was overseas on a match day, I would be following Yeovil by phone or the internet. Perhaps I could write an account of Yeovil's season from afar based on what I was doing on each of Yeovil's match days?

I am the chairman of a special-interest tour operator, employing forty staff divided between our offices in Sherborne and the US. I also own a small property development company, maintain homes in three countries, have three teenage children, am fifty per cent of a marriage that needs urgent attention (I hasten to add that I am responsible for eighty per cent of its failings) and I am renowned for doing and attempting too much. I am a compulsive traveller and lead at least one long-distance trek in the mountains each year for our specialist trekking division, 'Great Walks of the World'. Additionally, three years ago I tried to buy a shareholding in Yeovil Town Football Club.

'Write a book, Michael!? Just when will you have time for that? Why do you always have to be doing something? It's time to be winding down, not starting new projects.'

As always, Sharron might have had a valid point! I spent the summer of 2004 in Switzerland, watching England in Portugal, at our American offices and in Canada and all the time the idea of this book was bubbling away at the back of my mind.

When Yeovil galloped away with the Conference in the 2002/03 season and won by 17 points, I felt reasonably confident our young team would acquit themselves well in what was then Division Three. They might not win the division but I thought they had every chance of making the play-offs and, if they didn't go up in their first season, they surely would the second. 2004/05 was Yeovil's second season in the Football League and now I thought it could go one of two ways. We could either fade into mid-table mediocrity, having overachieved in our first League season, or we would build on the achievements and achieve even more the second time around.

I followed Yeovil's pre season from Canada and, at the end of July, when we won our final pre-season friendly away at League One Torquay, I decided we were likely to have a good season and if I was going to write a book this was the season to do it.

This book, then, is an account of two journeys. Firstly it describes the journey of one of England's best-loved football clubs as Yeovil attempt to launch itself on an ascent through the divisions of English football, and secondly of my own journey through five continents.

The bond between a fan and a football club is nothing unusual and a fan's account of their club's season is nothing new. Indeed, many accounts have been written by fans about their relationship with a particular club and the range of emotions experienced over a season or seasons. So the basic concept of this book is not unique, other than that this particular fan lives, by many people's assessment, a somewhat privileged life. And in this particular season I only got to see fifteen of the fifty-four games my club played as I travelled around the world... but always with Yeovil close to heart! Nevertheless, this is still a complete and comprehensive account of Yeovil's season, but as seen through the eyes of a fan who was often thousands of miles away and always 'up': either up to get the results, up high in the mountains, up for an adventure and just occasionally, as the reader will discover, up to no good as well!

As this is an account of two journeys and of the relationship between a fan and his club, it behoves me to introduce both to the reader.

The Fan

I am of the postwar 'Baby Boom' generation, being born in Bournemouth in 1949. I had no brothers or sisters, which I deeply regret, but I could not contribute to the solving of that particular problem! I shared a bedroom with my parents in my grandmother's small home and my mother insists we were not poor. 'We weren't poor, Michael. You wanted for nothing. It was just a shortage of housing and we had no room for a brother or sister. It wasn't because we couldn't afford one.' All I know is that I certainly thought we were poor because I once fabricated a story about a lost watch so I could go back and dig up potatoes from the school vegetable garden to take home for my parents because I thought we were too poor to buy them!

After we moved I grew up on a council estate. I failed my eleven-plus but eventually transferred to the local grammar school where I sat my 'A' levels. A school trip to Germany in 1963 that cost £10 for seven days gave birth to a lifelong love of travel that has now evolved into owning one of the world's biggest educational tour operators. I now organise tours for students to travel at the most impressionable stage of their lives, just as I did forty years ago. Our company motto is 'Learn to Travel. Travel to Learn' and that says it all as far as I am concerned.

I decided to apply for university, despite my headmaster's refusal to write me a reference, and I got into University College London anyway. I found the first year tough but I eventually parlayed my love of travel into an Honours degree in Geography and followed that up with a Master's degree in Soviet Foreign Policy!

I was always interested in sport in general and football in particular. I remember watching footage of the 1958 Munich Air Crash that decimated the Busby Babes on Pathé Movietone News at the cinema. A few months later, watching our neighbours' television, I saw Nat Lofthouse bundle Harry Gregg and Manchester United's dreams into oblivion in the FA Cup final. When we finally got a television and I didn't have to go next door to watch football, I remember watching Wolverhampton Wanderers' exploits in the early European Cups led by England's captain Billy Wright.

Living in Bournemouth I was fortunate to be able to watch Bournemouth one week and hitchhike up to Southampton the next. I was brought up on a diet of attacking football, which explains my empathy with Gary Johnson's commitment to attack. Southampton boasted forwards with an outstanding pedigree. With Terry Paine and John Sydenham on the wings and Ron Davies and Martin Chivers (sold to Spurs when Mick Channon was ready to replace him) in the centre there was always going to be a bagful of goals but Southampton and the word 'defending' rarely appeared in the same sentence. I once saw three games at the Dell in the space of eight days – a 6-2 win, a 4-4 draw and a 5-1 home defeat! David Webb's initial pre-Chelsea style of defending as a Southampton full-back was to chase after the winger shouting and trying to frighten him off the ball!

When John Bond arrived at Bournemouth in the early seventies he put together an attractive attack-minded team and came within a hair's breadth of taking the club into the Second Division. Ted MacDougal and Phil Boyer formed one of the most effective striking partnerships ever seen outside the Premiership and played together at Bournemouth, Norwich and Southampton. I was there in 1972 when Ted MacDougal set an FA Cup record by scoring nine goals against Margate!

Four years at university in London meant I had the pick of watching the week's top games at Spurs, Arsenal, Fulham, West Ham and Chelsea. Arsenal were probably my favourites and I was in a crowd of over 50,000 (and about the same outside!) at White Hart Lane in May 1971 when they became the second modern era team to clinch the double, courtesy of a Ray Kennedy header!

After completing my studies I taught in the East End of London before travelling through Asia for six months with my girlfriend and eventually arrived in Australia where I lived and worked for five years, initially as a prospector and thereafter as a teacher, of geography of course! In Australia my natural interest and love of sports developed into a fascination with gambling and it was in Australia that I honed my entrepreneurial instincts for the first time. In search of the perfect betting system (which of course does not exist) I developed several sensible staking systems and sold these to desperate punters (one cannot go wrong selling either gambling systems or beer to Aussies!). My teaching colleagues thought I was crazy until after three years they realised my yearly income from selling gambling 'systems' was four times higher than my teaching salary and they became quite envious. After five years in Australia and several forays around the South Pacific and South-East Asia I returned to the UK in 1977 with a sizable sum and the intention to work for myself.

I spent a year looking for a suitable property that I could use as a language school and, just when I was about to give up and return to Australia, found the former Merthyr Guest Cottage Hospital in Templecombe, about twelve miles east of Yeovil. By now I had decided that, rather than be one of the 400 language schools in England, I would set up the first residential summer school in England for American students.

I had met my wife to be Sharron in the highlands of Papua New Guinea two years earlier, and she joined me in England. Together we purchased the former hospital in Templecombe in September 1979 and have lived within three miles of Templecombe ever since. However, as I was born in Bournemouth, all of thirty-six miles away, I reckon I will need to put in another ten years or so before I am truly considered a local and not an interloper; after all, old habits die hard in the country!

For the next ten years, like many others starting their own businesses, Sharron and I worked very hard and at some cost to our personal relationship. We had started out thinking it would be fun to work hard in the summer and travel in the winter but, of course, things don't work out like that, as we were spending the winters promoting our business to schools, teachers and students in North America. Casterbridge Hall International Summer School evolved into Casterbridge Tours running historical, literary, concert and sports tours throughout Eastern and Western Europe. We opened our own sales office in the USA in 1987 and, by 2001, after twenty-one years, had forty staff, over £7 million sales and pre-tax profits in excess of £1 million. Casterbridge Tours has been my life but I believe there is more to life than work and, as the company evolved, I worked hard and played hard but sadly I have never learnt to do either in moderation!

Devoting my life either to work or travel meant I did not get to see a great deal of live sport through the 1980s and 1990s. However, while I have never drunk or smoked, I was a prolific and obsessive gambler so my idea of relaxation was to research form and bet on football, rugby, golf, American football and cricket, which meant I was always very much up to speed with what was going on in sport. Occasionally I would go with my friend and colleague, Tony, down to Southampton and once or twice a year I would go to nearby Yeovil. I remember taking my then-two-year-old daughter Sarah to a game at the Huish eighteen years ago and we missed Yeovil's two goals in a 2-2 draw when I took her for a pee!

As our business grew I had more spare time and especially so when I gave up gambling! I rediscovered my love of live sport and I found myself increasingly drawn to

The author near Everest Base Camp, Nepal.

Huish Park Stadium to watch Yeovil, seemingly forever destined to not quite secure a place in the Football League. I even found myself journeying to away games at such select destinations as Dagenham! With more time at my disposal and with Yeovil, under Colin Addison, challenging for a Football League spot, I was attending more and more Yeovil matches and I liked what I saw in the prospects for the club. So, in 2002, I arranged a meeting with chairman and chief executive John Fry, as I was interested in our company, Casterbridge Tours, buying a shareholding in the club. I felt there were synergies between our company and the football club that could be mutually beneficial. I also felt that Yeovil needed to grow and diversify its income stream and could perhaps introduce other income-earning activities to its site. I had grown a small company from zero turnover to making profits in excess of £1 million per annum but was not too proud to recruit directors with skills I did not possess and I felt Yeovil Town could also benefit from additional expertise.

At the time Yeovil was owned totally by Jon Goddard-Watts, a much-admired and respected man who had acquired the club to give something back to the community, although he chose not to be a director of the company he owned. The position of chairman and CEO were held by John Fry, who was no longer a shareholder and the club only had one other director. It was a strange and somewhat unusual situation and it seemed as if everything went through John Fry. Such a structure and situation could not last long if the club was serious about developing, because it would clearly need other skills, expertise and directors.

Casterbridge was a successful and cash-rich Queen's Award-winning local company and I confirmed to John Fry our interest in acquiring a significant minority shareholding and provide up to three experienced non-executive directors with the skills and time to help the club prepare for the inevitable changes required to diversify and expand its income stream. My proposal was not accepted as presumably the owners did not want to dilute their shareholding, but the board was subsequently expanded and strengthened and I remained in contact with John Fry, our paths crossing from time to time. I have always found him to be very transparent and helpful in our discussions.

Within twelve months Yeovil had secured a place in the Football League by romping away with the Conference in the 2002/03 season and, by this time, I was attending every home match and away games whenever possible. So this account of our 2004/05 season is written very much through the eyes of a passionate, committed and enthusiastic fan and I am very much aware that in this respect I am no different from thousands of other Yeovil fans except I am in the privileged position of being able to travel the world on an ongoing basis.

But I am only part of the story; the other part of the equation is the club.

Yeovil Town FC

Yeovil Town Football Club has rejoiced in (or suffered) the title of the most famous non-league club in Britain, rather like Davis Love III and Colin Montgomerie have in turn held the unwanted title of 'the best golfer never to win a major'.

Yeovil's roots as a prominent non-league club go back to 1895 when the club was founded as Yeovil Casuals FC and evolved into Yeovil Town before merging with Petters United during the First World War to become Yeovil & Petters United. The Petters United was dropped in 1945 and Yeovil have been known thereafter as Yeovil Town FC. The nickname 'the Glovers' comes from the town's history of glove-making, an industry that was at its peak in the Yeovil area when the club was formed.

To football fans throughout the country from Old Trafford and Highbury downwards the very word Yeovil is synonymous with giant-killing exploits in the FA Cup and, for older fans, also with the famous sloping pitch at the Huish, our ground until 1991, when the club moved to their current home, the then-new Huish Park Stadium on the Lufton Trading Estate. This was a move that crippled the club financially and, for a while, threatened to send it into extinction. So ingrained is the association of Yeovil with 'that sloping pitch' that many visiting fans still expect to see a sloping pitch, not realising it has long since been flattened (literally) and is now buried under a supermarket!

As a non-league club, Yeovil advanced to the first round of the FA Cup on over forty occasions and knocked out league opposition twenty times. Yeovil's first success against a Football League team came in 1924/25 when, after taking a shock 3-0 lead, they held off a determined fightback to defeat Bournemouth 3-2, but the club first reached national prominence with a spectacular FA Cup fourth round success beating table-topping First Division Sunderland 2-1 in front of a club-record 16,000 ecstatic fans. Yeovil were led that day by legendary player-manager Alec Stock, who maintained close relations with the club until his recent death. A less well-known fact was that, in the fifth round of the cup in 1949, after defeating mighty Sunderland, Yeovil were drawn away to Manchester United, then playing at Maine Road and, despite

suffering the biggest defeat in the club's history (8-0) they came away with the distinction of being one of the two sides responsible for attracting the biggest ever FA Cup
attendance excluding the final itself, as over 81,000 fans packed Maine Road to see
the Red Devils take on the mighty Glovers! That is a record that stands to this day.

From the fifties to the seventies Yeovil played in the Southern League and Southern
Premier League and won both league titles without gaining election to the Football
League. In 1976 we were runners-up to Wimbledon in the Southern Premier League
and now, after the two very different and equally improbable journeys, we are again
in the same league, albeit in Wimbledon's latest guise as the Milton Keynes Dons!
Managers during this period included Ron Saunders who, like Alec Stock before him,
was to achieve managerial success at a higher level after moving on from Yeovil.

1979 saw the birth of what was then the Alliance Premier League and subsequently the Conference, which became the game's 'fifth' division. Yeovil were founder
members and this marked the beginning of what was to be a twenty-four-year quest to
secure a Football League spot, but this was certainly not without hiccups. Life was not
always easy in non-league football's premier division and Yeovil were twice relegated, first in 1985, despite the assistance of 'local Yeovil boy made good' Ian Botham as
a player. Yeovil were relegated to the Vauxhall Opel League, only to return to the
Premier League three years later, but relegation was repeated again in 1995 when,
after a last-gasp escape the previous season Yeovil could not avoid the inevitable and
were relegated from the GM Vauxhall Conference to the ICIS League. Two years later,
winning the ICIS League secured a return to the Conference. While on each occasion
that Yeovil were relegated the club was able to secure promotion back to non-
league's premier division, the ultimate goal of promotion to the Football League
continued to be elusive.

In 2000/01 Yeovil led the Conference for much of the season after Colin Addison
took over as manager from David Webb (who, after transforming the club into a full-
time professional outfit returned to Southend) and it seemed the dream of league
football was finally to become reality, but it was not to be as Rushden & Diamonds
overturned a big Yeovil lead in the league and secured the sole promotion spot. To the
dismay of many fans Colin Addison was forced to resign at the end of the season. It
was, however, a resignation that was to change the fate and fortune of football in
Yeovil forever.

When Gary Johnson was appointed in June 2001 most fans' reactions were characterised by two words: 'Gary Who?' Some research revealed that he was the former
youth team coach at Watford, not quite famed throughout the world as an academy of
stylish football, and the former manager of Latvia. Some Yeovil fans had an idea
where Watford was located but very few knew anything about Latvia, expect it was
probably close to Transylvania and had something to do with Dracula (wrong on both
counts!). However, the significance and evident result of Gary Johnson's stint in Latvia
were to become clear when Latvia qualified for the European Championships for the
first time in 2004 as a result of the foundations and organisational structure that he put
in place. Unknown to the fans, John Fry had unearthed a gem and Yeovil have not
looked back since.

In Gary Johnson's first season (2001/02) Yeovil finished a credible third in the
Conference and a thrilling run in the FA Trophy (the main prize for non-league sides)

culminated in a 2-0 victory over Stevenage Borough in the final at Villa Park before a crowd of almost 19,000. Gary Johnson had secured his place in Yeovil's history, as this was the first major trophy that the club had won in their 106 years but, unbelievably, more was to quickly follow.

The following season saw Yeovil fans looking forward with great anticipation because, after years of speculation, there were finally two places available for promotion to the Football League, a play-off promotion being made available to one of the second, third, fourth and fifth-placed teams. Surely if we didn't win the Conference we could at least secure a play-off spot and a chance of glory? It was ironic that the first season when two places were available for Conference clubs to be promoted to the Football League was also the year when Yeovil did not need the assistance of a second chance! After a loss and a draw in their opening two games, Gary Johnson's young and attack-minded team only lost on two further occasions in the league and, playing a quality of football rarely seen in Division Three, let alone in non-league football, romped to the title by a record seventeen-point margin and scored 100 League goals in the process. It is a tribute to the calibre of our Conference-winning team that many of that squad are still with the club and acquitting themselves well at a higher level today.

So Yeovil's epithet as Britain's most famous non-league club could finally be discarded after 108 years and that was no mean sacrifice. After all, Yeovil had been the only non-league side that merited its own Subbuteo team!

Many pundits tipped Yeovil to go straight through Division Three and secure promotion at the first attempt in the club's inaugural Football League season but, ironically, it was fellow ex-Conference side Doncaster, who had trailed seventeen points behind Yeovil the previous season, that secured promotion as champions and, despite a thrilling 3-2 away win at play-off bound Lincoln City on the last day of the season, a Northampton goal twenty minutes from the end of their game at Mansfield ensured that Yeovil were excluded from the play-offs on goal difference alone.

Yeovil fans were devastated but, in truth, our form had not been either convincing or consistent since Christmas and there were many who wondered if the distractions of a third round FA Cup home tie against mighty Liverpool, when we played with distinction but lost to two late goals, was partly responsible for our campaign coming off the rails for a while. Gary Johnson for one certainly did not think so and maybe he was a little remiss in staying loyal to our Conference-winning squad without significant additions for rather too long, but that's the kind of club that Yeovil is – loyal, tight-knit and family orientated and players are treated like family. Upon reflection, after a 108-year wait, eighth in Division Three in our first Football League season was no mean accomplishment, but could we build upon this?

In three seasons Gary Johnson had won the FA Trophy, led us to the Football League as Conference champions and only missed out on the play-offs in our first season as a League club on goal difference. Clearly he was a god to all Yeovil fans and sent from heaven (or Latvia). Something special was happening and the club was certainly in the ascendancy. Was this another Northampton (Fourth Division to First Division in successive seasons) or Wimbledon (non-league to Premiership) story waiting to be written or were we just deluding ourselves with a couple of seasons of impressive form?

As the season approached I became convinced Yeovil had the ability to go all the way and, on 31 July 2004 in Canada, I started to record what I hoped would be a memorable season for Yeovil Town FC. In August both Yeovil Town and myself started on two separate journeys that would be linked together for the next nine months and I know that neither Gary Johnson nor myself could possibly conceive just what would transpire over the following nine months.

Read on, and I hope you enjoy the journeys that are described on the following pages.

A Commitment from Canada

Saturday 31 July 2004 – Locarno Beach, Vancouver, Canada

We are spending much of the summer in Vancouver, British Columbia, where we have spent fifteen of the last twenty summers. Our children all have joint Canadian-British citizenship and, three years ago, after many happy and rewarding home exchanges we finally bought the four-bedroom house we lived in when here for nine months in 1996. We are fortunate to be close to both the beach and the down-town area of what is surely North America's most beautiful and spectacularly located city.

It's a long way from this harbour-side beach where I am writing to Plainmoor, home of Torquay United. However, events at Torquay today have persuaded me to keep a journal of Yeovil's season, albeit through the eyes of a fan who will spend most of the season a long way from Huish Park Stadium!

At the end of the season before last Torquay barely survived in the Football League while Yeovil were promoted from the Conference. However, last season saw a change of fortunes for Torquay, who marked our card by winning 2-0 at Huish Park Stadium in September and many fans thought this the most impressive performance by a visit-ing team all season. Torquay finished the last third of the season in great form, secured automatic promotion and there are to be no local derbies with Torquay this season. But there was a pre-season friendly and that took place today! And, with due respect to Tiverton Town, this was the last of the 'serious' pre-season friendlies and a stern test for Yeovil.

When I got up today I checked the Yeovil Town website and the summary read, 'Full time Torquay 2 …'. Fearing the worst I clicked to get the full story and was more than pleasantly surprised to read Torquay 2 Yeovil 4, and that follows three goals against League One side Cardiff last week. Furthermore, there has to be some basis for thinking manager Gary Johnson may have made his most inspired signing yet, as our new twenty-nine-year-old striker Bartosz Tarachulski scored a hat-trick. As any Yeovil fan will tell you, a regular goal-scorer who could have knocked in twenty goals last season would have given Yeovil automatic promotion – no arguments!

So a 4-2 Yeovil victory at Torquay in a pre-season friendly may not have caused many ripples of interest on the global football scene but it has sent one wave of antic-ipation as far as the west coast of Canada. An away win against a newly promoted

Locarno Beach, Vancouver.

team preparing for life in a higher division makes me think that this could be a memorable season for Yeovil. We would all like to think that last season was a 'consolidation' season and assume we will improve this year but there has to be a distinct possibility that momentum, enthusiasm and team spirit could have combined with the result we actually overachieved last season. However, if some of the new signings come good, this could be a be a memorable season for Yeovil.

The signs from Torquay are encouraging so I have decided to definitely commit to this project. I'm scribbling my thoughts down as the sun sets over the Gulf Islands, with an eagle flying overhead and the snow-covered coastal mountains forming a wonderful backcloth to this spectacular city. The Symphony of Fire will start in forty-five minutes and the beach is crowded. One of the delights of Vancouver, in many ways my second home and where I was married twenty-one years ago, is that this is such a cosmopolitan city. As much as twenty per cent of the city is of Asian origin and the beach tonight and the parkland behind is packed with families walking, talking, playing and singing as twilight descends. I can hear Cantonese, Spanish and Russian spoken as much as English and everyone is waiting with anticipation for the fireworks to start. Of course, I hope that the fireworks will start in earnest next Saturday with Yeovil's opening game in the newly named League Two away at Bury!

As I start this chronicle of Yeovil's 2004/05 season, I hope that in nine months' time Yeovil will have secured a place in League One but I suspect there will be a lot of twists along the way, both for Yeovil and myself. However, all that lies ahead, and the first step is to profile the players whose names will appear frequently on the following pages.

Player Profiles

(All ages as on 1 August 2004)

Goalkeepers

Steve Collis (twenty-three) has been the back up to Chris Weale for the last two seasons but, when Weale got injured towards the end of last season, Collis impressed the fans as a very able substitute and the team was certainly not weakened by his presence. Apparently Gary Johnson is stating that they both go into the season as joint number ones. He has been with Yeovil for three seasons, although only made a handful of appearances before his run at the end of last season. Given that Steve is a similar age to Chris Weale and is such a capable goalkeeper, this probably makes it more likely that Weale will be sold at some point. Steve was a member of the Watford youth academy under Gary Johnson and linked up with him for a second time when he joined Yeovil at the start of the 2001/02 season.

Chris Weale (twenty-two) is one of the two local players in the team, the other being Andy Lindegaard. When I met with John Fry three years ago and Chris was the reserve team goalkeeper behind Tony Pennock, the chairman told me that 'our reserve goalkeeper is worth at least £100,000 and will be a very good goalkeeper in the Football League'. He was certainly correct and last year Chris was training with West Ham for three days a week and there was a lot of speculation that he was going there for £250,000. Both the speculation and training at West Ham went on for a number of weeks but the potential move collapsed after Chris was injured. Nevertheless, it is accepted that ultimately he will most likely join a Championship or Premiership side. Chris is a product of our youth team and was selected as goalkeeper in the PFA Division Three squad last year. He is a very sound and impressive goalkeeper who commands his area well. However, if he does have a weakness, I did find myself thinking last season that he rarely looked likely to stop a penalty. Chris was the regular 'keeper for the record-breaking promotion-winning squad from the Conference in 2002/03.

Defenders

Scott Guyett (twenty-eight) was playing non-league football with Chester last season and was signed in the off season as a central defender. I've yet to see him play but, by all accounts, he was quite impressive in the pre-season matches. Although Hugo Rodrigues was a real crowd favourite last season, I did not think that he was really a long-term solution to our weakness at the back when we didn't have our two first-choice centre halves playing. Hopefully, with Scott joining Skiverton, Miles and O'Brien, we will also not have to consider playing Lockwood as a central defender this season. Scott is one of two Australians in the Yeovil squad.

Adam Lockwood (twenty-two) – I don't think Adam did himself or his career any good by having to play so often as a central defender last year. However, I understand that this is his preferred position! As a tall, powerful, attacking full-back who is particularly effective at set pieces, I thought that he was one of the Yeovil players who had the potential to adapt to a much higher level than League Two. He is versatile enough to be an effective central defender when playing with Terry Skiverton but when he was paired with Hugo Rodrigues last season I was always afraid of the fragility at the centre of our defence. I did wonder if Michael Rose's signing meant that Adam's future prospects were not going to be so bright but, on the other hand, I think he rates highly with Gary Johnson. Adam joined Yeovil after a loan period from Reading and has always been a consistent goal-scorer for a defender. Was a regular in the squad promoted from the Conference in 2002/03.

Colin Miles (formerly Pluck) (twenty-five) is another who was in the Watford youth academy under Gary Johnson and has also played for Morton in the Scottish League. Always 100 per cent committed in everything he does, I think Colin has the potential to play at least as high as Championship standard. Unlike Adam Lockwood, I think that Colin Miles is equally effective as full-back and central defender and from last year's squad he would be my preferred partner to Terry Skiverton in the heart of the defence. Colin is without doubt the hardest tackler in the squad and also the possessor of the fiercest temperament. Totally committed, he is a great crowd favourite and was a member of the Conference promotion-winning squad.

Roy O'Brien (twenty-nine) has been at Dorchester, Bournemouth and Arsenal before coming to Yeovil and was very impressive as a central defender in the first two months of last season before getting a serious season-ending injury. Indeed, it was after his departure from our defence that our results started to be more problematic. Gary Johnson gave Roy until 1 July to prove his fitness and obviously he has done this effectively because he has played a fair amount in the pre-season matches. If he stays fit, Roy will be a welcome returnee to the Yeovil squad. Roy is one of the oldest players in the squad!

Terry Skiverton (twenty-nine) is another of the 'old hands', an elder statesman in the dressing room! Terry joined Yeovil from Welling five years ago in June 1999 and previously had experience with both Chelsea (where he was a junior) and Wycombe. He is the club captain and an inspirational presence on the pitch. His non-stop commitment and the threat he poses at set pieces in our opponents' goal areas make him one of the key players of the Yeovil squad. When we lost our big lead and failed to get promoted at the end of the 2000/01 season there was talk that many of the players would leave including Terry Skiverton, who seemed somewhat disillusioned with the future at Yeovil. However, the chairman and Gary Johnson persuaded him to stay and he has been a key presence in the last three years as Yeovil's fortunes have so dramatically improved.

Stephen Reed (nineteen) is a product of the youth squad. He made 4 league appearances last year as a full-back, looked very poised and accomplished on the ball and is a fairly regular substitute. I think he is an excellent prospect for the future.

Michael Rose (twenty-two) is an ex-Manchester United junior and was signed in the off-season from Conference side Hereford. The indications are that he is going to be one of the regular full-backs. Not having seen any of the pre-season matches this year, I have yet to see him play.

Midfielders

Adrian Caceres (twenty-two) is a young Australian/Argentinean who was previously on Southampton's books (shades of Dani Rodrigues) and actually was substitute for a game in the Premiership. He went back to Australia from Southampton and was playing for Australia's leading domestic side, the Perth Glory, when he was signed during the off-season. By all accounts very impressive in the pre-season and it seems he might have done enough to warrant one of the starting places in midfield.

Lee Johnson (twenty-three) is the manager's son, which can't be easy! During his first season I wasn't particularly impressed with Lee but over the last two years he has earned everyone's respect by his tremendous work rate and is another player who, despite his diminutive size, certainly has the ability to play at a higher level than League Two. My colleague, Tony, often surmises that eventually another club will come in and take both the Johnsons as a package! Lee is always trying to grab the ball and take quick free-kicks, whether it is a long-distance shot or a quick pass. Sometimes I wonder if he is so intent on taking the kick quickly that he doesn't give a thought to what he is actually doing with it! Notwithstanding this one negative element to his play Lee is a tremendous asset to the Yeovil team.

Andy Lindegaard (twenty-three) Despite the Scandinavian name, Andy was born and bred in Yeovil and has worked his way through the youth and reserve teams. He has scored a hat-trick as a striker, been very effective playing on either flank as a midfielder and has had some good games as an attacking wing-back but I often feel that his versatility has worked against him because he has never been able to make one position his own. Very popular with the fans and really turned the match round against Scunthorpe single-handedly last year when he made the equaliser and scored the winning goal. Since El Kholti has departed, he is now the only wing-back in the squad. I suspect he will be a substitute for much of the season but, as a result of his versatility, Andy is one of the most valuable members of the squad.

Nicolas Mirza (nineteen) is a Frenchman who was signed after a pre-season trial period. Nicolas was previously a youth player with Paris St Germain and his combative and impressive form pre-season led to the nickname 'Vieira'! We live in hope!

Paul Terry (twenty-five) was signed early last season from Dagenham after previous spells with Charlton and Millwall. I did not think he was particularly impressive in his early outings for Yeovil but he settled down to be a valuable member of the squad, whether playing as a full-back or as a central midfield player. His brother John is, of course, the Chelsea captain and England's form central defender of the past eighteen months. John came down last year to watch Paul play against Liverpool in the third round of the FA Cup. It would be good if the Terrys can make it a family double this season!

Steve Thompson (forty-two) is very much the oldest of the 'old hands' at the club and indeed is only registered as a player for an emergency and the occasional outing for the reserve team. He is the club coach and assistant manager, a position he also held under Colin Addison. Steve will surely be at least caretaker manager when Gary Johnson does eventually move on, or will Gary take Steve with him? Having been with Yeovil for seven years, Steve is an important member of the Yeovil family.

Darren Way (twenty-four) will be entering his fifth season with Yeovil and, together with Terry Skiverton and Colin Miles, very much forms the emotional heart of the team. He runs on adrenalin, never stops chasing and, for such a small midfielder, wins a very high percentage of all the balls he challenges for in the air, often outjumping players six to eight inches taller than him. When Way plays well, Yeovil usually play well and he never ceases to give 100 per cent effort. His style of play constantly reminds me of Billy Bremner. At the end of last season I thought that either Darren or Lee Johnson might be replaced as I felt that one of our weaknesses was that our two central midfield players were both small, the dilemma being that they were also our most effective and consistent midfielders! However, I suspect Gary Johnson is going to stick with Darren and Lee, add Gavin Williams for flair and the fourth midfield player will be a key position. Darren won Player of the Season honours in our Conference-winning season two years ago.

Gavin Williams (twenty-four) has a tremendous amount of ability and came to Yeovil from non-league Hereford and, in my opinion, has the skills to warrant a place in the Welsh squad. 'Super Gav' won all the Player of the Year awards last year and, despite speculation during the off-season that he might be moving on to either Hull or Doncaster, he signed a new contract to stay with Yeovil. Gavin probably possesses the best 'on the ball' skills in League Two but just needs to harness them so that he makes the final pass at the right time. Gavin has an excellent shot and likes to attack just behind the strikers. Indeed, when the goal supply dried up from our strikers last season, Gary Johnson decided on a couple of occasions to play with just one up front and had Gavin playing just behind the striker. It was not particularly successful but it accurately reflected the impressive nature of Gavin's attacking instincts.

Strikers

Kevin Gall (twenty-two) will always be associated in tandem with Kirk Jackson because the two of them played as a strike pair for the last half of our Conference-winning season and couldn't stop knocking in goals. One of the disappointments of last season was the failure of Kirk Jackson to be a regular scorer at league level. Kevin is a very fast and exciting player and one of the fleetest of foot outside the Premiership.

Last season his pace was still a very real threat to opposing defences but unfortunately his personal goal supply dried up after Christmas. The last half of the season was very much the story of waiting for Kevin to end his drought but, in truth, he looked woefully short of confidence whenever he was near the goal. He nevertheless earned a lot of credit from the fans for his non-stop efforts and for not letting his head drop. He has played at Under-21 level for Wales and did have some outings last year as a wide midfielder, using his pace on the flanks. Very much a fans' favourite, it would be good to see him scoring regularly again. However, with Tarachulski and Jevons now in the squad he is unlikely to be a regular first choice as striker, or at least not until the goals start appearing!

Phil Jevons (twenty-four) was signed from Grimsby in the pre-season, where he had a record of scoring a goal every three games or so (21 goals in 70 appearances, including 17 as substitute). He had previously made 9 first-team appearances for Everton and hopefully will be what Yeovil very much need, a regular goal-scorer. What we needed last season were two strikers each capable of scoring 15 goals. If Phil can replicate his efforts with Grimsby at Yeovil, he will be a positive addition to the squad.

Kezie Ibe (twenty-one) was signed late in the pre season, joining Yeovil from Staines. He was a prolific goal-scorer in the lower league and time will tell whether he is able to transfer his record to a higher level if he is given a chance.

Yemi Odubade (twenty) was signed during the summer after scoring more than thirty goals last season for Eastbourne United. If either Yemi or Kezie come up trumps then it can be assumed that these (speculative?) signings will have been well worthwhile.

Bartosz Tarachulski (twenty-nine) is a new name but, viewing the pre-season from afar in Canada, I think the signing of Bartosz was the most positive development of the summer. He has played for top-flight clubs in Poland and also at the highest level in Belgium and Israel. So, yes, he has moved around and does not stay at clubs very long but he has played regularly at a high level and anyone who can score a hat-trick at Torquay, albeit in a pre-season friendly, has to be seen as a very positive contribution to the squad. If Bartosz and Phil Jevons were to knock in thirty-five goals between them I feel the rest of the squad are more than capable of contributing another forty-five goals and in that case I feel we have an excellent chance of automatic promotion. From as far away as Canada, I will put my marker down now and say that Bartosz could be a key factor affecting the success or otherwise of Yeovil's coming season. I am looking forward to seeing him play.

Simon Weatherstone (twenty-three) was signed last January from Boston United. Whether playing as a striker or as a midfielder, I wasn't particularly impressed with Simon last season and felt he should join the likes of Lee Elam and Neil Mustoe as players who we just have to accept didn't work out and should move on. However, it appears that Gary Johnson sees him as an important squad member and he is going to have plenty of opportunities this year. He has played over 70 games in what are now the Championship and League One and was a fairly regular goal-scorer at Boston, averaging about one goal in every four games. It may be that Simon just needs time to settle down at Yeovil and it will be interesting to see how he turns out this season.

Dale Williams (seventeen) is the youngest member of the Yeovil squad, who has been given a contract after working his way up through the youth and reserve sides. I have yet to see Dale play.

Pre-Season Prospects
Wednesday 4 August 2004 – Princess Louise Inlet, B.C. Coast, Canada

Three days to the start of the season away at Bury. I am sitting at the end of the jetty at the head of Princess Louise Inlet, about 150 miles north of Vancouver. There are a dozen motorboats (power yachts) and a handful of sailing boats at the jetty or anchored nearby but otherwise no signs of civilisation. The sun has come out and the scenery is very reminiscent of Norway with towering, almost vertical, cliffs dropping hundreds of feet into the inlet named after Queen Victoria's mother. We've hired a thirty-eight-foot Bayliner Motor Yacht for four days at $500 (about £200) a day and my wife, Sharron, and children, Lisa (seventeen) and David (fifteen), have been joined by Sharron's cousin Marion and her daughter Kaia.

The boat has two sleeping cabins and a lounge/diner and the skipper, Dennis, sleeps on the covered bridge. We anchored in a little cove about sixty miles north of Vancouver last night and we motored for about two and a half hours up the almost-deserted Jervis Inlet, with forested slopes towering above us and occasionally glacier-clad peaks revealed in the distance when the cloud and rain permitted. We met with five other vessels and took our turn to go through the narrow and somewhat hazardous rapids into this beautiful narrow fjord and, after full steam (sorry, diesel) ahead, we secured one of the last berths at the public jetty.

It's been raining on and off on the last two days after three weeks of continual sunshine but, by late afternoon, it had cleared and we walked up to Chatterbox Falls, one of the most dramatic waterfalls I've ever seen. A sign proclaims not to go near the top of the falls where twelve people have slipped to their deaths! The west coast of Canada is a continual reminder that rainforest is not restricted to the tropics and the vegetation is dense with moss-covered trees.

I've brought a chair from the boat to the end of the jetty and boat owners stroll up. 'Howdee. Best seat in the house,' one comments and indeed it is, with the fjord stretched out in front of me and waterfalls cascading down the bare rock faces that separate the almost-vertical tree-clad slopes. The sky above is blue but cloudy remnants of the rainy day hover amid the trees. Like Switzerland you can hear the solitude, which is always the sound of running water.

The season starts in three days and I wonder if Bury away will yield as positive a start as last season's 3-1 win at Rochdale. That was Yeovil's Football League debut match with almost 2,000 Glovers fans travelling 300 miles to Lancashire. The omens seem good because it appears, after a dodgy first thirty minutes at Torquay on Saturday, the

Princess Louise Inlet, B.C.

defence tightened up and Tarachulski certainly had an impressive game. A regular goal-scorer will make all the difference and, if Jevons delivers, Gall can start scoring again and one of the two prolific non-league strikers we have signed come good, we should be able to get some goals from somewhere. I like both Way and Johnson but at this level I am not convinced we can afford two small players in the centre of midfield. From the internet I gather the young French player, Mirza, has been impressive pre-season and clearly Weatherstone is still in favour with Gary Johnson because, although never impressing the fans, he still appears to be in the shake up.

It does appear that this year Yeovil have a squad with more depth. At the end of last season we were playing with ten players on the pitch who were in the Conference promotion-winning squad and while I applaud the loyalty I think some fresh blood and more experience was required. I was sorry we didn't keep Dani Rodrigues but, fans' favourite or not, I don't think Hugo Rodrigues was a big loss. He was never as dominant in the air as a man of his size should be and as the tallest player in the Football League he was, not surprisingly, slow to turn. My heart was always in my mouth when Lockwood and Rodrigues teamed up as our two centre-backs because I thought this combination had the potential to be a lethally effective partnership – for the opposition! I suspect that Adam Lockwood might be relegated to be a bit player this season with Skiverton, O'Brien, Guyett, Miles and Rose all in contention for a defensive spot.

And where does this leave Andy Lindegaard, one of our two home-grown players? He has played well whenever he has had a chance over the last two years, whether as striker, in midfield or as wing-back, although last season I always thought playing him and the often-impressive El Kholti as twin wing-backs in the same team was a luxury.

Lindegaard is one of the lower league's best utility players, skilled enough to cover all positions but, sadly, as a consequence, never likely to make one his own.

I am in Canada until early September when I may have to go to New Jersey to meet with a church tour operator who has approached Casterbridge with a proposal that we might want to acquire her business. Her operation could dovetail and sit quite nicely with our existing concert-tour operation, many of which are church choirs. After visiting our US office in Virginia I will only be in the UK for a few days before leading the annual Chairman's Trek, this year for thirty-one days to Nepal and Tibet and (almost) halfway up Everest. So it could be mid-November until I see the Glovers play. It is possible to 'watch' each match live on the internet with a text commentary that is updated every two minutes. But believe me, that is like watching paint dry! However, I may go home earlier because I am not too happy about the current per-formance of our company and I have concerns that our CEO, David, and myself are not on the same page regarding several matters. Last night I tossed and turned with all my concerns and what ifs going through my mind and eventually I got up in the cabin and wrote down an outline of all my thoughts. I came to the conclusion that there were indeed a number of issues regarding Casterbridge that need to be addressed but I will leave off making a final decision about going back to England earlier until I return to Vancouver and read David's reports.

As I sit here pondering the future of Casterbridge, Gary Johnson is pondering his team selection. From halfway round the world I suspect: Weale in goal; Miles, Skiverton, O'Brien (or Guyett) and Rose forming the back four; Williams, Johnson, Way and Caceres in midfield with Tarachulski and Jevons as our two strikers. The subs will probably be Guyett (or O'Brien), Lockwood, Lindegaard, Gall and Terry. I won-der how accurate I will be? I think I can safely say at this moment in time I am probably the only person anywhere in the world writing about Yeovil Town FC and watching seals swimming offshore!

With my worries about Casterbridge, I suspect it is going to be an interesting season in more ways than one and it starts in less than seventy-two hours!

An Inglorious Beginning

Saturday 7 August 2004 – Vancouver, Canada
Bury v. Yeovil (League Two)

So here we are, day one of the new season proper. I won't go so far as to say every fan at every club envisages that they will have a winning and successful season but, at the moment, every team is unbeaten and all supporters can at least delude themselves into being optimistic until the final whistle of the first game! Although there was some unease about lack of transfer activity early in the pre-season, I think Gary Johnson has done a good job in making some significant additions to the squad, primarily with Jevons and Tarachulski as strikers. Strengthening the strike force has clearly been a priority so let's hope it pays off. Hopefully Caceres and Mirza in midfield and Scott Guyett and Michael Rose in defence will also prove to be positive additions.

The first day of the season is always special with eager fans anxious to evaluate their team's prospects for the new season, and this Yeovil fan, currently based in Vancouver, Canada, is no exception. However, as it happened, the first day of the season saw me waking up just over the border in the USA. We returned to Vancouver yesterday after our four-day charter and when we got back to our house there was a telephone message from a longstanding friend of mine, George Bottcher, an American who now lives in neighbouring Washington State in the USA. He was in Vancouver to buy some lumber for a construction project and was enquiring if it was possible to get together. I met George in Singapore in 1972 and he was the best man at our wedding in New Westminster (a suburb of Vancouver) back in 1981. How did George know we were in Vancouver? One of the advantages of e-mail is circulating details to friends and contacts when one moves around! We met up last night but first I had 'an appointment' with a famous celebrity who was visiting B.C. to give a lecture!

Doug Scott is one of the most famous mountaineers in the world. Accompanied by Dougal Haston, he was the first Briton to climb Everest, in 1977, and is world-renowned as a mountaineer's mountaineer, having climbed many of the major peaks in the Himalaya and mountain ranges around the world, often by new, innovative and challenging routes. He has made ascents of all the seven summits (the highest points on each of the seven continents) and, like Sir Edmund Hillary, has in recent years devoted a lot of his time to raising funds for poor communities in Nepal. Without their support many western mountaineers would not be able to climb successfully in the Himalaya. Doug was in Vancouver to give a lecture to raise money for a porter's shelter at Machermo in Nepal and I thought I would piggyback on his fame by going to the auditorium and promoting my own Chairman's Trek to Nepal and Tibet, which is taking place this coming October!

When I went to the venue, I saw Doug sitting close to the entrance as a very big crowd gathered and filled the auditorium. I sat on his left, put my hand on his shoulder and said, 'Well, fancy seeing you!' at which point a very surprised Doug Scott turned and said, 'Good God. What are you doing here?'

Doug was very much on form and I thoroughly enjoyed the lecture even though I had heard and seen much of the content before. I did manage to get a plug in for our trek and then, at the end of the lecture, Doug auctioned some photos to raise funds for the Machermo project and I ended up buying an original photo of the late Dougal Haston climbing the Hillary Step. The picture was signed by both Sir Edmund Hillary, the first to climb the Hillary Step, and Doug so I came out of a lecture I was planning to use to promote our own trek $520 the poorer!

Following the lecture we drove down across the border to the small town of Blaine, where our friend George was planning to sleep overnight in his sailboat, which he kept moored at Blaine for most of the year. We met up at the only diner in town that was still open and had a good hour and a half's chat catching up after ten years before going back to his boat to sleep for a fifth successive night on water. After coffee this morning we said our farewells to George, hoping it wouldn't be another ten years before we saw him, and then drove back across the border to Vancouver.

As soon as I got home I went to the computer to check the result of the Yeovil match, which had finished several hours earlier. However, before I found the Yeovil result, I noticed that Bury were sitting proud at the top of the league table.

George and my wife Sharron in the Blaine diner.

Shit! That meant that Bury had won convincingly and indeed the result was terrible: Bury 3 Yeovil 1.

There was no escaping the obvious! This was nothing other than an impressive win to Bury and not what Yeovil supporters, whether in Somerset or Canada, envisaged for the start of the new season. Had all the new signings and pre-season promise been a false dawn or was this just a one-off result? Who knows? After reading the account of the match at least I took something positive from it in that Yeovil had taken the lead and were winning 1-0 away from home at half-time.

I had checked the result on the computer in the (basement) den of our Vancouver home and, in truth, being somewhat superstitious I had not been too optimistic about checking the result there. Why? Because it was here that I learnt the results of two disappointing games that made significant contributions to our failure to qualify for the play-offs last season. These were the home loss to Kidderminster on Boxing Day followed two days later by going 2-0 down at Swansea, fighting back to 2-2 only to concede the winning goal in injury time. Those two successive defeats over the holiday period halted the momentum that Yeovil had maintained from the beginning of the season until Christmas and we fell out of the top three, never to regain an automatic promotion position. Now I was at the same desk, in the same den with another negative result! I did not feel any better when I noticed that both Northampton and Lincoln, who should both prove to be serious promotion challengers this season, won away from home.

I guess the only positive comment I can make is that, two years ago, when we won promotion from the Conference, we lost our opening match away from home but went on to have an outstanding season, only losing three matches all year. However, am I clutching at straws, trying to find a positive spin for what was clearly a very disappointing result? We'll have the opportunity to redeem ourselves against Darlington at home in three days' time but this wasn't exactly the start that I or countless other Yeovil fans had anticipated. Let's hope we can get things going on Tuesday!

Bury 3 Yeovil Town 1

Team: Steve Collis, Roy O'Brien, Terry Skiverton, Colin Miles, Michael Rose, Gavin Williams, Lee Johnson, Darren Way, Adrian Caceres, Kevin Gall, Bartosz Tarachulski

Subs: Phil Jevons (63 for Tarachulski), Simon Weatherstone (78 for Way), Nicolas Mirza (80 for Johnson)

Subs not used: Chris Weale, Andy Lindegaard

Goal-scorer: Adrian Caceres (39)

Attendance: 3,171

Position in League after match: 20th

Good News Required

Tuesday 10 August 2004 – Vancouver, Canada
Yeovil v. Darlington (League Two)

The last two days have been pretty tiring as I have been very concerned over some aspects of Casterbridge. Subsequently I spent almost the entire night (Sunday night/Monday morning) on the phone with managers, fellow shareholder, our accountant and advisors reviewing the various courses of action available.

I was meant to be going for a hike yesterday (Monday) with a friend of mine from Vancouver and I ended up ringing her at 8.50 a.m. yesterday morning, saying that I had worked all through the night but if I could get a few hours sleep, hopefully we could still manage a half-day hike. In the end I slept from 9 a.m. to 1.30 p.m. and then, together with my daughter Lisa, picked up Angeline, a bright and enthusiastic young lady in her mid-twenties. I met Angeline three years ago at a boat marina and she struck me as an articulate and enthusiastic young woman. We have kept in touch by e-mail while she has been working in France and Switzerland as well as studying for a degree in business management and marketing in Vancouver.

Mount Seymour is one of a number of peaks that overlook Vancouver from the north and the three of us drove to the Mount Seymour trailhead. We did not get there until 4.30 p.m. and then walked over the first two pumps (peaks) to the third peak, which is Mount Seymour itself and where there is a good view north of the Coastal

With Mike Mayer by Jericho Pier Vancouver.

Mountains and south, over the city of Vancouver, down to the San Juan Islands in the United States. We could also look south-east to Mount Baker, one of the seven great volcanoes that stretch along the western seaboard of North America and west across the Straits of Georgia to the Gulf Islands and Vancouver Island. Vancouver residents are fortunate to have such spectacular wilderness scenery quite literally on their doorstep. We hiked the last hour back in the gloom but got to the car all right and then went for a vegetarian dinner at the Nam, a Vancouver institution, where Sharron joined us for a late-night snack.

It had been very good for me to get out yesterday as, after ten hours working through the night on the phone to England, I really appreciated the opportunity to get out on the trail and not think about work-related problems. I was also quite pleased because, although the hike included about 500m (1,600ft) of ascent and was about six or seven miles return on a rugged trail, I managed the walk with no difficulty after less than four hours' sleep. Perhaps I am not as unfit as I sometimes fear.

I spent today at home considering how best to handle the situation with Casterbridge and then I called Tony, our UK schools sales manager and the other Casterbridge shareholder, who was at the Yeovil v. Darlington match.

I had obviously slightly miscalculated the time difference as he told me I was calling five minutes after half-time and Darlington had just equalised. Tony said it had very much been on the cards from the latter stages of the first half as Darlington looked very impressive and more likely to score than Yeovil. Indeed, it was only a great save by Steve Collis that prevented us from falling behind while I was talking to Tony. I could hear the crowd in the background as Tony commented that Michael Rose had had an awful game, being taken off after only thirty minutes. Not the most auspicious of home debuts!

I rang back fifteen minutes before the end to hear the score was still 1-1 and that Weatherstone had missed a sitter, according to Tony. He said that the new striker, Bartosz Tarachulski (my hope for the season), looked slow, ponderous and isolated and Yeovil's attack looked no more potent than it did last season. Tony commentated as play was going on and we ended our conversation with about five minutes to go. I didn't bother to check the final result immediately on the Internet, just assuming it was a 1-1 draw and another two points dropped. When I checked later in the day, hoping against hope that I was wrong, this was confirmed.

So we have hardly set League Two on fire, with one point out of six from our first two matches, although two years ago in our Conference-winning season we also started with an away loss and home draw (albeit at substitute home pitch, Dorchester) so let's hope this unexpected start is a portent for a similar conclusion! Like any football fan, I will clutch at any straw available!

A Canadian friend, Mike Mayer, now teaching in Hong Kong, rang a couple of times during the day to see if we could get together as he was in this part of Vancouver with his Filipino fiancée. I had put him off because I was trying to write up some memos and thoughts regarding Casterbridge but, feeling that I was not being particularly productive, I eventually agreed to meet them down at the beach. The three of us went for a walk on Jericho Pier, which is only a few hundred yards from our house and a repository for South-East Asian and Vietnamese fisherman and crab catchers. I enjoy watching them hurl their crab traps from the end of the pier into the harbour waters.

After supper overlooking the beach, I went back home to continue my work. Hopefully things will soon start to look better for both Casterbridge and Yeovil. I need some positive news from somewhere!

Yeovil Town 1 Darlington 1

Team: Steve Collis, Andy Lindegaard, Terry Skiverton, Colin Miles, Michael Rose, Gavin Williams, Lee Johnson, Darren Way, Adrian Caceres, Phil Jevons, Bartosz Tarachulski

Subs: Roy O'Brien (28 for Rose), Kevin Gall (64 for Caceres), Simon Weatherstone (74 for Miles)

Subs not used: Chris Weale, Nicolas Mirza

Goal-scorer: Phil Jevons (6)

Attendance: 5,116

Position in League after match: 18th

Finally on our Way

Saturday 14 August 2004 – Locarno Beach, Vancouver, Canada

Yeovil v. Boston United (League Two)

Canada is renowned for the Rocky Mountains, its pristine forests and the snow-covered wastelands of the far north, and few people would associate Canada with sunny beaches on a magnificent ocean inlet but that is exactly the vista before me as I write these comments. There can surely be very few more stunning locations on which to write a football report, albeit on a match that I didn't even watch!

I was up late this morning because we erroneously went on a hike in search of Pine Cone Lake about seventy miles north of Vancouver. I took my friend Mike Mayer from Hong Kong, my daughter Lisa and nephew Daniel and it was a scorching day with temperatures around 30°C in the shade and obviously hotter in the sun. Once we were above the tree line, we all found ourselves getting very tired and going through our water much quicker than anticipated as we didn't come across any streams. After a couple of hours we realised we had started too late to make it all the way to Pine Cone Lake, so decided we would come back next year with tents and make it a two-day expedition. We got back to Vancouver late in the evening and, by the time I had unpacked the hiking gear and sorted through some papers on my desk, it was 2.30 a.m. before I went and had a bath as my back, which is causing me a lot of problems, was pretty stiff after the day's efforts.

When I woke this morning I went straight down to the den to check the internet for the Yeovil result. My nephew Daniel had wanted to sleep in the double bed in the den but I told Sharron that he couldn't as I wanted to wake up around 7 a.m. to check the 'live' text commentary, which is really like watching paint dry as every two minutes they update the summary without any descriptive flair whatsoever! I tend to sit at the desk doing some form of work and every time the screen flickers I know something has been added and you hope against hope that the next entry is going to be a Yeovil goal! I 'watched' three matches like this from Vancouver last Christmas and not one of the results was positive so, in many ways, I was glad that I did oversleep, although poor Daniel could justifiably feel hard done by! I went down to the computer, switched it on and went straight to the Yeovil result with no faffing about. There it was: Yeovil 2 Boston 0. Great! Our first win and the season has finally got underway.

I read the report and it turned out that Paul Gascoigne didn't play for Boston. Even if he had I doubt whether it would have had an impact on the result. I've never had too much time for Gascoigne, although undoubtedly at his prime he was a great player. However, I did stumble across a documentary on him on BBC3 about six months ago and I found myself feeling very sorry for him as quite clearly he has to battle the addictive aspects of his personality. I am sympathetic to the continual battle he has with depression and I hope he manages to turn his life around, but I'm not holding my breath.

The match report indicated that it was a comprehensive Yeovil victory and both strikers scored. Tarachulski opened his account in the league with a header, following Jevons' second goal of the season. If our strikers score on a regular basis then Yeovil must have a good chance of success this year, despite their faltering start. I had

Lee Johnson helps secure Yeovil's first victory of the season.

noticed during the week that Yeovil already had some injury problems with regards to this match as O'Brien, Miles and Guyett were all out and, with Lockwood suspended, that meant we were thin on resources for our back four. Gary Johnson has signed two central defenders on a month's loan and Liam Fontaine from Fulham was particularly impressive against Boston. Furthermore, as Gavin Williams had broken a finger against Darlington and was likely to be out for up to six weeks the midfield that lined up against Boston was Johnson, Way, our Australian-Argentinean Caceres and... Kevin Gall!

This surprised me as I did not realise Gary Johnson was considering Gall as a mid-fielder (although he had a few runs on the flanks last year when the goals dried up) and I thought that he might have given Nicolas Mirza the opportunity to start in mid-field. It seems to me a midfield with Johnson, Way and Gall in it is particularly short of height but what do I know? Without Gavin Williams and with a very small midfield we obviously had a very convincing win over Boston and clearly Gary Johnson likes Kevin Gall. He certainly persisted with him last season even though he rarely looked like scoring.

With several teams bunched on four points, Yeovil are up to ninth on the league on the back of this one victory and, interestingly enough, the bottom two teams are Chester and Shrewsbury, both newly promoted from the Conference. Quite a contrast to last year when the newly promoted Conference sides did very well, Doncaster ending up as champions and Yeovil just missing the play-offs by a whisker. The early signs are that the Conference teams will not fair so well this season.

After checking the results I walked the 300 yards to Locarno Beach, where I spent the afternoon and early evening writing and reading. I have been fortunate enough to travel to forty-six of the fifty American states and most of the Canadian provinces and

I can unequivocally state that Vancouver is by far the most beautiful city in North America and without doubt one of the world's great cities. Within seven miles of the city centre one can be on the summit of several 5,000ft mountains with winter skiing and yet also within five minutes of the city centre one can relax on magnificent sandy beaches. We are indeed privileged to have a home where we can walk down to Locarno Beach and enjoy the magnificent urban, mountain and sea views laid out in front of us.

While Los Angeles is always associated with the archetypical West Coast lifestyle, I have always thought that in Vancouver a significant percentage of the population actually practice it! As I sit here on the beach I can watch people windsurfing on English Bay and participating in several spectacular volleyball games practically adjacent to me on the beach. Behind me families and friends are exercising their dogs, jogging and cycling along the beachside path while in front others are playing frisbee, skim-boarding in the shallow water and diving into the sea from a nearby float. It really is a glorious panorama and full of interest. I always take my binoculars down to the beach with me and spend time looking at vessels in the harbour, at the north shore mountains in front of me across the bay, many of which I have climbed, and my glasses have even been known to wander to some of the attractive young girls walking along the beachfront as well if truth be told! To my left the sun is setting behind Bowen Island and the snow-capped Tantalus Mountains that lie beyond the Howe Sound, and two magnificent ocean liners make their way out of the harbour heading north to Alaska.

I suspect that I am probably the only person on a Vancouver beach contemplating the make up of the Yeovil team and I think at this stage that Gary Johnson has got at least eight of his first-team preferences finalised. It seems the goalkeeper's position is up for grabs between Weale and Collis, although I suspect when push comes to shove Johnson will go with Weale. New acquisition Michael Rose is preferred for sure as one of the full-backs and Skiverton as one of the two centre halves. I think the other central defender's position is up for grabs between Miles, O'Brien and Guyett and that Miles probably has the inside running. The other full-back position is available for Lindegaard, Lockwood or Miles.

At this stage it is clear that Gary's preferred midfielders are Caceres, Johnson, Way and Williams but I just wonder if it needs a hard ball-winning midfielder to replace one of them. Up front his preferred pairing is Tarachulski and Jevons.

Well, we've broken the duck! Now let's see how we go away at Notts County next week.

Yeovil Town 2 Boston United 0

Team: Chris Weale, Andy Lindegaard, Terry Skiverton, Liam Fontaine, Michael Rose, Kevin Gall, Lee Johnson, Darren Way, Adrian Caceres, Phil Jevons, Bartosz Tarachulski

Subs: Simon Weatherstone (82 for Caceres), Keize Ibe (84 for Jevons), Paul Terry (90 for Gall)

Subs not used: Steve Collis, Roy O'Brien

Goal-scorers: Phil Jevons (49), Bartosz Tarachulski (65)

Attendance: 5,178

Position in League after match: 9th

Up to Fifth

Saturday 21 August 2004 – Vancouver, Canada
Notts County *v.* Yeovil (League Two)

I awoke at 9 a.m. and realised the game at Meadow Lane had finished just minutes earlier so I went downstairs to check the results on the internet. I am always a bit apprehensive about checking results in the den because, as I explained before, I always associate that room with the two poor results against Kidderminster and Swansea last year. I turned on the computer and went straight to the BBC website and noticed a story that Kathmandu was allegedly under 'blockade' by the Maoist rebels. I went to the League Two page, holding my hand up over the top and right hand of the screen so that I wouldn't see an errant headline giving away the score and then quickly looked for Notts County. There it was: Notts County 1 Yeovil 2. What a grand result!

With two wins in a row, including an away win with Notts County, the signs are that Yeovil are indeed going to be serious contenders in League Two this year. It seems that Notts County had the best of the first two-thirds of the match, but Paul Terry chose this match to open his Yeovil account with a spectacular header from a Phil Jevons cross, and Jevons kept up his almost goal-a-game average by scoring his third league goal of the season in our fourth game to clinch the win for Yeovil.

If we can win away when not playing well it shows we are capable of mounting a very formidable challenge in this division. Obviously Jevons is not going to keep a goal-a-game average up through the season but, if he can score on a regular basis and come close to twenty-five goals, he will make all the difference and I suspect we will be promoted.

I notice Gary Johnson kept the same team as last week (Paul Terry coming on as substitute) and, as the updated league table was not posted, I started checking all the results and I calculated that Yeovil were up to sixth but, in fact, when the league table came up, we were fifth, which was excellent. Last year we were third or fourth for much of the time until Christmas, hovered around fifth and sixth until March and then we were scrambling between seventh, eighth and ninth thereafter so, although we haven't made the most impressive start of the season, to be fifth after four matches is quite satisfactory.

I think Northampton and Bristol Rovers are both going to be formidable opponents and I did think, when Ian Atkins left Oxford to go to Bristol Rovers last year, he would make a positive impact. Indeed, their end of season form was quite impressive,

Paul Terry nets his first goal for Yeovil with a spectacular header at Notts County.

notwithstanding a 4-1 defeat at Yeovil! Atkins obviously felt there was more potential with a team flirting with relegation to the Conference than with Oxford, who had led the division for much of last season, so Bristol Rovers are my early season pick for success. If nothing else I'm sure our two matches against them will be among the season's highlights.

I'm obviously turning into a football anorak as I started to review the next two matches that all the leading teams have to play over next (Bank Holiday) weekend. The six leading teams at this point are Macclesfield, Bristol Rovers, Scunthorpe, Rushden, Yeovil and Northampton, and each of these teams have to play at least one of the other five next weekend. Indeed, Rushden and Scunthorpe both have two games against leading contenders, so some of these teams are going to be dropping points for sure. If Yeovil could pick up six points next weekend or even four, we should be very well placed.

After reading and re-reading all the football reports with regard to League Two, I checked the general news on Kathmandu because, in late September, I will be leading the Chairman's Trek, which will be flying in there. A close examination of the websites showed that, to an extent, this was little more than a normal day in Nepal but one of our Canadian clients had got hold of a very exaggerated news report and was obviously worried. Bob had got in touch with me planning to cancel his participation and I had patiently explained (whilst thinking 'what a prat!') that more people had died violently in Vancouver in the last two weeks than had died in Kathmandu! I found a couple of news reports about Kathmandu that gave a more balanced perspective and e-mailed them to him, together with a report of a missing hiker in British Columbia, which just confirmed that it was perhaps rather more dangerous to go hiking on your own in Canada than to visit Kathmandu!

Our son, David, flew back to England today (his pal, Nick, went home yesterday) and I was sorry to see David go because, as I have been working overseas, I have only seen him for a handful of days when I have been back in England since late March. He has gone back early so that he can go to the Reading Festival!

I am still pretty worried about the situation with Casterbridge but I know that worry and stress goes with the territory. At least Yeovil have bounced back from their disappointing start so there is light on at least one horizon!

Notts County 1 Yeovil Town 2

Team: Chris Weale, Andy Lindegaard, Terry Skiverton, Liam Fontaine, Michael Rose, Kevin Gall, Lee Johnson, Darren Way, Adrian Caceres, Phil Jevons, Bartosz Tarachulski

Subs: Adam Lockwood (38 for Caceres), Paul Terry (50 for Lindegaard), Simon Weatherstone (83 for Jevons)

Subs not used: Steve Collis, Roy O'Brien

Goal-scorers: Paul Terry (68), Phil Jevons (81)

Attendance: 5,024

Position in League after match: 5th

A Bizarre Hat-Trick

Tuesday 24 August 2004 – Vancouver, Canada
Yeovil v. Plymouth Argyle (Carling Cup First Round)

Yeovil v. Plymouth in the Carling Cup! In truth, I haven't been too excited about this match because our priority has to be the league and an extended run in the cup competitions, while potentially lucrative, could also be a distraction and a possible source of injuries.

Plymouth were guided out of League Two last year by Paul Sturrock before he moved on to Southampton and I thought that Gary Johnson was a possible contender for the Plymouth hot seat after Sturrock's departure. This is a match against a form team from the Championship and has the added spice of being a local derby as well so, if nothing else, I guess it will serve a good purpose as a yardstick to measure out progress. I have been checking the BBC 606 forum and noted some comments from Plymouth fans who realised that coming to Yeovil could be a tricky challenge. I thought a Plymouth victory was likely and did not bother to stay in to follow the internet commentary, which was going to be between midday and 2 p.m. in Vancouver.

After an afternoon at one of my favourite stores, the Mountain Equipment Co-operative, I returned home to check the results on the internet. I wasn't in the best of moods because I'd had further telephone conversations with Bob over Kathmandu and he had confirmed their pulling out. What a wimp! The glorious weather had given way to persistent rain throughout the day, I felt that I hadn't got a great deal done over the last few days and, all in all, my mood was neither positive nor optimistic.

I pulled up the page of results for the Carling Cup and of course there were so many matches that Yeovil was off the page. So I scrolled down and what's this? Yeovil 3 Plymouth 2? What an excellent result and, of course, let's not forget that, at this stage last year, we went out 4-1 to Luton, who were a division above us!

The more I thought about it the more I thought this was really a good result. Because the match had finished several hours earlier, I was able to access a couple of reports and it seems that not only had Lee Johnson scored his first hat-trick for Yeovil but the first had been a totally bizarre goal, which was only surpassed by the unique circumstances that led to Plymouth's equaliser! Apparently, because Plymouth had an injury, they had deliberately kicked the ball into touch and, when the Yeovil throw in gave the ball to Lee Johnson, he kicked the ball downfield towards the Plymouth goalkeeper so the game could restart with the ball in Plymouth's possession. However, Lee hadn't noticed that, after looking up to see where the goalkeeper was, the 'keeper had significantly moved his position and when he kicked the ball downfield, it inadvertently went into the Plymouth net with the goalkeeper totally stranded! Obviously the Plymouth fans were not too pleased, the Plymouth team were outraged and, after a quick conference between Gary Johnson and his team, the Yeovil players just stood like statues after the kick-off and allowed a Plymouth player to quite literally walk through their defence and put the ball into an open net! Given the circumstances, that was probably the fairest and best thing that Gary Johnson and Yeovil could do to get the team out of the some-what embarrassing position that they had inadvertently put themselves in.

Thereafter, Plymouth took the lead in the second half but two outstanding strikes from Lee Johnson, one a free-kick and one from general play in extra time had given the match deservedly to Yeovil, but it will be forever remembered because of the bizarre circumstances regarding the first two goals.

Lee Johnson is a fine player despite at times being a little too impetuous in trying to take quick free-kicks. Without a shadow of doubt he and Darren Way, despite their diminutive size, are still the driving force of this Yeovil team.

Bristol Rovers won at Brighton and I think this confirms that they are clearly going to be a force in League Two under Ian Atkins. As Plymouth were second in the Championship at the time of today's game this was a victory of some merit. All in all, things are starting to look quite promising.

Yeovil Town 3 Plymouth Argyle 2 (a.e.t.)

Team: Chris Weale, Adam Lockwood, Terry Skiverton, Liam Fontaine, Michael Rose, Kevin Gall, Lee Johnson, Darren Way, Adrian Caceres, Phil Jevons, Bartosz Tarachulski

Subs: Paul Terry (57 for Lockwood), Roy O'Brien (65 for Caceres), Simon Weatherstone (89 for Tarachulski)

Subs not used: Steve Collis, Kezie Ibe

Goal-scorer: Lee Johnson (28) (69) (109)

Attendance: 6,217

Reunion with Rushden

Saturday 28 August 2004 – Vancouver, Canada
Yeovil *v.* Rushden & Diamonds (League Two)

I woke up this morning feeling awful as I had been up until about 3.30 a.m., which is nothing unusual, but I had not slept well because of my concerns regarding Casterbridge. However, I quickly realised that Yeovil's game against Rushden was over and I could go downstairs and get the result. Maybe it would give me just the fillip that I desperately needed to kick my day off.

For all Yeovil fans, a fixture against our old nemesis and Conference rivals Rushden brings back a host of memories. I remembered the last time Yeovil had played Rushden, which was four seasons ago and before Gary Johnson arrived. It was the season when we had David Webb and Colin Addison as managers and eventually lost a commanding lead and watched Rushden get promoted. Towards the end of the season, when we weren't playing well but were still in with a chance of promotion, we entertained Rushden and had a sell-out crowd. I had explained to Sharron what an important match it was and went with her and our son David and, although the atmosphere and build-up was exciting, the game was an uneventful 0-0 draw and one of the final nails in Yeovil's coffin that season. I will always remember that Sharron was pretty unimpressed to be dragged to the game but there you go, one can only try!

The crowd relished having a go at Rushden's long-serving manager, Brian Talbot, that day and he has since left the club, realising that the financial writing was on the wall. When their benefactor turned off the money that had underwritten much of their success they had to sell a lot of their better players and were subsequently relegated to League Two. What goes around comes around and now we are again in the same league as our old rivals.

I realised that the reason I was reading the latest chapter of the Wayne Rooney transfer saga rather than going straight to Yeovil's result was because I was a tad nervous that it could be bad news! At least I can admit to denial! In the end I decided to stop prevaricating and went to the League Two section and deliberately diverted my eyes away from the league table because if Yeovil had dropped to a mid-table position that would indicate a poor result. I went to the results page and would you believe it? Yeovil weren't on the page! I scrolled down with my eyes shut, opened them, focussed on the last result and there it was... Yeovil 3 Rushden 1. From 6,000 miles away that looks a very good result and it was especially pleasing to me because looking up Yeovil's results in this room has not always been positive!

A further review of the results revealed that Mansfield and Lincoln had both lost. Indeed, Lincoln lost at home to Notts County, which makes our win there last week look good. Gary Johnson had said that Notts County were going to pose problems to many teams this season and that our win there last Saturday was a good result. Macclesfield and Scunthorpe, two of the four teams above us before today, both drew, which was good for Yeovil as both of them are now only one point ahead of us. Yeovil have now overtaken Rushden to go up to fourth, just one point behind Macclesfield and Scunthorpe and three points behind Bristol Rovers.

Yeovil's three goals were scored by Johnson, Tarachulski and Jevons. That's four goals scored over two matches in four days by Johnson and I'm very pleased that both Tarachulski and Jevons scored. That makes four goals for Jevons in five League matches and, if he was able to average a goal every two matches he will end up with twenty-three in the league. I think with Yeovil's small midfield there is always a danger we are going to be bossed out of a certain number of games per season but that won't matter if we've got the firepower up front to win between half and-two thirds of our games. If we can do that, we will be going up this year and it seems that, with Tarachulski and Jevons, we may just have the two reliable goal-scorers that we need at this level. If they can stay fit through the season, things are beginning to look very hopeful indeed.

Just as we have to accept our midfield will sometimes be overrun because of its size (or lack of it!) any rational fan will also understand that our attacking instincts will sometimes inevitably leave the defence exposed or shorthanded but, again, this will not be so significant if we have regular goal-scorers who can convert the chances our attacks create. Since football switched over to three points for a win, a draw now represents two points lost and plenty of teams are going to draw matches, so the key to success is to win a good percentage of your games. It really doesn't matter if you lose a fair number in going for a win because a loss is not much worse than a draw and it's wins that count. And you need goal-scorers to win, so step forward and take a bow Jevons and Tarachulski!

With three wins in a row and a match at Mansfield to come in two days' time on Bank Holiday Monday, I certainly feel optimistic that we can achieve a play-off place and, at this stage, it looks like we will be very much in the hunt for automatic promotion. I'm not sure about the depth of the Macclesfield and Scunthorpe squads but interestingly (or should it be ominously?) Oxford and Wycombe are now fifth and sixth. Oxford are a team that played well for most of last season and indeed were top of the division until the New Year and surely Wycombe, with Tony Adams in charge, can only improve after their horrendous season last year, which led to relegation.

I went upstairs to watch some Olympic coverage and Kelly Holmes did herself proud by coming from behind and winning the 1,500m to make it an 800m and 1,500m double, the first Britain to get a middle-distance Olympic double for almost ninety years. However, the real highlight for me was to see Britain unexpectedly win the 4x100m sprint relay. This was a fantastic result, considering that none of our male sprinters got to the finals in either the 100m or 200m and the victory is always sweeter when America is the loser!

During the evening I realised that I had not checked the Carling Cup draw. Would you believe it? We have drawn Bolton at home; just about the strongest of the Premiership teams involved in the second round. Giannakopoulos, who won a European Championship winners' medal with Greece this summer, is in their team, as of course is Jay-Jay Okocha, probably Bolton's best-known player. I checked the date for the second round and it is the week beginning 20 September, when I was definitely planning to be in England. Terrific! What a great prospect and something to really look forward to!

Yeovil Town 3 Rushden and Diamonds 1

Team: Chris Weale, Adam Lockwood, Michael Rose, Terry Skiverton, Darren Way, Paul Terry, Lee Johnson, Kevin Gall, Phil Jevons, Bartosz Tarachulski, Liam Fontaine

Subs: Roy O'Brien (16 for Lockwood), Adrian Caceres (61 for Jevons), Kezie Ibe (68 for Tarachulski)

Subs not used: Steve Collis, Simon Weatherstone

Goal-scorers: Lee Johnson (16), Bartosz Tarachulski (43), Phil Jevons (44)

Attendance: 5,088

Position in League after match: 4th

Problems at Mansfield

Monday 30 August 2004 – Vancouver, Canada
Mansfield Town v. Yeovil (League Two)

I woke up at 8.30 a.m. and realised that the game at Mansfield was still going on. I really didn't want to go downstairs and watch the commentary by text as I am convinced that brings us bad luck so I thought I would lie in for fifteen minutes then go down and check the results!

My eldest daughter, Sarah, is going back to England today. My brother-in-law, Wayne, has arranged a complimentary bus ride to Seattle for Sarah and her friend Rose, who have both spent much of the summer driving round America exploring the roots of rock and roll! Sharron and Lisa are going home this coming Wednesday and I'm still not sure what I'm doing. I might stay in Vancouver for another couple of weeks and try to clear all the outstanding work I brought out with me. I don't feel I have achieved a great deal over the summer as a lot of my time and energy has been focussed on worrying about the future of Casterbridge.

The match is over, so I go downstairs to check the results in the den. Yeovil have been doing so well that, to be honest, I am really expecting to win. We won at

One-way traffic as Mansfield put four past Yeovil.

Mansfield last year and they have made an iffy start but is a fourth win in a row a bit too obvious? After all, the run has to stop somewhere. 'A draw would still be good,' I think as I switch the computer on and start searching for the BBC website. I always get a little bit nervous at this stage as I begin to fear the worse and the first headline that screams out is that Newcastle have forced Robson out. Although a little bit idiosyncratic I rate Bobby Robson very highly as a manager. I always describe him as the best manager that England never had because he was treated appallingly by the press and was never really appreciated during his tenure in charge of the national team. Wherever he has gone on the Continent he has had an outstanding track record and, let's not forget, he was within a penalty shoot-out of taking us to the World Cup final, which is far more than Sven has achieved!

I arrive at the League Two results and – oh no! – it's Mansfield 4 Yeovil 1! It looks like the wheels have well and truly come off and possibly by so much that we'll have to take the result as a blip. Or is that just wishful thinking? Even worse, it means our goal difference is back to zero from +3. However, Bristol Rovers have only drawn and, despite losing 4-1, we are only a point further behind the leaders than we were three hours ago! Macclesfield and Northampton both lost whereas Scunthorpe (against Northampton), Oxford and Wycombe all won. As a result of all this we are down to eighth.

Before this match we were averaging two points per game with ten points from five games and, if we kept that average up throughout the season, we would get ninety-two points, which I suspect might be close to a record for League Two (or what was Division Three). It is highly unlikely that we will keep that average up through the season and I suspect we won't see it again.

I went to the text commentary to see how the game had panned out and, in fact, Mansfield took the lead in the seventh minute only for Terry Skiverton to equalise in the twenty-second minute. We were 1-1 at half-time and in fact the game turned on three Mansfield goals in five minutes between the sixty-fifth and seventieth minutes. Maybe I am clutching at straws again, but it looks as if the whole match turned in five minutes of mayhem so perhaps it wasn't quite as bad as it looks.

Anyway, the euphoria is over and it's back to reality. It looks like it's going to be a tough season and I am thinking if I went home earlier I would be able to see Cheltenham away on 11 September. That will almost be a local derby given that Plymouth, Torquay, Exeter and Bournemouth are now in different divisions. Next Saturday we are home to Swansea who are seventh, one place above us, and also on ten points. That is a clearly a game that we cannot afford to lose.

Mansfield Town 4 Yeovil Town 1

Team: Chris Weale, Roy O'Brien, Terry Skiverton, Liam Fontaine, Paul Terry, Darren Way, Lee Johnson, Michael Rose, Kevin Gall, Bartosz Tarachulski, Phil Jevons

Subs: Adrian Caceres (54 for Fontaine), Simon Weatherstone (69 for Tarachulski), Colin Miles (71 for Terry)

Subs not used: Steve Collis, Nicolas Mirza

Goal-scorer: Terry Skiverton (24)

Attendance: 3,826

Position in League after match: 8th

Clipping the Swans' Wings

Saturday 4 September 2004 – Vancouver, Canada
Yeovil v. Swansea City (League Two)

I am here on my own in Vancouver. I decided to stay and try to get a fair amount of work done before my friend Ian is due to arrive and spend a few days with me before visiting his brother on Vancouver Island. I am trying to use the opportunity to get as much work done as possible and I didn't get to bed much before 4.30 this morning. I awoke at 9.30 a.m. and immediately went down to the den to check the Yeovil result.

Swansea at home has the potential to be a tricky match because it was at Swansea last year when the wheels came off and our season really started to head south. Prior to that, in September, we had beaten them comfortably at home when they came to Huish Park top of the table. At that match I thought that Lee Trundle looked particularly impressive and indeed he went on to score a lot of goals through the season and there was speculation he might be signed by a club from a higher league. I always thought Trundle would make a very good signing for Yeovil because for a big man he is both very skilful and a consistent scorer and I imagine they are paying him money that is beyond Yeovil's budget to keep him at Swansea. Furthermore, I would have thought he would probably justify a transfer fee of at least £500,000.

I noticed during the week that Adam Lockwood had picked up a serious injury in the match against Mansfield and he will be out for four to six weeks, but I think we have a big enough squad for this not to be a problem.

As I am always apprehensive about looking up Yeovil's results on the internet and don't want to receive any bad news by an inadvertent headline. I covered the screen until I had the League Two page up and then looked for the 'Y' for Yeovil at the bottom and there it was: Yeovil 1 Swansea 0! That was close but a win is a win.

As I ran through the results things got even better, Wycombe and Oxford both drew last night so that in effect meant they both dropped two points. Bristol Rovers and Scunthorpe both drew and Macclesfield lost. So we are back up to fourth and only two points behind the leaders, which is actually a better position than we were last week so in fact seven days have repaired the damage of our 4-1 defeat at Mansfield. Great!

I went to the text commentary to see who had scored and it was Gavin Williams in the eighty-second minute with a penalty. I can just imagine him taking the penalty, as he always seems to hit the ball low and, on one or two occasions, without a great deal of power, so I wouldn't have wanted to have watched it myself. Gary Johnson's starting midfield line up was Terry, Way, Johnson and Gall, with Williams coming on as a substitute. Swansea had three players booked and one sent off and it seems Weale made some good saves during the first half to keep us in the match. It appears Swansea had the best of the first half but, on balance, Yeovil deserved to win as they were pressing throughout the second half. Mansfield on nine points and Northampton on eight still have to play but neither of them can overtake us and our position in fourth place is secure for at least a week. If we had drawn today we would have been ninth so that shows just how bunched League Two is at this stage.

At the moment we are averaging 1.85 points per game, which, projected over the season, would give us eighty-five points and deliver automatic promotion. Considering we only got one point out of our first two games, our last five games have resulted in four wins and twelve points out of a possible fifteen. Not at all bad.

I spent the rest of the day working and in particular reviewing Casterbridge's finances. In the evening I checked the internet for the results of the early World Cup qualification matches and England, after leading 2-0 in Austria, were held to a 2-2 draw thanks to a goalkeeping error from David James. After watching England play in Portugal this summer, I am very definitely not a fan of Sven-Goran Eriksson as I think he is far too conservative and picks players on reputation rather than their current form. With Butt injured and Scholes having retired from international football, Wayne Bridges started on the left-hand side of the midfield, which couldn't have been much encouragement for Joe Cole who finds that, even with other midfielders unavailable an attacking full-back is still preferred to him as a midfielder!

I'm torn between not wanting to see England do too well because I think it would be good to move Eriksson on but not wanting them to trip up during this qualification series as I am looking forward to the next World Cup in Germany in two years' time. It should be quite easy and fun to follow England from our Swiss home, unless of course we are drawn to play in Hamburg or Berlin, which would be quite a trek!

Yeovil Town 1 Swansea City 0

Team: Chris Weale, Roy O'Brien, Terry Skiverton, Liam Fontaine, Paul Terry, Darren Way, Lee Johnson, Michael Rose, Kevin Gall, Phil Jevons, Bartosz Tarachulski

Subs: Andrejs Stolcers (45 for Tarachulski), Gavin Williams (45 for Gall), Simon Weatherstone (87 for Terry)

Subs not used: Steve Collis, Adrian Caceres

Goal-scorer: Gavin Williams (82 penalty)

Attendance: 5,826

Position in League after match: 4th

Afloat in Vancouver

Saturday 11 September 2004 – Vancouver, Canada
Cheltenham Town *v.* Yeovil (League Two)

My friend, Ian, arrived from England on Wednesday and on Thursday we hired a motorboat and motored up the Howe Sound (every bit as spectacular as the Norwegian Fjords) with his brother, who came over from Victoria on Vancouver Island. Yesterday Ian and I took a small boat out and explored Vancouver Harbour, crisscrossing between the ocean liners and large cargo vessels before heading up Indian Arm until it started to rain. We are obviously fair-weather sailors so we turned around and, in any case, it was quite choppy!

We had a good meal at the Afghan Horseman last night and then I was up late as per usual catching up on paperwork and so, when I woke up this morning at 8.15, I felt really knackered as I'd only had about three hours' sleep. I realised it was halfway through the second half so I went downstairs and checked the latest scores – Yeovil were drawing 1–1 at Cheltenham and I noticed Bristol Rovers were losing 4-2. I switched over to the instant text commentary and saw that Gary Johnson had started the Latvian international Stolcers, who is on a weekly contract, as a striker, and Tarachulski was relegated to the subs' bench, which was the line-up that finished last week's match.

I had been checking the internet during the week and there had been a couple of comments from Gary Johnson implying that he would like to keep Stolcers but, as his

Exploring the Howe Sound.

salary was £15,000 a week at Fulham, he was going to have to take a wage drop if he wanted to stay at Yeovil. You're not kidding! Apparently Stolcers played for Latvia when Gary Johnson was their coach and was signed by Fulham for two or three million but never really cracked it as far as the first team was concerned.

Gavin Williams was deemed fit enough to start this week, which meant Kevin Gall was relegated to the subs' bench. Adrian Caceres was also on the bench, having lost his early season starting position.

I noticed that all the teams ahead of us were either losing or drawing so, although I consider a draw as two points lost, we wouldn't be in a worse position *vis a vis* the teams ahead of us. However, if we can get a win with a goal in the next fifteen minutes we will go top!

Cheltenham had scored halfway through the first half but Darren Way had equalised only a couple of minutes later. I watched the commentary for the next fifteen minutes and the final result was a 1-1 draw but, as Bristol Rovers lost 4-2, Oxford drew 0-0 and Scunthorpe lost 2-1 at home to Chester, I think that we can very definitely say it was a point won rather than two points lost. However, Wycombe won at Southend and we have in fact dropped down to sixth but, although we are three points behind the leaders Wycombe, we are only one point behind the four teams in joint-second place. It's going to be a tight old race for League Two this year, no doubt about that.

In the afternoon I planned to drive up to Whistler with Ian to take him on a hike in the Coastal Mountains but there was obviously a very big accident on the Sea to Sky highway near Britannia Beach and, after being deadlocked in traffic for an hour and a half, we decided to turn round and just went for a short hike in the very muddy North Shore mountains.

Oxford at home next week and I am planning to get to that game that via New York, New Jersey, Washington DC, Switzerland and Canada! Why do I think I have a tiring week ahead?

Cheltenham Town 1 Yeovil Town 1

Team: Chris Weale, Roy O'Brien, Terry Skiverton, Liam Fontaine, Michael Rose, Paul Terry, Lee Johnson, Darren Way, Gavin Williams, Phil Jevons, Andrejs Stolcers

Subs: Bartosz Tarachulski (61 for Stolcers), Adrian Caceres (77 for Fontaine)

Subs not used: Colin Miles, Kevin Gall, Steve Collis

Goal-scorer: Darren Way (28)

Attendance: 3,966

Position in League after match: 6th

The Mauling of Oxford

Saturday 18 September 2004 – Huish Park
Yeovil *v.* Oxford United (League Two)

So, here we are and finally, six weeks into the season, I get to see my first 'live' match after what has been a hectic week. I flew from Vancouver to New York on Monday and, after meeting another tour operator in New Jersey, drove to Washington DC on Tuesday. I missed my flight and caught a later overnight flight to Paris, a second flight to Zurich, a train to Bern, collected my car and then spent barely ten hours at our apartment collecting the work I had been doing in June and July before driving back to England. I stopped for a break in Frankfurt en route, parked near the station and went into an internet cafe. I checked the Yeovil website and noted that Simon Weatherstone had been sold to Hornchurch earlier this week. I had actually been surprised that he had continually made the bench as a substitute for most of our matches so far this season because in truth he was another, like Lee Elam, who didn't really make much of an impression during his short stay with Yeovil.

I wandered around the red light district near the station and popped into some of the infamous 'sex inns' where the girls stand at the doors of their little cubicles. There were about twenty of these establishments all within three or four blocks, most of them six floors high and not a lift in any of them, so one builds up a fair level of fitness walking around to view the scenery! In truth it was both amusing and a tad demoralising to see so many forlorn gents wandering around and checking out the action. And only 30 Euros a shot!

I decided I couldn't be bothered to look for accommodation and decided that, if I could stay awake, I would drive through the night to Calais and get the ferry to Dover. I arrived home yesterday morning at 10.30. Once home, I went straight to bed, only to get up mid-afternoon and stay pretty much glued to the television for the remainder of the afternoon and evening, watching Europe take a 6½ to 1½-point lead against the Americans in the Ryder Cup. Great stuff! We like nothing more than to beat the Americans, who often seem to come across as supremely arrogant however gracious they try to be superficially!

I had rung Tony yesterday afternoon to see if he was going to the match today but he had to look after his children and he thought his assistant, Patrick, was busy. However, when I rang Patrick, after only a moment's hesitation, he said, 'Of course I'm up for it. Going to see the match with the chairman? I wouldn't miss the opportunity Michael!'

'Been to any of the games so far, Patrick?' I asked, wondering if he had used the season tickets.

'It's not the same without you, Michael. I mean, half the fun is going to see the matches with the chairman, isn't it? You know what I mean?'

'Patrick, you're such a creep!' However, Patrick says everything so openly his comments come across in a very endearing way.

I was watching the beginning of the second day's play of the Ryder Cup when Sharron called me from Yeovil, saying that the traffic was really backing up from Pen Mill towards Sherborne and I'd better get on my way if I wanted to get to the match in plenty of time. I set off at once and by the time I met Patrick the heavy rain and squalls had blown through and the sun was beginning to shine. Indeed, a lot of blue sky was replacing the clouds, which was good as bad weather can be a great equaliser.

Patrick is an interesting character who is guaranteed to arrive with a combination of coffee, kitkats, peppermints and, occasionally, a gourmet sandwich! He works in our UK school sales department and has possibly read every book there is on the art of selling (or at least he gives that impression!) so Patrick is well versed on saying the right thing at the right time. He is also a dead ringer for Paul Terry! Last season, when we had three season tickets, he often came with both Tony and myself and he was particularly impressed by both Andy Lindegaard and El Kholti, so he was disappointed to learn that El Kholti was no longer with Yeovil. Some of our staff find Patrick and his non-stop extrovert in-your-face energy a little hard to handle but I have never taken him too seriously and always laugh at and with him. He has an army background and sometimes, partly in jest and partly serious, if I am walking through the offices and he catches my eye he will stand up and salute! I just shake my head and tell him he is a bloody creep! Most importantly he works hard, does his job well and I admire his work ethic and enthusiasm. I enjoy going to football matches with Patrick, who is entertaining company and enjoys having the chance to make a positive impression in front of the chairman, so it works well for both of us.

The stadium was bathed in sunlight, although the crowd didn't look as big as I expected. This was surprising as Oxford were strong opponents, only a point behind us in the table and not too far for visiting supporters to attend. With Weale in goal, the back four were Skiverton and young Liam Fontaine (still on loan from Fulham) as the two centre-backs with Roy O'Brien at right-back and Michael Rose, looking every inch a genuine skinhead, at left-back. In midfield we had Lee Johnson and Darren Way in the centre with Adrian Caceres on the left and Paul Terry on the right. Our strike force was Phil Jevons, with four goals from seven starts to date, and Andrejs Stolcers, playing rather than Bartosz Tarachulski who had really caught my imagination in Canada. I was disappointed that Tarachulski was not going to start but I suspected he would be brought on at some point.

So at kick-off, although sixth, we were only one point behind second place and three points could take us to first, depending on how the other results went. Despite the wind and rain that was hanging around we kicked off under blue sky in almost perfect conditions. For the first few minutes Yeovil played some very nice one-touch football but once the game settled down, it proved to be Oxford who were well on top. Paul Terry and Roy O'Brien didn't really seem to be on the same page on the right side of the pitch and Chris Weale made three outstanding saves to keep us level.

Oxford were proving to be a very well-coached and well-organised team and, with their manager Graham Rix standing prominently on the touchline being supported by his crutches after a recent training ground accident, I was quite surprised that there was no wag in the crowd shouting out ribald comments suggesting how his injury might have been acquired!

Andrejs Stolcers had been unable to find another club after being released by Fulham and had asked Gary Johnson if he could train with Yeovil on a week-to-week contract to maintain his fitness. Notwithstanding the fact that he is an international player I thought he looked particularly ineffective for most of the first half!

As usual Patrick was getting into the match, as he is nothing if not positive and enthusiastic. If he enjoys it this much when he comes to games with me, I can't understand why he doesn't come every week when I am not around. Ironically, although I have been overseas and it was my first match of the season I was having to identify all the new players for Patrick. I was getting quite distracted by the father behind continually explaining everything to his very young daughter but, hey, what goes around comes around and I wonder how many people were distracted by me explaining to Patrick who Rose, Fontaine, Jevons, Caceres, Stolcers and Tarachulski were!

Slowly but surely, as the half progressed, Darren Way and Lee Johnson were getting Yeovil back into the game and were proving to be the real engine room of the Yeovil team. How wrong I was in my pre-season ramblings to think that there was probably only a place for one of these guys in the Yeovil midfield because quite clearly Gary Johnson sees Way and Johnson as the first two midfielders selected out of whichever four he is going to play each week and quite rightfully so. In the fifteen minutes before half-time we were beginning to get on top again but were trying to walk the ball into the net. Both Paul Terry and Michael Rose were at fault in trying to pass rather than score when they had good opportunities but, in the thirty-seventh minute, the pressure finally paid off as Stolcers cut inside, delayed his shot to round a second defender and, when he finally shot, got a lucky deflection with the ball ending up in the back of the net.

We ended the half strongly and it was good to go in with a 1-0 lead. I pointed out to Patrick that, if you ignore our first two matches and we won this match, we were going

Latvian international Andrejs Stolcers scores the first two in Yeovil's 6-1 thrashing of Oxford.

to end up with five wins and a draw from our last seven matches. If we maintained that sort of form for a good part of the season we will inevitably end up as champions! At half-time Patrick went off for a smoke and I chatted with some of the fans around us. I asked if it was a Gary Johnson quip or whether Stolcers had indeed been on £15,000 a week at Fulham, and the consensus was that the figure was correct.

'Does anyone knows what he is on at Yeovil?' I asked.

'£1,000 a week,' was what one fan had heard.

The half-time scores from the five teams above us couldn't be better because all of the teams were either drawing or losing and if the results were frozen at half-time then Yeovil would be top! However, it was very unlikely that either Oxford wouldn't come back at us or that at least one of the other teams wouldn't manage to improve on their performances in the second half, so I was certainly not making any assumptions at half-time!

Yeovil started the second half really brightly with a great shot from Michael Rose and, before long, Stolcers had scored a second to give us a 2-0 lead and from then on it only got better. Paul Terry seemed to find a completely new gear and skill level to anything he showed last season and was playing very well as an attacking midfielder. Before too long Phil Jevons had hit a third with an accurate shot at an acute angle from just inside the penalty area. That made five goals in nine games for Phil. He is clearly just what we did not have last year: a consistent scorer.

Midway through the second half Kevin Gall came on for Paul Terry and within minutes hit a centre at pace to the far post, which will surely be remembered as one of the crosses of the season, and Jevons was on the spot to head into an empty net. It was an outstanding goal and not without considerable skill from Kevin Gall. We all know he has blistering pace but his accurate cross was very impressive. 4-0 up and, with two each from Stolcers and Jevons, it was a question of who was going to get their hat-trick first. I was already wondering how many more we could get in the last twenty minutes and what a difference this match could make to our goal difference. A four-goal victory here could put us up to plus five, nearly as good as anyone in our league. However, Oxford soon spoilt those calculations when Yeovil failed to clear a bobbling ball in our penalty area and it was finally struck past a hapless Weale. The Yeovil defence does tend to look a little flat-footed now and again but, as long as we score more than we let in, I think we can live with that.

Of all the newcomers, I was probably least impressed with Liam Fontaine, who has by all accounts been playing well in previous games. I didn't think that Adrian Caceres was a significant improvement over Nick Crittenden although in the second half Caceres did make a number of telling breaks and looked a good player.

Within five minutes of the Oxford goal, Rose broke out of defence on the left side and hit a glorious cross-field ball, which must have gone all of fifty yards and more to Kevin Gall, who collected it on the edge of the penalty area and, with just one touch, volleyed it over the goalkeeper and into the back of the net. It was an outstanding goal and indeed Kevin Gall's first league goal since last December at Swansea! That has certainly been a drought and a half that has eroded his confidence but what a goal to break his duck. It was an absolute cracker.

Unbelievably there was still time for Phil Jevons to get his third goal and complete his second-half hat-trick after Darren Way harried and darted his way around the Oxford penalty area and won the ball back before playing a pass forward to put it on an absolute plate for Jevons, which brings him up to seven goals in nine league games! Well done, Gary Johnson! Many of us had ever heard of Jevons but what an outstanding buy.

And there it ended, 6-1 against one of the potentially stronger teams in the league who had only lost one of their first eight matches before today. That was Yeovil's biggest win in the Football League and the somewhat disappointing crowd of about 5,400 gave the team a tremendous and well-deserved standing ovation. Patrick was overjoyed to have seen such an outstanding performance and, as soon as we got out of the ground, rang Tony to tell him he had missed a fantastic match. However, the three of us will be coming back here to see the Carling Cup tie against Bolton Wanderers on Tuesday. That should be a good match as earlier today Bolton drew 2-2 with Arsenal at Highbury to be the first team to take points off Arsenal this season.

So, what an unbelievable match to see on my return, the undoubted highlight of the season so far. Tarachulski looked quite useful when he came on for Stolcers with about fifteen minutes to go and Yeovil look a very much stronger and more cohesive unit than last year. Interestingly enough, this was another very impressive victory without Gavin Williams. There is speculation that Stoke City are interested in Gavin but it does seem that Yeovil can play effectively without Gavin in the team. And for the icing on the cake, as I drove home I found out that Yeovil were up to second in the table and would have been first if Scunthorpe hadn't got an eighty-ninth-minute winner in their match at Bury. That is the highest we have been since that one day in mid-August 2003 when we were top after winning our first two matches in Division Three. We spent most of last season in fifth or sixth position, although we were briefly third in December.

Although I do not expect to be scoring five or six goals every match for the remainder of the season, if we can maintain the same intensity, structure and purpose that we did for most of the game today, we are going to be promotion certainties without troubling the play-offs and I think we have as much chance as any team to be champions. I cannot see any other team in League Two who are likely to stamp their authority on the division to the extent that Doncaster and Hull did last season.

Indeed, after our opening defeat and draw, Gary Johnson did say 'Let's judge this team on where we are after ten matches rather than two.' And after nine games we are second! We couldn't ask for much more than that, could we?

Yeovil Town 6 Oxford United 1

Team: Chris Weale, Roy O'Brien, Terry Skiverton, Liam Fontaine, Michael Rose, Paul Terry, Darren Way, Lee Johnson, Adrian Caceres, Phil Jevons, Andrejs Stolcers

Subs: Kevin Gall (66 for Terry), Bartosz Tarachulski (70 for Stolcers), Nicolas Mirza (76 for Caceres)

Subs not used: Steve Collis, Colin Miles

Goal-scorers: Andrejs Stolcers (38) (49), Phil Jevons (59) (69) (79), Kevin Gall (75)

Attendance: 5,467

Position in League after match: 2nd

Up Against Big Sam
Tuesday 21 September 2004 – Huish Park
Yeovil *v.* Bolton Wanderers (Carling Cup Second Round)

So this is Yeovil's second big cup match of the year, following our third round FA Cup tie against Liverpool in January, which we lost 2-0 as a result of two late goals, including, notably, a disputed penalty when Harry Kewell appeared to dive in the penalty area, much to the chagrin of cult player Hugo Rodrigues. Obviously it will be great to watch the current team pit their talents against a high-flying Premiership team but, even down in the depths of League Two, this is really just a bit of icing on the cake and I'd prefer points for a league win at Shrewsbury on Saturday than a win and glory against Bolton tonight!

I spent the day at home in Stowell catching up on paperwork and preparing for the forthcoming Chairman's Trek to Nepal and Tibet. We have lived here since 1987 and it would be presumptuous to call it a village, as it is no more than a hamlet. At the beginning of the new millennium, the population of Stowell was about eighty spread between thirty-five families. That was some progress from the reference to 'Stanwelle' (the former name for Stowell) at the time of the Norman Invasion when the population was sixty, so that's a thirty-three per cent increase over a thousand years. Not bad! But still no shop or pub and I think we all like it like that. However, we do have a phone box, church and letterbox!

I picked up my son David from school in Sherborne and then met up with Tony and Patrick. When we got to the ground, it was a lovely mild evening and indeed Bolton had left out many of their star players, including Bruno N'Gotty, Gary Speed, Henrik Pedersen, Jay-Jay Okocha, Kevin Davies and Florent Laville. Jussi Jaaskelainen was replaced in goal by Kevin Poole and the back four also included the Brazilian Julio Cesar and the Israeli captain Tal Ben Haim. The veteran Les Ferdinand was Bolton's sole striker at the age of thirty-seven but was supported by the Greek European Championship-winner Stelios Giannakopoulos on one wing and El-Hadji Diouf on the other. Ten years ago I don't think many would have thought we would be seeing a current European Championship-winner playing at Yeovil and still less someone as famous as three times European Champion's League winner and ex-Real Madrid and Spain captain Fernando Hierro, who was making his Bolton debut against Yeovil. I am sure playing against Yeovil will rank right up there with his World Cup appearances and 89 Spanish caps as a highlight of his career!

My prediction just before kick-off was that Yeovil would win 2-0 because I thought that our attacking form on Saturday, against a team that had only previously conceded three goals this season, was more than capable of unsettling many Premiership defences. Once the game got underway, it was first blood to Yeovil with a long-range shot by Darren Way but Bolton soon settled into their stride and played a very nice one-touch passing game and it soon became evident that this 'reserve' Bolton team, which was littered with internationals, were going to be formidable opponents. Hierro played a holding role just in front of the back four and the Nigerian international, Blessing Kaku, was also prominent in the early exchanges. The crowd well remembered that El-Hadji Diouf had dived several times during the game against Liverpool last season (he is currently on a season-long loan to Bolton after two unimpressive seasons with Liverpool) so every time he got the ball the whole ground resounded with a crescendo of boos, which was very amusing.

After fifteen minutes it was clear that Bolton were very much in control but they were not really making their pressure tell and most of Yeovil's efforts were being channelled through Darren Way, who was having another very effective game in midfield. Chris Weale made an outstanding save from a Les Ferdinand header after a corner and Tony turned round and commented that West Ham really missed out by not buying him. Indeed, it seems inevitable that, at some point, Chris Weale will get transferred to either a Championship or Premiership team and, when he eventually breaks into a Premiership first team, I would have thought he will have every chance of getting into the England squad because there is a paucity of English goalkeepers in the Premiership. The early exchanges were taking a very similar pattern to Saturday's game against Oxford and at this stage it was very much Weale versus Bolton!

However, with about ten minutes to half-time, we made a very promising attack thanks to good work by Johnson and, within a minute, I wasn't quite sure how a header from Jevons stayed out in the mayhem in the far goalmouth. By half-time the game had evened up and Yeovil came off to a standing ovation. We had weathered the storm and were doing very well to compete with a strong 'reserve' Premiership team. I'll nail my colours to the mast and state here and now that there is no doubt that this Yeovil team is going to be too good for League Two.

The second half proved to be far more even and Yeovil looked very comfortable on the ball and were passing it well, although, when El-Hadji Diouf broke through, it looked ominous but he totally lost control in a forlorn effort to go past Chris Weale. I was never very impressed with Diouf at Liverpool but I thought much of his approach work had been effective tonight and it was as good a game as I had seen him play.

Darren Way's work rate was truly phenomenal and he never stopped running and hustling. Indeed, he again reminded me very much of Billy Bremner or Gordon Strachan with his combination of total commitment, non-stop effort and telling passes. When Darren got injured, he and Adrian Caceres, who hadn't been too impressive, were replaced with Kevin Gall and Gavin Williams, and both showed some nice touches.

Big Sam Allardyce, Bolton's manager, was obviously getting worried as he came down from his seat in the stand to stand on the touchline, perhaps with good reason because, within moments of coming on, Kevin Gall had whipped in another devilish cross that Stolcers tried to volley first time as he was free on the edge of the penalty area. Bolton brought on Kevin Davies, the former Southampton striker, who was an ever present and top scorer for Bolton last season, and followed that not long after by bringing on the Dane Henrik Pedersen, who scored against Arsenal on Saturday. Obviously Bolton were trying to kill the game off and decided to bring on some of their stars for the last quarter of the game.

A Hierro free-kick in a dangerous position caused some problems and, throughout the game, Yeovil had not looked too confident against the Bolton corners and set pieces. Just as I jotted in my notebook that Bolton's corners were causing problems, with the usual chorus of boos in the background, Diouf took a very good corner that Julio Cesar met with a bullet header and Bolton took the lead with just eleven minutes to go. That brought us all down to earth. Minutes later the game was killed off when Skiverton misjudged a long punt and it bounced over his head to leave Pedersen with just Fontaine between him and the goal. As they both ran on to the bouncing ball, it was Pedersen who brought it under control and shot through Fontaine's legs and past the outstretched arms of Weale into the corner of the goal. So, after competing for eighty minutes, all of a sudden we were 2-0 down and the game was dead and buried. That, of course, is how it ended.

C'est la vie! It was a good night out and we will not come up against many teams in League Two who are as strong as the Bolton outfit that we met tonight. In a curious sort of way, I felt quite positive when leaving the ground and tonight's performance only confirmed to me that, as a team, we are probably far too good for League Two. Maybe I am counting my chickens but there is even a little bit of me that is perhaps disappointed we will not be involved in the excitement of advancing via the play-offs because I believe that, at worst, we are going to win an automatic promotion place.

We had a long walk back to the car and David and I dropped Tony off in Sherborne and then went home. Although I had a lot of work to do, I actually ended up watching the video of tonight's match! The pre-game show featured the previous match against Plymouth so, for the first time, I saw the 'unfortunate' goal that Lee Johnson scored when just attempting to give the ball back to Plymouth after an injury stoppage and then how Yeovil stood like absolute statues to allow the Plymouth player to walk through their ranks to score an instant equaliser, a gesture widely applauded around the country and for which Yeovil have been nominated for a FIFA Fair Play Award.

It was interesting watching the match again after having seen it live because one saw it from a completely different perspective. One interesting observation that the commentators made was that the two eldest players in the Football League were both involved in tonight's match. Kevin Poole, the Bolton goalkeeper, was forty-one and of course Steve Thompson, the Yeovil coach, who has a few more years added on top of this, is still registered with Yeovil as a player for emergency purposes.

By the time I had watched the game again on video it was after 2 a.m. and I didn't feel up to starting any work at that stage, so I went off to bed thinking that I'd be in Kathmandu for Yeovil's next game!

Yeovil Town 0 Bolton Wanderers 2

Team: Chris Weale, Michael Rose, Lee Johnson, Terry Skiverton, Liam Fontaine, Paul Terry, Adrian Caceres, Roy O'Brien, Darren Way, Andrejs Stolcers, Phil Jevons

Subs: Gavin Williams (63 for Caceres), Kevin Gall (64 for Way), Bartosz Tarachulski (81 for Stolcers)

Subs not used: Steve Collis, Colin Miles

Attendance: 8,047

A Call to the Chairman

Thursday 23 September 2004 – At Home, Stowell

I spoke to John Fry, Yeovil's chairman, today on the phone to tell him about this book. He was aware of my escapades last year when I came back from Everest to watch the penultimate match against Hull. My reason for ringing him was to see if I could arrange some interviews with himself, Gary Johnson and some of the players. Given that the title is *Around the World with Yeovil Town*, I thought it would be particularly useful to include some interviews with the overseas players as well as the local lads, like Andy Lindegaard and Chris Weale, which would illustrate the diversity of the club as it is today.

John Fry thought the book and the theme was an excellent idea and said he would give me whatever help and support I needed. He was very helpful and I have a lot of respect for what he has achieved at Yeovil. Four years ago I wasn't sure whether he was the right man for the position but, in fact, if you judge people by their results, his stewardship is totally vindicated by the progress Yeovil has made over the last three years and I congratulated him on such an outstanding start to the season. Like me, he thinks that Yeovil have every chance of being promoted this year and he said that, as an organisation, we are better equipped to be promoted this season than we would have been last season. He had just returned from the League Two chairmen's meeting in Oxford and he felt that, in comparison with most of the clubs in the league, we were very much ahead of the game.

John Fry was obviously on the ball because, within an hour, I got a phone call from Adrian Hopper (the infamous Fat Harry), Yeovil's media and communications manager, who said he too would give me all the help I wanted as far as promoting this book was concerned. He thought it was a novel idea and something completely different. I was encouraged that both the chairman and Fat Harry were enthusiastic about the project as this book is already taking up a lot of my time!

Today is our daughter Sarah's twentieth birthday. We went to the Rajpoot Indian restaurant in Sherborne for a celebration dinner with Sharron, my mother, Lisa, David and Sarah's friend Rose. Sarah's teenage years have come and gone and like all parents I am sad to see our kids growing up so quickly.

Tomorrow I am off to Kathmandu in Nepal and on Saturday Sarah is off to the University of Sussex to study Sociology with Social Psychology so I probably won't see much of her until Christmas. I've always been friendly with the Bangladeshi team that run the Rajpoot and the manager was brimming with pride when we arrived. And just why was he brimming with pride? We found out five minutes later when he brought a selection of photos of a turbaned groom, which was clearly him with his new wife. He had apparently gone back to Bangladesh this summer to get married and told us that he had only met his wife for the first time on the day of the wedding. She was indeed a very attractive thirty-year-old. 'Not bad for a lucky dip,' I quipped and even my wife and mother found that amusing and he laughed as well.

When I got back home at about midnight, I made some headway with the files on my desk and completed some of the packing I had to do in preparation for tomorrow's five-week trip. I really didn't feel that positive about things in general, as there are a lot of issues regarding Casterbridge that I have yet to resolve. At least everything with Yeovil was looking pretty good, I thought as I went off to bed. Better to live to fight another day!

On Top in Kathmandu

Saturday 25 September 2004 – Kathmandu, Nepal
Shrewsbury Town v. Yeovil (League Two)

I woke on a Qatar Air Airbus A-300 between London and Doha after a two and a half hour sleep despite a heavy head cold and a very runny nose that was not helped by the air conditioning. I was en route to Nepal with thirteen clients and Caedmon, a professional filmmaker, to lead the annual Chairman's Trek, which this year is a thirty-

day adventure through western Nepal to Mount Kailas in Tibet. After a four-day cir-
cuit of this unclimbed and very holy mountain we will be transferred by five Land
Cruisers across the high, dry Tibetan Plateau to Rongbuk Monastery where we will
follow the route of the early British Everest Expeditions of the 1920s and 1930s from
Rongbuk Base Camp to Advance Base Camp and beyond to a famous pass, the
Raphu La at the very foot of Everest's long, dangerous and infamous North-East
Ridge. If we get to that point we will be above 6,500m (21,000 ft). Without doubt
this is genuinely the journey of a lifetime for our clients and I am not aware that any
other company has ever combined western Nepal, Kailas and the North-East Ridge
of Everest.

I felt quite exhausted last night at Heathrow. I was only back in the UK for a week
after five days' travelling and had a lot to do, let alone prepare for this trip! I did not
meet our CEO David, or go into the office at all, so the situation with Casterbridge is
unresolved. I feel comfortable with that and hope that he can prove that all my concerns about the company are unfounded. Worrying about Casterbridge has worn me
down this summer but I suspect interacting with new people and directing this trek
will be very good for me.

Caedmon, two clients and myself were on the Qatar Air flight and the other eleven
were on a Gulf Air flight about an hour behind us. Christine and Richard are friends
who have previously trekked together in Kenya and India and are good company.
Indeed, Christine is a former tour operator who ran her own ski company for over
twenty years and had sold her business to a former employee of ours, so she knew
quite a lot about Casterbridge. What a small world! She loves not having the responsibility of running her business any more and I am a tad envious, although I am not
ungrateful for the considerable benefits that I derive from Casterbridge.

After changing planes in Doha we were descending into Kathmandu and I remembered, as always, the PIA Airbus crash of 1991 when Mark Miller (our Great Walks of
the World manager Andy Broom's original partner in his previous company) had been
killed, together with everyone else on board when the plane slammed into a hillside.
Fortunately there was no cloud around today and we landed on the runway! At
Kathmandu's hot airport, surrounded by hills, we descended to the tarmac and then
got a shuttle bus to the terminal. By now I knew to get in the visa queue first and fill
the form out while queuing rather than fill it in first and end up at the back of the
queue! The visa was $30 but, after several close inspections, the visa officer instruct-
ed his assistant to refund my money because my last visit in April had exceeded
fifteen days and I therefore qualified for a free visa! How nice of them. The Nepalese
are such charming people although, in truth, the country, the tenth poorest in the
world, could better use the $30 than me.

I went out to the usual bustle of people, touts and waiting agents and quickly
recognised our agent, Suman. I arranged for Christine and Richard to be transferred to
the hotel while Caedmon and I waited for the other eleven in our group soon to arrive
on the Gulf Air flight. I talked my way past immigration officials and re-entered the
not-very-secure (after all this is Nepal!) arrivals area and met my friend Colin Tucker
coming out, so obviously their plane had landed and I quickly found the remainder of
the group processing their visas.

It was good to have the chance to have five minutes to chat with Ray Tempest as we

Ancient Kathmandu.

sorted out the baggage. He was a client I took to Everest Base Camp two years ago. Ray left school with no qualifications, tried for ten years or so to make it as a professional golfer, got his GCSEs and 'A' Levels in his thirties before getting an Open University degree in Psychology and becoming a counsellor. Ray is a real laugh and his private life is as interesting as his professional life. He stays one night a week with ex-wife number one, two nights with current but separated wife, one night with one son, one night with another son and one night on his narrow boat! I guess that leaves one night for getting lucky!

We loaded and boarded our bus for the transfer to the famed Thamel area in the heart of Kathmandu. Nepal is one of the world's poorest countries and we were immediately immersed in the real Asia as we followed one of the least ostentatious airport to city transfers in the world. No four-way highway here as we drove along narrow alleys and between shanty dwellings amid roadside vendors, repair shops, washing hanging out to dry and always hordes of people hanging around aimlessly. We drove past the Royal Palace, where three years ago a drugged Crown Prince murdered his parents and virtually the entire royal family. Finally, we turned into Thamel and arrived at the Marshyangdi Hotel where a big poster proudly bedecked the front of the hotel welcoming 'Michael Bromfield and the Great Walks Mount Kailas and NE Ridge of Everest Trekking Team'! As always I was greeted like an old friend, and eventually got everyone to register and checked into their rooms in this comfortable hotel owned by a Tibetan family from Manang.

I went out for a wander around the narrow streets of Thamel, a heady concoction of bars, restaurants, money exchangers, clothes stores, handicraft outlets and record shops before I met the group in the foyer at 7.30 p.m. and gave them a brief introduction to Nepal regarding hygiene, do's and don'ts, beggars, etc.

We had an enjoyable dinner at the famed Rum Doodle Bar and I felt considerably more relaxed than at any other period over the last few weeks. The group seems very congenial, with nice and interesting people, and all the signs indicate that this will be a positive experience, although I am loath to draw conclusions on day one of a thirty-day trip! By 10.30 p.m. we were ready to wander back through the dark streets to our nearby hotel. Technically there was a curfew because of the Maoist 'threat' but the occasional shop and several bars were open and the police were happy to let people wander around.

I felt tired but relaxed and what could be better than to find Yeovil have won away at Shrewsbury today and gone top! I bade farewell to the group only a hundred yards or so from the hotel and made my way to the internet shop that Sarah, Lisa and I used when we were out here in March. I am sure at least one or two of the group suspected I was making my way to one of the many brothels masquerading as massage parlours rather than checking on Yeovil's progress! Internet shops are all over Thamel at about 40p an hour and I turned to the League Two pages. As I waited for the page to flip to the results page, my eyes couldn't resist the temptation and strayed over to the league table where Yeovil were.... TOP! So we must have won. Fantastic!

The results page came up and confirmed Shrewsbury 1 Yeovil 2. What a fine end to a good day. Indeed, this result makes it a grand day! The clouds and stress that have hovered around me for weeks are beginning to lift; I am with a nice crowd, I'm looking forward to the trek and I can't be contacted by work! I've no immediate worries and Yeovil are top, having reclaimed the position they held for one week only after the first two matches of last season. But ten matches into this season is far more significant! All kudos to Gary Johnson who, after the disappointing first two matches, said 'No panic, it's early days, judge us after ten matches'. Well Gary, we are judging you after ten matches and you're top! Well done! So our record is six wins, two draws, two losses and actually 6-1-1 for the last eight matches. That's not promotion form; that's championship form if it can be sustained.

There was no report posted so I read the text commentary. Colin Miles and Gavin Williams had replaced Terry Skiverton and Adrian Caceres with Paul Terry retaining his place in midfield. We were 1-0 down at half-time but fought back in the second half with goals from Johnson, his fifth of the season, and Tarachulski, who came on in the second half. It seems we have three strikers all capable of putting the ball in the net with Jevons on seven, Tarachulski on three and Stolcers on two. That will pro rata to fifty-four goals over the season and the rest should score thirty. I think if we can score eighty-four goals this season we will win the league! Furthermore, Gavin Williams missed a twice-taken penalty so the victory margin could have been greater.

We have also achieved the very significant two points a game average, which I don't expect to maintain through the season. That will be virtually impossible but ninety-two points would bring us the championship for sure. Scunthorpe, Wycombe and Mansfield all drew 1-1 whereas Swansea and Macclesfield won 1-0. We are top with twenty points with Scunthorpe and Swansea on nineteen, Wycombe on eighteen and both Macclesfield and Mansfield on seventeen. It would be nice to net a couple of wins now and put some daylight between us and the pack, although Yeovil's position would be more dominant if not for our opening two results.

If we can get through the next couple of matches it's not inconceivable we could stay top from here on, just as in our Conference-winning season. Already there are some very uncanny resemblances, with an opening away defeat followed by a home draw and going top in late September!

I was in bed by 12.45 a.m. but woke after two hours and started reading Walt Unsworth's classic history of the exploration and ascents of Everest. It will help me be prepared with information and history by the time we get there! We won't be going to the top of the mountain but it will be nice if Yeovil are still top of the league when we arrive at Everest!

Shrewsbury Town 1 Yeovil Town 2

Team: Chris Weale, Michael Rose, Liam Fontaine, Colin Miles, Roy O'Brien, Gavin Williams, Darren Way, Lee Johnson, Paul Terry, Phil Jevons, Andrejs Stolcers

Subs: Kevin Gall (46 for Miles), Bartosz Tarachulski (60 for Jevons), Nicolas Mirza (84 for Stolcers)

Subs not used: Steve Collis, Adrian Caceres

Goal-scorers: Lee Johnson (69), Bartosz Tarachulski (72)

Attendance: 4,196

Position in League after match: 1st

Are There Rocks in These Clouds?

Tuesday 28 and Wednesday 29 September 2004 – Nepalgunj – Simikot – Masigaon (Western Nepal)
Torquay United v. Yeovil (LDV Trophy First Round)

As this game was played in the evening of Tuesday 28 September UK time, which was early morning Wednesday 29 September Nepalese time, this account covers both days until the result was known to me.

On Monday we flew to the hot, dry and undistinguished town of Nepalgunj, five kilometres from the Indian border in western Nepal. After staying overnight at a hotel with the plus points of a small swimming pool and armed guards patrolling the roof twenty-four hours (this is a town close to areas controlled by the Maoist guerrillas) we were hoping to fly to the remote Nepalese village of Simikot on Tuesday to begin the first stage of our journey, a six-day trek through the Himalaya to the Tibetan border.

Departing from Simikot.

We left the hotel at 5.45 a.m. yesterday and the ride to the airport was quite an experience. Although it was still dark, the road was alive with action. There were women in colourful saris, kids going to school on foot and rickshaws parked at the side of road waiting for business. There were buses parked and loading up, brightly decorated lorries and cows still sleeping on the road with the bus bearing down on them at a rate of knots. Even worse were those cows wandering aimlessly in the road with the driver throwing the bus around them and trying not to hit pedestrians, oncoming traffic or rickshaws during the process. Anything on the road was a potential target with our bus heading full speed at them, klaxon bearing!

However, our journey was in vain as it appeared there was bad weather at Simikot and, after waiting several hours and after a chat with the air traffic control manager in the control tower (there's nothing like getting first-hand information!), we loaded up the bus and rushed back to the hotel with a suicidal kamikaze driver who it seemed had only been taught to use the horn and not the brakes. Everyone broke into a round of sarcastic applause when our child-sized driver got us to the hotel alive!

I spent the afternoon around the pool telling Christine and Richard about the history of the early Everest expeditions. They seemed impressed but in truth my knowledge was pretty basic and no greater than anyone's with an interest in Himalayan exploration.

I thought everyone coped with the lost day very well. I went to bed last night around 11 p.m., 6.15 p.m. UK time, which meant another hour and a half before the kick-off of Yeovil's LDV Trophy game at Torquay. I went to sleep wondering if we would repeat our pre-season victory at Torquay, which spurred me to write this book, and I had a good night's sleep, waking up this morning with two things on my mind.

Firstly, how did Yeovil do at Torquay last night? I could not call home as it was about 1 a.m. in England! Secondly, if there was an extended period of poor mountain weather our itinerary could be shot to pieces.

After breakfast we got on the bus in the early morning gloom and there was some amusement (or disappointment) that our driver was the midget kamikaze driver who astounded everyone with his escapades bringing us back from the airport yesterday. I feared that the sardonic round of applause the group had given him for reaching the hotel alive would only encourage him to greater excesses. As we drove down the hotel drive I was about to comment that we had at least got to the road without him using the horn but I spoke too soon! For the second morning in a row we managed to get to the airport without hitting anything and this time we were in luck. After a few hours our agent, Jiban, took me out to the tarmac, the plane was in and he introduced me to his friend the pilot who said we should be okay. I returned to join my group in the waiting room and I gave 50 rupees to the deaf mute who seemed to live at the airport in a dirty David Beckham T-shirt. He had always tried to be helpful during the three days we had spent passing through the airport.

The plane was a small eighteen-seat Twin Otter, which fitted our group of fifteen and we were soon tearing down the runway and lifting off, but there was still a lot of low cloud around and I thought 'Here we are flying into the high Himalaya with clouds everywhere – that's a really clever idea!' I couldn't see any land below and there was still some cloud above us, and I wondered how the pilot picked our route out as there are no navigational aids here! I was reminded of the sign that they used to have at Kathmandu airport: 'In Nepal we do not fly whenever it is cloudy because our clouds sometimes have rocks in them'!

There was so much cloud around I thought there must have been a fair possibility that we might turn around and go back to Nepalgunj. My altimeter said we were at 3,585m and as we barely cleared a ridge I estimated we were no more than 100m above the trees. Our journey thereafter consisted of crossing a succession of forested ridges with deep valleys between them, inevitably with a stream rushing along at the bottom. After about fifty minutes I saw some isolated houses and narrow terraces carved out of the precipitous slopes below and when I looked forward I saw there was land filling our windscreen as the pilot had left the cockpit door open so that we could see what was going on. As more houses came into view through the cockpit window it was clear we were on our final approach to Simikot. The pilot made a quick turn to the left and we came down rather heavily on a short dirt runway.

Our sirdar (leader), who had been waiting in Simikot for two days, welcomed us. His name is Dakipa and I later learnt he had climbed to the South Col of Everest on four occasions and had reached the summits of Shishapangma and Cho Oyu, the sixth and thirteenth-highest mountains in the world respectively, and both over 8,000m. He had been at our briefing meeting in Kathmandu on Sunday and then flown here to begin recruiting the forty/fifty porters, yak herders and horse handlers that would accompany us for the next six days.

Our plane was ready to return to Nepalgunj so I thanked the pilot and co-pilot for delivering us safely to Simikot. The plane went to the end of the runway, and with engines blaring started building-up speed, bouncing a couple of times before finally lifting off just before running out of runway. This was just as well because, like many of Nepal's remote mountain airstrips, the runway ends on a sharp slope and if you don't lift off, you go cart-wheeling into the valley below! Within seconds the runway resumed its prime use as a pedestrian thoroughfare with people crossing it and milling around.

We walked through Simikot to an enclosed area, which was obviously used as a preparatory area for expeditions as there were areas for the cooks to prepare food and several trestle tables had been put together for lunch. The cooking staff were all crouched over pots, pans and primus stoves and there must have been at least fifty or sixty horses and yaks gathered in the adjacent paddock waiting to be loaded up with supplies and baggage for the trek north to Tibet.

Dakipa wanted all our passports so that he could take them to the immigration office to get our exit visas for Nepal stamped. Although it is a six-day walk to the Chinese border it is considered too dangerous for the government to keep an immigration post any closer to the border than Simikot as most of the country that we would be walking through is under the control of the Maoist rebels trying to overthrow the Nepalese government.

The hustle and bustle was amazing, with animals, porters, prospective porters, cooking staff, onlookers, women and children all mingling around and meanwhile our group were having a gourmet lunch on trestle tables complete with table cloths in the middle of everything. It was really quite surreal. The security forces in Nepal are not too keen on people using satellite phones so I did not want to use my phone in Simikot to find out how Yeovil did last night at Torquay. I decided I would call home in the evening when we had made camp and finally, after the yaks and mules were loaded up, we were on our way at 2.30 p.m., climbing out of Simikot on the first of what I estimated would be fifteen days of challenging walking.

Going on trek in Nepal can be a very interesting experience. On this occasion we had ten Nepalese trekking and kitchen staff accompanying us, fifteen trekkers and probably about fifty animals carrying bags with perhaps twenty-five herdsmen each cajoling two or three animals along precipitous trails, whacking them with sticks, pulling ropes or propelling rocks into the rump of any animal they considered to be either tardy or wayward!

We reached our campsite after about four hours and we hadn't erected the tents when Dakipa told me that a Maoist had come and said it was traditional for every group passing through to donate three camera films and some clothing! The problem was that we all had digital cameras! Our professional photographer, Paul Quayle from South Cheriton, jokingly said he was happy to turn over some out-of-date films as long as he could get a photograph of the Maoist but when he saw the kid, who looked no more than a schoolboy, he didn't even bother to take a picture!

The young Maoist did come back again after dinner, this time with two others and in the end were satisfied with a sleeping bag, waterproof trousers and an all-weather jacket. Quite clearly our trekking crew were not going to be arguing with anyone who said they were a Maoist whether or not they looked like an overgrown schoolboy! Clearly the government does not have any real authority or control over this remote part of western Nepal.

I went out at a quarter to midnight to ring home on the satellite phone, although I was very conscious that if there were any Maoists hanging around the camp who saw me they would be sure to want the phone as a 'gift'! I got through to Sharron and she told me that last night's LDV game at Torquay resulted in a 4-3 loss, which I considered to be a good result because if Yeovil are out of the tournament then that is one less distraction. Secondly, to score three goals away against a League One team shows that Yeovil will be more than competitive in League Two.

So I was well pleased and hoped that Yeovil could take that form into next Saturday's match against Northampton. I told Sharron I would ring her on Sunday to get the Northampton result as the match won't be over until midnight local time, and told her to also check the Mansfield, Macclesfield, Scunthorpe, Wycombe and Orient results. Meanwhile, we're finally heading for Tibet!

Torquay United 4 Yeovil Town 3

Team: Steve Collis, Stephen Reed, Liam Fontaine, Roy O'Brien, Andy Lindegaard, Adrian Caceres, Paul Terry, Nicolas Mirza, Kevin Gall, Bartosz Tarachulski, Andrejs Stolcers

Subs: Lee Johnson (72 for Mirza), Michael Rose (72 for Reed), Yemi Odubade (74 for Stolcers)

Subs not used: Chris Weale, Kezie Ibe

Goal-scorers: Andrejs Stolcers (42), Adrian Caceres (67), Bartosz Tarachulski (84)

Attendance: 1,610

Held-Up by Maoists

Saturday 2 and Sunday 3 October 2004 – Yangar – Thado Dunga, Humla Region, Western Nepal
Yeovil v. Northampton Town (League Two)

Although the game was played in the late evening of 2 October Nepalese time, I did not get the result until the following afternoon so this account spans both days.

Yesterday I woke thinking Yeovil had a tricky game at home to Northampton but thoughts of Yeovil were quickly dismissed as I had three interlopers at the door of my tent! Whenever we camp near a village people appear and yesterday was no exception as three Nepalese kids stood in my tent doorway watching me sort myself out. It always seems to take an hour to wash, get dressed and put everything away in my kit-bags. There's not much to do but it always takes an hour!

I felt a tad listless yesterday and was glad it was going to be a short day, which it was as we were at our campsite by lunchtime. The day's progress was limited by not wanting to ascend too far in a day to ensure proper acclimatisation. Last night's dinner was good – vegetable and garlic soup, beautiful roast potatoes, parsley in cheese sauce, boiled cabbage but still no sign of the cakes that Andy had packed for desserts! The Sherpas do a wonderful job of cooking in such remote locations.

'I wonder when we'll see the Maoists,' Andrew asked.

'Maybe they're at the border,' someone replied.

'There's 600 million of them at the border!' I commented.

Last night I had the mess tent to myself to finish my journal and, when I went to bed, noted there was still half an hour of Yeovil's home game against Northampton left. I had a feeling this could be a tricky game and suspected we might not be winning. As I was tired I decided to call home today when the final result was known.

Today was the fifth day of our six-day trek from Simikot to the Tibetan border and generally we are doing fine, although the fifteen participants have had their expected selection of colds, coughs and tummy upsets. I am glad that I resisted the temptation to try and do the trek in five days to regain the day lost waiting for our flight in Nepalgunj. It would have been possible to have done so but yesterday this would have involved gaining almost 800 metres of altitude in one day and there would have been a good chance that at least one of the fifteen of us would have suffered from altitude-related problems, so I have stuck to a conservative level of ascent, which means we will still do the trek in six days.

It is an interesting group that came from a very varied selection of backgrounds – Richard, an accountant aged sixty, who only signed up for the trek eight days before departure, is the eldest and Rohit, twenty-seven, of Indian origin, is the youngest. There have been no arguments and everyone gets on very well. There has not been much more than about forty-five minutes between the first and last of our group arriving at any given destination after a day's walking so there are no weak links. Everyone has been wondering if and when we will meet the Maoist insurgents who control much of Nepal, and how much we will have to pay to be able to pass on our way.

I didn't sleep particularly well last night, which is not unusual as one gains altitude, but dozed on and off until one of our Sherpas came to my tent with a hot drink at 6.30 a.m. Another Sherpa brought a bowl of hot water to my tent so I was able to have a good wash, which made me feel a lot fresher for the day, and I was also pleased that, when I checked the colour of the urine in my pee bottle, it was much clearer than yesterday (the clearer the urine the more body fluids I am retaining and the better I am adjusting to altitude).

After the usual hour to sort out my tent and get the sleeping bag rolled up and everything packed away into my kit bags I emerged from my tent to a very cloudy day. Despite the Cheerios and hot milk (!) I had a good breakfast and the cheese omelette and chapatti went down particularly well. I had a couple of coffees and felt more energetic for today's hike than I did yesterday. Rohit came up to thank me for arranging for him to have a single tent last night, as he felt much better on an uninterrupted night's sleep. I got my woolly hat out to keep my head warm then I went to Dakipa and asked if we could start off.

After a couple of hours we came to some ruined buildings on the trail, which were several hundred feet above the much bigger settlement of Yari where two valleys met below us. There must have been at least fifty or sixty dwellings in Yari village but most of the houses on the trail seemed abandoned. However, there were canvas tarpaulins spread over two of the buildings, forming a makeshift roof, and a man emerged from one and a woman from another to stare at us with great interest. It was bleak, windy, the surrounding slopes below the low cloud were dry and arid and I couldn't help describing our location as the arsehole of nowhere!

The group was pretty much all together and we all set off again with people stopping from time to time to look at the activity in the fields several hundred feet below. After traversing around a couple of ridges on our still-level track I could see the trail beginning to zigzag upwards in the distance, which I assumed was the beginning of the ascent to the Nara La pass, which I wanted to cross tomorrow. My intention was to sleep below where the ascent to the pass began at around 3,900m.

As we walked along the bleak trail it turned out we had been joined by a young boy on a horse who had probably ridden up from the village of Yari. He told one of our Sherpas that he was a Maoist and asked if we had paid the expected 'donation' for using the trail. Our Sherpa told him that we had paid the fee earlier on the trail (which was an outright lie) and said he didn't know which of us was the group leader. Caedmon was quite optimistic that he had persuaded this kid that we probably had paid and that maybe we could fluke it. However, it turned out the Maoists were not that naïve!

We finally arrived at our campsite at Thado Dunga at noon after a very easy three and a half hour walk. It was still cloudy but not too windy and occasionally a snow-covered peak emerged from the clouds around us. It turned out the boy on the horse had come back and was accompanied by an older guy and my group had heard from our trekking crew that these were the Maoists and they wanted payment. Some of the group questioned if they were genuine Maoists or perhaps just 'Johnny come lately' extortionists who were using the Maoist insurgency as an excuse to take money from travellers. We had briefed the group before departing England that it was quite probable we would be stopped by Maoists and asked to pay a fee of between $20 and $100 so the group were prepared for this eventuality, but nevertheless there were some comments as to how one single guy with a boy and a donkey would propose halting fifteen adults and a large trekking crew if we refused to pay and just continued on our way. Our blunt Lancastrian, Dave, was typically forthright and blunt: 'It's nothing more than fucking extortion. Tell him to fuck off and if he doesn't I'll give him a fucking head butt to send him on his fucking way. Let him come back with his fucking Kalashnikov if he wants his $100 and then I'll change my mind pretty quick.'

The mess tent and kitchen tent went up pretty quickly and then Dakipa came over to tell me that the Maoists were here and asked me to go into the tent to talk to them. I took Caedmon with me to film the whole episode. Ray came in as well so there was at least one of the group who could report to the clients on the negotiations that took place.

The small guy opposite me looked tired and wore a fez-type hat and I jokingly nicknamed him Mustafa, to which Ray quickly added 'Must have $1,800' because that was the sum that he wanted! He had established that there were fifteen in our group and he wanted $120 per person. The first thing I had to do was verify whether he was a genuine Maoist or just trying to take advantage of the situation, and he showed me two receipt books that were printed Nepal Communist Party (Maoists) for the Humla area, containing stubs for payments made by individuals and legitimate trekking groups dating back to April that were the equivalent of 100 Euros or $120 per person. Mustafa and his sidekick were the real deal so it was game on!

I suggested that, as we had a large group of fifteen people, we should pay a lower per-person fee. Furthermore, I said it was not appropriate for Caedmon or myself as staff to pay, although I quickly explained to the group members who were listening that this was only to reduce the net amount payable and we would still divide the total amount payable by fifteen. I asked for Chola, the younger Sherpa who had been talking to the pony boy on the trail, to be brought into the tent as his English was better than Dakipa's and Chola understood the concept of negotiation. I explained to Chola that we would only pay $50 per person and he should translate this to Mustafa. Ten minutes of discussions followed before Mustafa put his head on the table to indicate he was obviously not budging and was bored with the debate.

I asked how he proposed to stop our party and no response was forthcoming. The group, who had now all crowded into the mess tent, suggested we just call his bluff and sit it out. I knew sooner or later we were going to have to pay something but at this point Mustafa walked out of the tent, went over to three of the tents that had been erected and started pulling out the tent pegs. The message was clearly 'you are not going to stay here' and our Nepalese trekking crew, who had to stay in Nepal and would possibly return to this area were hardly going to continue against the Maoists' wishes.

Chola thought we could probably just pay $100 but Mustafa was now so pissed off that he wasn't returning to the tent unless I went to him! He eventually returned and I wrote 15 x $100 = $1,500 on a piece of paper. Out came Mustafa's calculator, a few buttons were pressed and the figure was shown to me as $1,800. He was not budging and there were a few jokes about being held up by a calculator and not a Kalashnikov! Mustafa then made it clear that he was not accepting any tens, fives or singles so we had to exchange denominations until we had $1,800 in notes that were acceptable to him!

One of our group members then asked if we could have individual receipts rather than a group receipt, as donations to the Nepalese Communist Party would make great souvenirs! With the cash safe in my pocket I had to write out fifteen individual receipts in his receipt book, which were then carefully removed and distributed before I finally gave over the $1,800 which had to be recounted! Bloodshot and bleary eyed he may have been but the eagle-eyed Mustafa had already pointed out one (genuine) mistake with my addition when I had previously counted the notes in front of him!

What a bloody pantomime. All I wanted to do was to get this over with as quickly as possible so I could call home on the satellite phone and get the result of Yeovil v. Northampton! During these protracted negotiations two hot drinks were supplied for myself and Mustafa. I did not appreciate the significance of being told which was 'my' drink but, unbeknown to me, a substance or two was added to Mustafa's which would result in a few extra visits to the toilet over the next twenty-four hours, if he stayed awake!

We finally got a wry smile from Mustafa and a cursory handshake acknowledging that the transaction was complete, and our cook ushered us into the mess tent for our long-delayed lunch. The conversation naturally revolved around the payments the group had to make to the Maoists. We were all interested to learn exactly where the

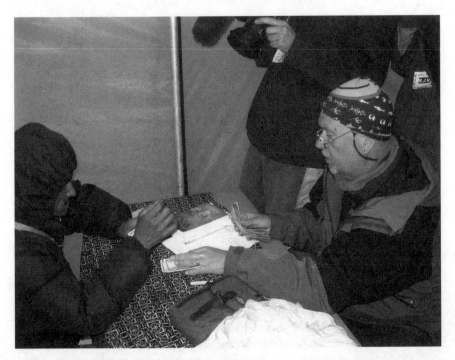

Pay-off time! Negotiating with the eagle-eyed Mustafa.

money went because with the average annual income in Nepal being only US$130 per person (about £80 a year), Mustafa had walked away with the equivalent of fifteen years' salary! Some of the group, and Dave in particular, felt that he was nothing more than a brigand and directed a fair amount of venom towards him.

I explained that the situation wasn't quite as clear cut as that. The Maoists controlled about sixty per cent of Nepal and had a lot of support for their drive for increasing democratisation. However, it might well be that Mustafa was not a Maoist himself but more likely that the nearby village had been threatened with reprisals if they did not collect a tariff from each passer-by over a year. Mustafa struck me as a tired and rundown individual who had an uncomfortable job to do, rather than a zealous Maoist. Indeed his unwillingness and inability to enter into any form of negotiation convinced me that he was the bagman or collector for a third party and I had no doubts that the entire $1,800 would be delivered intact to a higher contact. However I had no idea if the funds were then used to provide some degree of health care, education and services for the local people in remote villages or were used to buy arms.

By the time I had given this scenario for consideration Dave felt quite contrite. 'I feel a right bastard now because Mustafa was probably a real nice guy and is probably going home to a real bollocking from his wife. She's probably going to nag him for being out robbing and pillaging all day and ignoring his family at home.' We all had a good laugh at that one!

Although we had arrived here just after noon, by the time we had finished lunch and I had unpacked my gear, it was after 4 p.m. and time to ring home to find out how Yeovil had performed yesterday against Northampton. As far as I was concerned this had the potential to be a real bogey match. It was Northampton who denied us the last play-off place twenty minutes from the end of last season and when they came to Huish Park they really did outmuscle Yeovil and easily beat us 2-0. It was like watching men taking candy from boys because, although we were the more skilful team they were far more clinical in their finishing and much stronger. This game certainly had every prospect of being a difficult contest irrespective of our recent outstanding form.

I wasn't sure if the Maoists were still in the camp so I thought it prudent to go out of sight and sit behind a big rock before I got my satellite phone out. A satellite phone would be very useful to an insurgent group and I didn't want the ante to be upped if they realised we had one in our possession. Despite the low cloud cover I was able to get a good signal and I rang home and Sharron answered. It really is quite bizarre being 13,000ft up in the high Himalaya, freezing one's butt off and ringing home as if it were next door. It is indeed a very small world as a result of modern technology and it never fails to impress me.

I didn't think it was prudent to ring home and make my very first question an enquiry as to how Yeovil did yesterday, so I asked about the arrangements that Sharron was making for our holiday in Dubai at the end of this trip. Then, just as I was about to ask for the result of yesterday's match, I lost the satellite signal! I redialled several times and eventually got through and, as I suspected, we did not win but drew 1-1. Sharron had no idea who the scorer was nor who scored first. However, second-placed Scunthorpe lost 2-1, third, fourth and fifth-placed Swansea, Wycombe and Mansfield all drew and sixth-placed Macclesfield lost, so we remain top and didn't really suffer from dropping two points at home as none of the challenging teams made ground up on us. Nevertheless it was a lost opportunity because, if we had won, we would have been three points clear in first place instead of still just one point ahead. However a tricky match had been successfully negotiated without losing ground, just as we had eventually negotiated our way past the Maoists!

Bristol Rovers and Leyton Orient were the only teams in the top nine to win yesterday, and the first thing that I did on returning to my cold tent was to work out the current league table. Yeovil, with twenty-one points, are still one point clear of Swansea but it is a very tight table with four teams (Scunthorpe, Wycombe, Bristol Rovers and Leyton Orient) now on nineteen points and just two points behind. Mansfield have eighteen points and Macclesfield are on seventeen. We are now one point under our target two points per game average. However, a win next week at Rochdale will put that right.

I dismantled and hid my satellite phone amid all my kit before getting inside my sleeping bag fully clothed and started dictating my notes for this day. It was too cold to sit and write! Dinner was served at 8 p.m. in the mess tent and, after a delicious soup with pastry croutons, we enjoyed potatoes, cauliflowers, green beans and a delicious spaghetti with tomato sauce followed by fruit salad.

Tomorrow we will cross the Nara La Pass at 4,500m (just under 15,000ft) the highest point of this initial six-day trek. We will then have a 1,000m descent into Tibet, where we have five Toyota Land Cruisers and a lorry waiting at the border to transport us the 100 miles or so north into Tibet to Mount Kailas.

Together with my invaluable pee bottle I climbed into my sleeping bag just before 10 p.m., thinking that without doubt I was the only person the length and breadth of the high Himalaya sleeping on the side of a bitterly cold mountain and thinking about Yeovil's position sitting proudly at the top of League Two. I also wondered how Mustafa was doing because it was confirmed at dinner tonight that the ingredients slipped into his hot drink during the negotiations should ensure that he daren't stray too far from a toilet over the next twenty-four hours if he managed to stay awake. The consensus was that his twice-spiked drink would have him shitting in his sleep! Just as well I took the correct drink!

Yeovil Town 1 Northampton Town 1

Team: Chris Weale, Paul Terry, Roy O'Brien, Liam Fontaine, Michael Rose, Kevin Gall, Darren Way, Lee Johnson, Gavin Williams, Phil Jevons, Andrejs Stolcers

Subs: Adrian Caceres (46 for Williams), Bartosz Tarachulski (46 for Jevons), Andy Lindegaard (76 for Gall)

Subs not used: Steve Collis, Colin Miles

Goal-scorer: Phil Jevons (14)

Attendance: 5,944

Position in League after match: 1st

Rochdale Fans in Tibet?

Friday 8 and Saturday 9 October 2004 – Jarok Donghank – Lake Manasarova, Tibet
Rochdale v. Yeovil (League Two)

Although the game was played on the evening of 8 October UK time, this was early morning on Saturday 9 October in Tibet, so this account spans both days.

It is Saturday 9 October and we have been in Tibet for six days now since we crossed the 4,600m Nara La Pass last Monday. We then made a spectacular descent to the Nepalese/Tibetan border around a large amphitheatre with the path precariously clinging to the side of a 5,000m peak, before making a very steep descent to the Tibetan border. We were met by a lorry and five Land Cruisers and spent the following day driving to the godforsaken town of Darchen, where we commenced a four-day trek around holy Mount Kailas.

Our Tibetan agent Pemba wanted to cut down on the number of yaks he was going to supply to carry food, fuel and camping equipment and there were a few problems between him and the yak people that he recruited as to how far they would go each day and the exact places they would camp. As we were crossing a 5,630m/19,000ft pass I did not want to ascend too quickly to ensure everyone acclimatised properly, but our agent did nevertheless unsuccessfully try and persuade me to do the circuit in three rather than four days.

Yesterday was the crux of this walk as we crossed the Dolma La, the highest point on our circuit of Kailas, but I had slept well the previous night considering that we had camped above 5,200m. I emerged from my cold tent to be greeted by John Burton advising: 'Apparently the yaks are lost and have wandered off.' John always has good news! 'The first aid case is broken,' or 'Ray is ill,' have been other early morning greetings!

Actually, the yaks had not wandered far in search of pasture. It was a beautiful sunny day and Kailas looked superb. I froze in the dining tent until the sun came out and had porridge, omelette and chapatti for breakfast. Our doctor, Matt, did not feel so good, John B. had taken some Diamox for his headaches and Ray had suffered a bad night with lots of visits to the loo and not much sleep. Other than that we all seemed in reasonable shape and as I sat in the mess tent I could see pilgrims going past on the trail. We had taken two days to get to this point and they had probably set off after midnight and caught us up in six or seven hours!

After a good breakfast we were on our way. I felt particularly strong and climbed the 400 metres from our campsite to the pass in an hour and forty minutes. At one point I had come across a pile of clothing on the trail and had assumed it was an offering of discarded clothing left for the gods of Kailas, as we had passed several such piles of clothing over the previous two days but it turned out to be the Tibetan lad I was following who was having a rest! Twenty minutes later Ray and Caedmon, who was feeling pretty rough, came up. 'God, I'm knackered,' said Caedmon, who is an outdoors instructor as well as a filmmaker. 'I'm going to give up mountaineering and take up bloody table tennis!' and then promptly started retching!

It was a spectacular and colourful spot with thousands of prayer flags fluttering and a dramatic hanging glacier dropping down from one of the many surrounding 6,000m peaks. The rest of the group came up over the next hour and, after taking a series of group pictures, we started to descend and continue our journey.

We camped last night in a beautiful valley by an icy river with several people saying it was their toughest-ever day in the mountains. I think all of us had set a height record, although we will be going almost another 1,000m higher in just over a week.

I had found some of the relatively 'easy' days in Nepal more tiring and I think I tend always to struggle more with the early days on trek and then build-up fitness and fortitude. I am encouraged that I appear to handle altitude well as this was the fifth time I had been to 5,400m or more with no problems and I am hopeful that I should be able to get to ABC (Advance Base Camp) and even the Raphu La in the final section of this trip. As I was the second to reach the pass I must be reasonably fit, despite my fifty-five years and cough, which I still cannot shake off.

I finished my journal alone in the dining tent after dinner last night, totally unaware that Yeovil would be playing Rochdale a few hours after I drifted off to sleep as I had not realised it was a Friday evening fixture.

Dave exercising and Caedmon filming at our Lake Manasarova campsite. Gurla Mandata (7,728m) is behind.

Last night was cold... and I mean cold. I wore my trainers as well as fleece trousers and jacket inside a sleeping bag liner inside my main sleeping bag! When I woke up I looked at my watch and noted it was at least -10°C inside my tent. My watch cuts off at this point!

Today was going to be the fourth and final day of our circumnavigation of Mount Kailas and we had agreed that we would have the kitchen crew cook us lunch when we arrived in Darchen, which was about an eight-mile walk. I suggested people take a cold pancake from breakfast in case they wanted to snack on the way.

The scenery was really beautiful and, as we were walking down a 'U'-shaped glaciated valley, we had to cross over several frozen streams that were running down across the trail to the main river. This four-day circumambulation of Mount Kailas is one of the world's famous walks but for many it is a spiritual journey and the spiritual significance was even greater for our good doctor Matt, who was inadvertently locked in a cave monastery that we visited en route. He was left to contemplate rather longer than anticipated while the group looked for the monk with the key!

After another couple of hours, we were gazing over the Barsar Plain ahead and the spectacular mountain of Gurla Mandata, which really looked magnificent, emerging to almost 7,800m from the Tibetan plateau and, before too long Darchen came into view and I have to say the architecture of this remote Tibetan town can only be described as spectacularly unimaginative.

The hotel where we had lunch was grubby, the décor was worse and we were served drinks by three Chinese girls in a rather strange-looking Teutonic uniform. I cannot understand why the standard of Chinese hotels that we have experienced in Tagalot and Darchen are so abysmal and I say this as someone who has experienced accommodation throughout the Third World and is not particularly demanding. But why build hotels and forget to plumb in the water, and then ask clients to empty their water bowls and discard rubbish out of the window? The Chinese are capable of much better than this, or is Tibet just being starved of invest-ment and management?

There was a moment of great hilarity over lunch when Caedmon was filming every-one eating their noodles and Christine noticed that Colin was having difficulty with his chopsticks. 'Just put it in your mouth and suck,' she instructed. To which one wag could not resist responding, 'That sounds like something they teach you in brothel school.' Of course the whole group disintegrated into laughter, much to Christine's amusement!

After lunch we wandered around Darchen. As well as being the repository for such dismal architecture, Darchen's inhabitants appeared to enjoy a standard of living best described as squalid. A stream ran down part of the main street, which seemed to be the main receptacle for rubbish as well as a venue for people washing their bodies, clothes and possessions. I found Darchen an interesting place to photograph, but a poor advertisement for Chinese hegemony over Tibet. As Mount Kailas is one of the most important tourist attractions in Tibet and the most important in western Tibet, you would think the Chinese would have done something to smarten the town up. Indeed, as one of our group said when driving across Tibet to get to Darchen four days ago, 'You wonder why the Chinese bother!'

We left Darchen to drive to Lake Manasarovar. Roads in Tibet are really nothing more than a graded strip on the high plateau and whenever the road surface deterio-rates or there is some obstruction, alternative routes just fan out across the plain to either side of the main route so it was not unusual to see our five Land Cruisers driving abreast across a 100m strip of the desert as they all chose a different route to get to our destination. Each vehicle leaves its own dust trail, which is why the vehicles often fan out rather than blithely (or is it blindly?) follow the vehicle in front. Sadly, in contrast to the magnificent landscape, it was rather depressing to drive through the squalid set-tlements that dotted the landscape.

We drove along the northern edge of Lake Manasarovar, with rolling hills and snow-dusted mountains on one side and the towering peaks of Gurla Mandata beyond Lake Manasarovar on the other. It was a magnificent landscape and two or three times we asked our driver to slow down so that we could take photos, but unfor-tunately we were not always quick enough to get shots of the white horses galloping across the plain with the mountains rising behind.

After a while we turned off the 'road' to find a campsite close to Lake Manasarovar. You would only know it was a designated camping spot by the amount of rubbish that dotted this particular wilderness area and a ramshackle building that was probably occupied intermittently by a Chinese administrator. The Sherpas did a magnificent job in erecting ten tents, a kitchen tent and a mess tent very quickly in the most ferocious winds. Although we had blue skies above the winds were coming down from the 7,700m peaks of Gurla Mandata, whistling over the lake and hitting our campsite about 400 metres from the lake shore with great velocity. Whatever image the reader might have of Chinese-occupied Tibet, let me tell you that first and foremost it is bloody cold and I knew I was in for a chilly night. As the last to get to the dining tent it was my privilege to be at the draughty end and to serve up the dinner, which consisted of tomato soup and prawn crackers, boiled cabbage, mixed vegetables in a spicy sauce, mashed potato and cauliflower au gratin, followed by warm fruit salad and Christmas cake that Andy had sent out as congratulatory fare for successfully circumambulating Mount Kailas.

It was cold when I got back to my tent at 10 p.m. Nepalese time or 12.15 a.m. Chinese time, which meant it was 5.15 p.m. Saturday UK time so I decided I could ring home on the satellite phone to check Yeovil's results. As Yeovil had played at Rochdale the previous evening I could have called at any time during the day! As there was a clear sky outside I was able to get a fantastic signal from inside my tent but sadly, when my son David answered the phone, like any laid-back fifteen-year-old, he was not excited to hear from his father who he had not spoken to for two weeks. Clearly it was nothing unusual that Dad was calling up from the middle of Tibet! I told him to check the results on the internet and I would phone back in five minutes, and meanwhile I made a foray across the freezing cold Tibetan plateau to our nearby two toilet tents. Thankfully I have now mastered the art of getting my trousers down and sitting on the usually secure toilet seat that was perched above a hole dug in the ground. I was very grateful to follow Christine into the loo as her posterior had warmed the seat to my advantage!

I went back to the tent and again got a great signal. David ran through the results and sadly it was not good news. I could not believe what I heard… Rochdale 2 Yeovil 1. Swansea beat Mansfield 1-0 and Scunthorpe beat Wycombe 2-0 so it meant Yeovil were down to third, two points behind the leaders. So much for our two points a game average.

Swansea are now top of the league and I fancied them to do well last year before they tailed off. Of course, with Lee Trundle they have a striker who is always likely to give their team a good headwind when he is on form. Macclesfield and Oxford apparently are playing tomorrow and although David had given me all the results, it was far too cold in my tent to be able to work out the league table in any detail. I thought I would at least go to bed with some reassurance if I knew that Yeovil had an easy home match next week but the high altitude and cold temperatures meant that the battery in my palmtop had died! As a result, it was a miserable group leader who climbed into his sleeping bag with no positive crumbs of comfort to hold on to.

This was a disappointing result, as we should be beating the likes of Rochdale. We only lost three times all season when winning the Conference two years ago and it seems we are not going to dominate League Two to the extent that we did when winning the Conference. It seems that everyone is going to be beating everyone else.

The following morning I went in the dining tent and said, 'Okay, who lives near Rochdale?'

Everyone looked up with blank faces. 'Why?' a couple of people asked.

I sat down and just said 'Rochdale 2 Yeovil 1'.

'Oh, bad luck Michael but there you go.'

'Bad luck guy,' drifted up from the far end of the tent.

However, a few minutes later the knives went in! 'Of course I've always supported Rochdale from afar.'

'Good team Rochdale, I heard they were doing well this season.'

'Oh yes, Rochdale. I always try and go to their home matches.'

And so it continued all through the day. Come on Gary, sort them out. I'm suffering out here in Tibet when the results go against us!

Rochdale 2 Yeovil Town 1

Team: Chris Weale, Paul Terry, Roy O'Brien, Liam Fontaine, Colin Miles, Kevin Gall, Lee Johnson, Darren Way, Michael Rose, Phil Jevons, Andrejs Stolcers

Subs: Andy Lindegaard (46 for Gall), Terry Skiverton (46 for Miles), Bartosz Tarachulski (74 for Fontaine)

Subs not used: Steve Collis, Adrian Caceres

Goal-scorer: Phil Jevons (48)

Attendance: 2,402

Position in League after match: 3rd

This is Getting Tricky

Saturday 16 and Sunday 17 October 2004 – Everest Base Camp – Everest Camp 2 (6,010m), Tibet
Yeovil v. Macclesfield Town (League Two)

Although the game was played in the late evening of 16 October Tibetan time, it was so cold I did not obtain the result until Sunday 17 October so both days are covered in this account.

Our four-day drive across the Roof of the World – the high, dry and arid Tibetan Plateau – took us through an amazing variety of landscapes, always with the backcloth of the high snow-clad Himalaya to our south. After forming the 'Gay Bathing Society of Tingret', when we had a communal bath at the nearby hot springs to remove eighteen days' worth of dust and grime, we finally arrived at Tingret, the closest settlement to Everest, and then continued on to Rongbuk Monastery, where we camped. On Thursday we walked the five miles to Everest Base Camp from Rongbuk in atrocious weather to find the conditions so cold and the ground so frozen our Sherpas could not erect our tents and make them secure from being blown away. We paid the princely sum of about $3 each to stay in three 'guesthouses' that had been erected on a semi-permanent basis by enterprising Tibetans, primarily to offer overnight accommodation to visitors who wanted to break the journey between Lhasa and Kathmandu with a detour and overnight stay at Everest Base Camp. They were really enlarged yak herders' or nomads' tents with half a dozen chairs, four or five beds and a multitude of mattresses and blankets. We woke to find that the condensation rising from our bodies overnight had frozen and formed icicles inside the tent. Each morning we were woken by them melting and dripping all over us as the sun hit the outside of the tent.

Because of the bad weather our yaks, supplied by the monastery, were delayed in arriving from their pastures in a lower valley. Pemba and I had returned to Rongbuk on Friday to look for the missing yaks. Pemba was highly embarrassed as he clearly considered he had lost face with us and he really let rip at the head monk who was supplying our yaks. However, all's well that ends well, as the yaks eventually turned up just as we set out to search for them and the enforced extra day at base camp on Friday has given us an extra day for acclimatisation.

My friend Colin particularly appreciated this as he has been quite listless and poorly. However, Colin being Colin, he will not take advice from either our doctor Matt or myself about whether he should continue. I have told Colin I already have concerns about him getting down from ABC (Advance Base Camp) in a single day as he is already the slowest of us. Although very fit, Colin has difficulty on the terrain with his hip and I cannot allow him to be an encumbrance or put the group at risk. We also used Friday to check out and test our Gannow Bag, a portable decompression chamber into which we can immerse anyone who suffers severe altitude sickness (pulmonary or cerebral oedema) and simulate a rapid descent in altitude by raising the pressure inside the sealed bag.

So we finally set off at 9.55 a.m. yesterday morning to follow the route made famous by all the pre-war British expeditions of the 1920s and 1930s who attempted to climb Everest from the north. Our route was planned to take us in three days to ABC, just below Everest's infamous North Col, and is in truth one of the most challenging mountain walks anywhere in the world that is attainable to fit walkers as opposed to technical mountaineers. If we get to ABC we will then have the option of continuing on to the Raphu La, which is the col at the very foot of Everest's North-East Ridge. However, our initial aim is to get to ABC, a major adventure in itself and normally only visited by hardcore climbing groups heading for Everest's summit and the occasional trekking group.

We walked slowly towards Everest, which was dominating the view in front of us. It was an absolutely magnificent sight. It looks a very, very big mountain with the North-East Ridge extending to our left and the North-West Ridge to the right. Everest looks a much bigger and more impressive mountain from the north in Tibet than from the south in Nepal. Indeed, the mountain cannot be viewed from the Nepalese Base Camp and when you climb to the famous viewpoints of Kala Pattar and Gokyo Ri, it is only the top third of the mountain that is viewed, thrusting above the surrounding peaks. In Tibet, however, you can view the entire massif from base to summit together with the various ridges, and without doubt it is one of the most compelling and magnificent sights I have ever seen.

Camp Two at 6,010m by the East Rongbuk glacier.

We walked in the ablation valley between the moraine on our right and the steep slopes on our left, and we slowly but surely made our way towards Everest with the magnificent snow-clad mountain dominating the vistas ahead. The summit could not have been more than six miles away!

We stopped to eat our packed lunches and let the yaks catch up with us, and climbed up onto the moraine. The view ahead of Pumori, Lingtren, Khumbutse and Nuptse was without doubt one of the finest mountain panoramas I had ever seen. In Nepal you can just see Changtse rising beyond the Lho La but now we were actually approaching the flanks of Changtse and looking south-east towards Nepal. The view up the Khumbu valley in Nepal towards the Nepalese Base Camp is magnificent but this view of·Everest and its surrounding peaks was was incomparable. I felt really privileged to have now been able to view this unique collection of spectacular peaks from both the Nepalese and Tibetan sides of Everest.

Despite the distractions of Everest I remembered that, in a few hours, Yeovil would be kicking off and I could not imagine more contrasting locations than Huish Park and the dramatic landscape of mountains and glaciers in front of me. I thought we could not afford another slip up after only one point from our last two games.

As we started to climb up the East Rongbuk valley we came across a group of four who were descending. They were led by an English guide from Southampton who was now based in Denver and he explained that the blind German lady he was leading ran a school for blind Tibetan children in Lhasa and they had brought eight of their students up to Everest Advance Base Camp. This was the highest altitude ever attained by a group of blind people and explained the reason for the film crew we had seen at Rongbuk. He introduced me to the German teacher and the other blind person in their group called Erik, and I immediately interrupted him. 'You're Erik Weihenmayer, the only blind person to climb Everest.'

Erik confirmed that this was so. What a coincidence! I had left a copy of Erik's book in Kathmandu to read in Dubai next week. We chatted about his book and Paul and I took photos. Then the guide announced, 'We had better get on our way as we need to get down before it gets dark.'

'I wouldn't have thought it would make any difference!' I replied flippantly and Eric cracked up laughing.

'Well I need to see where we are going even if the others don't!' replied the guide.

When we arrived at the old British Camp One at an altitude of 5,530m, Caedmon was continually teased for having missed filming the only celebrity on the trail. He somehow resisted our suggestion that he might want to hike back a couple of hours to get some footage of Erik Weihenmayer.

Over dinner last night Paul asked me who Yeovil were playing and I said I did not know because my organiser's batteries had died in the cold and that was where I had the fixtures recorded. 'Surely a real Yeovil fan would know their entire fixture list off by heart!' quipped Caedmon, trying to get his own back.

I went to bed in a very cold tent and when it was 10 p.m. realised that it was probably just that time when the crowds were leaving Huish Park Stadium with the result known. However, it was far too cold for me to get the satellite phone out and call home, so I decided to wait until tomorrow afternoon when it would be warmer. That would be Sunday morning in the UK and if I called when the weather was a bit milder I would be able to write down all the results and work out the league table.

When I went to the mess tent for breakfast this morning I cracked up when I heard our resident wit Dave say, 'I don't need a packed lunch today as I'm breeding a fantastic culture on my teeth – I'll just snack on that!'

It was nice and warm in the mess tent once the sun was out. John B. was not feeling too good and is on antibiotics and said he would have to review his situation about continuing when he got to Camp Two. By contrast I felt absolutely great and was really looking forward to today's walk, although Andy said it was likely to be the toughest of the whole trip. Although we only go up about 500m, Andy said that it was tough going and there was a lot of up and downing between Camps One and Two. Back in the mess tent I asked Dave if he'd read *The Road to Wigan Pier* (he and John O. are both from Wigan) to which Dave, in his own typically blunt manner replied, 'I think that guy Orwell's a real fucking bastard.'

'Do I take that to be a negative response then Dave?' I replied in a deadpan fashion.

'People all round the world think we're as thick as fucking bricks as a result of that bastard's book.'

'Oh well, Dave. You can't win them all and think positively – maybe Wigan will get promoted this year!'

I confirmed to Dakipa that we were going as far as Camp Two today and not just to the Intermediate Camp between Camps One and Two. Dakipa said that this should be about a six-hour walk. I should perhaps point out that these campsites are just loosely defined rocky areas where generations of mountaineers and the occasional trekking groups have erected tents on their way up Everest. The Intermediate Camp was a fallback position for the early British expeditions and groups who got hit by inclement weather or needed an extra day to journey between Camps One and Two. Before leaving I gave the group a bit of a pep talk, stating that I wanted them all to walk together because of the uneven terrain on ice and moraine, and I did not want anyone getting lost.

We set off at 10 a.m. and were walking at a good pace, although we made a couple of stops. We crossed to the south side of the East Rongbuk valley by a frozen lake, finally arriving at the Intermediate Camp at 1.10 p.m. The camp was quite high and looked down over the glacier. It was nothing more than a few piles of rocks forming windbreaks and producing some very basic shelter.

I was trying to keep out of the wind and eat a typical lunch of Tibetan bread, hard-boiled egg and cheese together with biscuits, when all of a sudden Matt came to me and announced that he was sending Brian down! It turned out that Brian had been talking to Andrew when he had suddenly started slurring his words for about thirty seconds and couldn't think straight. Matt's diagnosis was that a very small blood clot might have formed and touched his brain before dispersing and for 30 seconds or so this had the effect of a minor stroke. The danger was that if Brian was predisposed to forming clots at altitude he could have a more serious attack at a higher height.

I suggested that Brian might want to descend to Camp One with a Sherpa and a tent and, if there was no repetition, follow us up tomorrow after additional time for acclimatisation but Brian's preference was to turn around at this point and return immediately to base camp. He explained that he had seen some magnificent scenery, it had always been his ambition to get to view Everest at close quarters and he felt he should pay heed to the warning and descend. We waited for the yaks to catch us up and made sure we identified his kitbag, and Dakipa selected Bima to descend with Brian. This was a good choice. He had joined us at Tagalot, having come with supplies from Kathmandu and he was congenial, his English was passable and he could never do enough to help us.

No sooner had we continued our journey from the Intermediate Camp area after Brian and Bima's departure than we came to a halt because we had to make a very steep descent to cross a stream emerging from a glacier, and then faced a very tricky climb up onto the median moraine. The group had stopped to watch the antics of the yaks, who were crossing over the crevasse and stream at the bottom of our slope and then hauling themselves precariously up the steep and slippery slope. One yak actually slipped and slithered a few feet, but didn't panic, until he came up against some rocks that held his weight. It was quite a spectacle to watch twenty-five yaks strung out in a line valiantly climbing this steep icy slope.

Then it was our turn and I followed one of our climbing Sherpas, Kami, up what turned out to be the most precarious and steepest part of the slope! At one point I slipped and grabbed onto a rather large boulder, which I prayed would remain frozen in the ice, and rather unceremoniously hauled my way up. Apparently this was all being filmed by Caedmon, who said he was waiting for the boulder to give way so he had some really outstanding footage for our film!

Soon we were on George Mallory's famous 'Magic Highway' as we followed a narrow strip of rocky moraine with towering ice pinnacles to both our left and right. It really was spectacular. After Mallory had discovered the North Col route up Everest from the Lhakpa La in 1921 he returned to the North Col in 1922 via the East Rongbuk

Glacier and it was this stretch of median moraine that provided relatively easy access to the North Col area. Hence the name 'Mallory's Magic Highway'.

We had come around the south slopes of Changtse, now towering above us to the right and adorned by hanging glaciers, and we stopped for group photos as there was a magnificent view ahead and to our right of Everest in its entirety with the entire North-East and North Ridges extending to the very summit. I could also see the Raphu La, our eventual destination, on the left beyond the East Rongbuk Glacier that we were following. However, before long it was 5 p.m. and every time I asked Chola how far it was to Camp Two all he would say was 'one hour'. As Andy had warned, there were an awful lot of ups and downs. At one point Colin commented we were at 6,000m, to which I sharply replied, 'I couldn't give a shit. I just want to find Camp Two!'

Finally one of the Sherpas was waiting for us on the trail with a lamp, and led us down to Camp Two, which was a cold and bleak campsite nestled up against towering ice pinnacles, each the size of a three-storey house! Everyone was pretty exhausted when they arrived and there was a common agreement that this had been the toughest day of the trek so far. As ever it was a comment from Dave, made in his indomitable blunt style, that summed up how we all felt: 'I'm as fucked as a Blackpool donkey on Whit Monday!'

I went to my tent and rang home as I was in need of good news, which Sharron duly did not deliver! She immediately me advised me that Yeovil had surprisingly lost at home 2-1 yesterday! That wasn't exactly the fillip that I needed after today's exertions! Apparently there was a late goal scored by whoever we were playing and Yeovil have dropped a position to fourth but are still only two points behind the leaders (Leyton Orient with twenty-three points), despite only securing one point out of the last nine. All the other teams are clearly doing us a favour by not breaking away. Swansea and Scunthorpe are both on twenty-two points and Mansfield on twenty-one points. So Yeovil are having a bad run now with only one point from their last three matches, and here's one of their most devoted fans halfway up Everest in desperate need of better news than a 2-1 home defeat!

Dinner was good: soup, chips, vegetables and then custard, but my feet felt as if they were freezing in the mess tent, which was understandable as we were camped on a glacier at just over 6,000m, or 20,000 feet in Somerset language! Only ten of us turned up for dinner as the others had retreated to their sleeping bags with various ailments, exhaustion and the cold. I did make a pithy comment at dinner criticising Roger and Andrew for going on ahead today, saying I had enough to worry about without having to look down gullies and ravines as we were going along to see if either of them had slipped down and were in trouble.

I went to bed at 9.44 p.m., took my watch off and hung it in the tent and before long it displayed -9.9°C, which is the lowest it registers. When we stopped yesterday for lunch I took my watch off, put it in the shade and it also registered -9.9°C. That was with the sun out so God knows what the temperature was falling to inside the tents at night, but probably at least -25°C, as we were surrounded by ice above, around and below us.

As I lay above at least 100 feet of ice I wrote in my notebook 'It's so cold it will freeze my heart'. I then thought a good result from Yeovil would have gone some way to warming it up!

Yeovil Town 1 Macclesfield Town 2

Team: Chris Weale, Paul Terry, Terry Skiverton, Liam Fontaine, Michael Rose, Kevin Gall, Darren Way, Lee Johnson, Gavin Williams, Phil Jevons, Andrejs Stolcers

Subs: Bartosz Tarachulski (65 for Stolcers), Roy O'Brien (72 for Skiverton), Adrian Caceres (74 for Gall)

Subs not used: Steve Collis, Colin Miles

Goal-scorer: Darren Way (51)

Attendance: 5,313

Position in League after match: 4th

Halfway up Everest

Tuesday 19 to Thursday 21 October 2004 – Everest ABC –
Raphu La – Rongbuk – Zhangmau
Bristol Rovers *v.* Yeovil (League Two)

Without access to my organiser and fixture list, I was blissfully unaware that the day that represented the culmination and greatest challenge on our thirty-day expedition also coincided with Yeovil's midweek fixture away at local rivals Bristol Rovers. I was unaware of the fixture and the result until almost forty-eight hours later, so this section covers the three-day span.

We arrived at Advance Base Camp (6,340m) on Monday evening without any further problems or mishaps and I thought it was a tremendous reflection of the group's willpower and resolve to get fourteen out of fifteen to such a high point. I might also add that it was a fine testimony to the excellent planning provided by our trekking division, Great Walks of the World!

On Monday night it seemed likely that only three of the thirteen clients, excluding myself, definitely wanted to push on to the Raphu La and, if that was the same on Tuesday, I decided it would not be fair to keep the other ten waiting for at least half a day in the cold at such a high altitude. I advised the group that if it was only three wanting to continue we would turn around and if necessary take two days rather than one to descend to Rongbuk.

Consequently I spent part of Monday night, when I wasn't sleeping, worrying about the likelihood of going to the Raphu La and particularly with regards to Colin. He is very target-orientated and was determined to ski to and from the Raphu La but I could see him having difficulties in getting back to Rongbuk in a day if he did go on to the Raphu La.

After getting up I went around all the tents and was surprised by the various responses. Richard confirmed that he was definitely up for going to the Raphu La. Ray, who I had presumed would not want to go, said that he would give it a go, as did John O. Matt said he was staying in his tent but within ten minutes was up and announced that he was definitely going! So all of a sudden we had nine who were definitely going, Paul, Colin, Roger, Matt, Richard, Caedmon, John O., Ray and myself. It was now a no brainer and the final challenge was definitely on! Andrew, John B. and Christine decided that they would prefer to go down and leave as soon as possible that morning and descend to Rongbuk.

This left two who were staying at ABC while we went to the Raphu La – Rohit, who was just going to immerse himself in the surroundings and Dave, who was going to wait until his mate John O. returned and then descend with him the following day. We said goodbye to Christine, Andrew and John, who were setting off down with Naru as their guide, and remembered to 'borrow' their crampons so that the climbing Sherpas could use them! I was not impressed that some of Suman's Sherpas had not been provided with crampons.

Finally we set off, making our way through the ice towers and then following an easy route across the East Rongbuk Glacier. We carefully made our way over a crevassed area and when we reached a flat area of ice we stopped to put our crampons on. The Raphu La looked very close and appeared to be not much more than an hour's stroll up a gentle snow slope! Of course these things are never quite as easy as they look! The scenery was magnificent and I felt totally comfortable and in my element as we made our way towards the Raphu La while the East Rongbuk Glacier continued towards to the North Col on our right.

The North Col did not look an easy target, as it sat at the top of some very steep cliffs and almost as jumbled a collection of seracs as the Khumbu Ice Fall was on the Nepalese side of Everest. I remembered that it was there where George Mallory was avalanched in 1922 and lost seven porters, a loss that weighed heavily with Mallory for the remainder of his life and which nearly brought a permanent end to the early Everest expeditions. I felt privileged to be able to view the famous North Col that had played such a significant role in those attempts.

We were alone in this pristine area except for three Chinese who appeared to be planting poles in the ice. I assumed they were planning to return in future years and measure glacier movements. I felt that this was the day that Dakipa was really earning his money because he was making the route selection. He used his ice axe to tap the snow immediately in front of him and in some places we were definitely walking over what sounded like very hollow snow and ice. I wondered if he tapped too hard whether he would actually go through but he seemed to be stopping and assessing the route continually, which was good.

Other than the three Chinese we had the entire area to ourselves as there were no climbing groups at ABC or the North Col, as the climbing season is pretty much now restricted to the April-June pre-monsoon period. Neither the altitude nor the gradient was causing too much of a problem and I was quite comfortable with our progress. However, as we made our way up it got increasingly windy and strong gusts of winds would blow spinthrift and snow all over the place and sometimes slow down our walking. Finally, the world's fifth-highest mountain Makalu came into view above the

Raphu La and then we found the snow getting a lot more difficult. Richard in particular kept calling for an increasing number of stops and eventually, at around 6,480m, said he felt he could not go on any longer and Ray on the other rope also decided to turn around, and the two of them descended with Kami. At this point the nature of the snow had changed quite significantly. I was by far the heaviest person of the seven of us and I was increasingly falling through the crusty snow up to my knees or further. Because I was falling through the snow it was taking me two or three times as much effort to make any progress. Previously the calls from behind were to slow down but now I could hear Caedmon commenting that if we didn't get a move on he was concerned about getting frostbite.

It was now me who was slowing the rope down because I was finding it so difficult to advance through the deep snow and at one point Roger, who was behind me, asked if I had given any consideration to a turnaround time and enquired whether we would actually make it to the col. I said that that wasn't an issue yet and we probably had until 2.30 p.m. before we needed to turn around.

We made painfully slow progress and at one point both Caedmon and Roger said they were thinking of turning around because of the cold, but I told them that our destination was only ten minutes ahead so we might as well keep going. I dined out on this on several occasions over the next few days by commenting to super-fit Roger that he wouldn't have made it to the Raphu La if it hadn't been for me telling him to go on when he wanted to turn around!

I wouldn't go as far as to say that I was crawling but certainly with me part flailing, part falling, we finally got to the point of the Raphu La where two of the Chinese had dug quite an extensive pit and Temba, who had gone on ahead, was sitting in the snow hole with them! I was quite tired and, although the first three-quarters of the climb had been very easy, I had found the last fifty minutes really hard work and I fell backwards quite inelegantly and needed some extricating from the deep snow on the col!

The seven of us who had made it to the Raphu La had got there on two ropes. Roger, Matt, Caedmon and myself on one and John O., Paul and Colin on the other. Up on our right we could see part of the Kangshung Face of Everest, which looked very dramatic, a jumbled mass of ridges, seracs and scarred ice. It looked very inhospitable and very difficult.

Our three Sherpas were clearly pleased and started congratulating us, cheering, laughing and shaking hands and I took quite a few pictures. Despite the strong winds we managed to get the banner out that Suman had displayed outside our Kathmandu hotel and we posed as best we could for a group picture with the wind trying to blow us off the col. My eyes were continually drawn to the North-East Ridge of Everest, which rose and stretched away above us to the Pinnacles where Pete Boardman and Joe Tasker were lost in 1982. Opposite us at the end of Everest's eastern ridge was Pethangtse, to the west of the Arun Valley, and Makalu, the world's fifth-highest mountain and its twin peak of Chomolonzo to the east of the valley. This was a magnificent mountain panorama that encompassed two of the world's highest five mountains.

Roger, Caedmon and John O. were feeling cold so they turned around and went down sooner rather than later, but I hung around at the top for a bit longer taking pictures before we broke up the party to go down. It was only on the way down that I

Super-fit Roger, photographer Paul, filmmaker Caedmon, Dakipa and our good doctor Matt at the Raphu La, 6,548m.

started thinking 'Well, we did it.' I hadn't felt particularly elated when I reached the Raphu La, as I was exhausted after my efforts getting through the brittle snow. However, on the way down, I did feel quite proud that I had managed to keep the group together, got fourteen out of the fifteen to ABC and seven of us had actually got to the Raphu La and stood within a couple of hundred metres of the foot of the famous North-East Ridge of Everest.

The weather was perfect as we descended with no problems whatsoever and eventually we picked up the flags and wands left by the Chinese and started to weave our way over the crevassed area. We made our way through a narrow passageway to cross the final part of the glacier and then had a short haul back up to get to ABC where Richard was waiting for us with both congratulations and his usual enthusiasm. Before long we were enjoying noodle soup in the mess tent. It turned out Ray was in his tent asleep as he was obviously pretty exhausted. Dave wasn't feeling too good but Rohit had had a typical upbeat day exploring the ABC area and appreciating everything around him. Colin looked rough and was complaining about being hypothermic so I gave him my down jacket.

After finishing my soup and noodles I went back to my tent, which was a lot warmer than the mess tent and just relaxed. I had a pleasant feeling of a job well done and mission (almost) accomplished. I rang Sharron to tell her we had reached the Raphu La and returned okay and she said well done. I then called Andy, who was pleased at our success and asked me if I'd enjoyed it. I avoided giving him a direct reply but said it had been an experience, the scenery was magnificent but I wasn't sure about leading any more Chairman's Treks! Andy said he could hear the wind howling (just as I was wondering if it was likely to take the tent and me with it!) and commented that every-one feels the cold and cannot wait to get away from Everest but that after a few days 'You will doubtless start planning a return trip.' Of course, he was right!

After dinner I was quite happy to lie in my sleeping bag catching whatever thoughts drifted through my mind, but I did have four potential problems as far as getting down the following day was concerned. Colin and Ray were obviously pretty exhausted and neither had appeared for dinner tonight. Dave was not feeling too good and John O. had snow blindness so it may be tricky getting him down. I had two thoughts in my head. Firstly, in three more days I'd be back in Kathmandu and flying off to see Sharron, Lisa and David. Secondly, the following day was clearly going to be an inter-esting day with its own set of challenges!

I was pleased that we had accomplished our goal and was blissfully unaware that, as I dozed through the night looking forward to seeing Sharron, Lisa and David in a few days, Yeovil were playing at the Memorial Stadium against Bristol Rovers. Last year ten-man Yeovil secured a memorable 1-0 victory thanks to a magnificent Nick Crittendon strike. Little was I to know that this year's game and result would be even more dramatic, but I would not be aware of the result for another two days.

After our successful ascent to the Raphu La, the following day's fourteen-mile descent to Rongbuk was, if not epic, certainly an interesting journey. When I had asked Colin how he felt yesterday morning he had replied, 'Just wondering how to get off this bloody mountain.' But more worrying was that John O. was pretty much 100 per cent blind as he paid the price for not wearing any sunglasses or goggles when he went up to the Raphu La. None of us had picked up on this at the time. Matt had got up twice that night to administer eye drops and pain relievers to John. Dave however, was obviously on the mend because, when I asked him what he thought of the spec-tacular location, he replied, 'The views are the least of my fucking worries!'

We considered using yaks for both John and Colin who had clearly, as I had pre-dicted, pushed himself too hard to get to the Raphu La. He had been feeling hypothermic but I didn't think it was that cold and his body was obviously weak and run down. The yak men had refused to let the yaks carry people but one enterprising yak man offered to piggyback Colin eleven miles for $200, and I countered with $25 an hour. However, after 300 yards Colin decided he would rather walk than be piggy-backed down the precarious trail. John O. was faithfully supported by two Sherpas for the best part of fourteen miles. He looked like death but got down, and so did Colin, not too long after the remainder of the group. We spent last night at the Rongbuk Monastery guesthouse reunited with Andrew, John B., a fully recovered Brian and Christine with a streaming cold.

Today, Thursday, we had a wonderful drive over the Pang La (Pass), nursing our Land Cruisers up to over 5,000m before taking a most spectacular drive along the Friendship Highway towards the Nepalese border. As we drove along the dry, arid, rolling hills of the high Tibetan Plateau, majestic snow-clad peaks emerged from the horizon like icebergs stranded in a desert. It was stunning! This was perhaps the most spectacular drive I had ever undertaken. I hoped the drive would last forever but eventually we arrived at Zhangmau, which was situated in a spectacular gorge as we descended through the Himalaya towards Nepal.

Gavin Williams scores his final goal in a Yeovil shirt, at Bristol Rovers, before moving on to West Ham.

Zhangmau has the reputation of being a bit of a frontier town and indeed our hotel was festooned with the only neon lights we saw in Tibet! Apartment buildings, shops, hotels and restaurants were all crammed around the single road clinging to the side of the gorge. I thought I would wander around the town before sorting out all the tips to be handed out at tonight's farewell dinner. Pemba and our faithful but mad Land Cruiser drivers would leave us in the morning at the border and our Nepalese trekking crew would disperse as soon as we got to Kathmandu the following afternoon.

Andy had told me that Zhangmau was an interesting town, not least because of a proliferation of Chinese ladies of the night who offered their services to the passing lorry drivers! I bought some snacks and sat on the steps of a shop, strangely at one with myself and very content just to sit outside with no worries and watch life go by.

As well as noting there were indeed a number of bordellos in the town, I found an internet shop, only to discover that the BBC was one of the banned websites to which access was withheld in China, or at least this part of Tibet. However, I could access my e-mail and as well as a host of congratulatory messages from friends who had received the e-mail I had dictated to my P.A. Wendy by satellite phone from ABC, was a note from Sharron telling me that I might have missed that Yeovil drew 2-2 at Bristol Rovers on Tuesday.

She was right! With my organiser dead I didn't even realise any midweek League Two games were scheduled and assumed this might even be the Somerset Premier Cup! It was only the following day in Kathmandu that I learnt that it was indeed a League Two game and not a point gained but very definitely two points lost, as we surrendered a two-goal lead to Bristol Rovers. My God! Even worse was that Bristol Rovers had been reduced to nine men. Gary Johnson must have been distraught at throwing that lead away!

However, I was in blissful ignorance of these mishaps as I trudged back to the hotel restaurant to join everyone for a merry celebration and distribution of tips to our trekking crew and Tibetan Land Cruiser drivers. These farewell dinners are a tradition and much enjoyed by clients and the trekking crew alike, and are a way of letting the trekking crew know how much we appreciate their efforts.

One day back to Kathmandu and then it's off to Dubai for a real holiday! And surely Yeovil's results have to start improving soon?

Bristol Rovers 2 Yeovil Town 2

Team: Chris Weale, Roy O'Brien, Liam Fontaine, Colin Miles, Michael Rose, Paul Terry, Darren Way, Lee Johnson, Gavin Williams, Phil Jevons, Andrejs Stolcers

Subs: Kevin Gall (79 for Terry), Bartosz Tarachulski (79 for Stolcers), Adrian Caceres (90 for Rose)

Subs not used: Steve Collis, Andy Lindegaard

Goal-scorers: Paul Terry (27), Gavin Williams (57)

Attendance: 9,295

Position in League after match: 5th

Fancy Meeting You!

Saturday 23 October 2004 – Kathmandu, Nepal – Hatta Fort Hotel, Dubai
Scunthorpe United *v.* Yeovil (League Two)

We got back to Kathmandu yesterday afternoon and had an informal farewell dinner for most of the group members at the Rum Doodle last night, when I presented our mad but capable doctor, Matt, with a gift on behalf of the group. I was pleased to personally have been one of only three of our fifteen who didn't need his services over the last month but he was an absolute godsend and kept us all amused as a bonus. Thank you, Matt. Sadly, he could only attend briefly as Colin was taken quite ill and was in considerable pain. Matt decided to stay with Colin in his room through the night to monitor the situation and administer painkillers.

Back at the Hotel Marshyangdi I got my wake-up call at 5.45 a.m. and was very tired as I had only had three hours' sleep. As I lay in bed preparing to get up I reflected that it was thirty days ago that we all met at Heathrow and I don't think I have ever travelled with a more congenial group of people. Now I was looking forward to having a relaxing and restful half-term week in Dubai with Sharron, Lisa and David. I thought that the day would be really capped off well if Yeovil were to get a win at Scunthorpe!

When I got down to reception this morning there were no messages from Matt so I assumed that Colin had not got any worse overnight. There was no time for any breakfast and I managed a quick cup of coffee and met with Richard at reception. We made our way to the airport through the early morning activity of Kathmandu and the check-in officer was insistent on charging me some excess baggage for the 100 'Made in Nepal' kitbags I was taking home for Great Walks clients but, fortunately, after a great deal of effort, I talked my way out of this!

I had my usual two nice milky coffees at the friendly restaurant in the departure lounge before boarding our plane and, as there weren't too many people on it, Richard and I had four seats each and were able to lie down. I woke up after about two hours of our four-hour flight to Qatar and when I went to the loo I noticed a tall South African in a Springbok shirt sitting by the gangway as I made my way to the back of the plane. After another couple of hours' sleep I again noticed the South African before landing at Doha and thought, 'Bloody South Africans can't go any-where around the world without wearing something to reflect their identity!'

I made my way off the plane at Doha thinking I had earned the degree of satisfaction I felt for a job well done. The clients had enjoyed themselves, we had got up to a great height on the flanks of Everest and I felt I deserved a week's holiday in the sun. As I made my way into the transit lounge, I could see Sharron waiting at the end of the security checkpoint but I had to blink and make a quick double take because she was standing next to Chris Elsworth, a senior anaesthetist at Yeovil Hospital and a very good friend of mine. Indeed, Chris had once stayed at our apartment in Switzerland with me for a week's hiking.

So what is Chris Elsworth doing with Sharron at Doha airport, I thought? And then I remembered the tall South African on the plane with the green Springbok shirt. It had been my good friend Chris and I had walked past him twice without realising it! I was flabbergasted to see such a good friend in the Middle East and to think that I had been on the same flight as him and neither of us had recognised the other!

After a coffee and a good chat, when Chris told us about the trek to Gokyo that he had just completed, it was time for Richard and Chris to board their flight back to the UK and Sharron told me that she had paid a fee to allow her, Lisa and David to sleep in the executive lounge during their six-hour wait at Doha. That was why I hadn't seen Lisa and David, who were both sleeping. However, I was wandering around the duty-free shop ten minutes later when the tall, laid-back guy standing next to me turned out to be my fifteen-year-old son David, who had come to look for me! Hugs all around, and he explained that the music in the background that I had been trying to identify was an American group called Hoobastank and the song I liked was *The Reason*. It's handy having teenage kids if one wants to keep up with contemporary music!

When our flight was called Sharron woke up Lisa and we all boarded the plane for the short one-hour flight. An hour later we landed in Dubai, which is a fascinating destination. I first came here four years ago for a half-term holiday with David and then after the first operation on my spine came back for a week's holiday on my own as part of the recuperation. My third visit had been a family holiday when all three kids, Sharron and myself had come together. Lisa, whose eczema has got worse in the

On top for much of the game but Yeovil and Phil Jevons could not find a way through the Scunthorpe defence.

last couple of years, had not been too keen on a beach holiday so this time we were staying inland near the desert. Sharron had been able to get a good deal at the Hatta Fort Hotel and so we collected our rental car and set off.

My cold had really freshened up on the plane and I felt it would be a good idea to try and get some cough medicine, so we managed to get lost a few times as we drove around looking for a pharmacist. We went to a small mall but, because it was Ramadan, most of the shops were closed until sunset. We eventually found a pharmacist and then, after a final stop to buy some pastries and a coffee, we were on our way for the 120km drive inland. We did most of the journey across the desert in the dusk with Sharron commenting that it was meant to be a very pretty drive (translated as we spent too long in Dubai City!) and me with a terrible rasping cough that meant I was coughing quite severely every ninety seconds or so. Nevertheless, it was good to be with the kids and to be somewhere with a guaranteed hot climate for the next week.

We got to our hotel at Hatta and checked into our palatial adjacent rooms. After unpacking we went down to the restaurant to have a very nice meal, and then it was time to go to the internet to check the result of Yeovil's vital and difficult game at second-placed Scunthorpe. The hotel let me use the computer next to the reception and I went directly to the BBC League Two pages. The headline story came up 'Laws hails important Iron victory.' Uh oh! Wasn't Brian Laws the manager of Scunthorpe? Aren't Scunthorpe known as 'the Iron'? This isn't looking good.

I clicked on to the results and there it was: Scunthorpe 1 Yeovil 0. It was a Scunthorpe goal in the closing stages. This isn't good because, since beating Shrewsbury on 25 September, we've drawn at home to Northampton 1-1, lost away to Rochdale 2-1, lost at home to Macclesfield 2-1, drawn away at Bristol Rovers 2-2 and now lost away at Scunthorpe. That is two points out of fifteen, which is hardly promotion form!

The brief report on the web indicated that Yeovil might have been unlucky but we need to regroup now and desperately need a run of wins. The consequences of our loss were compounded by the fact that both Leyton Orient and Macclesfield won, which is not good and we are now down to eighth in the league and, having played fifteen matches, have only got twenty-two points, which is a long way off Gary Johnson's target and my hopes of a two points per match average. The tide has really turned after those magical first ten games where we had twenty points and we were indeed averaging two points per game. In fact, to get back to that two points average we will need to win our next eight games in a row (!), which would give us forty-six points from twenty-three matches, and that just is not going to happen, is it?

I don't think we are going to come close to that two points per game average this season again but that does not mean that we cannot get promotion. However, with only two draws in the last five matches, next week's visit of Chester to Huish Park Stadium is going to be a really important game if we are to re-establish some momentum.

I went back to our room with my head full of cold to sleep in the most luxurious bed that I had seen anywhere in the last thirty days and drifted off hoping that Yeovil can soon get the season back on track.

Scunthorpe United 1 Yeovil Town 0

Team: Chris Weale, Andy Lindegaard, Liam Fontaine, Colin Miles, Michael Rose, Paul Terry, Lee Johnson, Darren Way, Gavin Williams, Andrejs Stolcers, Phil Jevons

Subs: Adrian Caceres (76 for Stolcers), Scott Guyett (76 for Miles), Bartosz Tarachulski (84 for Terry)

Subs not used: Steve Collis, Kevin Gall

Attendance: 4,470

Position in League after match: 8th

In the Desert

Saturday 30 October 2004 – Hatta Fort Hotel, Dubai
Yeovil v. Chester City (League Two)

We have had a nice relaxing break, and it has been interesting to stay inland and see a different aspect of Dubai, although we went back to Dubai City to celebrate David's sixteenth birthday with a visit to Wild Wadi water park. The hotel is very comfortable, almost palatial, although the reception is a little small for a hotel of this stature and they perhaps don't promote the various attractions and facilities as well as they might. It's easy to be critical when you're a tour operator!

This very impressive country is built on the back of great wealth but not a wealth generated by oil. Dubai is an entrepôt port and only about twenty per cent of the nation's revenue comes from oil, the remainder from trading activities. The Al Maktoum family have certainly been driving Dubai dynamically forward for the last twenty-five years and the city is now undoubtedly one of the greatest in the world and a fascinating destination for short-break holidays.

The feature that has impressed us most on this visit is the most extensive series of dual carriageways stretching all over the desert, but often without any traffic! The distance from Dubai City to Hatta is 110 kilometres and yet the entire road is perfectly illuminated. Sharron has reminded me that when one flies over the Middle East in general and Dubai in particular, it is not unusual to see these lights from high in the air. However, despite the impressive road network it is impossible to buy a road map! I must have pulled into at least ten garages to ask if they had a map and I could have been asking for a return ticket to Mars!

The United Arab Emirates is a collection of small Sultanates that together have formed one nation. Dubai itself has a population of approximately two million, of which only about twenty-five per cent are indigenous Arabs, the bulk of the remainder being expatriot workers, not educated Westerners but cheap labour from India, Sri Lanka, Pakistan, Nepal and the Philippines. The prosperity of this nation is quite clearly built on the back of this cheap labour, typically earning about £200 per month in wages, which is very attractive in comparison with the wages available in the labour-supplying nations.

The first time I came to Dubai I was amazed at the scale of development and in the last four years both Dubai's rapid growth and stunning architecture continue to impress. The world's tallest hotel is already built here and the world's tallest building is under construction, as well as three offshore developments – the Palm, Palm 2 and The World, where islands are being created offshore in the shape of massive palm trees and the continents of the globe! A multitude of trucks are criss-crossing Dubai bringing rocks to be dropped in the sea to build these artificial islands, and there appears to be no limits to the entrepreneurial dreams of those who are driving this nation forward. This is certainly no Third World country but it is being built on the back of cheap Third World labour, although there doesn't seem to be any resentment from the population of immigrant workers.

One day we hired a Land Cruiser and a driver to go dune driving in the desert, as we knew this was something that the kids would enjoy. I had to chuckle that we ended up paying about US$180 to drive up and down sand dunes in the desert for a couple of hours when I had recently been in a similar Land Cruiser for upwards of a week in Tibet and got all the rough riding I wanted without having to pay a premium! However, I have to admit our friendly Indian driver really did make it very exciting and interesting as we drove up and down the dunes at very steep angles. I was amused that Sharron enjoyed it because if I was to drive at a tenth of that speed off road with my Ford Explorer I know she would be moaning at me!

The other event of significance this week and very much the end of an era for Sharron, myself and our business was the sale of Casterbridge Hall at auction in England. We purchased the former Merthyr Guest Hospital for £57,000 in 1979 and it was our home for five years as well as the foundation of our business, a base for

Looking slim in the Dubai desert after a month at altitude!

thousands of American students on our tours and the Casterbridge offices for twenty years. It sold for £722,000 against a reserve of £650,000 and there goes twenty-five years of hard work and memories both good and bad!

When reading this morning's paper I caught up with the news regarding the US election. The polls cannot really separate Bush and Kerry and although it looked certain that Bush was going to be re-elected, there now seems to be a real chance that Kerry could get in. Although, in my opinion, Kerry is not an attractive candidate I cling to my hopes that he can replace Bush.

We spent the day relaxing at the hotel and over dinner tonight David announced that he wanted to be an actuary! My God! I told him that being an actuary made even an accountant's job look exciting! A son of mine as an actuary? It doesn't bear thinking about!

After dinner I went to the reception to log onto the internet and get the result of Yeovil's match this afternoon against Chester. I went straight to the League Two pages and didn't even have to go to the results because the headline story this week was a positive one: 'Yeovil end Chester's run'. Chester had gone about eleven matches without defeat under Ian Rush as their manager but Yeovil had won comprehensively 4-1 and now possess the second-best goal difference in the division thanks to a hat-trick from Phil Jevons, now clearly the leading scorer in League Two with 12 goals. All Phil's goals have been in the league and with 12 goals from 16 matches that is a strike rate of three-quarters of a goal per game. If he kept that up would net 33 League goals this season. That will do very nicely! When Torquay secured promotion last season the difference between Yeovil and Torquay was the fact that they had David Graham, who scored 22 League goals. If Phil Jevons scores 25 goals for Yeovil this season I am sure we will be promoted because as well as Phil there are plenty of other players in the squad who are banging them in as well.

The rest of the results went well for us although Bristol Rovers were able to salvage a point as a result of a last-minute equaliser. Swansea only drew, as did Leyton Orient against Scunthorpe. Wycombe lost, which was good because we are playing them next week. As a result of this win we have improved our position from eighth and out of the promotion frame to fifth and in a play-off position.

Tomorrow we fly home and I went back to our room to finish packing, content that Yeovil had won for the first time in a month.

Yeovil Town 4 Chester City 1

Team: Chris Weale, Paul Terry, Colin Miles, Liam Fontaine, Michael Rose, Gavin Williams, Darren Way, Lee Johnson, Adrian Caceres, Phil Jevons, Andrejs Stolcers

Subs: Scott Guyett (36 for Miles), Andy Lindegaard (84 for Caceres), Kevin Gall (87 for Stolcers)

Subs not used: Steve Collis, Bartosz Tarachulski

Goal-scorers: Phil Jevons (25 penalty) (63 penalty) (90), Adrian Caceres (56)

Attendance: 5,741

Position in League after match: 5th

Three Points from Bartosz

Saturday 6 November 2004 – Huish Park – Amsterdam
Wycombe Wanderers *v.* Yeovil (League Two)

I have spent the last week in England and pretty much at our home in Stowell. I was hoping to go to Switzerland for a week to continue the research work I was doing in preparation for a new division selling holidays in alpine villages. I was originally planning to fly to Switzerland on Tuesday but when it got to Thursday I decided I might as well stay until Saturday and go and watch Yeovil at Wycombe on the way to the airport. I think this was lurking in my sub-conscious as a possibility through-out the week and perhaps contributed to the lack of urgency in some of the things I was doing!

The main event of this past week of has been the US election and I watched the election results from 10 p.m. until 7 a.m. on Wednesday morning when sadly it was clear there was to be no change. I fear for out future with four more years of Bush.

On the way to Wycombe, I stopped to look at a cottage that was for sale in nearby Charlton Horethorne. Although Casterbridge Tours has in every way been my life for the last twenty-five years, about ten years ago I set up a small family company grandly entitled Leisure and Property International Ltd to have some diversity and new challenges in my working life. Over the years LPI, with two permanent staff, has bought and renovated a number of cottages and properties in Sherborne, Yeovil and the surrounding villages. I thought the listed cottage was full of potential and the guide price of £175,000 was not unrealistic but it was probably a buy up to £225,000.

I drove to Wycombe in a little under two hours. After parking the car it began to drizzle as I walked through the trading estate (similar to the location of Huish Park Stadium) and I hoped that it would not rain, as I believe that the better the conditions the better Yeovil play.

I thought that the Wycombe programme was excellent and very informative. There was a very good article on Phil Jevons and how his career was handicapped by not being given the opportunity to play at Grimsby because it would have meant them making more payments to his previous club Everton. Considering how few games he played, his record at Grimsby meant that he had the potential to be an outstanding goal-scorer when playing regularly and Gary Johnson did very well to make him our first priority as an off-season signing. I have quite a good feeling about this match as Wycombe have only won two of their last eight matches and the Wycombe fans did not seem very enthusiastic, either when their team was announced or when they ran out!

Our back four of Rose, Guyett, Fontaine and Terry had a completely new look as none of them played regularly at the back last year. Indeed, this showed the current depth of our squad because an alternative four could be chosen from O'Brien, Skiverton, Lockwood, Miles and Lindegaard. Of the four playing today, Guyett and Rose were with Chester and Hereford in the Conference last year, Fontaine was a Fulham reserve player and Terry was primarily a midfield substitute last season. It was interesting to note that, although we are in a higher position than we were at this time last year, two of our back four were playing non-league football a year ago!

The first half was uneventful with the ground as quiet as a graveyard and the only noise coming from the Yeovil fans. The game was desperately in need of a goal and Wycombe looked to be a poor team or at least one that didn't have much confidence. Paul Terry was very sound at full-back, Adrian Caceres was by far our least effective player and Gavin Williams was having one of those frustrating days when he looked lazy and I felt we would be better served by Kevin Gall's pace and energy. The highlight of the closing moments of the first half was the Wycombe goalkeeper making a good save from a Lee Johnson free-kick. I kept thinking that we had to be capable of putting this poor Wycombe side away but only a fine Chris Weale save after a sloppy back pass prevented us from going in at half-time 1-0 down.

It was crazy that only three minutes got added on at the end of the first half as there had been several stops and I would have thought that a minimum of four if not five minutes had been lost. I fail to understand why football cannot have a clock, like most American sports, that is stopped and everyone can see how much time is remaining and we get the correct amount of playing time.

As the players went in for half-time I was certainly hoping that Gall would be introduced as we desperately needed some pace because Wycombe were playing a desperate but effective smothering game with only one player up front and nine outfield players in midfield and at the back. A check of the half-time scores showed that both Scunthorpe and Swansea were winning. We really can't afford to let them get away from us so this was a game we needed to win. It's usually Gary Johnson's style to go with the starting eleven for at least the first ten minutes of the second half but to give him credit he usually does bring people on so they have enough time to get into the game and be effective rather than just come on for the last five or ten minutes. Sure enough, as the players came back on the pitch, there were no changes.

The second half started with a completely different complexion to the first half as Wycombe had plenty of possession and, furthermore, the Wycombe fans had discovered a drum, which we never heard in the first half. With the drum beating, the Wycombe fans had finally woken up and were making themselves heard. I couldn't believe that these were the same fans that had watched the first half, and the drumming was now so incessant I wondered if the club had put on a record to wake up the fans! Both the noise that their supporters were making and the possession that Wycombe had on the field were quite in contrast to the first half and Wycombe were now well on top. It looked as if Gary Johnson was planning to bring on Bartosz Tarachulski but then Liam Fontaine got injured and it was in fact Roy O'Brien who came on as Fontaine had to be helped from the field. Nathan Tyson was looking particularly effective for Wycombe and the programme notes indicated that he was probably their leading player and returning after an injury.

The game turned again as a result of a Gavin Williams run that almost set up a goal for us. This was Yeovil's best move by far and was soon followed by another Williams run and then, obviously inspired by him, Caceres finally began to make some positive contributions to the game including a very dangerous cross that almost resulted in a goal for Yeovil. Yeovil were now playing far better as a unit and Gavin Williams in particular was more effective than he had been in the first half.

As I predicted Gall came on (for Caceres) with twenty minutes remaining, which was hopefully going to be long enough for him to make impact and, as far as I was concerned, it wasn't soon enough. Tarachulski also came on and had a wonderful chance that was only denied by a great save from the Wycombe goalkeeper. Yeovil were now well on top and a great crossfield ball found Gall on the right who, despite overrunning the ball was able to recover and still get in a good cross. And in came Tarachulski with a stooping, glancing header to give us the lead with six minutes to go. This has been the difference with Yeovil this year. We now have two regular goalscorers in our team with Jevons and Tarachulski.

Tony commented to me during the week that he rated Tarachulski as a much better player than Stolcers but at the moment it does seem that Gary Johnson prefers his Latvian international as a starter. I hadn't been particularly impressed by Stolcers today, whereas Tarachulski forced one excellent save and scored a goal in the limited time that he was on the field. Tony, you were right!

Now we just had to hold out for the last four minutes and, infuriatingly, we wasted two corners when trying to be too clever in holding on to possession, and each time gave the ball away. Why do players persist in short corners, which are rarely productive and only frustrate fans? Gavin Williams managed to kick the ball right out of the ground and seemed to get a booking for his efforts. I didn't realise there was anything in the rules about clearing from your defence as high and as far as you could in any direction!

Time ran out and we held on for the win. Great! We are beginning to haul ourselves back after what was a disastrous run of six games with only two draws, and achieving two wins in a row should do a lot for the team's confidence. After applauding the team I was out of the ground pretty quickly and drove to Heathrow without there being anything like the delays that I anticipated. I listened to the results on Radio Five and, although Scunthorpe and Swansea both won at home, this win put us up to third in the table.

I arrived at Amsterdam around 11 p.m. and decided to have a walk around the always interesting red-light area with a variety of girls of all nationalities on display in the windows of their cubicles, before retiring to my airport hotel for a night's sleep and continuing my journey to Switzerland in the morning.

Wycombe Wanderers 0 Yeovil Town 1

Team: Chris Weale, Paul Terry, Scott Guyett, Liam Fontaine, Michael Rose, Gavin Williams, Darren Way, Lee Johnson, Adrian Caceres, Phil Jevons, Andrejs Stolcers

Subs: Roy O'Brien (57 for Fontaine), Bartosz Tarachulski (60 for Stolcers), Kevin Gall (71 for Caceres)

Subs not used: Steve Collis, Andy Lindegaard

Goal-scorer: Bartosz Tarachulski (84)

Attendance: 5,453

Position in League after match: 3rd

Last-Gasp Equaliser

Saturday 13 November 2004 – Mürren, Switzerland – Stowell
Darlington v. Yeovil (FA Cup First Round)

I am returning to England after a week at our apartment in Switzerland, and it is on the days that I travel that I realise there are advantages in having a second home close enough to get to without spending a whole day travelling! It usually takes nine hours or so between Stowell and Mürren by car to the airport, plane and then train in Switzerland. It's not really worth coming to Mürren unless it is for the best part of a week if you have to spend a day travelling in each direction. Nevertheless I do realise we are fortunate to enjoy three homes and I am certainly not complaining! However early the hour I start my journey home I never fail to be impressed by the magnificent scenery of one of the world's most spectacular train rides, which follows the flat balcony route from Mürren to Grutschalp. From the comfortable train seat (and indeed the footpath that follows the tracks) there is an incomparable panorama of the Eiger, Mönch and Jungfrau, rising above 4,000m, just kilometres away on the far side of the Lauterbrunnen valley. It is without doubt, one of the most spectacular rail journeys that one can find anywhere in the world.

One of the attractions about travelling in Switzerland, a country whose total population is less than London, is that there is a most comprehensive rail service that always runs on time. Whether it is a local mountain train creeping along the edge of a 1,000m drop, a steep funicular descending down a forty-five-degree gradient, a post bus connecting up a remote alpine valley or an intercity express, the system always run on time and never fails to connect.

My journey home was uneventful and I was soon on the M3, heading west to Somerset. The main story on Radio Five was the amazing result of the early match, with Arsenal winning 5-4 at Tottenham! Of course, Jose Mourinho was quick to comment that it was neither a football match nor a result anyone could take seriously!

Today is the first round of the FA Cup and perhaps an opportunity for Yeovil to start writing another chapter in their history of outstanding cup exploits. However, first we had to get past the very tricky away fixture against a strong Darlington side. As I drove westwards from Heathrow I heard no mention of any scores from Darlington so assumed the score was 0-0, and was disappointed to hear a half-time score of Darlington 1 Yeovil 0 as I pulled into a supermarket car park at Wincanton. However, as I drove out of Wincanton and onto the A357 the radio announced an equaliser courtesy of Colin Miles!

I was driving to nearby Templecombe to visit my mother. Our trusty NHS had once again (not) delivered, as her planned hip replacement operation was cancelled last Monday but no one had had the courtesy to tell her and she was left at home for three hours waiting for an ambulance to arrive! I flipped and, from Switzerland, got the surgeon on the phone and was promised a new guaranteed theatre date and we meanwhile decided my eighty-nine-year-old mother was better off in a nursing home for the ten days prior to her rearranged operation.

My buoyant spirit was further improved when I was parking the car at the nursing home as another updated score was announced: Darlington 1 Yeovil 2. Fantastic! The FA Cup is now very much secondary to the leagues in which all teams play. Survival in every division and the chance of promotion to the next means the FA Cup is nothing like the institution it was when I was a teenager. Nevertheless, all lower division clubs still dream of getting to the third round and then drawing a big club.

I went into the rest home and spent half an hour chatting to my mother, who is very alert and with a much better memory than me. Earlier this year she flew alone to Switzerland and spent ten days with me in Mürren. For eight of those days we went out sightseeing and took cable cars and funicular railways to the top of mountains. I even pushed her to the summit of one peak in her wheelchair, with her complaining that I was about to tip her out of her chair. I try and ensure my mother remains very active for her age!

When it got to 4.40 p.m. I suggested we switched the TV on so that I could check the final results, and the latest score came up as Darlington 2 Yeovil 2. Not to worry. That would mean a replay on Tuesday 23 November, when I was going to be in England, so I wouldn't be disappointed if the game ended up as a draw! However, as we sat waiting for the final score to come up the next time the scores scrolled around, it was Darlington 3 Yeovil 2 with the Darlington goal being scored in the 86th minute! That was a blow. It seemed every time I had checked with the radio or TV today another goal had been scored but I commented to my mother there were still four minutes left and we could hope against hope for a miracle to occur.

The results kept on scrolling over with no change to Darlington 3 Yeovil 2 but nor with the letters FT going up to indicate that the game was over. Fully ten minutes had gone since it had announced Darlington taking a 3-2 lead and I wondered if there was a technical problem preventing the teleprinter from updating the Darlington result to final. Finally the coverage switched to the full time results and amazingly it now showed Darlington 3 Yeovil 3 with a ninetieth-minute equaliser from my hero Bartosz Tarachulski! What a great result. We had made the long journey to the North-East to play against a team in good form who had beaten us 3-2 last season. To draw 3-3 was a very commendable performance and, as a bonus, I will see an extra match the week after next!

Excitement over, and after a visit of an hour or so to my mother (most of which was spent monitoring the Yeovil result!) I said it was time to go home because Sharron and I were going out in the evening with my longstanding friend, Brian Nettley and his wife Enid, who had agreed with some reluctance and reservations, to make up a team of four for a general knowledge quiz at the Charlton Horethorne village hall. We had a good evening and did not disgrace ourselves.

It will be Lisa's eighteenth birthday tomorrow and then it's back to Switzerland on Monday, although I am coming back to England next Friday to attend the Kendal Mountain Film Festival in the Lake District. Then I will be home for when my mother has her postponed hip replacement operation and, as a result of today's final score, I will be watching the Darlington replay on Tuesday week!

Darlington 3 Yeovil Town 3

Team: Chris Weale, Paul Terry, Colin Miles, Scott Guyett, Michael Rose, Kevin Gall, Lee Johnson, Darren Way, Gavin Williams, Bartosz Tarachulski, Andrejs Stolcers

Sub: Andy Lindegaard (74 for Stolcers)

Subs not used: Steve Collis, Adrian Caceres, Roy O'Brien, Yemi Odubade

Goal-scorers: Colin Miles (46), Bartosz Tarachulski (55) (90)

Attendance: 3,698

At the Film Festival

Saturday 20 November 2004 – Kendal, Lake District
Yeovil v. Southend United (League Two)

I am in Kendal attending the Kendal Mountain Film Festival. I flew from Basel to Liverpool yesterday and then took the train to Warrington, where Sharron and Andy from Great Walks met me as they had driven up from Somerset. Our son David and eldest daughter Sarah also came.

We were all at the festival by 9 a.m. and the highlight of the morning films was *North West Passage* about an Irish sailing expedition that went through the famed North-West Passage to the Bering Strait. I have never been particularly interested in either the Arctic or the Antarctic although in 1969 I did hitchhike to Europe's most northerly point, the North Cape, and climbed a minor peak in Arctic Norway. On that trip, when hitchhiking, I was picked up by a very glamorous Belgian poet who introduced me at the tender age of nineteen to some of the more delicate arts of lovemaking. The term 'land of eternal sunshine' certainly had more interpretations than one for me that summer! I repaid her affections by losing my concentration while driving her car and turned it over three times. I told her that when I had the money I would buy her a new car and we are still friends but, alas, I've never delivered with the car!

Last year we showed the film *Everest Base Camp: One Man's Odyssey* about Ray Tempest who I had taken to Everest Base Camp in November 2002. I knew Ray, one of the stars on our recent trek to Tibet, and many of his friends and family were coming to Kendal again and I met them in the bar at lunchtime. It was great to see Ray who I had last seen a month ago in Kathmandu. Of course Ray being Ray, he had booked some accommodation but hadn't thought to buy any tickets and all the tickets for Saturday were sold out! I quickly concocted a plan whereby I would get my group in the various screens and then bring the tickets out for Ray's group to use again! This involved more complex logistical planning than travelling around Tibet and Ray now owes me big time!

However, first I wanted to check if Tony was going to watch Yeovil play Southend this afternoon. I rang Tony at home and he didn't seem too enthusiastic about going. He said his home was warm, it was raining outside and he was trying to toss up whether to go or not. 'If you don't go it will be a good match and if you do the conditions will be against Yeovil and it will be a boring match. Either way you can't win so just go!' I suggested. He agreed that he would probably go and we arranged that I would ring him at half-time.

I watched a couple of excellent films (*The Conquest of K2* and *Nima Temba Sherpa*) before leaving the auditorium at half-time to call Tony, and immediately bumped into Matt, our doctor from the trip to Kailas and Everest. He had just driven up from his home near Dorchester. I explained I had to get my order of priorities right and call Tony to get the Yeovil update before I could chat! 'Good news, Yeovil are playing well, Michael. Tarachulski and Jevons are looking effective up front and Stolcers is playing in midfield. Jevons hit the bar and then scored just before half-time.' Tony sounded very upbeat about our prospects.

Great! Just what I wanted to hear and I chatted with Matt before he went off to watch a film and I called Tony back halfway through the second half. 'Not so good, Michael. We seemed to be sitting back on the goal and letting Southend come at us and we conceded a header from a free-kick. It's 1-1 but we are getting back on top. It's a good match and I'm glad I came.'

I watched twenty minutes of a rather arty Spanish film that, in my opinion, just did not work and then called Tony who was on his way home. 'It was comfortable in the end. Bringing on Gall and Lindegaard for Stolcers and Terry made all the difference. Gall created havoc. Guyett scored from a Johnson free-kick and then Bartosz from a Gall cross.' Tony said it was a good game and repeated that he was pleased he had gone.

The film festival was due to recommence at 7 p.m. for the evening session, so I had a snack in the bar, met up with Sharron, Andy, Sarah, David and Ray and his crowd and we agreed we would all go out for a late-night Chinese after the films ended together with Matt and Brian from Tibet who had also come up to Kendal.

I went to bed pleased that, after three league wins in a row we are secure in third place on thirty-one points and, as well as beating Southend, fellow contenders Swansea, Leyton Orient and Macclesfield all lost. All round, not a bad set of results!

Yeovil Town 3 Southend United 1

Team: Chris Weale, Paul Terry, Colin Miles, Scott Guyett, Michael Rose, Andrejs Stolcers, Lee Johnson, Darren Way, Gavin Williams, Phil Jevons, Bartosz Tarachulski

Subs: Kevin Gall (77 for Stolcers), Andy Lindegaard (77 for Terry)

Subs not used: Steve Collis, Adrian Caceres, Roy O'Brien

Goal-scorers: Phil Jevons (43), Scott Guyett (83), Bartosz Tarachulski (85)

Attendance: 5,839

Position in League after match: 3rd

Despite the Linesman!
Tuesday 23 November 2004 – Huish Park
Yeovil v. Darlington (FA Cup First Round Replay)

My mother had hip replacement surgery today and I picked up David from school in Sherborne and then went straight to the hospital to visit her. Considering she had been under anaesthetic for two and a half hours this morning at the age of eighty-nine she was looking remarkably well. We stayed talking with her for about forty-five minutes until 7 p.m. and then left to meet Tony and Patrick at the ground for this evening's match.

There were certainly not more than about 100 Darlington supporters in the away end although we did actually have two sitting in the row behind us. Tarachulski's recent goal-scoring form, with three goals in the last three games, meant that he is guaranteed a start and Stolcers was playing on the right side of midfield where I would have preferred to see Gall playing. Paul Terry's form is currently so good that if he cannot get a place in midfield he is going to get a place in the back four and he was playing at right-back. He is probably the most improved player at the club this season. Fontaine has returned to Fulham, so our back four was Rose and Terry as full-backs with Miles and Guyett in the centre. The line up had six from last year and five new-comers, namely Jevons, Tarachulski, Stolcers, Guyett and Rose. Without a shadow of a doubt it is the additions who are going to give Yeovil an excellent chance of being promoted this year, as the squad is a lot stronger.

For the first ten minutes Yeovil played some sublime football with some flowing pass-ing movements that would have graced the Championship if not the Premiership and, as early as the second minute an excellent move produced a Darren Way cross and a scor-ing header at the far post by Tarachulski, which was disallowed. It looked fine to me although a voice behind said there was no doubt he was offside. For a moment I thought this was an objective Yeovil supporter who had seen something I had missed, but it turned out this was the first contribution from our friend from Darlington!

Darren Way and Lee Johnson were very active and controlling the opening parts of the game but, sadly, we had a very fussy referee who was continually halting the action. Indeed, there was one very long stoppage of about three minutes that came when Yeovil were well on top. I really thought they should be taking the Darlington player off and this stoppage, combined with a linesman on our side of the pitch who was contin-ually raising his flag for offside decisions, halted Yeovil's period of supremacy. A lot of the decisions were marginal but I found it difficult to believe that he was right on more than fifty per cent of the occasions. Of course, it seemed that the more the crowd got at the linesman the more determined he was to raise his flag whenever any ball was played towards a Yeovil forward. Williams was as frustrating as only Williams can be, making two or three runs where he breezed past a number of players but then either overran the ball or lost possession because he delayed playing the final ball. Yeovil's play became more and more predictable and the Darlington supporters were getting more and more encouraged by their team's performance. It was certainly Darlington who were pressing and Yeovil's passing began to look very ragged.

It deteriorated into a poor and disjointed first half and the officiating had not helped. To cap everything off, it was unbelievable that only a minute of time was added on! Why can we not have electronic timing on a clock, which can be stopped by the referee and which is visible to everyone? Fans were denied three minutes of a forty-five-minute half, which is about seven per cent of the first half or three per cent of the match. It is ridiculous that the timing is so subjective and when the referee cannot keep track of the time properly it does not give you much confidence in his overall competency!

At half-time I chatted with Tony and the Darlington supporter sitting behind us. He said that the referee was awful and conceded that he had hurt Yeovil a lot more than he had hurt Darlington. He felt that Darlington were worth parity, which indeed was true.

The second half started with an excellent contribution from Paul Terry, who went on a long marauding run from the right-back position into the heart of the Darlington goal

Colin Miles, Scott Guyett and Phil Jevons pressurise the Darlington goal.

area. Now Yeovil were coming far more into the game again despite Lee Johnson having one of his less effective games, as he had gone missing after the first ten minutes. Gavin Williams followed Paul Terry's example by going on a long mazy run and Yeovil were playing much better. Finally, in the fifty-sixth minute, Yeovil scored a great goal. Darren Way got the ball on the left, cut in, moved to the right to avoid two defenders on the edge of the box and then hit a long hard shot that gave the goalie no chance. The entire stand stood to applaud, including the Darlington supporters behind us! It was an excellent goal from the most effective player on the pitch. However, from the kick-off Darlington immediately went on the attack and we were lucky not to concede an instant equaliser to Darlington after a Weale fumble. The crowd began to sing their salutations to Gary Johnson, who immediately responded with a clap. The deep affection and indeed adulation that the crowd holds for Gary Johnson and the ritual singing to the manager and acknowledgment in return is not something you see in many grounds. It must mean an awful lot to Gary to know that he is held in such high regard and I am sure that when push comes to shove and he has an offer to go to a bigger club this adulation and respect will be a significant factor in his decision about whether to move on or stay and try and get to the same higher level with a club where he is already worshipped. I know which I would choose so keep singing all you Yeovil fans! I suspect my comments have been prompted by some paper speculation that Gary Johnson may be linked with the current vacancy at Wolves. Yeovil controlled the remainder of the game and we ended up as comfortable a winner as a 1-0 scoreline will allow.

I left the ground to drive home with David thinking that, although we cannot take anything for granted, an away game at lowly rated Histon in the second round means that we have every chance of reaching the third round again. It's beginning to look like a very promising season on all fronts.

Yeovil Town 1 Darlington 0

Team: Chris Weale, Paul Terry, Colin Miles, Scott Guyett, Michael Rose, Andrejs Stolcers, Lee Johnson, Darren Way, Gavin Williams, Phil Jevons, Bartosz Tarachulski

Sub: Kevin Gall (71 for Stolcers)

Subs not used: Steve Collis, Roy O'Brien, Andy Lindegaard, Terry Skiverton.

Goal-scorer: Darren Way (56)

Attendance: 5,365

No Luck at Lincoln (Again)

Saturday 27 November 2004 – Stowell
Lincoln City v. Yeovil (League Two)

I thought of taking one of the supporters' coaches up to the tricky game at Lincoln today but, as I am flying to the States on Monday, I thought it was best I tried to catch up with some paperwork at home.

I switched the radio on at ten past three. Lincoln was where we had that memorable day at the end of last season, a great 3-2 win but denied the play-offs as a result of Northampton's win at Mansfield. So near but so far! It would be great to win again today but Lincoln are a strong team and, despite their faltering start, have to be one of the favourites for at least a play-off position at the end of the season. It seemed from the radio commentary that Lincoln's long-ball game was keeping Yeovil pretty much on the back foot and it was no real surprise when a good through ball found the Lincoln striker Richardson, who put Lincoln in the lead. By all accounts Chris Weale did well to keep us only one goal behind with a series of outstanding saves as half-time approached.

However, disaster struck and the game's fate was sealed when we suffered our first sending-off of the season as Gavin Williams was judged to have deliberately gone into the goalkeeper as he challenged for what the radio described as a fifty-fifty ball resulting from a Lee Johnson through pass. But worse was to follow because, within a minute, as Yeovil were still coming to terms with their being reduced to ten men, the Lincoln player Fletcher hit a second past poor Chris Weale. In just a minute the complexion of the game had changed. It is one thing going into half-time a goal down but quite a separate matter to go in two goals adrift having lost a player in the minutes before half-time. Bristol Rovers came back from two behind with nine men against us so I guess I should never say never, but I think this one is well and truly written off.

Gall was brought on for Stolcers and a glimmer of hope appeared when the Lincoln defender, Ben Futcher, was sent off for what sounded like a pretty innocuous shirt pull on Tarachulski after fifteen minutes of the second half. Terry Skiverton came on for Colin Miles and joined the attack and not without causing the Lincoln defence some problems. The commentator thought he had scored at one point but it seemed the ball didn't cross the line. It appeared Yeovil were dominating the game but, wouldn't you know it, as so often happens, the defending team broke away, Richardson grabbed his second goal and put the result beyond doubt! Shit.

There was time for Terry Skiverton to grab one goal back but it was going to be a long drive home for the boys with very little to show from the game, and for the second time in just over six months! It seems that Sincil Bank is not a good destination for Yeovil and a quick check confirmed that our last match of the season is at home to... Lincoln! That will be the second season in a row, but at least we will be at home this time. Is that ominous or what?

It was a mixed day as far as other results were concerned. Scunthorpe won convincingly at home against Shrewsbury so are now seven points ahead of us and, if they win again and we lose, could open up a ten-point gap and be pretty much out of sight. Swansea slipped up at home to Bury 3-1 and are still only two points ahead of us and we remain third, but Leyton Orient, who won 1-0 at Mansfield, are level with us on thirty-one points and both Lincoln and Macclesfield, who won 2-0 at Rushden today, are only a point behind on thirty points. Then there are another seven teams (down to and including Rochdale) in thirteenth place who are within four points of us, so if we slip up again we could quickly find ourselves in a mediocre mid-table position.

After ten games we were first with a two point per game average but, although we have been in third place throughout November we are barely holding on to one of the automatic promotion places and now have a host of teams on our heels. There are too many teams within striking distance for my liking.

I spent the evening working in my library, not quite sure why I always have so much to do. At fifty-five and with thirty staff and a successful business, shouldn't I be enjoying myself a bit more?

Lincoln City 3 Yeovil Town 1

Team: Chris Weale, Paul Terry, Colin Miles, Scott Guyett, Michael Rose, Andrejs Stolcers, Lee Johnson, Darren Way, Gavin Williams, Phil Jevons, Bartosz Tarachulski

Subs: Terry Skiverton (63 for Miles), Adrian Caceres (82 for Tarachulski)

Subs not used: Steve Collis, Kevin Gall, Roy O'Brien

Goal-scorer: Terry Skiverton (81)

Attendance: 4,714

Position in League after match: 3rd

Avoiding a Tripwire

Saturday 4 December 2004 – Staunton, Virginia, USA
Histon v. Yeovil (FA Cup Second Round)

I am at the Casterbridge offices in Staunton, Virginia, about 150 miles south of Washington DC. Whenever I come here I am always infected by the energy that is evident from our American sales director, Peter, and his team. The historic and attractive town of Staunton in the Shenendoah Valley isn't at all a bad place for our staff to be based, the only downside is that many of the charming inhabitants could best be described as 'rednecks' as far as their political outlook is concerned. We're in George Bush country folks and this is the South, even if we are within two hours of Washington DC!

Earlier in the year Tony suggested to me that it was important I put together a summary of both the ethos upon which I had founded Casterbridge Tours and the standards to which we should always aspire. After reading this Ron Blake, the manager of our American concert tour division, thought that the more his staff heard directly from me about my early experience in setting up Casterbridge, the more it would reinforce his team's belief that they were working for a quality company. So this week I have made the time available to go out with each of our three American sales teams – schools sales (north and east), school sales (south and west) and concert sales.

I told them how in 1981 and 1982 my wife Sharron and myself had driven 30,000 miles one winter and 50,000 miles the next criss-crossing North America, making cold calls and doing presentations to schools in the middle of nowhere. I hoped that by telling the staff that I had been in the trenches too and that much of our success had come because of persistence, it would encourage them to follow all sales leads and not just the promising ones!

Today was also the end of an era as we were having an auction of the contents of Casterbridge Hall, and was really the final chapter that brought to an end our twenty-five-year association with Casterbridge Hall. Much of the furniture that was being sold I had bought myself at auction for next to nothing in 1979 and 1980 when Sharron, myself and my then-sixty-four-year-old mother spent practically a whole winter decorating the building and furnishing it before we started trading as an international holiday centre aimed at American students. I rang Sharron to find out how the auction went and she was busy with bidders and really very short with me. She obviously couldn't understand that I would be interested in learning how the final stage of the disposal of Casterbridge Hall, which had been part of our life for so long, had gone. It wasn't worth persevering with the conversation so I just hung up. I guess in her defence she was thinking that if I was interested I should have stayed and helped! Sharron certainly has the knack of killing my enthusiasm stone dead at times and often I think we are not on the same planet, let alone the same page!

Last night I went and saw a film in Staunton at the Dixie Theatre! It was Richard Gere, Susan Sarandon and Jennifer Lopez in *Shall We Dance?* It was a very light movie but it made some very pertinent points. The film revolved around an older family man who had everything he wanted in life materially but had something missing in his life. Sounds familiar? Of course, woven into the strand of the plot was his fascination with a younger woman, in this case Jennifer Lopez, which was the prime reason he took up ballroom dancing. However it wasn't so much that he wanted to have an affair (he didn't) but the fact that he just wanted a change. 'And why do you need something else?' his wife, played by Susan Sarandon, asked him. 'Because I want to be happy.' Gere replied. Amen to that.

As it was now mid-morning I decided it was time to go to our offices and check the half-time results on the internet and see how Yeovil were doing in their second round FA Cup game. Surely we, the perennial giant-killers, were not going to be tripped up by the lowest-ranked non-league side left in the competition?

I was not sure if I had read that Yeovil were playing at an earlier kick-off time and, indeed, when I got to the BBC football page it already had the result showing as a headline. Histon 1 Yeovil 3 confirmed the potential hurdle had been successfully negotiated.Of course, these matches are always potential tripwires but being honest that was what I expected and I was pleased that we got through that test without any hiccups. I think something like Manchester United, Chelsea, Newcastle or Arsenal away would be my preferred tie for the next round as that would be good for the club's finances. Failing that, a match against top opponents at home or against poor opponents at home. The last thing we want is an away match to either a League One or a Championship side. The goals were scored by Jevons, Johnson and Odubade in injury time, by my calculation his first goal for the club.

I checked the Yeovil site and there were two stories of interest. Gary Johnson had apparently stated that the sale of Gavin Williams to West Ham (that I had noted was in the offing earlier in the week) was definitely going to take place subject to a medical and would be quickly completed. Secondly, there was speculation that Chester were going to make a bid for 'unsettled' Yeovil striker Phil Jevons. I just can't see that story having legs. Jevons has come to a successful club where he is having a great goal-scoring run and is in a team challenging for promotion. Chester is close to his home city (Liverpool) but I would have thought it highly unlikely that an ambitious player would leave a successful club like Yeovil for a team only a few places off the bottom of the division.

In the afternoon I went to see the movie *Ray*, which was showing as an afternoon matinée at the Dixie, an old art deco cinema that is almost adjacent to one of the company's apartments where I am staying. Jamie Foxx was outstanding as Ray Charles and must be a shoo-in for Best Actor at next February's Academy Awards. He was really excellent.

I went back to the office and checked both the BBC news and sport websites to see if there were any additional comments about the Yeovil match. I also went to the 606 discussion forum for League Two and there were a lot of postings concerning the transfer of Gavin Williams to West Ham. The general consensus was that he was one of the better players in League Two and deserved his chance to play at a higher level. I certainly think it will be a good sale for Yeovil because Johnson and Way have proved that, despite their diminutive size, they are more than capable of driving Yeovil forward. Paul Terry has been in such outstanding form this season that he more than warrants a starting place, whether in the back four, where we seem to have a sur-plus of candidates if everyone is fit, or preferably in midfield. That still leaves four other candidates for the fourth starting place in midfield. My own preference would be to play Kevin Gall, whose pace can be just as effective as Gavin Williams' silky skills. Whenever he has come on this season he has proved to be very effective when breaking from midfield and also in providing some first-class crosses. So I certainly do not think it is a bad move to take the £250,000 that's on offer from West Ham. Yeovil have won four out of their five matches when Gavin was out injured and there are times when he can be a luxury. By delaying the playing of the final ball we haven't always capitalised on the advantages that his skills have produced.

It was 8.30 p.m. and another day had gone! Not a great deal achieved but at least Yeovil are in the third round of the cup.

Histon 1 Yeovil Town 3

Team: Chris Weale, Terry Skiverton, Scott Guyett, Colin Miles, Andy Lindegaard, Lee Johnson, Darren Way, Michael Rose, Phil Jevons, Kevin Gall, Bartosz Tarachulski

Subs: Yemi Odubade (77 for Gall), Andrejs Stolcers (90 for Tarachulski)

Subs not used: Steve Collis, Adrian Caceres, Adam Lockwood

Goal-scorers: Phil Jevons (52), Lee Johnson (59), Yemi Odubade (90)

Attendance: 2,564

Determined Opponents

Tuesday 7 December 2004 – Huish Park
Yeovil v. Kidderminster Harriers (League Two)

My overnight flight from Washington DC landed at 6.45 a.m. but, after stopping for a sleep in the car, it was almost 11 a.m. before I got to Casterbridge Hall and met Wendy and Sharron to decide what to do with the items not sold in the auction. With the exception of a few trinkets that we would take back to our home I decided we would leave everything else in the building and let the new owners have the problem of disposal! Realising this situation might occur I had sensibly incorporated into the special conditions for the sale a clause that if we did not clear the building it was the buyer's responsibility to do so! Clever move Michael, which I gather the purchasers did not notice because they were now asking Wendy whether we were going to clear it all! I then went on to the cottage in Charlton Horethorne that Wendy successfully bought at auction on behalf of LPI and met our building consultant to discuss when we will begin the renovation works.

After unpacking, I rushed into Sherborne to visit my mother in hospital before picking up Tony, as we were off to see Yeovil against Kidderminster who are rock bottom of League Two with just twelve points. They had only scored two away goals all season and were four points adrift of the next team above them. This looked a nailed-on certainty to be either 5-0 or 6-0 to Yeovil with a Phil Jevons hat-trick! Of course, that means that current form will quite likely be turned on its head and it will probably be a tricky match for Yeovil. It was last year's home defeat against Kidderminster on Boxing Day that started a run of only one win and one draw in seven matches, which really knocked the impetus out of Yeovil's season. So in truth I was approaching today's game with some degree of apprehension.

We were in our seats fifteen minutes before kick-off and a glance around the ground indicated that this was going to be one of the smaller gates of the season. Yeovil started off with a 3-5-2 line-up with Miles, Skiverton and Guyett at the back and Rose, Lindegaard and Gall playing in midfield together with Johnson and Way, and Tarachulski and Phil Jevons up front. Swansea, who are two points ahead of us, are playing away at Oxford tomorrow night and are then at Scunthorpe on Saturday, so I think they are highly unlikely to take all six points. I feel that, if can we win our home matches tonight and against Grimsby on Saturday, there is every possibility that we will go second by the end of the week.

Bartosz Tarachulski showed some lovely touches in the opening period of the game and the highlight of the first fifteen minutes was a very nicely worked Yeovil free-kick when everyone was expecting a shot from Johnson, but instead it was played gently forward to a Yeovil player in front of the wall and laid off to Jevons, who found himself in space but side-footed it wide. Tony turned to me and commented, 'That was a beautifully executed training ground move. And it almost came off.'

Kidderminster looked a poor team and, as the game wore on, it was clear they were pulling Yeovil down to their standards (always blame the other team, eh?). I turned to Tony and said, 'If Yeovil get an early goal I can see them getting a hatful. But if they don't, the longer this goes on the more Kidderminster are going to be encouraged and they could be very difficult to break down.'

Darren Way was Yeovil's best player and Tarachulski was playing well up front, but Yeovil weren't really making much headway and consequently Kidderminster were encouraged to stick with their ultra-defensive game. Eight of the Yeovil starters were playing Conference football two seasons ago and six of them were in our successful Conference-winning team – Weale, Skiverton, Miles, Johnson, Way and Lindegaard. It is a tribute to Gary Johnson that he has brought these players on to a point when they are in an automatic-promotion spot in League Two and that he can strengthen the team by unearthing additional talent from the Conference, namely Rose and Guyett.

A third of the game had gone and there was a glimmer of hope when Jevons shot and Tarachulski followed up and put the ball in the net, but it was deemed to be offside. However, Kidderminster then mounted one of their rare attacks at our end of the pitch and it appeared that the ball had gone out over the dead-ball line but the referee allowed play to continue and the Kidderminster player passed the ball back to his wide midfield player, who put in a high, looping cross that was headed home by on-loan striker Darryn Stamp. A rather pedestrian goal but an effective header at the end and that was the worse scenario possible.

Kidderminster have only scored two goals away all season and they chose to score their third one here! They were now going to be even more difficult to break down with probably all ten players defending for the rest of the match and trying to secure a win for new manager Stuart Watkiss. The game certainly needed a goal but I wasn't anticipating it coming from Kidderminster! To their credit, Yeovil immediately hit back and we were privileged to see one of the moves of the season when Colin Miles brought the ball out of defence and, from well inside his own half in the old left half position, hit a glorious cross-field ball to Andy Lindegaard in the right winger's position. The ball must have travelled all of sixty yards and, as it did so, Tony turned to me and said, 'He hits a lovely long pass, doesn't he?' Just as Tony spoke, Andy Lindegaard, with his first touch, brought the ball beautifully under control, moved to his left and bought himself some space to the right of the defender in front of him. Then, from a good five yards outside the penalty area, he hit a beautifully flighted curling left-foot shot that hit Kidderminster's right-hand upright and cannoned into the back of the net. We won't see a finer long pass nor a better flighted shot all season. It was a beautiful move and local-boy Lindegaard should be justifiably proud of such a marvellous first goal of the season.

Half-time brought the news that Scunthorpe were losing 1-0 at Cambridge, which means that if Yeovil were to win tonight and Scunthorpe lost we would be well in contention, only four points behind them.

When the game resumed for the second half, Yeovil were well on top and I predicted a 3-1 victory. Darren Way was having an outstanding game and I think Darren would be a much more difficult player to replace in the Yeovil team than Gavin Williams. I turned to Tony and said, 'What was it that Eric Cantona used to call the French captain, Didier Deschamps – the Water Carrier?' That was exactly what Darren Way was doing so effectively. He was continually bringing the ball out of defence and feeding it to the flanks or to the strikers, just like the water carrier continually going to the well and carrying the water for the benefit of everyone.

After fifteen minutes of the second half, Caceres came on for Miles. Unfortunately, Andy Lindegaard, who had played well on the right-hand side, picked up a knock and went off to be replaced by Adam Lockwood, and our shape changed to 4-4-2. Yeovil's passing game was working well, we were well on top and I was quite confident we were going to win this match. Pedro Matias was substituted by Kidderminster and he was not a happy lad. He threw off his armband and disappeared down the tunnel. Not a very clever way to create a positive impression with a new manager!

I have to admit I am not over keen on Adrian Caceres and I am not sure he is a significant improvement on Nicky Crittenden. He has scored three goals this season but too often he is out of position and his passing game can be wayward. By contrast I have been very impressed with Chris Weale's distribution. The way he releases the ball very quickly with long throws to his wingbacks is very reminiscent of Peter Schmeichel.

Stolcers came on for Rose and we reverted to 3-5-2 again with Lockwood, Skiverton and Guyett at the back. The ball was eventually worked out to the right to Lee Johnson, who put in a cross met by a Stolcers' header that found the back of the net. Another of Gary Johnson's inspired substitutions had paid off! In truth it was a great move that fully deserved a goal. We had the chance to make the game secure but the Kidderminster goalkeeper made a fantastic double save to defy both Jevons and Stolcers. Stolcers certainly looked more impressive in the closing minutes of this match than in all of his other appearances I have seen this season and we held on for the win, which was a great relief!

Tony thought we had played poorly but I thought we had done well to overcome a dogged and determined team. If your opponents are rock bottom and facing an exit from the Football League, you can hardly expect them to come to Yeovil and try to outplay us with flowing football!

We checked the other results at Tony's house and would you believe it? Scunthorpe scored twice in the last five minutes to win 2-1 at Cambridge and are still seven points clear, but we are up to second by default as Swansea are not playing until tomorrow. Lincoln lost 2-1 at Macclesfield and Leyton Orient salvaged a 1-1 draw at home to Southend.

When I got home, after just forty-five minutes' sleep in the car this morning and two hours on the plane last night, I was really looking forward to a good night's sleep and thankfully, after our win, I was not going to be distracted by worrying about Yeovil!

Yeovil Town 2 Kidderminster Harriers 1

Team: Chris Weale, Terry Skiverton, Scott Guyett, Colin Miles, Andy Lindegaard, Darren Way, Lee Johnson, Michael Rose, Phil Jevons, Kevin Gall, Bartosz Tarachulski

Subs: Adrian Caceres (61 for Miles), Adam Lockwood (68 for Lindegaard), Andrejs Stolcers (80 for Rose)

Subs not used: Steve Collis, Yemi Odubade

Goal-scorers: Andy Lindegaard (38), Andrejs Stolcers (83)

Attendance: 4,634

Position in League after match: 2nd

Your Club has a lot of Momentum
Saturday 11 December 2004 – Huish Park
Yeovil v. Grimsby Town (League Two)

I am trying to arrange all my visits to England in periods when Yeovil have got two home matches within a short period of time, so that I get two matches in less than a week's visit! My P.A., Wendy, is originally from Grimsby and her parents have come down this weekend so I am using the second of our season tickets to take Wendy's dad Barry, a lifelong Grimsby supporter, to the game. I hadn't seen Barry for the best part of six years and he remembered me as having a bit more weight. I remembered him as having a bit more hair!

While we were waiting for the kick-off I told Barry which of our players had come up from the Conference and that the best signing Yeovil had made in the last two years (or should it be the best decision?) was at the beginning of our Conference championship season, when we widened the pitch and relaid it to provide an excellent playing surface that enabled us to play attacking football thoughout the season. Today the pitch looked immaculate, there was not a cloud in the sky and conditions looked perfect.

Since last Tuesday Gavin Williams has signed for West Ham for the sum of £250,000, and I think this was a good move for both Gavin and for the club. With Stolcers, Terry, Rose and Gall all being able to play in midfield and the promising French junior, Mirza, in the reserves, it strikes me that we have plenty of depth in midfield. Today our midfield players in a 4-4-2 formation were Gall on the right and Caceres on the left, with the two regulars Johnson and Way in the centre.

Barry told me Grimsby are a good footballing team and their main problem was that they didn't score goals. Although they are seventeenth in the league, which is fifteen positions behind us, they only have seven fewer points and I suspected Grimsby would be dangerous opponents today.

Although Yeovil started brightly it was clear that Grimsby were a strong and capable team and I commented to Barry that last year we sometimes got muscled out of games against teams like Huddersfield and Northampton. Was that going to happen today, I wondered?

'Come on,' Barry shouts when Grimsby mount an impressive attack, and no-one has any problem with there being a Grimsby supporter in among the crowd as my guest. Three weeks ago we had a Darlington supporter sitting behind us and everyone was able to talk with him quite congenially, and why not? Grimsby were playing some good football and Yeovil weren't really putting any flowing moves together after the first five minutes, but we came to life with a great run from Kevin Gall and an excellent cross. I think Kevin has been an absolute revelation this year. Last year he couldn't buy a goal as a striker after Christmas. This year, by having the ball played to his feet and then using his speed to go past opposing defenders, he has been far more impressive and a real star. I would suspect that the single most important factor behind Gary Johnson's decision to sell Gavin Williams was because he knew that, although his ball skills may not be so silky, Kevin Gall is equally as effective in pressurising opponents by his sheer pace from midfield.

We were not playing well. Darren Way, who I consider to be the best header of the ball at the club, was hardly winning anything in the air. Of course, the players he was jumping against were always six or eight inches taller but that is not normally a problem for Darren, who has such a leap and purchase when he leaves the ground that he usually wins more balls than not! Phil Jevons was not having a particularly effective game against his old club and clearly this was not going to be an easy match for Yeovil. Kevin Gall was the only threat to Grimsby and I felt that we really needed Darren Way to be more involved in this game if we were going to make any headway. Another free-kick for Grimsby in a dangerous position and Barry turned to me and said, 'I think this is going to be the first goal, Michael.' He wasn't far wrong because the resulting shot eluded Weale and hit the crossbar!

We were seeing a lot of nice approach work from Grimsby who were more than holding their own in the game and it appeared certain we were going to go into half-time at 0-0. However, in the forty-third minute Yeovil were awarded a free-kick about seven or eight yards outside the penalty area. I was explaining to Barry that this was a prime position for Lee Johnson, who was an excellent striker of a dead ball. Exactly on cue Lee Johnson runs up and hits a marvellous thirty-yard shot into the top right-hand corner. 1-0 to Yeovil.

We held on to half-time and went in ahead whereas, in truth, I think that Grimsby had done enough to shade the half. It had been quite entertaining but neither goal-keeper had really had to make any significant saves, except for one smothering save from Chris Weale at the feet of a Grimsby player.

Gavin Williams made a farewell appearance at half-time and chants of 'Super Gav' went up all around the ground. There was no resentment regarding his departure as Gavin served us well and everyone knows that he is a good player who, if given a chance at a higher level, will probably go on to represent his country. The fans also appreciate that the signing of one of our Conference players by a team challenging for a Premiership place is a reflection on how far the club has come. Barry was impressed that one of our star players was leaving on good terms with the club and fans.

The half-time scores were going well for us with Macclesfield and Lincoln both drawing and Darlington leading Leyton Orient. Obviously we would prefer Scunthorpe to draw with Swansea and for both teams to drop points but in fact Scunthorpe were winning 1-0, which meant that, if the results stay as they were at half-time, we would be second in the league at 5 p.m. Scunthorpe is quite close to Grimsby and Barry said he found it difficult to believe they can sustain their current form and position right through the season. Let's hope he's right but, at the moment, they would appear to be the favourites for the championship and certainly the most consistent team in the league to date.

No sooner had the second half started then there was a very good Yeovil move working its way down the left and a long cross came to Tarachulski, who placed an easy header to the goalie's right and we were 2-0 up. What a great start! The second half was entertaining, with Yeovil playing much better and Gall continuing his good form, and I was hoping for a third goal that would move our goal difference up to +12. Phil Jevons worked hard to get on the scoresheet and appeared unlucky not to win a penalty at one point. However, it was Grimsby's stocky-looking substitute, Ash Sestanovich, who threatened to turn the game on its head when, with five minutes left, he made a very impressive run across the edge of the Yeovil penalty area and with excellent close control for such a big man took the ball past three Yeovil players before drilling it into the corner, which meant we had a very difficult last five minutes to survive. Surely we would not concede a second when we had been so dominant for much of the second half?

Yeovil tried to take the game to Grimsby in the last five minutes but Grimsby did nevertheless have two corners. Each time the ball was swung over my heart was in my mouth. There was only a minute of added time and it seemed to drag on forever but, eventually, the referee blew for full time. I was certainly right about my pick for man of the match as Kevin Gall was chosen.

As we walked back to the car Barry commented that he certainly got the feeling that Yeovil were a club that were going somewhere, and there was certainly a lot of momentum with the team, fans and overall organisation. As I drove out of Yeovil and was listening to BBC Five Live I heard that Scunthorpe had beaten Swansea 1-0, so we were up to second. I drove to Sherborne Hospital in good spirits to visit my mother before going home to pack as we were flying to Canada for Christmas the following day. It was last year when we were in Vancouver for Christmas that the wheels started to come off Yeovil's season with defeats at home to Kidderminster and away at Swansea. This year I will be away for next week's games at Leyton Orient, at home to Cheltenham on Boxing Day and away to Cambridge, but I am planning to come back on 31 December so that I can spend New Year's Eve with my mother and then go to the crucial match away at Swansea on New Year's Day. I just hope Yeovil's form can survive my visit to Canada and we will still be in contention in three weeks' time when I return.

Yeovil Town 2 Grimsby Town 1

Team: Chris Weale, Scott Guyett, Terry Skiverton, Colin Miles, Michael Rose, Kevin Gall, Darren Way, Lee Johnson, Andrejs Stolcers, Phil Jevons, Bartosz Tarachulski

Subs: Adam Lockwood (62 for Guyett), Yemi Odubade (78 for Tarachulski), Stephen Reed (90 for Stolcers)

Subs not used: Steve Collis, Adrian Caceres

Goal-scorers: Lee Johnson (43), Bartosz Tarachulski (47)

Attendance: 5,733

Position in League after match: 2nd

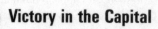

Victory in the Capital

Saturday 18 December 2004 – Vancouver, Canada
Leyton Orient v. Yeovil (League Two)

We are back in Vancouver for Christmas at our Canadian home after flying over last Sunday. I haven't done a great deal this past week but I have caught up on one of the great loves of my life, going to the movies! After watching *Spanglish* an excellent feel-good movie and *Sideways*, a road movie with a difference, I went for a drive last night around the lower east side of Vancouver along Hastings Street. This is one of the poorest and most-deprived areas of Canada with the most unfortunate collection of misfits and lost souls, jettisoned by society, parading along the streets. Drug addicts, prostitutes, their pimps and a wide range of strange characters that have slipped between society's cracks were on every street corner. It was depressing yet fascinating to observe and it was 4.30 a.m. before I got to bed, having pledged to keep more sensible hours and find more productive pastimes for late-night entertainment in the future!

I woke, tired of course, at 8.30 a.m. and lay in bed dozing. I finally went down to the den at 9.30 a.m. (5.30 p.m. in England) a little bit apprehensive and fearing the worst. Was it going to be Orient 4 Yeovil 0? It would be good if we could win and open a gap on all the clubs clustered behind us. I covered the screen so that no errant headline or league table would reveal the result and clicked to the League Two page. My heart was pounding as I removed the paper covering up any headlines to reveal Orient 2 Yeovil 3! What a fantastic result because, despite recent poor form and injuries, Orient are well placed in the play-off zone and could easily overhaul us, so this was a very, very good result.

Furthermore our new signing from Southampton, Arron Davies, came on as substitute and scored. What a dream debut. Tarachulski also scored, as did our most improved player of the season, Paul Terry. We can certainly perform without Gavin Williams, and I say this without any rancour as both Terry and Gall are in such good form they deserve to play. Our midfield is currently strong in both depth and ability.

Darlington, Macclesfield and Lincoln all lost but Swansea had a convincing 4-0 win at home to Notts County. What about Scunthorpe? I quickly checked the results again and unfortunately they had a good 3-0 win at Rushden. I discovered that Southend played on Friday evening and won 1-0 at home against Chester with an eighty-eighth-minute winner! It seems everyone is getting late goals as last week Scunthorpe scored twice in the last five minutes to beat Cambridge. Still, I mustn't complain. It was late when Tarachulski and Stolcers scored our winners against Wycombe and Kidderminster respectively!

I read the details of our match again. We were 2-0 up but Orient pegged us back to 2-2 before Davies scored the winner. It showed some resilience to lose a two-goal lead away from home but still score a third to win. This really was a good result and perhaps we will look back and see today as the day that confirmed we will probably go up? More importantly, we are building up some momentum, as that is four wins in a row and three in the League. We have now played twenty-two games for forty points, which is getting back near the golden target of two points per game, which looked a forlorn hope in November. We are still seven points behind Scunthorpe but there are now only six teams within seven points of us and a five-point gap to fourth. So a gap is definitely beginning to form with Scunthorpe, Yeovil and Swansea pulling away. Is the league finally shaping itself and are these three teams going to be the front runners for the remainder of the season?

Our next games are Cheltenham at home on Boxing Day, Cambridge away, and then the big match at Swansea on New Year's Day, followed by Shrewsbury at home. If we don't slip up and win three of these matches, we could still lose at Swansea and be very well placed in the New Year. Scunthorpe don't really have any difficult matches until 11 February when they play Southend, Yeovil and Swansea, all away, in a fifteen-day period.

If Yeovil can stay in touch, that could be when Scunthorpe start to feel the pressure and wilt as they are definitely due a bad run, having won six in a row. Indeed, their last nine League games have resulted in eight wins and a draw! That is some run but it cannot go on forever and we have to stay in contention for when they do slip up. However, I must concede that their December and January fixtures do not look particularly challenging.

This could be the defining day of our season as we are now five points clear of Southend in fourth and now have a great opportunity to consolidate our position in the automatic promotion frame. I checked our position at this point with the corresponding point last year, which was as follows:

	P	W	D	L	GD	Pts	Pts/game
2004/05	22	12	4	6	+11	40	1.8
2003/04	21	13	1	7	+13	40	1.9

What an amazing similarity in results, in fact almost identical on forty points with goal differences of +11 and +13 and either 1.8 and 1.9 points a game average. This year we currently have the second-best home record in the league; last year it was third best, but this year our away form isn't so good. It is only the twelfth best whereas last year it was the fourth best. Nevertheless, today we are second in the league, whereas last year we were fourth at this time and the big difference this year is the fact that we have a regular goal-scorer. Phil Jevons is going to be our key to a successful season.

After this flying start to the day, I spent the rest of the day and evening sorting through thousands of digital images of Nepal, Tibet, Canada and the Alps and putting them in categories in order to make image selection for next year's Great Walks of the World brochure a lot easier. It sounds soul destroying but I enjoy working with images. If I had my time again I would aspire to be a professional photographer. Then again, everyone's job is always more interesting than your own!

Leyton Orient 2 Yeovil Town 3

Team: Chris Weale, Paul Terry, Terry Skiverton, Colin Miles, Michael Rose, Kevin Gall, Lee Johnson, Darren Way, Andrejs Stolcers, Phil Jevons, Bartosz Tarachulski

Subs: Arron Davies (46 for Jevons), Scott Guyett (46 for Rose)

Subs not used: Steve Collis, Adrian Caceres, Yemi Odubade

Goal-scorers: Bartosz Tarachulski (26), Paul Terry (45), Arron Davies (77)

Attendance: 3,867

Position in League after match: 2nd

No Boxing Day Blues

Sunday 26 December 2004 (Boxing Day) – Vancouver, Canada
Yeovil v. Cheltenham Town (League Two)

It is Boxing Day and, after a somewhat understated Christmas as everyone else was in bed by 10 p.m. last night, I stayed up quite late reading until about 2.30 a.m. – so not much difference there! When I woke at 8.30 a.m. I had some trepidation about going to check the Yeovil result. We were home to Cheltenham and last year on Boxing Day we lost at home to Kidderminster!

I went downstairs, got straight to the results page and it showed an updated score that Yeovil were beating Cheltenham 3-1, Great! Jevons had scored and Davies has come on as a substitute and has scored for the second game in a row, which continues the excellent start to his Yeovil career. Furthermore, at present it is Chester 1 Scunthorpe 1, which means we could reduce Scunthorpe's lead to five points. While I was reviewing the scores, Yeovil scored again to make it 4-1 with a goal from Paul Terry. That is a terrific result because three goals will be very good for our goal difference. The team that played today seems to be what I would consider our strongest with Weale in goal, Rose, Skiverton, Miles and Terry as a back four, Gall, Way, Johnson and Stolcers in midfield with Tarachulski and Jevons as the strike force, which is seven of last year's team and four newcomers who seem to have made quite a difference. The subs were Andy Lindegaard, Arron Davies, Adrian Caceres, Scott Guyett and Steve Collis, which just about means that our strongest sixteen were all available. Other than Adam Lockwood and Stephen Reed I cannot think of anyone else I would consider for my first sixteen.

The final results confirmed that Southend won 1-0 at Wycombe. Damn! However, Macclesfield drew, which means they lost two points in comparison with us and we are now only five points behind Scunthorpe. Swansea are third, one point behind us. There is then a further gap of four points to Southend, which means they are five points behind us. Macclesfield are fifth, eight points behind us, and Northampton sixth, nine points behind and they did not play today.

I noticed that we were a goal down again today and came from behind. We are becoming quite a resilient side and I hope such a positive result on Boxing Day is going to be symbolic for the rest of the season. We have now won four League games in a row and seven out of our last eight. I will be more than happy if we can get a win at lowly Cambridge in two days' time and then a draw at Swansea.

Today's was a very good win because if Cheltenham had won they would have been only five points behind us, so they had every incentive to do well. We are now at the halfway point of the season and amazingly, despite being so far behind the curve, we are now approaching the two points a game average again. I have to say that, ten matches ago, I never thought that would be a remote possibility for the remainder of this season!

I don't want to tempt fate but it now seems that four teams might be breaking away and be fighting for the three automatic promotion spots: ourselves, Scunthorpe, Swansea and Southend. However I mustn't be premature because last December I thought that we were so far in front of the eighth team there was no way that we weren't going to get into the play-offs! Hopefully I have learnt my lesson not to take anything for granted!

By the time I had finished on the computer David and Lisa were up and they were planning to go over to their cousins and watch the expanded version of the three *Lord of the Rings* films back to back through the day! Is this torture or what? Apparently this is about twelve hours of footage and if they can start by late morning they'll have finished by midnight! So there won't be any family activities with the children on this Boxing Day! Sarah and I went to see the new Martin Scorcese film *The Aviator*, featuring Leonardo DiCaprio, based on the life of Howard Hughes. When we came out of the movie we drove to New Westminster to join the rest of the family for brother-in-law Wayne's annual Boxing Day bash, where he has friends and relatives around. As the night proceeds he and some of his former band colleagues start playing Blues, Country and whatever type of music takes their fancy.

We left at about 1.30 a.m. in the morning to return home with me hoping for another positive Yeovil result in a little over twenty-four hours' time.

Yeovil Town 4 Cheltenham Town 1

Team: Chris Weale, Paul Terry, Terry Skiverton, Colin Miles, Michael Rose, Kevin Gall, Darren Way, Lee Johnson, Andrejs Stolcers, Phil Jevons, Bartosz Tarachulski

Subs: Arron Davies (68 for Jevons), Andy Lindegaard (80 for Stolcers), Scott Guyett (88 for Tarachulski)

Subs not used: Steve Collis, Adrian Caceres

Goal-scorers: Kevin Gall (30), Phil Jevons (44), Arron Davies (80), Paul Terry (86)

Attendance: 7,320

Position in League after match: 2nd

 ## Five Away from Home
Tuesday 28 December 2004 – Vancouver, Canada
Cambridge United *v*. Yeovil (League Two)

I got up at 9 a.m. after another late night and went down to the den to check the result from Cambridge. I was a little bit apprehensive because although we had done well to win at Orient and then at home against Cheltenham with their very strong defence, this was an obvious away win against the bottom-but-one team. However, it was so obvious that it was also a potential banana skin! And it would be awful to dilute all the benefits of our good results so far over the holiday period by screwing up at Cambridge.

When I got down to the den Sharron was on the computer and it seemed the death toll from the tsunami in South-East Asia had risen from the 3,000 that was reported on Boxing Day to 38,000. Three of the worst areas to be affected were Phuket in Thailand, that I visited ten years ago, Galle in Sri Lanka where Sharron and I had stayed in 1979 and 1983 and Penang in Malaysia where we have had two family holidays. Of course, our former tour guide Chris Williams lives in Phuket, so hopefully he and his daughter are okay. It's certainly one of the worst disasters in living memory and puts the importance of football into proper perspective.

When Sharron left I scrolled to the football pages and the only headline for League Two was 'Cambridge appoint Thompson'. I wondered if this story was about to continue 'Cambridge appoint Thompson as manager after great victory against Yeovil'. I hoped not. My heart was beating quite quickly as I turned to the League Two page to get the results and I scrolled down, making sure the league table that would give the result away was covered. I quickly came to Cambridge 3 Yeovil 5! What an amazing result and what's this? Scunthorpe drew at home against Notts County so I was right, the wheels are coming off their season (but rather earlier than I anticipated) and Southend lost 1-0 at home to Macclesfield. It couldn't be better for us as far as the other results were concerned.

Bottom-but-one team or not, it is still a fantastic achievement to score five goals away from home against anyone, especially when you come from 2-0 down! It seems Yeovil had the best of the first half and squandered a lot of chances before Cambridge scored either side of half-time. Jevons then scored twice, the second from a penalty and, as Yeovil re-established their dominance, Jevons set up Lee Johnson to put us ahead before completing his hat-trick with a second penalty. Cambridge then pulled one back but Stolcers completed the rout with a delicate lob with the president of the Latvian FA watching, so that will do his prospects for an international recall no harm! Swansea won 3-1 at home to Boston so everything is all nicely set-up for Swansea v. Yeovil on New Year's Day, and I will be there. Great!

This has been an outstanding holiday period so far with three wins from three games. What a difference to last year when everything went pear shaped between Christmas and New Year. With Scunthorpe drawing their last two games, we are now only three points behind them rather than seven just three days ago. What a turnaround!

Scunthorpe have forty-nine points, we are second on forty-six and Swansea are third on forty-five, so both Swansea and ourselves have everything to play for on New Year's Day. The game should be an absolute cracker! Then there is further seven-point gap to Southend on thirty-eight, who are now eight points behind us! Macclesfield are also on thirty-eight and Northampton, with a game in hand, on thirty-seven. It certainly looks as if the front three are breaking away and it was excellent news that Southend faltered today.

I spent the rest of the day working at home and went out in the evening to watch the movie version of *Phantom of the Opera* with Lisa. It was less than riveting but I could live with that; after all, we've just won five on the spin in the League!

Cambridge United 3 Yeovil Town 5

Team: Chris Weale, Paul Terry, Terry Skiverton, Colin Miles, Michael Rose, Kevin Gall, Lee Johnson, Darren Way, Andrejs Stolcers, Phil Jevons, Bartosz Tarachulski

Subs: Arron Davies (55 for Gall), Scott Guyett (82 for Jevons), Andy Lindegaard (82 for Tarachulski)

Subs not used: Steve Collis, Adrian Caceres

Goal-scorers: Phil Jevons (55) (81), Darren Way (56), Lee Johnson (69), Andrejs Stolcers (90)

Attendance: 3,828

Position in League after match: 2nd

Happy New Year in Swansea
Saturday 1 January 2005 – Vetch Field
Swansea City *v*. Yeovil (League Two)

I flew home from Canada yesterday arriving at Heathrow at 11.30 a.m. to be met by my P.A.'s partner, Neil, who drove me home. No sooner did I get in than my eldest daughter Sarah turned up. She had flown home from Vancouver two days before me and is going with her friend Rose to our Swiss apartment for a week's holiday. Here is another page of family history turning. This is the first time one of our kids has used our apartment on their own.

Last night I went into Sherborne to see my Mum still in the Yeatman Hospital. She looked good, was moving well and had been pleased to be kept in over Christmas where they could look after her. I didn't stay long as I was tired. I slowly drove the five miles home from Sherborne to Stowell along the country lanes and found I was driving with one eye closed, a sure sign of tiredness, and kept hitting the verge and hedge even though I was barely driving at 10mph. I should have stopped and slept in the car but I only had a mile to go so kept going. Big mistake! I fell asleep and ended up in a ditch hitting a tree! Luckily I had my safety belt on. I was now fully awake and nursed my vehicle home the final mile to Stowell. The car could well be a write-off and I'll have to see what the insurers say. They'll never believe I wasn't drinking on New Year's Eve but I am a teetotaller and don't drink!

The accident woke me up so I finished unpacking after calling my friend Ian and saying I wouldn't come over to see in the New Year with him and his wife as any more driving probably wasn't a good idea!

I called Tony at 7.30 this morning as I was tempted to get a lift with him, but I was not sure about going to Swansea via Heathrow (where Tony was collecting Patrick who is flying in from New York) and continuing to Taunton after the game to drop Patrick off. After confirming that my mother's car, which had been left at our home, actually started I decided I would drive to Bristol and meet Tony and Patrick there as planned.

So this is it. The match of the season by far with both teams in superlative form. I have to say I fancy Yeovil's chances and I am sure we will score at least one goal. As for Swansea, it is in our favour that Bristol City have recalled Marc Goodfellow, who scored four goals in eight games while on loan at Swansea. However I believe the biggest danger for Yeovil today is without doubt Lee Trundle.

Tony called at about 10 a.m. from Heathrow and we arranged to meet near the M32 in Bristol in about seventy-five minutes but, of course, it took me about thirty minutes to get everything together and I then discovered that my Mum's car was low (read empty!) on petrol. It was 10.45 a.m. and I drove to Anchor Hill Service Station near Wincanton... and it was closed. On Saturday morning? Of course – it's a Bank Holiday. Shit! At least Morrisons in Wincanton will be open. I drove another mile. Wrong! I eventually limped into the Sparkford Shell station in a state of desperation as I was driving on fumes at this point, and then drove like the clappers to Bristol and met Tony and Patrick. No sooner did we continue than Patrick presented me with my New Year's gift, a T-shirt from New York! Patrick was in good form and excitedly told us all about his trip. I didn't know if Patrick had gone for a short-break holiday or for the company and it turned out the latter. So I guess I paid for the trip and it was a pretty expensive T-shirt!

As Swansea were at home and in good form Patrick went for 1-0 or 2-1, Tony opted for a 2-2 draw but I was reasonably confident we could win. As we discussed the game driving into Swansea we passed a very impressive new stadium under construction. We parked by some sand dunes and headed for the ground and it was like entering a time warp. Vetch Field was located in the midst of a working-class community, which presumably formed the foundation of Swansea's original roots. There were rows and rows of terraced houses and a few rough and ready pubs, which were so packed we decided not to try and get any food. Posted above an alley providing rear access to two sets of terraced houses was a sign: 'Welcome to the Vetch Field: Players' and Directors' Entrance.' We were incredulous but, yes, there was the Yeovil team bus parked outside and almost blocking the narrow street! We turned a corner and were amazed to stumble upon a terraced house with the lower floor converted into the club shop! Obviously Swansea supporters are desperate for gear at any time because the entire shop front was covered by safety wire, giving the impression of a prison camp, and you had to enter through a cage. Unbelievable!

We turned the next corner and walked along the back of the north stand, which seemed to be built out of corrugated iron interspersed with broken panes of plastic and glass. We eventually found our turnstile and wanted to go for a pee... or did we? The toilet was a concrete structure maybe twelve feet square with a little channel along the foot of three walls, which seemed barely capable of draining anything away! It did not bother me as I have survived some pretty disgusting toilets in the Third World but I'm amazed that was on offer to punters in 2005. How did it pass a Health & Safety inspection?

We ascended the dark, poorly maintained stairs and at least there was the courtesy of a sign apologising for the state of the ground and stating that the club would soon be moving, so that impressive new stadium is for Swansea. We emerged at the top of the covered terracing (as long as the wind didn't blow the roof off) and moved forward so the view was not obstructed by the countless support pillars of the rickety old stand and settled for a place near the corner where the pillers caused minimal interference. Patrick and Tony went for a coffee and the world's worst hot dog and yes, even the vending unit was protected by a wire cage!

The ground was already almost full but what a strange ground, with a high, large modern stand running just half the width of the home end and the only other seating being a low stand to our right that ran the length of the pitch! Most of the home supporters were in the pitch-length terrace to our left and not behind a goal. I noted from the programme that Swansea were selling parts of the pitch and ground to supporters as souvenirs and thought if the fans hang around long enough it will all fall down soon enough and they can get their souvenirs for free!

There was a great atmosphere and we finally got going at 3 p.m. Of course, there was no clock so I started my stopwatch. The rain had stopped, conditions didn't seem too bad and the sun had appeared. Yeovil were unchanged, except Scott Guyett came in for Colin Miles. Most of the early possession was ours and, although we couldn't get our passing game going, the ball was certainly more down the far end, which we were attacking, but was that because of the wind? When Chris Weale kicked downfield the ball landed well in Swansea's half, but their goal kicks didn't make the halfway line. I turned to Tony and, although I had predicted a win, I commented, 'You know, against this support, a draw would be a great result.'

Swansea's dangerman, Lee Trundle, showed some nice touches including a good shot comfortably saved by Chris Weale. Michael Rose had the distinction of taking probably the worst corner of all time at the far end. He must have scuffed it or misjudged the wind as it went along the ground and behind the goal! Kevin Gall was struggling to get in the game or use his pace and I reckoned Arron Davies could be on for him at half-time. Just as I thought that at least Swansea had not jumped to a quick 3-0 lead, as they did in their last home game against Boston, Paul Terry gave away a free-kick on the edge of our box for a foul on Trundle, who was looking very assured on the ball. I really rate him as a player although, like Wayne Rooney, he often looks to be carrying a bit of condition! This was Swansea's first opportunity, but the ball cannoned into the wall and, as the half continued, all the passing was now coming from Yeovil, who were playing well without threatening Swansea.

However, in the last fifteen minutes of the first half, Swansea started getting in the game and then Trundle produced a bit of absolute magic, turning on a sixpence, making space to move away from two Yeovil players and producing a curling left-foot shot that beat Weale all ends up and only missed his right-hand post by inches. The Yeovil fans were chanting 'Fat Boy' and trying to wind Trundle up, which I suspect would give him some satisfaction. He must know he's playing well if the fans pick him out, and I thought he showed commendable restraint not to respond. It was a great piece of skill but it would have been unfair to have gone in 1-0 down. We got to half-time more than holding our own at 0-0. I thought we won the first half on points and Tony thought it was even. Scunthorpe were only drawing at home to Darlington. Of course,

At least Swansea had the good grace to apologise for their abject stadium!

if we lost and they won we would be six points adrift but if we draw and don't lose ground to Scunthorpe that would be a real bonus.

Davies came on at the start of the second half for Gall, as I predicted, but none of us initially noticed that one of our favourite players, home grown Andy Lindegaard, had replaced the injured Michael Rose at half-time. As Andy was playing left-back at the far end of the ground, I think we can be forgiven.

After a clash of heads, Swansea were awarded a free-kick on the edge of the box. I desperately hoped all our good work was not to be undone by an early Swansea goal in the second half but the Yeovil fans' chant of 'Johnny, Johnny, Johnny Wilk-in-son' will tell you where that particular free-kick ended up! Almost immediately Phil Jevons was clear through after a slip by a Swansea defender and with the best chance so far and the goal at his mercy he sadly pushed the ball well wide. He soon burst through again and put in a wicked cross that the Swansea 'keeper, Willy Gueret, did very well to gather, but then it was Swansea's turn and a great shot was destined for the top corner when Chris Weale made a world-class save to turn it over the bar.

There had been more chances in the first ten minutes of the second half than the entire first half but more was to come as Swansea broke through and scored... but the referee gave offside. Phew! That was a let off and, soon after, a trademark header from Tarachulski with the goal at his mercy was sadly directed straight to the goalkeeper. It could easily have been 2-2 at this point! Arron Davies was making some nice contributions and I thought that, with this great atmosphere and crowd, he couldn't be regretting the move from Southampton and the very real likelihood of playing in League One next year.

Arron Davies, Paul Terry, Scott Guyett and Bartosz Tarachulski pressurise the Swansea goal. Yeovil fully deserved their vital New Year's Day victory at the Vetch Field as a result of taking the game to Swansea.

The match was now being played at a quicker pace and the Swansea player, Tate, headed against his own bar trying to clear a dangerous Yeovil cross. Darren Way was booked for shirt tugging by a referee who had generally done his best to let the game flow. You had to hand it to Yeovil who, with two strikers, a very attack-minded midfield and full-backs always willing to push up, were really taking the game to Swansea, who hardly got a kick for a ten-minute period. Our passing game was really working well.

The pattern of the game remained unchanged with Yeovil totally dominant and finally, twelve minutes from the end, we got the breakthrough we deserved. After more Yeovil pressure a headed clearance dropped to Stolcers at the edge of the box and he made space before hitting a great shot that I thought was going narrowly over. However it was a beautifully flighted shot, judged to perfection and hit with pace and it found the top right corner. Goal! The Yeovil fans erupted and the rest of the ground was silent. The longer Stolcers is around the more impressively he performs and immediately the Yeovil fans were chanting, 'He's a Latvian ooh ah'.

Caceres came on for Johnson, who had taken a knock. Could we hold on? We did at Bristol Rovers last year and that was with ten men, but too much of the game was down the far end for my liking and Trundle shaved our post with an overhead kick. Weale tipped over a goal-bound header and Swansea had three very good corners. This was nail-biting stuff and far too much pressure before a season-high crowd of 11,225. We survived the ninety minutes and then the ref added on a full three minutes so I reset my stopwatch. We finally got a free-kick, which gave us the chance to relieve the pressure, and with a minute left Davies took the ball to the corner to waste time and somehow the ball broke free. Stolcers worked it along the line and into the box and, after a couple of attempts the ball flew into the net from Jevons! Absolutely fantastic!

Clockwise from top left:

1. At Lincoln, 8 May 2004.

2. Patrick and his infamous gourmet rolls.

3. The all-seeing eyes of Buddha overlook Kathmandu from Bodnath.

4. Our good doctor Matt and Colin descending into Tibet, 4 October 2004.

5. Sunset over Locarno Beach, Vancouver.

Clockwise from top left:

6. A study in concentration and excellent technique resulted in Phil Jevons converting all 11 penalties during the season. At Notts County, 21 August 2004.

7. Despite his lack of height Darren Way has outstanding heading ability. 18 September 2004.

8. Michael Rose's consistent performances earnt him a place in the League select team. 14 August 2004.

9. Darren Way was always at the heart of all Yeovil's efforts. 18 September 2004.

Clockwise from top left:

10. Scott Guyett and Paul Terry keep a close eye on the ever dangerous Lee Trundle in the New Year Day's clash at Swansea.

11. Goal! We saw this 29 times from Phil Jevons.
1 January 2005.

12. Phil Jevons goes close against Shrewsbury,
3 January 2005.

13. Darren Way in typically combative form against Shrewsbury, 3 January 2005.

14. Calling home from Aconcagua Base Camp,
22 January 2005. We beat Cambridge 2-1!

Opposite page, clockwise from top left:

15. Tibetan Pilgrims circumnambulating Kailas, 9 October 2004.

16. Majestic Gurla Mandata rises to 7,728m behind Lake Manasarovar, 10 October 2004.

17. Life on the Tibetan Plateau, 10 October 2004.

18. Yak Herder and his daughter. Tibet, 12 October 2004.

19. Nomads, Tibet. 12 October 2004.

This page, clockwise from top left:

20. Smiling below freezing point! Near Rongbuk, 14 October 2004.

21. Approaching Everest, 16 October 2004.

22. On Mallory's Magic Highway, 18 October 2004.

23. At the Raphu La (6,548m) with Makalu (8,463m), the world's fifth highest mountain behind. 19 October 2004.

24. Approaching Advance Base Camp, Everest, 18 October 2004.

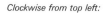

Clockwise from top left:

25. Our Nepalese sirder Dekipa and Tibetan Agent Pemba at our farewell dinner in Zhangmou. 21 October 2004.

26. Dekipa keeps an eye on Colin as we descend to Rongbuk, 20 October 2004.

27. In the desert, Dubai. 29 October 2004.

28. Dune driving in Dubai, 29 October 2004.

29. The Himalaya rise from the Tibetan Plateau like icebergs in the desert. 21 October 2004.

Clockwise from top left:

30. Plaza de Mayo, the historic centre of Buenos Aires. 15 January 2005.

31. Dancing in the street, San Telmo, Buenos Aires. 16 January 2005.

32. Art (67) being passed by three gauchos on the approach to Aconcagua, 21 January 2005.

33. Our guide Motoco leading us up the slag heap, 23 January 2005.

34. Aconcagua (6,960m), the world's highest mountain outside the Himalaya, from Base Camp. 22 January 2005.

Clockwise from top left:

35. 'I didn't know they had players like this in League Two!' Hermann Hreidarsson's expression says it all after tangling with Bartosz Tarachulski. 29 January 2005.

36. Kevin Gall was the FA Player of the Fourth Round for his scintillating performance at Charlton. Here he leaves Jerome Thomas and Hermann Hriedarsson in his wake. 29 January 2005.

37. Chairman John Fry applauds the 4,000 Yeovil supporters at Charlton. 29 January 2005.

38. Kevin Amankwaah made his Yeovil debut at Macclesfield on 5 February 2005.

39. Club captain Terry Skiverton, seen here against Bury, has risen through the leagues with Yeovil. 19 March 2005.

40. Darren Way helps inflict another heavy defeat on local rivals Bristol Rovers. 12 February 2005.

41. Local boy Andy Lindegaard, seen here in action against Leyton Orient, is one of the most versatile players at the club. 5 March 2005.

Clockwise from right:

42. Kevin Gall is one of the quickest players outside of the Premiership. Against Bury on 19 March 2005.

43. Terry Skiverton wheels away after heading Yeovil's first goal at Boston. Phil Jevons, Darren Way and Adam Lockwood seem pleased! 26 March 2005.

44. Captain Terry Skiverton, seen here challenging against Mansfield, 9 April 2005, is always dangerous from set pieces.

45. Arron Davies, seen here in action at Rushden, 2 April 2005, scored a succession of spectacular goals after arriving from Southampton.

46. *Above left:* At the Bar Sur, Buenas Aires, 25 January 2005. The Tango is a national institution in Argentina.

47. *Above right:* Prague has a wealth of historic buildings. 9 February 2005.

48. The old town square, Prague, 8 February 2005.

49. At the opera, Prague, 9 February 2005.

50. *Top left:* With my former personal assistant Wendy, 17 February 2005. Sadly, her next visit to Mürren was not so happy and she quit after nine years.

51 & 52. *Above left and right:* My favourite place. Mürren with the Eiger behind, in summer and winter.

53. *Below:* Home in the mountains. Just a fraction of the view from our balcony, Mürren.

54. *Above:* Relaxing at the Beach, Ko Samet, 12 March 2005.

55. *Left:* You are never far from delightful company in Thailand. Ko Samet, 11 March 2005.

Opposite page, clockwise from top left:

56. 'If you don't tip, we kill you!' Entertainment African style, approaching Sabi Sabi, 7 April 2005.

57. 'Now that's what I call a centipede!' Lisa, Sarah and David at Sabi Sabi, 7 April 2005.

58. A hungry elephant by the Sabi Sabi lodge, 8 April 2005.

59. Can you see the Rhinos? Sabi Sabi, 7 April 2005.

60. Lion spotting, Sabi Sabi, 8 April 2005.

Opposite, clockwise from top left:

61. The arrival of Nigerian international Efe Sodje saw a boom in bandanna sales! At Kidderminster, 9 April 2005.

62. After a long wait Steve Collins finally secured the 'keeper's spot on merit for the vital closing games of the season. 9 April 2005.

63. Marcus Richardson's first-half effort at Southend was disallowed. 30 April 2005.

64. Efe Sodje goes close against Wycombe, 23 April 2005.

65. Gary Johnson applauds the Yeovil supporters at Southend, 30 April 2005.

This page, from top:

66. 'Gary who?' the fans said but now a living legend in Yeovil with three trophies in four seasons. Soaked in champagne, 7 May 2005.

67. Darren Way was most fans' choice for Player of the Season. 7 May 2005.

68. Top from 3 January for all bar two weeks but the championship was only secured on the last day of the season. 7 May 2005.

69 & 70. With friend, colleague and fellow Casterbridge shareholder Tony supporting England in Portugal (*left*) and at Huish Park.

71 & 72. The author at work (with Prince Edward and Sophie Countess of Wessex)… and at play in his beloved Bernese Oberland.

A 2-0 win, which we thoroughly deserved on the back of our second half performance. The game barely had time to restart when the whistle blew and it was all over. Absolutely bloody fantastic! 'What a great day,' beamed Tony, who at first hadn't been sure about coming.

Many Swansea fans were applauding Yeovil's efforts and the team came over to salute the fans. Gary Johnson was really pumped up and had every right to be. This is without doubt the result of the season. We scored twice before 11,000 fans away from home against one of the league's meanest defences and our defence was superb, holding out and keeping a clean sheet against the ever-dangerous Trundle and a team who had scored 12 in the past 4 matches.

Tony commented that the team spirit at Yeovil was obviously superb. The most thankless job in the squad has to be reserve goalie as you have little chance of coming on and yet Collis looked as pleased and excited as anyone. He is a very good goalkeeper and will thoroughly deserve his chance when Weale follows Super Gav and moves on to greener pastures.

We learnt about the icing on the cake as we left the ground. Scunthorpe lost at home to Darlington! So they have well and truly hit the buffers and I thought their difficult games started in February! Instead of being six points behind if we had lost and Scunthorpe had won, we have closed that recent seven-point gap and are now equal top on points and only in second place due to an inferior goal difference of a single goal!

What a start to the New Year. We have won four out of four over the holiday period if you include Leyton Orient. This is a dream run and we have to be favourites to win the league outright now, although there is still a long way to go. After being dropped off to collect my car I continued home to watch *Match of the Day* and checked the impressive Swansea website, which already had a match report up that said Yeovil fully deserved their win.

It was 4 a.m. before I went to bed. Old habits die hard, even in a New Year, but I could not have imagined a better start to this particular year.

Swansea City 0 Yeovil Town 2

Team: Chris Weale, Paul Terry, Terry Skiverton, Scott Guyett, Michael Rose, Kevin Gall, Lee Johnson, Darren Way, Andrejs Stolcers, Phil Jevons, Bartosz Tarachulski

Subs: Arron Davies (45 for Gall), Andy Lindegaard (45 for Rose), Adrian Caceres (79 for Johnson)

Subs not used: Steve Collis, Stephen Reed

Goal-scorers: Andrejs Stolcers (78), Phil Jevons (90)

Attendance: 11,225

Position in League after match: 2nd

Fighting Back to the Top
Monday 3 January 2005 – Huish Park
Yeovil *v.* Shrewsbury Town (League Two)

Sharron, Lisa and David came home yesterday but unfortunately, just like Sarah who came home earlier, their baggage did not accompany them! Hopefully it will soon be found and delivered to our home.

It was a glorious day but I was a little apprehensive about the game. We should win and win well against Shrewsbury, who are third from bottom, but both Michael Rose and Lee Johnson picked up injuries at Swansea, although with our strong squad this should not be a problem. However, Shrewsbury have hit a bit of form and won two in a row so it won't be easy. It looks an obvious home banker and indeed, if we win by a few goals, we should go top as Scunthorpe, with two points out of nine, are having their dodgy run somewhat earlier than I anticipated. Scunnie will also be without two key players for their visit to always-dangerous Mansfield today.

Patrick and Tony both rang to say they were going to the game and we arranged to meet up at 2 p.m. I read some postings on the *606* League Two web forum and posted a couple myself. I noticed one posting referring to Yeovil being 2/1 favourites to win the league and that struck me as a good price as I know more than a little about gambling. From 1972 to 2001 gambling was my main hobby. I was not a mug punter as I mainly bet on sports where the knowledge was in the public arena, e.g. football, American football, rugby, cricket, golf, tennis and boxing, and I kept detailed records of each sport and every bet on an annual basis for thirty years. If I saw myself losing in certain sports on a regular basis then I cut back. To me my love of gambling was the thrill of the chase and of backing your own judgment, not actually trying to accumulate more wealth.

Was I a big gambler? You tell me. To someone who has a £5 or £10 bet, the £50 gambler is a big gambler, to a £50 punter the £500 gambler is a big better, the £500 better sees the punter who puts down £1,500 as a serious gambler and so on. Professional gamblers will often bet £10,000, the mega rich will back their judgement with £50,000 and £100,000 bets and the likes of Kerry Packer and Middle Eastern Sheikhs will stake £500,000 a night in the casino without blinking. My average bets were £100, a big bet was £300-£500 and my biggest bets occasionally totalled £1,000. I used to bet about £10,000 to £15,000 a year and I used to win or lose about 25 per cent of this turnover. I lost £30,000 in thirty years, which averages out at about £20 a week and as I don't drink or smoke it's not quite as much as it seems.

My wife Sharron never had a problem with my gambling because in the early years she always used to say it gave me an interest and diversion from work. Sharron and I are very different characters and we tend to argue over everything, so ours can be a rocky household. We never agree on anything but we have never had an argument about money. Sharron says it is because we have always had money, but I disagree (there you go!), because when we started Casterbridge Tours we put all our combined savings up and borrowed from the bank via an overdraft. In the latter years, Sharron probably felt it was not money I was wasting but time when researching form, watching games on TV and above all keeping records, checking statements, etc.

Do I regret it? Not really. I thoroughly enjoyed testing my judgment and following most sports and being a disciplined gambler taught me to manage risk and take (calculated) chances. As a result, I chose to back my own judgement and work for myself, and our company has grown to have years where it has produced over a million pounds of profits in a year. Set against £30,000 of gambling losses over thirty years, it's a no brainer!

Was I an addict or should I say, am I an addict? I used to say no because my image of an addict was someone out of control and I was usually pretty disciplined. But I have now realised that, yes, I was addicted and I do have an addictive personality. Obsession and addictions can be focussed on a variety of activities and alcohol, drugs, sex, eating disorders, gambling, working habits and shopping are all very different activities associated with addiction. However, there are identical patterns of behaviour that characterise the behaviour of addicts, who often transfer their addictive behaviour from one fixation to another, as I well know. I can now see that my thirty-year love affair with gambling was an addiction that, by and large, I kept under control and which did not threaten our family assets.

Three years ago I hit a run of form when I couldn't have won the Yeovil to Bournemouth bicycle race in a Maserati! I went about three months without winning a bet, my bets got bigger and bigger and I found I was not betting logically but in effect chasing my losses. So I stopped, just like that! Why? I lost about £7,000 in three months, which in the context of £23,000 in the previous twenty-nine years was a bit out of proportion. I wasn't enjoying my betting anymore and so I said 'I'm stopping'. Of course, this 'all or nothing' behaviour and not doing anything in moderation is very characteristic of an addict!

But back to the plot and Yeovil. Yeovil at 2/1 was very interesting but three things went through my mind:

1) A bet on Yeovil would surely be the kiss of death to their promotion prospects.
2) I get enough pleasure out of Yeovil winning. I don't need the extra buzz of a wager to add icing on the cake.
3) I have an excellent salary plus serious dividends from Casterbridge Tours. Winning a thousand pounds or so is neither here nor there so why bother? Any bet would need to be big enough to provide interest and a decent pay off.

I went to the company offices in Sherborne where I knew there was cash and travellers cheques in the safe that I had brought back from Tibet, and then I popped into Stanley's on Cheap Street, the only bookmaker readily accessible between home and Huish Park Stadium. My original thoughts of betting £1,500 had grown to £2,200 and if I could get 2/1, (or at worst 7/4) that would be a £4,000 pay out if Yeovil ended up winning the league. However, all they could offer was 11/8, which wasn't good enough so, together with my son David, I drove to Yeovil, met with Tony and Patrick and I guarantee I was the only person to go into Huish Park Stadium with £2,200 in my rucksack – and no, the stewards did not confiscate it.

The weather was good, there was blue sky above and the ground was pretty full with about 500 Shrewsbury supporters. We have changed our season tickets much further back to row L in block C and the elevated view made it much easier to see the far end. Great seats, so let's hope it's a good game.

There were two changes from the team at Swansea with Colin Miles and Andy Lindegaard coming in for Michael Rose and Lee Johnson, two ever-presents this season. Shrewsbury seemed a very big team and that's always ominous.

There was a minute's silence for the tsunami victims, now sadly above 100,000, and as it should be this was impeccably observed. I'm not sure it is appropriate to applaud at the end of the minute and I'm never sure whether the applause signifies 'Thank God no one misbehaved,' or 'Let's get on with the game!'

The referee showed he meant business by booking Stolcers for diving in the first minute and rightly so. Andrejs should have stayed on his feet as he had the ball under control and the skill to stay up. The first time Gall got the ball and ran at an opponent there was a real buzz of expectancy in the crowd. He is a real crowd pleaser and I am glad to see him doing so well this year. He was involved in our most promising early move – a good cross to Tarachulski, which was headed down to Jevons, who found the side netting! Soon after, another Gall cross found Stolcers, who blasted the half volley over from five yards out.

However, Shrewsbury weren't afraid to take the game to us and their speedy left winger looked useful. Our elevated position gave us a good view of the flow of the game and I felt fairly confident that we could handle Shrewsbury and get a result. Miles hit a great left-footed cross-field ball of all of sixty yards to Gall on the right wing, which was reminiscent of the ball he hit to Lindegaard for the equaliser against Kidderminster. To show it was no fluke, Miles hit three more such passes during the half. He really does have a sweet left foot for a defender.

As the half went on Gall struggled to stay involved after his promising start but, as per usual, Darren Way was everywhere. He is having a great season and is more than able to play in a higher division.

Mr Singh the referee missed a questionable handball, which upset the crowd, but then increased his unpopularity by missing a definite tug on Tarachulski's shirt as he was bearing down on goal. Yeovil were well on top, the passing game was working well and we looked dangerous. Stolcers was more involved than in any other game I've seen this season. The Shrewsbury goalkeeper was infuriating the crowd by moving very slowly for every dead-ball kick and capped this time-wasting performance by walking to collect the ball from near the corner spot and then walking even slower across the goalmouth to take the free-kick from the opposite side of the goal area!

Darren Way was still driving Yeovil forward and, after thirty-three minutes, hit a speculative shot from just outside the penalty area, which was deflected into the goal with the 'keeper stranded. No more than we deserved and, of course, sarcastic shouts of 'Take your time' and 'No hurry' echoed round the ground the next few times the goalkeeper touched the ball! At half-time we learnt that Scunthorpe, Northampton and Macclesfield were all losing while Southend and Swansea were both winning. I thought I'd settle for a 1-0 win and those results remaining unchanged , as we would be top and three points clear.

The second half got off to a slow start and the game deteriorated into a poor and scrappy affair and needed some fresh blood. I expected Arron Davies to come on for Gall, who had not been effectively involved since the first fifteen minutes. Then out of nowhere – disaster! A Yeovil defender misjudged the ball and let a Shrewsbury player clear on a one on one with Weale, who appeared to grab his ankle as the attacker tried to go round him. The ref had no doubts it was a penalty, which was duly converted. It was now 1-1 and the Shrewsbury fans were chanting, 'You're not singing any more'. I would have taken Lindegaard off but Reed came on for Guyett, who was apparently injured, and Miles moved to the centre of the defence. This was a rare opportunity for young Reed, who looked a good player when I saw him last year. Davies also came on for Jevons rather than Gall, which surprised me.

I felt Yeovil had to get Gall more involved if Gary Johnson was keeping him on and, lo and behold, in the space of five minutes he put in three good crosses and then a fourth. Although there was no one on the far post this was more like it but, just when we were getting back into the game, we had another disaster. Shrewsbury broke away and Miles came in at 100mph with what my notes described as a scything tackle, and the ref had no doubts it was a red card. And it got worse! The visitors quickly broke again after a Yeovil attack ended on the edge of the Shrewsbury box and the overlapping striker Edwards made no mistake with the quick low cross. Ten-man Yeovil were 2-1 down.

It looked like we weren't going top and, with Swansea leading at Rushden, they could only be a point behind. All the good work done at Vetch Field just two days ago would be quickly undone. So ten-man Yeovil had sixteen minutes left to get a point when, right in front of us, there was a skirmish between a Shrewsbury player and Lindegaard, who definitely overreacted. All hell broke out with a dozen players all grappling and the ref sent off a Shrewsbury player, Luke Rodgers, and booked Paul Terry and another Shrewsbury player. Shrewsbury had lost their advantage and it was ten against ten with the crowd really fired up after the Shrewsbury dismissal.

Caceres came on for Tarachulski and I looked at my watch. There were thirteen minutes remaining. If we could equalise by the eightieth minute maybe we could still pinch this game. Unbelievably, we did equalise when a Terry Skiverton header from a Kevin Gall free-kick was only partially saved and Paul Terry headed home to make it 2-2 just a minute after Shrewsbury were reduced to ten men. We were well on top and I felt the game was ours for the taking. The crowd was announced as being 7,250, which was the second 7,000-plus crowd of the holiday fixtures. Arron Davies was playing well and put Gall away, who crossed yet again and, although his effort seemed to be a mishit, the ball looped up and into the net courtesy of Adrian Caceres' shin! However, they all count and he won't score a more important goal for Yeovil.

You can't say Yeovil aren't exciting. From ten men and 2-1 down with fifteen minutes left, we were ahead and amazingly it got better. A beautifully judged through ball by Caceres put Gall clear and, with his blistering pace, he bore down on the goal from near the halfway line and an accurate finishing shot saw the ball buried in the net. Fantastic! What a run by Gall. What a team. What a match. We are 4-2 up and certainly going top unless Scunthorpe have turned their match around and are 3-1 up!

This was beyond our wildest dreams; seven wins in a row and, if you count the Orient match six days before Christmas, five out of five over the hectic Christmas/New Year programme. Our resilience in recent matches has been amazing as we have come from behind to win four times in the last month, including today. As I left the ground Scunthorpe were still losing, so we are top. I caught up with Tony and his children outside the ground. He couldn't believe how exciting it had been although he thought we hadn't played that well, but if that is the result when we play badly then we are going up for sure. I thought we played well in the first half and were outstanding for the last twenty minutes.

We now have just twenty games to the season's finishing line. When we were in the Conference we closed out our last eighteen matches with fifteen wins and three draws. Surely we can't do it again at this higher level, although at present no one can touch us.

As soon as I got home I went to the internet to get the results. Scunthorpe lost so we are three points clear at the top with Swansea, who won 2-0 at Rochdale, third. Today's win has also taken us back to the magic two points a game average – played twenty-six, points fifty-two, goals scored fifty-six, and so we are on course to get 100 league goals and two points a game, either of which would surely guarantee the championship.

Now we have a twelve-day mini break as far as the league is concerned because, on Saturday, it is Rotherham away in the cup, an awful draw but we must have a good chance as they are rock bottom of the Championship and we are top of League Two. We will probably be in the same league next year so we should be well capable of a draw, but do we want an extra match and the distraction of a cup run? Many fans think the distraction and hype of the Liverpool match contributed to us going off the boil last season. Indeed, this holiday season Scunthorpe have just got two points from four games and next week they play Chelsea in the cup. Coincidence, or have they had half an eye on that fixture?

In the evening I checked the Shrewsbury website and the Shrewsbury manager Gary Peters' post-match comments said there was no doubt that Yeovil are the best team and will easily win League Two. He seems sure so let's hope he's right!

Yeovil Town 4 Shrewsbury Town 2

Team: Chris Weale, Andy Lindegaard, Terry Skiverton, Scott Guyett, Colin Miles, Kevin Gall, Darren Way, Paul Terry, Andrejs Stolcers, Phil Jevons, Bartosz Tarachulski

Subs: Arron Davies (66 for Jevons), Stephen Reed (66 for Guyett), Adrian Caceres (77 for Tarachulski)

Subs not used: Steve Collis, Nicolas Mirza

Goal-scorers: Darren Way (34), Paul Terry (78), Adrian Caceres (84), Kevin Gall (89)

Attendance: 7,250

Position in League after match: 1st

Interviews

Monday 6 January 2005 – Yeovil Town Football Club

At very late notice I went in to interview some of the foreign players, which will be very helpful for the theme of *Around the World with Yeovil Town*. I saw Andrejs Stolcers, Bartosz Tarachulski, Nicolas Mirza, Adrian Caceres and then Gary Johnson.

My initial assessment was that Andrejs Stolcers was a very impressive and articulate individual and, although some fans have got the impression that he's only here for the money before moving on, he seemed totally committed. It was interesting to talk with him about Latvia as he clearly had a sense of nostalgia for when Latvia was part of the USSR and the state provided a safety net. His wife and a lot of his family are of Russian origin even though they are Latvian, so perhaps it was not surprising he was sympathetic to remaining in a Russian-dominated Soviet Union. I was told he could only maybe spend five or ten minutes with me but in fact he was more than willing to stay as long as it took, and we had a very interesting twenty-minute chat. He impressed me as a serious and likeable individual, and he has certainly run into some good form of late. He appeared to be really pleased when I told him that the fans and the press seemed to be really warming to him and were very receptive to his skills.

I had been told that Bartosz's English was not too good and a conversation might be difficult but, although he struggled with some words, we were certainly able to have an intelligible conversation, although he misunderstood one or two of my questions. It turned out that he was a real footballing gypsy, having played on three separate occasions for the Polonia club in Warsaw as well as in Belgium and in Israel. He seems to enjoy living in England and hopes that he will get another contract at the end of the season.

I felt a little bit sorry for Nicolas Mirza who I think is a player of some potential but is not really having the chance to show his wares. However, at eighteen, his time will come and I did try and say to him that doubtless as Yeovil succeeded some of the other midfield players would move on to other clubs. I was surprised that he was living on his own and so far away from home when he is really not much more than a schoolboy. His English was quite good but I suspect he is getting a bit frustrated at not getting a chance in the first team, and it wouldn't surprise me if he moved on at the end of this season.

Adrian Caceres came across as a very much jack-the-lad, slightly cocky and brash Australian who was been born to an Argentinean family that relocated to Australia. He has twice gone back to Argentina for six months so felt he had roots in both countries, although his body language and demeanour was very much that of an Aussie! He enjoyed winding up Scott Guyett, who was sitting at a table across the lounge, by saying that although Scott Guyett considered himself to be an Australian (this was where he had grown up) he was really a pom because he had born in England. The longstanding rivalry between England and Australia is alive and well at Huish Park! Adrian was apparently offered contracts by both Yeovil and Oxford and is very much aware that Gary Johnson feels he is underachieving and that he has got to prove himself by the end of the season if he wants his contract to be extended.

As for Gary Johnson, I was very, very impressed. It struck me that he was person-able and articulate and really what you saw on television was very much the real man. I certainly did not feel he was going through an act for me and I was surprised at how open he was with regard to his assessments of players in his squad. I believe that what you see is what you get with Gary and you can take everything that he says at face value because he is not a person who plays games. I think his management skills would be very transferable to running a business and that he would have every chance of being a success in any field of endeavour. I suggested to him that it must be more rewarding to stay and succeed with Yeovil rather than take the chance with a struggling club in a higher league, but he guarded his cards by saying that there was no decision to make until actual proposals were put on the table. However, I suspect that when push came to shove he'd be inclined to stay with Yeovil. It was also nice that, when I asked him what the highlight of the season was, he said, 'It doesn't come much better than having won seven in a row in the league, being awarded Manager of the Month and sitting here being interviewed about our success.' Gary was gener-ous with his time spending well over an hour with me.

I came away from the club thinking that the players I had met had very much got their feet on the ground, with the possible exception of Adrian Caceres, who certainly did not come across as conceited or big-headed, just your usual slightly cocky Australian who wants to be a winner and is confident of his own ability. There is noth-ing wrong with that. The players are certainly not taking anything for granted, the manager is realistic and a great motivator and I felt that there was no reason whatso-ever why Yeovil should not get one of the three automatic promotion places, or indeed sustain their current position and end up as champions.

It was a very revealing few hours and I felt both pleased and honoured that Gary Johnson had spent so long with me. I left Huish Park Stadium very confident that Yeovil are destined to be playing next season in League One.

Cup Glory Again!

Saturday 8 January 2005 – Stowell
Rotherham United v. Yeovil (FA Cup Third Round)

I thought I would wait until the result of today's cup tie before deciding on my travel plans. If we do get through to the fourth round, I would have one eye on the draw when deciding where to go, and if it was a plum draw against the likes of Manchester United, Chelsea, Arsenal, Tottenham or Newcastle, I would be very tempted to put in a shorter overseas trip so that I could come back for the fourth round tie. Maybe this is a little bit premature, as we have to get through today's match first!

I am considering going to Argentina as I have the opportunity to join a group climb-ing Aconcagua (6,950m), which is the highest mountain in the world outside of the Himalaya. Aconcagua is certainly not to be sneezed at, although by all accounts the main challenges are just coping with the altitude and inclement weather, as there is every possibility of strong winds and very cold temperatures. Notwithstanding this, technically it is really no more than a very tough high altitude walk that requires a good level of fitness. I had given up any thoughts of climbing any of the world's great mountains until my recent trip to Tibet, where I got over 6,500m, and now there's a little part of me wondering if I can climb Aconcagua and some of the other 'Seven Summits', such as Kilimanjaro in Africa, Denali in Alaska and Elbrus in Georgia.

This week the auditors' visit confirmed that Casterbridge's profits for last year on sales approaching £6m were only £100,000, which is a tremendous disappointment. Just four years ago our company made in excess of £1m profit on sales of £7m and now we are down to £100,000, so we have some major problems to address. Our CEO, David, was really surprised as he was predicting a profit of £220,000, which in itself was disappointing enough! Of course, last summer I had serious reservations about the company's performance but decided to postpone any judgement until this financial year was over. The implementation of our new software system has not been well managed or planned out as there is still disagreement between divisions and, all in all, this has been a very negative week for feedback on how Casterbridge is performing.

So I am thinking of flying to Argentina, possibly on Tuesday of next week, but meanwhile I am using today and the weekend to try and catch up on paperwork.

The third round of the cup is always a glamorous day and one of the most exciting of the football calendar, but we have a tricky away tie that will hardly be a money spinner, with the attendance likely to be less than if the game was at Yeovil. However while I might not be too disappointed if we went out of the cup, when I spoke to Gary Johnson this week he was quite keen to have a good cup run and a challenging draw against a Premiership team.

By the time I had got my act together and made myself some lunch, it was 3.15 p.m. when I switched the radio on and I continued to work with the game going on in the background. Yeovil seemed to be holding their own throughout the first half of an understandably scrappy game and it seemed that we were playing the best of the football. At half-time I went upstairs to make myself a coffee and when I came down Yeovil had been awarded a penalty that Phil Jevons duly dispatched so that we were 1-0 up. Over the radio I can hear the crowd shouting Gary Johnson's name in the background, and it sounds as though Stolcers was having a good game and displaying some sublime skills. He hit a fantastic effort that went narrowly wide.

Towards the end of the game I called Tony to update him on the score and while I was dialling Darren Way scored. I was telling Tony that we were 2-0 up, when blow me down but in almost the last minute, Stolcers scored and Yeovil had won 3-0!

What an absolutely incredible result, even by the standards of our current form. We have now won seven straight in the league plus two cup victories, which makes nine successive games in total! We've also won twelve out of the last thirteen and this has to be not only the run of the season, but almost the run of all time. A 3-0 score away from home against a team two leagues higher is an unbelievable result and, although Rotherham are bottom of the Championship, they had won two of their last three games. To travel half the length of the country and win 3-0 away, let alone against a Championship team, is a pretty good result by any standards.

Well Gary Johnson wanted to stay in the cup and he's got his wish. How long can this run go on for? There can be no shadow of a doubt whatsoever that Yeovil are well above League Two standard and let me now state the following with the same confidence that I had when we were running away with the Conference: I said at best we would spend no more than two seasons in League Two before going up to League One. I am now equally confident that if we can keep Gary Johnson and have a year or two to consolidate we will be very near the Championship within three years in League One.

I listened to the summary on the radio, which said there was no doubt that Yeovil were well above League Two standard, playing a passing game that is rarely seen at the lower levels and our victory was well deserved. And we've now reached the fourth round of the cup for the first time in fifty-six years!

I continued to work at home through the evening with a very satisfied smile on my face. I have now decided that I won't make any confirmation on my travel plans until after Monday's cup draw!

Rotherham United 0 Yeovil Town 3

Team: Chris Weale, Paul Terry, Terry Skiverton, Scott Guyett, Andy Lindegaard, Kevin Gall, Lee Johnson, Darren Way, Andrejs Stolcers, Bartosz Tarachulski, Phil Jevons

Subs: Arron Davies (79 for Jevons), Roy O'Brien (84 for Tarachulski), Adrian Caceres (89 for Gall)

Subs not used: Steve Collis, Nicolas Mirza

Goal-scorers: Phil Jevons (61 penalty), Darren Way (87), Andrejs Stolcers (90)

Attendance: 5,397

Sex Tourists in South America
Saturday 15 January 2005 – Buenos Aires, Argentina
Oxford United v. Yeovil (League Two)

I am in Buenos Aires, the capital of Argentina. I finally left on Thursday, arriving here yesterday morning. It is unusual for me to come to a new destination and although I know Europe, Asia, Australia and North America very well and have visited several areas of Africa, I had never visited South America until yesterday!

It was midday before I went out into what was a very, very hot day, and my plans were to go to the nearby Recoleta Cemetery, as this is one of Buenos Aires' leading attractions and one of the most famous and interesting cemeteries in the world to wander around. As I explored the cemetery I discovered that some of the ornate mausoleums were the size of small houses and the grandiose vaults were always placed in close proximity to one another. Of course, the main attraction was the vault that marked the final resting place of Eva Peron (Evita).

Dancing in the street, Buenos Aires.

After leaving the cemetery I took one of the taxis that had stopped outside the cemetery to the Plaza de Mayo, the main square around which some very famous old landmarks of Buenos Aires are situated. The jovial and overweight taxi driver spoke excellent English and told me he was educated at the British School of Buenos Aires. As we drove through the city I admired the red British-style telephone booths and the beautiful art nouveau street lamps, which are both characteristic of this very cosmopolitan city.

Like all Latin American countries the inhabitants of Buenos Aires enjoy their afternoon siesta, so there were not so many people on the street by the time I got to the Plaza de Mayo in mid-afternoon. At one end was a low but imposing building called the Casa Rosada, which was where many famous Argentinean leaders have addressed the people, including Eva and General Peron and General Galtieri during the Falklands War. Eva Peron had always addressed the crowds from the low balcony because she wanted to be close to 'her people'.

I walked along the Avenue Mayo and came to the famous Café Tortini, where I went in for some coffee and cake. It was very opulent with wood panelling and bronze plaques commemorating famous Buenos Aires literary figures who had frequented the café in the past, and all the waiters were smartly dressed in waist jackets and white gloves. At the end of the restaurant was a billiards and snooker room and it was all very ornate and reminiscent of either Parisian or Viennese café society around the turn of the twentieth century.

I continued along the Avenue Mayo until I came to an internet shop and decided it was time to check the Yeovil result. In truth I could have done this before I went into the Recoleta Cemetery, as the match at Oxford was over by 2 p.m. local time.

Despite the efforts of Bartosz Tarachulski, a wonderful nine-game winning run came to an end at Oxford.

However, I think I put it off because I wanted to enjoy my first sightseeing in South America without the risk of being upset by a disappointing result!

I clicked on to the League Two results and scrolled down in alphabetical order. Orient lost at home to Grimsby, which was good. Lincoln drew 1-1 which is also good because they dropped points, Macclesfield won 2-0 and oh dear, here we have it, Oxford 2 Yeovil 1!

It had to happen and, after nine straight victories, we have finally been beaten. My immediate thoughts were firstly that I was probably the only person in Buenos Aires who had been anxious about Yeovil's result and secondly that we can bounce back next week with a relatively easy game at home to Cambridge. Surely we won't let that one become a banana skin?

What about Scunthorpe? I hadn't got to their result yet, and if they had lost as well then the loss wouldn't be too bad. I carried on down and came to it: Scunthorpe 3 Bury 2. Would you believe it, it was another late winner in the 87th minute! So Scunthorpe are level with us at the top of the table but we have the better goal differ-ence. I continued down the results: Swansea drew 2-2 at home with Wycombe and Southend were held at home 0-0 by Notts County so, with the exception of Scunthorpe, our loss hasn't hurt us too badly.

I noticed that Roy O'Brien and Andy Lindegaard had played as full-backs today and that, with an attendance of 6,778 fans, a lot of Yeovil fans had understandably made the relatively short trip to Oxford. I checked the League Two table. Yeovil and Scunthorpe are on top with fifty-two points with Swansea on forty-nine and then there is a four-point gap to Southend on forty-five (having played one game more) and then Northampton on forty-four with Darlington and Macclesfield on forty-one. It's still all looking pretty positive despite today's defeat.

It was now about 6.30 p.m., it was still light outside and I was planning to continue my walk along the Avenue Mayo but I thought maybe I should check my e-mail. Little did I know that by doing so I was setting in motion a series of events that would dominate my travel plans for several weeks.

I replied to an e-mail from Chris Curling, one of our former non-executive directors, and I think I used my reply to get a lot of my anxieties and concerns regarding Casterbridge off my chest. No sooner had I sent it than I came across a memo that Sue, a senior manager who has been with us for fifteen years, had sent to David, our CEO. This outlined a number of serious concerns and after reading it, I was very despondent. However, I also realised that this issue was now finally resolved. We have already lost one senior manager and I could not afford to risk losing any more valuable staff. My concerns were now shared by others and it was clearly time to act. It was in Buenos Aires on this Saturday evening that I definitely decided that I was going to proceed with a restructuring of the company that would possibly result in the redundancy of our CEO.

I had left the UK deeply concerned over several matters concerning Casterbridge but it had proved to be Sue's memo that was the final straw that broke this particular camel's back. I composed a memo to David, outlining the steps I wanted him to take to resolve the problems between our finance and operations departments, and I finally got out of the internet shop at midnight. But at least after months of worrying I was resolved to proceed with definite action to improve the situation at Casterbridge.

I walked to a nearby café for a late supper. It had a lovely ambience and it seems there are beautiful historic cafes dotted all over Buenos Aires. I took a taxi back to the hotel but didn't feel too tired, so I popped into the bar opposite the hotel called Affair. The admission cost of 20 pesos (about £3) included two beers or in my case two colas. It was an interesting venue because it was quite obviously populated by a number of young ladies who were available for rent!

As I sat on a stool at the bar nursing a Coca-Cola and taking in the attractive surroundings, a number of very attractive young women came up and started talking to me, mainly in Spanish, and I usually managed to kill the conversation stone dead by replying in English! When he heard me, the customer sitting next to me introduced himself as Jack from Canada. I told him that my wife and children were Canadian and I knew his country well.

He was an interesting guy who owned a Texaco petrol station and a Subway franchise in one of the prairie provinces of Canada. He was in his late forties and this was his third visit to Buenos Aires. He was currently in a hotel and was moving into an apartment for a three or four-week stay. The main reason for his visit was quite clearly to enjoy the company of a different young lady every night and he had a string of girlfriends to look up from previous visits! I belong to the 'old school' and tend to be very English in never discussing one's sexual activities with other people. However, Jack was quite open about all the activities that he had paid for on his previous visits but not in a boasting or bragging manner. He was both intelligent and articulate. While I was more comfortable talking about Canada and the pros and cons of running a Subway franchise (my family are great Subway fans!) it was also very pleasant to admire the nice scenery walking up and down inside the bar and Will gave a running commentary about the prospects parading before us. He made the observation that this bar was a very interesting example of international commerce in action: 'They've got the pussy and we've got the money and it's just a question of where negotiations end up!'

It sounds crude in print but actually Will was both courteous and respectful when talking to all the young ladies who came up and obviously took a great deal of interest in the family life and background of the girls he met. He talked about his love life and the multitude of young partners he had enjoyed on his previous visits in a very open and convivial manner. It was certainly a first for me to be sitting next to someone I did not know and listen to them talking about their sexual adventures!

The girls in the bar mainly came from Argentina but there were also dark-skinned girls from the Dominican Republic, Paraguay and Brazil. I chatted for a while with a very attractive blonde Brazilian girl in her early thirties while Will considered whether he should approach the two friendly Argentineans, best described as well endowed in their tight T-shirts, to see if he could negotiate a group discount for both accompanying him back to his hotel!

We exchanged e-mail addresses and hoped we would meet later when I returned to Buenos Aires from Mendoza. Jack was a typically understated Canadian (rather than a brash American) and was in fact the first 'monger' that I had ever met. A 'monger' is a middle-aged male who goes to distant destinations primarily to combine sexual adventure with a holiday – or in short a sex tourist! As a non-drinker, I do not normally gravitate to bars in the first place so Will's companionship had provided both interesting conversation and a pleasant diversion.

It was 3 a.m. and there were still many attractive young ladies in the club. Apparently the practice was to pay a 'bar fine', which equated to 30 pesos ($10 or £6) to the bar to have the young lady accompany you outside of the club. According to Will the going rate for an hour or two's passion in your hotel was about 150 pesos ($50/£30) and apparently a couple of hours could end up as all night for little or no extra charge.

So my day ended at 3.30 a.m. and this report from Buenos Aires can close confirming that, unlike Yeovil at Oxford, their globetrotting supporter found himself with plenty of scoring opportunities!

Oxford United 2 Yeovil Town 1

Team: Chris Weale, Roy O'Brien, Terry Skiverton, Scott Guyett, Andy Lindegaard, Kevin Gall, Darren Way, Paul Terry, Andrejs Stolcers, Bartosz Tarachulski, Phil Jevons

Subs: Arron Davies (58 for O'Brien), Adrian Caceres (66 for Jevons)

Subs not used: Steve Collis, Nicolas Mirza, Dale Williams

Goal-scorer: Scott Guyett (82)

Attendance: 6,778

Position in League after match: 1st

On Aconcagua

Saturday 22 January 2005 – Aconcagua Base Camp,
Argentina
Yeovil v. Cambridge United (League Two)

After some enjoyable sightseeing in Buenos Aires, a city I really liked, I flew to
Mendoza last Monday to join my group and I am now attempting to climb Aconcagua,
with an elevation of 6,950m. This is day four, a rest day and I need it as I was really
tired after yesterday. It was a long day, four hours into the wind before lunch and
another four hours after lunch and the final 200m climb was exhausting. I would have
scheduled an extra day for acclimatisation on the walk in but the approach is somewhat constrained by the campsites designated by the National Parks Authority.

Today we are at Aconcagua Base Camp, which is massive and has hot showers
from $10, fifteen minutes' internet access for $10 and places to hire mules, porters,
guides, etc. All in all it's rather like a small town!

The scenery is so-so, the walking is quite tough and I'm not happy with the ascent
rate, as we ascended to 4,300m in three days, whereas in Nepal I would take four or
five days before arriving at this altitude. I celebrated my fifty-sixth birthday on the walk
in when the cook prepared a birthday cake, complete with candles! I am not particularly enjoying the trip so far and in truth I am not expecting to summit. I am a lot more
tired than normal but we all get 'down' days at some point and maybe this is mine.

My group has six others: four Americans, one Brit and one Irish. Hank, a dentist
from Dallas, is making his fourth attempt on this mountain; Art, sixty-six, a New
Yorker who now lives in Seattle, is very fit for his age but quite overweight and this is
his third attempt; Roger, a single lawyer from Texas, is the only Republican of the
three and quite goal orientated; Voreeta is fifty-six and has a son aged thirty-seven,
so she was a child bride! Robin is a forty-nine-year-old English guy who has failed
before and his friend Jack, from a wealthy Irish family, runs a very successful internet
dating company, market leaders in Australia, Ireland, Holland and Scandinavia it
appears! He and Robin make an amusing pair and I probably get on better with Jack
than anyone else.

After today's rest day, the plan is to have two load-carrying days and then a rest day,
before spending five days pushing camps upwards – to camps Canada, Condors Nest,
Berlin and then finally White Rocks at around 6,250m. We will then have a tough
summit day with almost 900 metres of ascent. Our Argentinean guide, Motoco, is in
his mid-twenties and has impressed me greatly.

If I am not enjoying myself I may call it a day. Four months ago I had no problem
going up to 6,550m in Nepal but then as group leader I had responsibilities and couldn't
quit even if I wanted to. We have had a lot of debate as to whether to try the summit
attempt from Camp Berlin at 5,800m, White Rocks at 6,250m or the Independente Huts
at 6,550m. For some reason few groups camp by the ruins of the highest man-made
structure in the world but I would have thought the benefit of a shorter summit day far
outweigh the difficulties of sleeping at altitude. I favour sleeping high and having a
shorter summit day because I know I can sleep high, whereas the guides want to sleep
lower and avoid carrying the tents up any further than necessary.

Approaching Aconcagua (6,950m) on the long walk in.

I went to the mess tent for breakfast at 9.30 a.m. I wasn't really hungry but needed to eat to acclimatise properly – but toast, bland porridge and cold crepes and pancakes didn't really do much for me. The food is much better when we trek in Nepal. After breakfast and two coffees I still felt tired so went back to my tent and dozed for a couple of hours. It was warm in the tent with the sun overhead.

At 1 p.m., about half-time in England, I rang Tony's mobile from the satellite phone but it wasn't on so I got him at home. He said he hadn't gone to the match but had watched Southampton 2 Liverpool 0 on Sky. After telling me the Premiership updates, he said the last time he had looked, which was probably in the first half, Yeovil, Scunthorpe, Swansea and Southend were all 0-0. I said I would call back in an hour's time. I continued to lie in the tent, feeling listless and very stiff. I was not feeling very positive about anything. Surely Yeovil won't slip up at home to Cambridge when just a few weeks ago we came from 2-0 down to win 5-3 there?

I waited until 2.15 p.m. (5.15 p.m. UK time) and rang Tony again. Jack took a picture of me on the satellite phone for the book.

'Hello,' said a positive Tony and I immediately suspected that Yeovil had won. Tony said it had been a day of mixed results but he obviously had his Southampton hat on at this point, telling me (again) that Southampton had won 2-0 but Palace had also won, Norwich had come back from 4-1 down to draw with Boro and WBA were leading Man City in the late game. This was not what I had rung home for, Tony!

'Now for League Two,' he continued. 'Leading club Yeovil were held by lowly club Cambridge... until a late winner secured a 2-1 victory!' You bastard, Tony! Why string it out?

He said Paul Terry scored the first goal just after half-time, then Cambridge equalised but with five minutes or so to go Yeovil had got the winner. Scunthorpe lost 2-0 and Swansea won 3-2 with a last-minute penalty. Southend drew. That's good as they have dropped two points. Northampton lost and Lincoln won. I wanted to save my battery so terminated the call.

Tony reckoned Yeovil had fifty-two points and Swansea and Scunthorpe both have fifty with Southend on forty-six, but poor old Tony has it wrong. Halfway up Aconcagua, I made it Yeovil fifty-five points, Swansea and Scunthorpe fifty-two points, Southend forty-six points, having played one more game, and Northampton forty-four points. So I calculated that we were nine points clear of the fourth and nearest team who could rob us of automatic promotion. Well, at least that's looking pretty positive!

At 3 p.m. we donned plastic boots and walked to a nearby glacier for some crampon and ice axe practise. I can't get excited by the scenery as it's a bit too dry and arid for me, but at least this was something to do. I was quite short of breath with just modest ups and downs as we crossed the rubble to the nearby glacier ,where we practiced walking, ascending and traversing as we climbed a way up the glacier. The large red rocky massif of Aconcagua had a golden glow in the late afternoon sun, and we could follow the route of tomorrow's carry, which looks steep and high enough. I walked back to base camp with Motoco and Robin, who has an infectious enthusiasm but is also clearly beset by self doubts. I don't think he'll make it.

I wrote my journal and chatted to Hank about films and to Jack, who comes from a publishing family, about this book. Art is big, blunt and affable and thinks he knows it all. He and I disagree on rates of ascent and altitude. He reckons local guides always know best but that's not always so.

I spoke with Robin, our extrovert Englishman who sells software. He failed barely above base camp last time. I get the impression he is very up and down with mood swings, despite coming over as a confident extrovert (it takes one to recognise one!). Apparently he had an anxiety attack last night in his tent and I reassured him that we all had doubts at times and I wasn't sure how far I would go. I said I wasn't expecting to summit and if, for whatever reason, this trip was too much, I'd quit. I'll just take every day as it comes.

Over dinner Motoco talked about tomorrow's load-carrying to Camp Canada, only 5kg extra per person (Roger expressed surprise and wanted to carry more!) and Motoco said if people didn't want to carry to Condors Nest the following day and have a second rest day here instead they could. I suspect I will probably avail myself of that option because I think, after two rest days, I will be better prepared for moving up the mountain.

The base camp services operated by the Argentinean ground handlers include a range of permanent mess tents available for each group. It is somewhat regimented and I have never seen 'camps' like these before. Confluencia even had sit-down flush toilets set up in a container that had clearly been helicoptered in! Dinner was the best yet, although ridiculously small portions so I had two helpings to ensure I was getting enough fluids in. During the evening I talked to the Welsh guide, Dean, who has worked for Andy in the past. His two clients are strong but have already failed four and two times respectively. Not as easy a mountain as it seems!

I drifted off to sleep thinking that Yeovil have now won eleven out of our last thirteen League games. Keep that up and we'll be champions for sure and with a new points record as well.

Yeovil Town 2 Cambridge United 1

Team: Chris Weale, Paul Terry, Terry Skiverton, Scott Guyett, Stephen Reed, Kevin Gall, Darren Way, Lee Johnson, Andrejs Stolcers, Phil Jevons, Bartosz Tarachulski

Subs: Arron Davies (70 for Gall), Yemi Odubade (84 for Tarachulski), Adrian Caceres (90 for Stolcers)

Subs not used: Steve Collis, Roy O'Brien

Goal-scorers: Paul Terry (46), Phil Jevons (86 penalty)

Attendance: 6,204

Position in League after match: 1st

Scoring in Buenos Aires
Tuesday 25 January 2005 – Buenos Aires, Argentina, Yeovil v. Rochdale (League Two)

So what am I doing back in Buenos Aires when I should be climbing Aconcagua? I decided on Sunday that the climb and this mountain were not for me on this occasion. I don't really enjoy walking in high winds,this mountain is a lot windier than any other that I've come up against and my mind just wasn't in the right place. It's not really my sort of mountain or scenery to be honest but perhaps I'm just making excuses.

On Sunday we did an acclimatisation walk up from base camp to Camp Berlin, which was at about 5,000m and, although I felt a little tired, I wasn't significantly slower than the rest of the group, and indeed was ahead of some of them, but the others came down a lot quicker than I did and I didn't particularly enjoy the descent nor the fact that I was behind the others. Nevertheless, these are pretty minor issues and in truth I have spent a lot of my time thinking about the possibility of our CEO David being made redundant as a consequence of my plans to restructure Casterbridge. Jack commented that it was usually the victim who worried, not the executioner.

The excuse that perhaps I was looking for not to continue came when I rang home to speak to Sharron on Sunday and she explained that there were a number of procedures that we needed to go through regarding redundancies and I probably needed to get home a few days earlier than planned and that sealed it. The others were obviously disappointed that one of the group was dropping out so early. I am honestly not sure whether I used the situation at Casterbridge as an excuse or that was genuinely the reason why I really couldn't focus on the climb. Of course, the opportunity to watch Yeovil's glamour fourth round FA Cup tie at Charlton did not come into the reckoning; or did it?

I made the very long fourteen-mile walk from base camp to the trail head yesterday and, as I walked out, I was thinking that as long as I get my head prepared I will give it a good shot next time. Next time? So I guess I am thinking of coming back! I will, however, allow a few extra days for acclimatisation if I organise the trip myself and will also want to put in one very high camp at around 6,500m. While hiking out I rang the office and both Patrick and surprisingly Andy allowed their arms to be twisted, and both are going with me on Saturday to Charlton. It's rather reminiscent of last year's journey home from Everest as now I'm returning from the Andes to see another important match.

When I got to my hotel at Mendoza last night I used the free internet access and caught up with all the news from Yeovil. Most significant was the fact that Gary Johnson had turned down the offer to be interviewed by Coventry for the vacancy as manager of the Championship club. I was not surprised because it has to be far more satisfying to be on the ascent with a team that he knows well and at a club where he is appreciated rather than jump into the hot seat of a struggling club. I had also forgotten that Yeovil had a match tonight at home against Rochdale. This will be a great opportunity to go six points clear of our challengers as neither Scunthorpe nor Swansea are playing tonight.

I have decided that I really love Argentina. A linguist I am not but I am really inspired to learn Spanish. Perhaps I'll come back to Argentina to learn Spanish and the tango!

Mendoza is a flat town in the centre of a wine-producing region with some nice squares and trees everywhere and, after breakfast this morning, I went to the Aerolineas Argentinas office to rearrange my flight back to Buenos Aires. When I got there I was quite amazed to meet Tony and Pauline, who were in the group that I took to South Africa in October 2003! This was our second meeting as I had already been very surprised to find myself seated next to them on the flight from Madrid to Argentina ten days ago when I learnt that they too were attempting Aconcagua. Apparently Pauline had damaged her back and they had had to be helicoptered out! What a sorry pair (or threesome) we made!

I used the flight to Buenos Aires to plan what I would like to see on this brief second visit to Buenos Aires. My initial impressions from the previous weekend that I spent in Buenos Aires was that it would be an excellent destination for week-long holidays with a lot of interesting sightseeing, some outstanding and varied architecture, outstanding craft markets, impressive shopping and of course the magic of the tango, which is enjoying a renaissance around the world.

My baggage was quickly through and I got a taxi back to the attractive Recoleta area where I stayed before and, after unpacking, I gave Sharron a quick call, but she was pretty short with me as *The O.C.* had just started on television! While I was on the phone I realised that, as it was 9 p.m. in the UK, we were midway through the first half of Yeovil *v.* Rochdale and no, Sharron didn't know the score and no, I certainly was not about to risk her wrath and ask her to switch off the television and find it on Teletext! I terminated the call and I headed out pretty speedily to check the score.

I found an internet café just a couple of blocks away and I switched to the BBC sports pages and to the Yeovil score. It was half-time and we were losing 1-0. Damn and shit! I really don't want to follow this internet commentary with an update every two minutes so I read the detailed stories about the Oscar nominations, which had been announced today but, before too long, I switched back to get an update on Yeovil. Great! Tarachulski had equalised and it was 1-1. We seemed to be on top because possession was 60/40 in our favour, shots twelve to seven in our favour, and corners seven to one. There must be a chance that we were going to get all three points. Andy Lindegaard came on for Colin Miles at half-time, but I was worried that Arron Davies had come on for Phil Jevons. I know Gary really likes Arron Davies but I am surprised he would take Phil Jevons off this early in the game and hopefully he's not injured. Maybe Gary wanted to save him for Saturday, but we also needed three points today.

I flicked between news stories, the Oscar nominations and the Yeovil commentary and the next time I went back there had obviously been plenty of action because it was 2-2! Rochdale had taken the lead in the seventy-seventh minute. Odubade made a rare appearance, coming on for Tarachulski who had hit the woodwork twice in the first half, so we were finishing the game without both our starting strikers. Six minutes after the substitution Lee Johnson equalised with a penalty. Like watching paint dry or not, I had to 'watch' the text commentary for the last ten minutes but the game ended in a 2-2 draw.

So we have missed our chance to go six points clear and are now four points ahead of Swansea and Scunthorpe but with both teams having a game in hand. However I've got to think positively and although this wasn't a good result for us we've still managed to score two goals. I sit in the internet café going through all the season's statistics. After our glorious run of seven League wins in a row, we have now only taken four points from our last three games but at least no one else is putting in a good run. Scunthorpe have only got one win and two losses from their last three matches and it is Swansea, with two wins and a draw, who are the current form team.

I look at our rivals' fixtures, when we will be playing Charlton on Saturday, and Swansea are at home to Chester and Scunthorpe at home to Boston, so that should be three points for each of our rivals. I noted that Macclesfield had a very impressive 5-0 win away at Notts County tonight and we have to go there in a couple of weeks' time. At present we are ten points clear of Southend and eleven clear of Macclesfield, who are the nearest two sides who can rob us of an automatic promotion place.

I went back to the hotel to drop my bag off and decided I wanted to go to a tango club. One of the guidebooks said that Bar Sur was a long-established authentic tango club where one got a real feeling of tango culture, so I took a taxi to the historic area of San Telmo and the Bar Sur, which really looked nothing more than a neighbourhood pub. The old doorman explained that there was a cover charge of about 80 pesos (£13) and that allowed me to have a complimentary drink, several plates of appetisers and ongoing entertainment until 4 a.m.! I was not sure if it was for me, walked out and then

The Rochdale defence frustrate Andrejs Stolcers and hold Yeovil to a 2-2 draw.

decided it was an opportunity that shouldn't be scorned so I went back and was shown to my own table next to the small dancing area.

There were probably about sixty guests in the audience, either sat at tables around the small dancing area or at an elevated dining area, and the entertainment was absolutely fantastic. There were three couples who performed spectacular tango dances, sometimes one couple alone, sometimes two and sometimes all three performing in the confined area at the same time. I could see why the tango is so popular as it is a very sensual dance. One of the three dancing pairs had a very slim, almost waif-like female partner. Her movements were both dramatic and graceful. She erotically wrapped her legs around her partner and to me she was the very epitome of what the tango represents.

The excellent backing trio sometimes performed alone and there were also two solo singers. One, a lady in her late sixties or early seventies, sang in a style very reminiscent of Edith Piaf. She was excellent and also did great renditions of *New York, New York, The Shadow of Your Smile, Autumn Leaves* and *Unforgettable*, so she was obviously used to having tourists in the house! Her voice control and interpretation was really outstanding and it just showed me what a fine line there is between being a very good club singer and an outstanding international jazz talent like Cleo Laine or Diane Krall. There was also a male singer, complete with the obligatory fedora, who sang some husky vocals. He was also a very impressive pianist and played instrumentals.

I finally left the Bar Sur at about 1.15 a.m. but the night was still young as Buenos Aires is a city where the entertainment continues until the sun starts to rise! As this was my last night in Argentina I decided to go to the Madahos Club, which was the

Outstanding musicians at the Bar Sur, Buenos Aires.

other side of the Recoleta Cemetery. I wasn't sure if it was a bar, nightclub or disco so I didn't know what to expect, but I did know that Madahos was by all accounts well worth visiting and not to be missed by any single male passing through Buenos Aires!

I paid my 30 peso cover charge and went inside to what was a throbbing and heaving atmosphere. There must have been about 350 people inside, with a DJ playing songs and music videos being projected on one of the walls and with lounge seats everywhere, but its most distinctive feature was that it was papered wall to wall with very attractive and very available young ladies of every possible shade, complexion and build.

I parked myself at the end of the bar with a soft drink and was amused as literally dozens of the young women who had seen a potential punter enter the club nonchalantly strolled past or even brushed up against me trying (not so very!) discreetly to ascertain if I was showing any interest! I had never seen such a collection of young and attractive ladies gathered in one spot and one or two of the more adventurous would even make an inadvertent grope as they walked past to ensure that I was aware of just what was on offer! However, after about forty minutes of watching the very attractive entertainment (and I'm not talking about the music videos) I decided to go back to the Affair Club near the Recoleta Apartments, where I was staying. I thought that there might be a chance tof meeting Jack, the friendly Canadian, or Ivanir, a nice Brazilian girl who spoke good English.

I walked around the Recoleta Cemetery and got to the Affair Club at about 2.30 a.m. wherel sat on one of the bar stools with yet another coke! It was certainly a lot quieter and more laid back than Madahos, with about ten male patrons like myself and about twenty young ladies lounging around and trying to look attractive. I was enjoying my drink when the very attractive young girl on my left said something in Spanish, which I did not understand. As soon as I replied, 'I'm sorry. I only speak English,' her friend, who I hadn't noticed standing the other side of me, asked 'Where do you come from?' and we were soon chatting away. It turned out my two companions were both Argentinean, one of whom spoke reasonable English and the other none. 'Would you like one of us to come back with you?' the elder of the two (twenty-three and twenty-two) asked, 'Only 250 pesos and a 30 peso bar fine.'

As the night went on the price came down from 250 pesos to 200 pesos and then, as closing time approached, 'Are you sure you wouldn't like us both to come back with you, only 150 Pesos each?' Now what on earth is one meant to say to that? 'I'm sure you would enjoy it,' was the follow up before I even had a chance to say no, and with bodies being pushed even closer against me and hands beginning to wander, I decided that this was the opportune time to retire for the night. After all, I've got to save my energy. I have a transatlantic flight tomorrow, a drive to Somerset to follow and I have to be on top of my game for the Charlton match on Saturday!

Yeovil Town 2 Rochdale 2

Team: Chris Weale, Paul Terry, Terry Skiverton, Scott Guyett, Colin Miles, Kevin Gall, Darren Way, Lee Johnson, Andrejs Stolcers, Phil Jevons, Bartosz Tarachulski

Subs: Arron Davies (45 for Jevons), Andy Lindegaard (45 for Miles), Yemi Odubade (77 for Tarachulski)

Subs not used: Steve Collis, Adrian Caceres

Goal-scorers: Bartosz Tarachulski (54), Lee Johnson (85 penalty)

Attendance: 5,180

Position in League after match: 1st

A Day Out at Charlton

Saturday 29 January 2005 – The Valley – Geneva, Switzerland
Charlton Athletic v. Yeovil (FA Cup Fourth Round)

So here I am back in England when, in truth, I should really be in Argentina at the Condors Nest Camp on the slopes of Aconcagua. Did I wimp out? Did I need to come back to deal with this ongoing problem with Casterbridge? Who knows?

I spent most of yesterday unpacking everything that I brought back from Argentina and was too tired to get around to reading all the papers that Sharron had prepared for me regarding redundancy procedures, but I am planning to take them all to

Switzerland to review. Meanwhile, today's priority is very much Charlton v. Yeovil in the fourth round of the cup.

As we drove to Charlton, I asked Andy and Patrick if they would mind dropping me off at Gatwick after the match. Of course, at this point they have no option but to say yes! It only adds about half an hour to their return journey so it was not a problem.

As we drive up the A303 I realised I couldn't find the keys to our Swiss apartment, so I rang Sharron at home, who was really not impressed and said I've really got to stop trying to cram so much into each day that my mind can't concentrate on what I have to do. She added that it might help if I managed to get a few hours' sleep occasionally and wisely suggested that I carefully look through all my pockets to ensure that I definitely didn't have the keys before we started looking at fallback plans.We stopped on the M25 for petrol and Patrick produced his gourmet sandwiches that he always prepares for away games that involve the chairman!

I was quite amused that Andy and Patrick have come together with me as they are complete opposites. Patrick is brash, extrovert, full of himself, positive and the consummate salesperson, who always tries to say the right thing although his in-your-face attitude can wind a lot of people up. Andy, on the other hand, is supremely competent in most things that he does but keeps a very low profile, and in fact you almost have to tease information out of him. When Andy lost his driving licence Patrick used to rib him mercilessly greeting him with 'Good morning, Andy "Great Walks to Work" Broom,' which I thought was quite witty but probably wore thin after the first three-dozen repetitions. I remember Andy saying on one occasion, 'I would like to knock that silly grin right off the side of his face.'

However one of the things that David has encouraged as CEO is for Patrick to sell some Great Walks products, and there have been many times when Andy and Patrick have gone off and done joint presentations. Indeed, this marriage of opposites has, on several occasions, worked quite well with Patrick engineering the breakthrough and Andy impressing clients with his competence thereafter and now they both respect each other.

We hadn't got a road atlas or a set of instructions between us but eventually found our way to within about a mile of the ground and then walked the rest of the way with Patrick managing to wind up most of the Charlton supporters in the vicinity! Once I had got out of the car I was relieved to find the missing keys. As per usual I don't actually lose items, I just seem to misplace them!

We had good seats and the Charlton ground looked very impressive, although the other three sides were taking a while to fill up, whereas the Yeovil end was pretty packed with the best part of 4,000 travelling fans in place at least an hour before kick-off. Patrick got his amusing little French rattle out and gave it a twirl, and its high-pitched whine put a smile on the faces of those Yeovil fans close to us.

As per usual, in the lead up to the match, Patrick asked us both what we thought the score would be. I ventured 2-0 for Charlton and Patrick bravely went for 2-2. I think Patrick had to ask Andy about ten times before he finally prised 'Charlton 1-0' out of him. In passing, Andy mentioned that the last time he said he had seen a top division team play was as a young teenager in the early 1970s!

The teams were announced and Yeovil's was Weale in goal and a back four of Lindegaard, Guyett, Skiverton and Terry, our usual four in midfield of Stolcers,

Kevin Gall leaves Talal El Karkouri and Jerome Thomas in his wake with another impressive burst against Charlton.

Johnson, Way and Gall with Tarachulski and Jevons up front. I was a bit surprised that Andy Lindegaard was playing and I think I would have preferred either Michael Rose if fit or my favourite, Colin Miles, to add some bite against a strong Charlton team. In the lead up to the match I had noticed that Paul Terry had been a junior at Charlton and that his brother-in-law, Paul Konchesky, was one of the Charlton substitutes today. Was this an omen for Paul to do well today? We would find out soon enough and apparently John Terry was present to watch his elder brother play.

The game was finally underway and all the early pressure was Charlton's and it was a good five or six minutes before Yeovil made their first promising move, which involved Gall on the left. Charlton were winning all the fifty-fifty balls and I had one eye on the programme, as I was trying to work out who was playing for Charlton. Their front two were the 'long on ability but short on delivery' Francis Jeffers and the South African Shaun Bartlett. In midfield Charlton had the Irish international Matt Holland, Danny Murphy, who scored the penalty against Yeovil last year for Liverpool, Jerome Thomas and Brian Hughes. I have long thought that their Irish international goalkeeper Dean Kiely was one of the most impressive goalkeepers in the Premiership and I finally worked out that Charlton's back four was Luke Young, Hermann Hreidarsson, Talal El Karkouri and Jonathan Fortune.

It was really important that Yeovil weathered Charlton's early pressure and did not give away a goal or two. Yeovil's second attack also went through Kevin Gall, who looked if he was going to have a good game today, and we forced a couple of corners and finally began to play it around and enjoy some possession. However, we had a lucky escape when a Charlton forward shot over at the far end when it seemed almost easier to score, which was an impressive response to Jevons' first attempt that had narrowly sailed over the bar.

Yeovil were now looking dangerous when they attacked and a good cross-field ball found Lindegaard in an attacking position but, instead of shooting, he cut inside and then passed the ball and the advantage was lost. However, the next Yeovil attack had Paul Terry pushing forward and forward and still further forward until he shot, beat Kiely and it came back off the upright! That was in the twenty-fourth minute and certainly, for the previous fifteen minutes, Yeovil had been giving as good as they received and were pretty much matching Charlton.

The Yeovil fans were in good voice and the chant went up 'we're going to score in a minute'. It sounded as if we were making far more noise than the Charlton supporters, though it would if you're sitting in the middle of 4,000 Yeovil supporters! At this point Yeovil were well on top and 'Shall we sing a song for you?' was teasingly sung to the Charlton fans, but I was concerned that we were getting a little bit too cocky with our chants and, sure enough, Charlton broke away and it seemed that it would have been easier for Jeffers to have scored when he shot over the crossbar. Not to be left out, Charlton's other striker Bartlett then volleyed over when, again, it seemed easier to score.

There were about ten minutes to go to half-time and the game was going backwards and forwards with first Yeovil and then Charlton on top. I commented to Patrick that if we could hold on until half-time we had every chance of taking Charlton back to a reply at Huish Park. However, just when we didn't want to concede a goal, that's exactly what happened. The ball was bobbing around in the penalty area, Brian Hughes took a snap shot and the ball passed the possibly unsighted Weale to nestle in the corner of the net. Thirty-eight minutes had gone and we had conceded a goal just before half-time. Shit!

Darren Way was having a good game for Yeovil and was pushing Yeovil forward in the last minutes before half-time. The ball was played to Kevin Gall in our own half and he was rushing towards us, holding off one man and a second as he continued right on into the Charlton area. Just as he was preparing to shoot he lost possession, the ball ran loose to his left and Paul Terry, who has followed Kevin into the Charlton box, swept it into the corner of the net. Unbelievable! We were back in the game at 1-1 and what a fantastic time to equalise, just a minute before half-time. The Yeovil fans went absolutely crazy. This was an absolute crackerjack game.

Yeovil went off level at half-time to a standing ovation from the ecstatic travelling supporters. Andy seemed to be enjoying the match and said there certainly didn't seem to be three divisions between Yeovil and Charlton. In truth, any neutral supporter would be hard pushed to tell which was the Premiership club, because Yeovil were playing their natural attacking, passing game and playing it well.

The second half started exactly as the first, with a lot of pressure from Charlton. 'Come on Yeovil!' Patrick bellowed out in a solo voice to get the crowd worked up and the response was that Charlton broke away with a good ball down the wing to the winger, who out-paced the Yeovil defender, crossed the ball and Jeffers had an easy tap in for Charlton to take the lead again. Shit and double shit! The Yeovil supporters were stunned and although a voice quickly rose from the back of the crowd 'Stand up if you love Yeovil,' there was not much of a response. However, 'Come on Yeovil, come on' got the crowd singing but Yeovil were still wobbling when Charlton's most impressive player, Jerome Thomas, set up Bartlett with some good skills and trickery

Skiverton, Guyett and Tarachulski do their best to prevent a 3-2 defeat. Yeovil completely dominated the final fifteen minutes and were desperately unlucky not to secure an equaliser at The Valley.

and Charlton scored an easy third goal. Oh no! We played so well in the first half but was this now going to deteriorate into a 5-1 or 6-1 defeat?

Michael Rose came on for Paul Terry but Charlton were on the attack again and it was only a great one-handed save by Weale that stopped Charlton extending their lead. Arron Davies was sent on for Tarachulski in the sixty-third minute and Yeovil finally got their passing game going again.

I turned to Patrick and commented that if we could score a goal in the next ten minutes that would make for a very interesting ending and no sooner had I uttered that comment than a good cross-field ball from the left wing found Davies on the right side of the penalty area. He cut inside and unleashed a great shot across the face of the goal that ended in the corner of the net. Unbelievable! It was the sixty-sixth minute, there were still well over twenty minutes left and Yeovil were back to 3-2. This was a classic cup tie and surely one of the matches of the season anywhere! 'We've got every chance of getting a result out of this,' I said and another good ball out of midfield found Stolcers on the left, who cut in and his cross-shot just landed on the top of the netting.

Darren Way was still playing well and broke up a Charlton attack. He put the ball through to Phil Jevons, who rounded the goalkeeper, but somehow the ball was cleared off the line by El Karkouri when it seemed it would be easier for Jevons to score. This was a fantastic game. Yeovil were well on top and I've rarely see us maintain such a sustained period of pressure against any team, let alone one of the better Premiership teams! Charlton were absolutely on the ropes and Yeovil's passing game was magnificent as we retained all the possession. What an advert this was for League Two football, and it hardly seemed possible that most of our team were playing in the Conference just two years ago!

The tannoy announced a crowd of 22,863, so hopefully that's a healthy gate revenue for Yeovil, and the game continued with Jevons bursting through two defenders but just failing to control the ball at the crucial moment. Even restrained Andy was getting into this game and he leapt to his feet when yet another Yeovil attack broke down. I commented to Andy and Patrick that Yeovil have scored a lot of late goals this season, but it was not to be and the game ended with a 3-2 victory for Charlton and the Yeovil fans singing 'We are top of the league'!

What a match! That was absolutely fantastic and what an advert for Yeovil Town FC. The Charlton fans sportingly applauded both teams, and in particular Yeovil, off the field and deservedly so, because the only other teams to have scored two or more goals at Charlton this season have been Middlesborough with two, Arsenal with three and Chelsea with four, so that's not bad company to be keeping.

The Charlton public announcer congratulated Yeovil on their performance and wished the club well in their efforts to secure promotion from League Two. That was a nice touch from what appears to be a friendly and family orientated club, which has maintained strong links with the local community. Indeed, Charlton are an excellent model for Yeovil to follow, being ambitious, well run, financially responsible and with a well-respected and capable manager providing continuity.

As we left the ground most of the talk from the Yeovil supporters was of how pleased and proud they were of the team and how it had probably been the best result possible. We can now concentrate on the league without the distraction of the cup, but we had performed really well against strong opponents as Charlton are seventh in the Premiership at the moment.

We found our car thanks to Andy's navigational skills and I was soon being dropped off at Gatwick. I asked Andy and Patrick to keep my presence at the game to themselves, and Patrick immediately chirped 'Game? What game?' to demonstrate he was toeing the chairman's line! I did not want there to be any speculation among the staff as to why I had returned to England.

My flight to Geneva was delayed and I eventually got to my hotel at 12.30 a.m. to be greeted by a very pleasant and amiable Portuguese night porter. We spent ten minutes talking about the European Championships and how he was following Mourinho's exploits in charge of Chelsea. I went up to my room and eventually put the light off and went to sleep at about 2.00 a.m., although that night a very bizarre incident occurred that I recount with both some amusement and a little shame!

I woke at about 4.30 a.m. dying for a pee and with the room in complete and utter darkness. I was only half awake and for some reason thought that I was in my tent in Argentina, so I got out of my tent (bed) and took a few paces away from it before I had a pee! It was only as I walked back to my 'tent' and walked into the end of the bed, that I mumbled 'Oh shit' (perhaps this isn't quite the appropriate exclamation, given this story) and thought, 'My God. Am I in Argentina or am I in a hotel in Switzerland? Please don't tell me I got out of the bed, took three paces and peed over the carpet in the middle of the night?' Surely not!

I got into my bed and went back to sleep and, when I woke up a few hours later, wondered if it had all been a bad dream. I could not see any discolouration on the carpet and decided I must have been dreaming, which was a relief, but I only took two paces away from the bed in my bare feet to land on a saturated patch of the carpet and my worst fears were confirmed! I must be going crazy! I will put my hand up and confess that, like many males, there have been occasions when I have been known to pee in the hand basin in a hotel room without en suite facilities but never, ever would I remotely conceive of peeing on the carpet!

So if you stay at the Hotel Modern in Geneva can I suggest you avoid room 228, although I can recommend the hotel for a very convenient and central location!

Charlton Athletic 3 Yeovil Town 2

Team: Chris Weale, Paul Terry, Terry Skiverton, Scott Guyett, Andy Lindegaard, Kevin Gall, Lee Johnson, Darren Way, Andrejs Stolcers, Bartosz Tarachulski, Phil Jevons

Subs: Michael Rose (58 for Terry), Arron Davies (63 for Tarachulski), Adrian Caceres (81 for Stolcers)

Subs not used: Steve Collis, Colin Miles

Goal-scorers: Paul Terry (44), Arron Davies (66)

Attendance: 22,873

Clinging to the Top
Saturday 5 February 2005 – Stowell
Macclesfield Town *v.* Yeovil (League Two)

I arrived back in England yesterday for what was one of the most difficult meetings that I have had in recent years with regard to Casterbridge Tours. I was in Switzerland from Sunday to Friday and, while there, reviewed all the work that had been prepared for me regarding redundancy as it applied to our chief executive David.

An interesting diversion during the week was when I had phoned an insurance loss assessor in Glasgow to discuss my car, which was indeed a write off after my accident on New Year's Eve. He was a Celtic supporter and knew all about Yeovil as many Celtic supporters were following Yeovil's results because we are the only other British team sporting Celtic's famous green-and-white hoops! They had even sent a coach load of supporters to watch our game at Carlisle last season!

I explained to David, our CEO that the financial situation had been very, very disappointing and if we restructured the company to give divisional managers more responsibility, we would remove the need for a CEO, which was a luxury we could not afford at current levels of profitability. I had to advise him that his job was at risk and that this was the beginning of a consultation period and that we would meet next week to discuss the matter properly. I stressed that no final decisions had been made. It was clearly an awkward meeting that I did not enjoy and it must have been a great blow to David. After telling him that if he wished he could take additional paid leave to prepare for our meeting next Thursday I brought it to an end.

During the last week when I was in Switzerland I read Brendon Owen's *Behind the Green Door*, an account of Yeovil's first season as a Football League team. I was interested to read how Brendon, like many other fans, tends to get into certain routines on match days and feels if he breaks his routine (or doesn't wear his lucky scarf!) it's going to be the kiss of death as far as the team is concerned!

I mention this because in Switzerland I also reviewed all the outstanding fixtures that Yeovil had for the rest of the season. I listed them all on my organiser and projected what I thought the results would be for each game and the points I thought we would accumulate match-by-match. I felt very guilty about doing this. Why? Because I did exactly the same last season around Christmas and it was at that point that our season went off track! However, I went ahead and what did I come up with? We have eight home matches left and I predicted six wins and two draws, and for us to get twenty more points at home. As far as our away fixtures are concerned, I've gone for just two wins, four draws and three losses, which means we should pick up ten points. My total for the balance of the season is that we will have eight wins, six draws and three losses representing an additional thirty points, making eighty-six in total. Eighty-six points will clearly be enough to give us promotion, though not necessarily as champions. What had I given for today's match against Macclesfield? In truth a big fat zero, so I'm expecting the worst and if we achieve anything from the match it will be a bonus. Macclesfield are fifth and this will clearly be one of the most difficult games that we have remaining this season.

Before I knew where I was it was 3 p.m. and I tuned into Somerset Sound to listen to the commentary about two minutes into the match. It seemed Yeovil were holding their own in the early stages, although quite clearly the duel between Skiverton, as our key central defender, and Parkin, Macclesfield's top scorer, was going to be crucial. The commentator and his assistant were talking about a player called Amankwaah. What's this? The way they are talking it sounds as if this Amankwaah is playing for Yeovil but the commentators were not the best and it was difficult to pick-up exactly whether this new signing was playing for Yeovil or for Macclesfield! I had been checking the Yeovil and BBC sites during the week from Switzerland and had not seen anything about a new signing.

The atmosphere sounded awful, as if they were commentating from, and the game was actually being played in, a cowshed and, after a comfortable first five minutes, it did seem as if Yeovil were having difficulty clearing their lines whenever Macclesfield attacked.

My initial thoughts were that we would do well to get a point from this match the way things were going but, after ten minutes, things seem to settle down and it was clear Amankwaah, whoever he was and wherever he came from, was definitely playing for Yeovil! There was no mention of Darren Way either, is he not playing? And how come Arron Davies has started?

It soon became clear that Arron Davies was playing up front as a striker instead of Tarachulski, and Darren Way's name did eventually pop up. Meanwhile I went to the BBC website and discovered that Kevin Amankwaah has been signed on loan for a month from Bristol City as cover for Paul Terry. It surprised me that Gary Johnson had gone for a loan player and put him straight in the team, rather than use Michael Rose, who was fit enough to come on as substitute last week at Charlton and who had been one of our best players through the season until his recent injury.

The first testing shot in the match came from Macclesfield, which was no more than a reflection of their superiority. Wait a minute, did the commentator say that Reed is playing as well? No he didn't, it is Stephen Reed, who is obviously sitting next to the commentator and giving a player's perspective on the game. The midfield was our strongest four with Way, Johnson, Stolcers and Gall. Davies and Jevons were playing together up front, with Skiverton and Guyett as our central defenders and Andy Lindegaard and this new guy Kevin Amankwaah as the two full-backs. We are playing with seven of my preferred first eleven, as I would rather see Colin Miles, Paul Terry, Michael Rose and Bartosz Tarachulski in for Scott Guyett, Andy Lindegaard, Kevin Amankwaah and Arron Davies, who would be my designated super sub!

The commentary was one of the most pedestrian I have ever heard and effectively managed to communicate all the excitement of a funeral parlour! Another shot from Macclesfield prompted the commentator to remind us that Macclesfield are the only team to have won at Yeovil so far this season, although Yeovil are coming back into the game and a good shot from Arron Davies was deflected for a corner. The commentator wasn't conveying the flow of the game, or was it that bad a game?

Apparently Macclesfield were playing five in midfield plus three central defenders but Yeovil were coming into the game and, when Arron Davies had a third shot at goal, I wondered if we could hold out until the second half and I even nurtured the possibility that we could sneak a 1-0 win, which would be excellent, as last night's results went very much for us. Swansea and Southend drew 1-1 so even if we lost we should be able to retain our position at the top of the table. We could only be dethroned if we suffered a big defeat and Scunthorpe won handsomely.

Skiverton went off with an injury, although he was quickly back on the pitch and Parkin scored a goal that was disallowed for offside. Parkin sounded as if he was causing a few threats and in fact the ball was soon bobbing around in the goal area. It looked as though we had dealt with the threat when a massive cheer rose from the radio and, about five seconds later, the commentator belatedly advised us that Matthew Tipton had volleyed the ball into the corner of the net after thirty-eight minutes. This is a bit like déja vu; wasn't it in the thirty-eighth minute that Charlton scored last week? Maybe we can get an equaliser just before half-time just like last week as well.

It was not to be but, thanks to a good save by Chris Weale, Macclesfield did not improve their lead and we went in at half-time 1-0 down. Right Gary Johnson, weave your magic.

At half-time I discovered that the commentator was one Phil Tottle. Phil advised us that Tarachulski was suspended and, although it sounded as if Davies had an impressive first half, Phil's observation was that he seemed to be too small to trouble the three central defenders. I checked the half-time scores and Scunthorpe, Mansfield, Lincoln and Darlington were all 1-0 up, which wasn't a very good scenario for Yeovil. However as well as Swansea and Southend both dropping two points last night, Northampton only drew at home against lowly Cambridge. I still think that Northampton could break from the pack and possibly pose a threat but, in truth, their

Some typical Arron Davies trickery could not save Yeovil from a 3-2 defeat at title-challenging Macclesfield.

form hasn't been impressive so far this season and it may well be that it's Southend or Macclesfield who will challenge the top three rather than Northampton.

Gary Johnson's half-time substitution was Adrian Caceres for Andrejs Stolcers, which I found surprising because I know that Gary Johnson is a big fan of Stolcers and has found Caceres a frustrating player. Perhaps deep down Gary has faith that Caceres will eventually deliver.

Macclesfield went straight on the attack from the kick-off and yet again the ball was bobbing around in our penalty area. It seemed that we had finally cleared it and just as I was wondering whether we could score two quick goals at the beginning of the second half goal number two was nestling in the back of Yeovil's net. It must have been less than sixty seconds from the kick-off. Shit! That's probably killed this game stone dead.

Rose came on for Gall and it seemed that Andy Lindegaard moved up into midfield, but the commentary team seemed unable to work out whether we were playing 3-5-2 or 4-4-2! If they can't tell and they are there, how the hell am I meant to know what's going on! I can't understand why Rose wasn't playing from the start rather than Amankwaah who, from the sound of it, is an attacking full-back but seemingly prone to making a few mistakes in defence. No sooner did I think that than he lost control at the back and gave away a corner. It didn't sound an impressive debut from the radio commentary! Why wasn't Colin Miles playing? This sounded just like the type of game where we needed his sort of muscle and commitment at the back. Stephen Reed's gentle West Country burr cut in, commenting that if we could get one goal he fancied us for getting two. Sure, Stephen! But from the radio that sounds like wishful thinking!

Now it was getting to be desperation time as Odubade came on to replace Andy Lindegaard. The bare facts were that Yeovil weren't really getting involved in the second half and it seemed that Macclesfield's second goal had absolutely killed the match dead. This was the second week in a row we'd conceded an early goal right after half-time and this is something Gary's going to have to work on with the boys. Caceres has a good shot deflected for a corner, which comes to nothing, but there is a glimmer of hope because when checking the updated scores on the internet I note that Kidderminster have equalised at Scunthorpe and if Scunthorpe draw they will still be two points behind us.

Macclesfield get a third with what seems to be Potter's second. That brings our goal difference down from +20 to +17, which isn't very clever and it's only going to be goal aggregate now that is going to keep us on top ahead of Swansea rather than goal difference if results stay as they are at present. To make things worse, Scunthorpe retake the lead against Kidderminster and that means that they are going to go on top on goal difference because, as things stand, they are +18 and Yeovil are +17. The commentator is so up to speed he hasn't made any reference to what's going on in the other matches and the importance of goal differences. Just as I scribble that unless we get one back we're not going to be top of League Two at the end of this game, a Macclesfield own goal in the ninetieth minute brings the score to 3-1 and puts our goal difference back up to +18, the same as Scunthorpe's. Of course, Gary Johnson's attacking philosophy means that on goals scored we are way ahead.

Other than the fact that we have just remained on top due to a ninetieth-minute own goal it's a dismal day and, although I was looking forward to the commentary, it was all for naught.

We now have three interesting matches coming up. I fancy us to do really well in the home derby against Bristol Rovers next week, but they have won 3-0 today, and will feel it's their turn to get a result against Yeovil at the fourth attempt. We are then away against Chester, who also won today. I would certainly not want these two away defeats against Oxford and Macclesfield to be continued with a third away loss on the trot at Chester. Then, of course, we're home against Scunthorpe, which is the big match, first against second. It would be really good to win one of these important home games in contrast to the poor results we got last year against high-flying Doncaster and Hull. I really think these next three games could be the most important phase of the season for us and if we could get seven points from the nine available it would set us up nicely for the final run in.

Despite our great performance at Charlton last week, the reality is we've only picked up four of the last twelve points in the league after our previous seven wins in a row, and we need to quickly put this dodgy spell behind us. There are now three teams tied at the top on fifty-six points. Yeovil and Scunthorpe have got goal differences of +18 and Swansea are on +17. It certainly could not be any tighter!

I go back to perusing the fixtures for the next few weeks. Is this a sign of desperation as I look for a glimmer of hope? With the play-off system leaving so many teams in contention our rivals are always going to have competitive games and that's exactly what is happening next week, when Scunthorpe travel to Southend and Swansea have a potentially tricky match at Orient. Am I clutching at straws to hope that it's now Swansea who are due a bit of a bad run, as they've had an impressive January?

I am off to Prague tomorrow where I will check and inspect hotels and review concert venues for some new tours we want to operate. I also plan to take some files with me so that I can give the situation regarding our CEO the consideration and attention that it deserves.

Macclesfield Town 3 Yeovil Town 1

Team: Chris Weale, Kevin Amankwaah, Terry Skiverton, Scott Guyett, Andy Lindegaard, Kevin Gall, Darren Way, Paul Terry, Andrejs Stolcers, Arron Davies, Phil Jevons

Subs: Adrian Caceres (46 for Stolcers), Michael Rose (61 for Gall), Yemi Odubade (75 for Lindegaard)

Subs not used: Steve Collis, Colin Miles

Goal-scorer: Danny Whitaker (90 own goal)

Attendance: 2,471

Position in League after match: 1st

Ho Hum, It's Another Six-Goal Thriller
Saturday 12 February 2005 – Huish Park
Yeovil v. Bristol Rovers (League Two)

It has been a very hectic and rather tiring week as per usual. I was in Prague until Thursday, a city that I had not visited since 1968 and the heady days of the 'Prague Spring', under the liberal Communist leader Alexander Dubcek, which many had hoped would herald a period of reform in Eastern Europe. Sadly this was quickly and cruelly put down by Soviet troops and Eastern Europe was condemned to another twenty years of Communist rule. My visit in 1968 only lasted a day and a half but was long enough to realise that this was one of the world's most attractive cities. Prague was as beautiful as I remembered and very, very cold! I took about 500 digital images, which will be useful for future brochures and presentations, and enjoyed the opera at a fraction of the price one would pay in London.

I came back on Thursday for the consultation meeting with David and surprisingly David did not really raise any points to argue against being made redundant! He had a few minor questions and, although I had detailed explanations prepared for specific points that I had expected him to raise, all my work was superfluous and not required. Consequently we had another meeting yesterday afternoon when I confirmed his dismissal by reason of redundancy and we were able to sort out a mutually agreeable package.

David, Lisa and Sharron are off to Switzerland for half-term and I am following them tomorrow. I am staying an extra day to watch Yeovil v. Bristol Rovers this afternoon. During the week, Kevin Gall had amazingly won the FA player of the fourth round award for his performance at Charlton, with over half a million votes and had beaten Wayne Rooney, Peter Crouch and Cristiano Ronaldo into the bargain. Well done, Kevin!

I must admit I now thought this game could be a banana skin waiting to happen. Rovers' manager Ian Atkins had been making provocative comments on the Rovers website that had been widely reported in the press, doubtless in an effort to stir up his players and fans prior to the match. Of course, earlier this season Yeovil were 2-0 up and were pulled back to 2-2 by nine-man Bristol Rovers, but this was still the only point Rovers have secured against us in three attempts. So far we have very much had the best of Bristol Rovers, but clearly this isn't going to last forever and sooner or later Rovers are going to win, and I had a feeling that today could go horribly wrong for us.

It was very blustery, which would not help us play football, and there would be a full contingent of Rovers fans. The last variable in the equation was that the Bristol Rovers striker Junior Agogo was acquitted yesterday of attempted rape, and he scored against us in the controversial draw earlier this season. Both he and Ian Atkins had said that if he was cleared he would be playing and I could see the headlines just waiting to be written: 'Acquitted on Friday, scored the winning goal on Saturday.' It was all very ominous as far as I was concerned.

As we were driving to the ground I got a call on my mobile from Paul Quayle, who was on my trip to Nepal and Tibet in October. He was at the ground and wondered if we had any spare tickets, because he hadn't realised that the game was all ticket. I told him to hang around the ticket office and see if any tickets were uncollected by kick-off time.

There was a good atmosphere building up inside the ground and the away end was full with a large contingent of travelling Rovers fans. When the team was announced the full-backs were Andy Lindegaard and Michael Rose, and I was surprised that Colin Miles was starting after his recent injury. I thought this might have been a game for Scott Guyett. When the game kicked off I really hoped that the strong, gusty wind didn't spoil it but I was very wary about Junior Agogo. I turned to Tony and said, 'I wonder how long it will be before the fans start having a go at him?'

The answer was all of ninety seconds; after Rovers' first attack the crowd immediately started singing 'You should be in jail' when Agogo weakly mishit his shot.

Arron Davies was starting in preference to Stolcers so he has finally managed to prise one of the midfield starting spots from one of the regular four. Gary Johnson told me he was keen to get Arron in the team on a regular basis but the midfield were all playing so well that Arron was continually coming on as a sub. He was the best and busiest Yeovil player in the opening ten minutes, although of course he doesn't add any weight at all to our already small midfield!

Kevin Gall was seeing a lot of the ball but Michael Rose was looking distinctly rusty from his lack of recent action and, when trying to trap the ball, allowed it to run under his foot and out of play. The next Michael Rose mistake proved costly, when he mishit a pass straight to a Rovers player in the middle of the field, which launched a Rovers attack, resulting in a long shot that evaded Chris Weale and it was 1-0 to Bristol Rovers. This was the first direct shot on goal and the game needed a goal as it was beginning to get rather scrappy in the wind. However, it was a Yeovil goal I had in mind and this just confirmed all the concerns I had about this match.

The wind was making it difficult to play football at times and when Agogo shot well wide again the crowd started singing 'You can only score in a bathroom' as his recent trial had been as a result of an alleged incident in a hotel bathroom – oh dear! But of course it was amusing for the crowd, if not for Agogo, who showed commendable restraint. I ask you, who would want to be a footballer?

It was now Bristol Rovers who were well on top and passing well until, in the twenty-sixth minute, after a quick throw in just in front of us, the ball was played forward to Jevons, who caught it beautifully on the volley and the ball rifled over the goalkeeper, just dipping under the crossbar and into the back of the net. What a goal! I'd like to see that again on TV. That was the best goal I had seen anywhere this season and just what we needed to get back in the game. It came from absolutely nowhere and after a wonderful first touch Jevons had produced a magnificent strike.

The game was now truly on but Michael Rose was still looking unbelievably rusty and could hardly do anything right. After a poor first home game he has played himself into some very impressive form this season, but this was probably the worst performance I've seen by a Yeovil player either this season or last. He looked absolutely awful today.

A great shot by Tarachulski went narrowly wide as Yeovil were getting far more into the game. Indeed, Bartosz was playing well and very effectively holding the ball up before releasing it wide to Arron Davies and Kevin Gall. Another attack ended with a Jevons header going narrowly wide, which clearly demonstrated the main difference between this year's Yeovil and last year's Yeovil. We now have an effective and consistent strike force who already have more than thirty goals between them and this is going to make all the difference at the end of the season.

Yeovil were well on top as the first half came to an end and Tony and I were discussing the prospects for the second half when all of a sudden a Scouse voice next to me said, 'Hi Michael, I thought I'd find you in here somewhere.' It was Paul Quayle, who I had last seen in Kathmandu! Paul had managed to get a ticket and, being the persistent guy he is, had walked up the entire length of the stand scanning the crowd until he found us. As there was a spare seat directly in front of us, I told him he should sit there and watch the second half with us.

No sooner had the second half started then Yeovil were well on top and pressing forward, and Davies side-footed it wide when it seemed to be easier to score with an open goal in front of him. I was afraid that if we did not put our opportunities away, it would come back to haunt us but, within minutes, Yeovil were awarded a bizarre penalty decision when an attempted clearance appeared to hit a Rovers player on the hand. It may have been a little premature but I turned to Tony and said, 'I don't think Jevons has missed one yet for Yeovil, has he?'

However, the wind was gusting all over the place and this was certainly not a gimmie. I remember when we were in Portugal at the European Championships and Beckham prepared to take the first penalty against Portugal. Tony had asked me where I thought he was going to put it and I replied, 'Sadly, right over the crossbar,' and that's exactly what happened. I wasn't expecting Phil to miss but I did realise that if he blasted it in this wind it could go anywhere so I wasn't totally confident that this was going to be a goal.

Step forward Phil Jevons and take all the kudos possible, because he very calmly side-footed it along the ground and into the corner of the net. That was a really excellent thinking-man's penalty, considering the potentially treacherous conditions. I was very impressed and we were 2-1 up. Great! Now we needed to keep the pressure on Bristol Rovers and make sure we secured all three points.

The skyline of Prague – probably Europe's most beautiful city.

Yeovil were playing some outstanding football in the very windy conditions and before too long Andy Lindegaard burst clear on the right and delivered a beautiful cross that was dispatched by a soaring Phil Jevons header to secure his hat-trick. I was impressed that Yeovil were playing so well in such difficult conditions and that they had converted their pressure into an additional goal.

Michael Rose was still on the pitch and still making mistakes, although his second-half performance was much better than his first, which was not difficult to achieve! However, he began to look more like the player we admired for most of the first half of the season. Indeed, he fed Arron Davies, who put in a long cross met by a Tarachulski header and the ball was dispatched into the back of the net. Oh my, oh my, oh my! It was 4-1 to Yeovil and the crowd were singing, 'Ooh-ah, it's a massacre!'

At this rate the strong local rivalry that has quickly developed between Bristol Rovers and Yeovil isn't going to have the opportunity to be continued next year. At the beginning of the season I picked Rovers as one of my tips for promotion, but if this is how they close out their matches after taking the lead, they certainly have no prospects of emerging from mid-table into the play-offs this year.

The attendance was announced as 9,100, which was only a couple of hundred short of the record against Liverpool last year, and 400 more than for the correspon-ding fixture last season. We were now well on top and launching wave after wave of attacks on Rovers and getting another two goals and ending up with six before the final whistle was not unrealistic. Kevin Amankwaah, who came on for Andy Lindegaard, put in a great cross but there was no one in the centre to apply a finishing touch. Soon after, Rovers made a rare attack, the ball was not cleared from the Yeovil penalty area and it ended up in the back of our net. A 4-2 scoreline was a more realistic reflection of the game than 4-1 but I was very keen that we had as big a goal difference as possible. However that was the end of the scoring and, ho-hum, it was just another typical Yeovil game, with six goals scored, and we ended up comfortable 4-2 winners after coming from behind!

I couldn't help thinking that Ian Atkins had ended up with a lot of egg on his face after making so many derogatory comments about Yeovil in regard to the earlier game between the clubs this season. I thought Gary Johnson was commendably and typically restrained in not responding and letting his team do the talking on the pitch rather than in the papers. Rovers have now secured one point out of twelve against Yeovil in the four games over the last two seasons!

Chester away next Saturday and then I'm flying back from Switzerland on Tuesday week for the match against Scunthorpe, which will surely be one of the highlights of the season.

Yeovil Town 4 Bristol Rovers 2

Team: Chris Weale, Andy Lindegaard, Terry Skiverton, Colin Miles, Michael Rose, Kevin Gall, Darren Way, Lee Johnson, Arron Davies, Phil Jevons, Bartosz Tarachulski

Subs: Kevin Amankwaah (74 for Lindegaard), Kezie Ibe (80 for Tarachulski), Andrejs Stolcers (89 for Gall)

Subs not used: Steve Collis, Scott Guyett

Goal-scorers: Phil Jevons (26) (56 penalty) (64), Bartosz Tarachulski (72)

Attendance: 9,153

Position in League after match: 1st

Success in the Alps

Saturday 19 February 2005 – Mürren, Switzerland
Chester City *v.* Yeovil (League Two)

This is the first match day that I have I spent at our second home, a three-bedroom apartment in Mürren, Switzerland, although I have spent plenty of time out here over the last twelve months. Mürren itself is perched on a terraced ledge about 3,000ft above the valley floor, and is only accessible by funicular and train via Lauterbrunnen and Grutschalp, or by cable car from Stechelberg. One cannot drive to Mürren, which is a car-free resort and one of the most spectacularly located villages in the Alps.

The pace of life is slow but the scenery is absolutely magnificent, as Mürren is sur-rounded by an incredible panorama of mountains, which are truly Himalayan in scale. In the mid 1990s Casterbridge Tours became quite a profitable company and we decided to indulge ourselves by investing some of our dividends in the purchase of an apartment in Mürren, which means we have a permanent base here. The chil-dren enjoy the winter skiing and I use it as a base for hiking.

I have no doubts in saying that the most spectacular scenery in Europe is located in the Swiss Alps and from our balcony we have a wonderful panorama that stretches around about 270 degrees and includes a dozen nearby peaks either approaching or surpassing 4,000m. Most famous is the triumvirate of majestic peaks that dominate both the view and the entire Bernese Oberland – the famous and foreboding Eiger (ogre), which has played such a dramatic role in the history of Alpine climbing, the proud Mönch (monk) and the Jungfrau (young girl).

As a tour operator I have travelled the world and I feel really privileged and fortu-nate to say that for spectacular scenery the view from our apartment surpasses any view I have ever seen from any other building. Of course, people always think I am exaggerating until they visit and then they agree! The Eiger, Mönch and Jungfrau are three of the most famous mountains in the world and yet they are so close I feel I can reach out and touch them from our balcony, as the summits are only between three and six miles distant.

We had a board meeting in Mürren this week so that we could discuss the situation regarding Casterbridge, and in particular our finance department, the implementation of our new integrated software and the implications of David's departure as CEO. With Sharron having to clean up the apartment and prepare it for the meeting it has not been the normal relaxing half-term stay in Mürren for either of us and I am hoping the week can come to a positive end with today's match at Chester. Scunthorpe (against Orient) and Swansea (against Grimsby) are both at home today and it would be nice if one of the two could slip up. The way the results have been going the pack is closing up behind us, but we still have a game in hand over most of the other teams. A win today and a poor result for Scunthorpe could put us in a very strong position.

At 3.15 p.m. I check on the internet and the news couldn't be better, because Yeovil are leading 1-0 at Chester with a goal from Arron Davies. However, the form team Macclesfield are already leading 2-0 against Rochdale, Northampton are 1-0 up at Oxford, but both Swansea and Scunthorpe are drawing. I check the line-up and it is clear that Arron Davies is now preferred to Stolcers as Gary Johnson's first choice on the left of midfield as he has started again today. Terry Skiverton is out, Colin Miles is a substitute and both Paul Terry and Adam Lockwood are on the bench. I check the internet commentary, which tells me that Yeovil have had sixty per cent of the posses-sion so far and seem well on top. We have had four shots to Chester's two, so keep it up boys and let's get a second.

Bartosz was booked in the twenty-fourth minute and I thought it would be great if we could get a second goal so we had a bit of a cushion. Next time I check it's 2-0, thanks to a Jevons penalty in the thirty-second minute, and Scunthorpe, Swansea, Wycombe and Darlington are still all drawing. Great! I return to the internet commen-tary again at 5.10 p.m. Swiss time, which is 4.10 p.m. UK time, but it seems to be frozen on the half-time situation.

Just a fraction of the view from our balcony in Mürren, Switzerland.

Well this isn't any good! I know I complain that I don't like watching the text commentary, but I like referring to it to get an update and I go back three or four times in the next ten minutes and indeed there is no update whatsoever! What's happening at Chester? We're now halfway through the second half and I've got no idea, so I find the soccer pages on the Sky Sports website and they have a ticker tape which has all the scores. I decide to use the Sky site to follow developments for the rest of the afternoon.

Northampton are drawing 1-1 with Southend, which would be a good result for us as both teams will be dropping two points. Scunthorpe have gone ahead but Swansea are still drawing 0-0. A good feature of this Sky website is that it has an updated league table, according to the status of all games in play at any given moment. Southend get a late goal at Northampton, which is bad news for Yeovil, but the teleprinter confirms that we have won 2-0 at Chester. Well done boys!

I've got my eye glued on the results coming through on the ticker tape, hoping that Swansea don't get a late winner and that Orient can equalise at Scunthorpe. There is a late goal but it is Dion Dublin getting a late goal for Leicester in the fifth round of the cup at Charlton so Charlton were there for the taking! We softened them up and Leicester came along and finished the business! Southend held on and won at Northampton, which was a pity. I would have preferred that to have ended up as a draw, but Swansea do draw so we've gained two points on them. Macclesfield end up winning 3-0 at home to Rochdale, Lincoln win 2-1 against Cambridge, and shit... Scunthorpe hang on to win 1-0 against Orient.

It is indeed going to be a very big match on Tuesday with Yeovil (first) playing Scunthorpe (second) and with us currently leading by two points and with a game in hand. Poor old Scunthorpe have to follow-up their midweek visit to Yeovil with a visit to Swansea, so it's not going to be an easy week for them.

In the evening I checked the Chester website, and most of the comments by their fans said that Yeovil were diving all over the place, the Jevons penalty should never have been awarded and that Chester were well on top for all of the second half. However, when I checked the Yeovil supporters' Ciderspace website, it seemed all of the entries were pretty unanimous in that Chester were probably the most physical and dirty team that Yeovil have played all season. As per usual there are two sides to every debate!

It seems once we went 2-0 ahead Yeovil decided to shut-up shop and protect what they had for all of the second half, conceding possession but not goals to Chester. This had been a result that I had not expected as I had predicted a draw in my calculations!

Sharron, Lisa and David go back to England tomorrow and I follow on Tuesday for what will surely be the match of the season: Yeovil v. Scunthorpe.

Chester City 0 Yeovil Town 2

Team: Chris Weale, Andy Lindegaard, Scott Guyett, Colin Miles, Michael Rose, Kevin Gall, Darren Way, Lee Johnson, Arron Davies, Phil Jevons, Bartosz Tarachulski

Subs: Kevin Amankwaah (21 for Miles), Paul Terry (70 for Jevons), Andrejs Stolcers (80 for Way)

Subs not used: Steve Collis, Adam Lockwood

Goal-scorers: Arron Davies (12), Phil Jevons (32 penalty)

Attendance: 3,072

Position in League after match: 1st

It Could Only Happen at Yeovil

Tuesday 22 February 2005 – Mürren, Switzerland – London Heathrow – Huish Park
Yeovil v. Scunthorpe (League Two)

I was pleased to learn that there was a 7.15 a.m. train that would get me to Basel in time for my flight home, which meant that I had an extra lie-in. This was just as well because I was up until about 4.00 a.m. as per usual sorting out the apartment and getting everything done that I hadn't done in the last week!

At Heathrow my car was delivered by the meet and greet service and I was soon on my way driving home. It was extremely cold and I hoped that it wasn't freezing in Yeovil, as I didn't want tonight's big match against Scunthorpe to be postponed, as it should be one of the highlights of the season.

I got into the office at about 5.10 p.m. and I made a short statement to the staff explaining that, because of our poor financial results and my desire to reorganise, we had sadly made David redundant. It is difficult to know what people were thinking, but there weren't any great gasps of surprise or disappointment and I thought the announcement went reasonably well. Once that job was out of the way I could concentrate on the day's priority and it was on to Yeovil and the game against Scunthorpe!

As we walked into the ground I commented to Tony that I was far more confident about this match than I was about the game against Bristol Rovers. I have been saying all season that I think Scunthorpe have been overachieving, so I was fairly confident that we would get a win tonight.

There always seems to be a bit more atmosphere at evening matches with the ground bathed in electric light. Tony and I had our new seats, which were three-quarters of the way back in the main stand, but the tickets we had for the other five were only two rows from the front. Now I had a major problem. Did I let someone else sit with Tony and go down the front and sit with my son, David, or did I sit at the back, knowing that David didn't have such a good view at the front? In the end journalistic integrity won out and I soothed my conscience deciding I had to take the better view so I could accurately record the game for this book! And David wasn't bothered anyway!

The Yeovil team was pretty much as expected, with Chris Weale in goal and a back four with Michael Rose and Andy Lindegaard as full-backs and Colin Miles and Scott Guyett as the centre-backs. I think I would have been tempted to play Paul Terry rather than Andy Lindegaard, as he has a little bit more muscle and power, although he is not as quick at chasing back as Andy, nor as penetrating if asked to play wide. Paul Terry has been having such a good season that I would have found a place for him somewhere in my starting line-up. The midfield was Kevin Gall, Darren Way, Lee Johnson and Arron Davies, with Bartosz Tarachulski and Phil Jevons up front.

There couldn't have been many more than 100 Scunthorpe supporters in the away end, which was otherwise deserted! I know it's a long way from Lincolnshire to Somerset on a Tuesday night, but this was a top-of-the-table clash that could have put them in top place. Obviously there is no great tradition of travelling support as far as Scunthorpe are concerned!

Just before kick-off Tony advised me that Yeovil had released Adrian Caceres, which did not surprise me. When I spoke to him, Adrian was clearly aware that Gary Johnson felt he was underachieving and Gary had said that Caceres had to start showing his outstanding skills on a regular basis. I guess that, with no subsequent improvement in his form, they agreed to go their separate ways.

The ref blew to get us going and the first six minutes were all about Yeovil with Bartosz and Phil Jevons looking particularly effective up front. Both of them looked very sharp, and Yeovil really looked up for this match. I turned to Tony and said, 'I really do have a very good feeling about this match. It would be great if we end up five points clear and with a game in hand at the end of the ninety minutes.' However, the game then got somewhat scrappy and Scunthorpe started coming into it but, after fifteen minutes, just in front of us to the left, Bartosz collected a ball after a Yeovil throw-in, kept possession well, shimmied around and, from outside the penalty area, curled over what I initially thought was a low cross but it evaded the goalkeeper, hit the far post and went into the net! Absolutely fantastic, and that's just the start that we wanted. My own gut feeling was that it was a cross not a shot but it doesn't matter as we were 1-0 up.

However, there was then an extraordinary scene because Brian Laws, the Scunthorpe manager, was absolutely furious with his goalkeeper, Paul Musselwhite and encroached onto the side of the pitch to rant at his goalkeeper. Laws was clearly very upset with his goalkeeper's positioning and I have never seen a manager berate his player so publicly, which couldn't have done much for Musselwhite's confidence. On two occasions the fourth official had to restrain Laws and bring him back into the technical area. Of course, the Yeovil crowd behind the dug out found this very amusing, and whenever Yeovil mounted an attack there were shouts of 'shoot' to reiterate the crowd's amusement at Laws' obvious lack of confidence in his own goalkeeper!

I couldn't help thinking that, indeed, it's a funny old game. In the middle of December we were seven points behind Scunthorpe and now we have every chance of being five ahead with a game in hand. That's some turn around. However, Scunthorpe were coming back into the match and Chris Weale made a good save, which of course prompted a few chants of 'don't you wish you had a good goalkeeper Laws?' to the Scunthorpe manager! When Musselwhite made a very poor clearance not long after the crowd made his obvious discomfort even worse!

After thirty-six minutes there was a scramble between a Yeovil and Scunthorpe player with the linesman flagging very vigorously for an obvious foul on the Yeovil player by his Scunthorpe opponent. However, the ref awarded a free-kick to Scunthorpe just inside the Yeovil half, and the crowd went absolutely ballistic because the ref had ignored his linesman's signals. 'It will be ironic if this leads to a goal,' I thought and, sure enough the long free-kick into the Yeovil penalty area was headed down and Paul Hayes was on the spot to sweep it home and make it 1-1. Jesus! The crowd of course were absolutely furious because the free-kick shouldn't have been awarded in the first place and the ref was now clearly in for a torrid evening.

Scunthorpe were now very much in the game, although Arron Davies had a tremendous run, passing several Scunthorpe players before shooting narrowly wide, and then Darren Way set up Kevin Gall for a great run. Ominously, however, it seemed that whenever Yeovil attacked, Scunthorpe were looking very dangerous with the counterattack and serious damage was almost done by a poor Terry Skiverton clearance, leading to a dangerous cross that was headed narrowly wide.

There are a number of people around us who obviously think that Terry Skiverton is close to his 'sell-by date' and he has made a few poor clearances in recent matches. However, we have to remember that Yeovil are always committed to attack and, with both full-backs and the midfield continually pressing forward, it is inevitable the two central defenders in particular are going to be stretched more often than not. Indeed, the cost of scoring 72 goals so far is the 49 that we have let in and I think some of the fans around us were being a little hard on Terry.

The ref awarded two minutes of added time at the end of the first half and Scunthorpe won a corner. The last thing we wanted was for Scunthorpe to score now, so what did we get? Yes, a Scunthorpe goal right on half-time! The corner came over and Darren Way, on the near post, either stooped, ducked, or misjudged the bounce, and an easy header right on the stroke of half-time put Scunthorpe in a 2-1 lead. That was a colossal blow and, as the teams went off, the crowd had to take their anger out on someone. Of course, it was the referee, and as a result the ref and the two linesmen were escorted off by a couple of bobbies!

I was reminded that last season we had two big games at home that we failed to win against Doncaster and Hull. I had a sense of déjà vu and wondered if yet again we were going to slip up despite our normally impressive home record. I certainly hoped not.

At half-time the good news was that Swansea were losing at Darlington. I told the others there were five seats free next to us and they all came up. Andrejs Stolcers came on for Kevin Gall at the start of the second half and no sooner had the second half started than Tarachulski was fouled on the edge of the Scunthorpe box. Lee Johnson lined up the free-kick. Was this going to be a Johnson special? It would be fantastic to get an equaliser right at the start of the second half, which would very quickly puncture the positive spirits with which Scunthorpe went into their half-time talk. Scunthorpe formed a wall, Lee Johnson took a long run up and blasted it low. I didn't quite see if there was a deflection but, sure enough, the ball was nestling in the back of the Scunthorpe net. Was that another mistake by the goalkeeper? I hoped so and of course I now fully understood why Gary kept his son on the pitch and took off Kevin Gall! So it is game on for sure as that was an excellent and immediate response from Yeovil. I turned to Tony and said 'I fancy 4-2 now.'

So for the third time that evening an alternative set of supporters chant 'We are top of the league, we are top of the league,' and this time it was the turn of the Yeovil fans. However, as the second half progressed Scunthorpe played really well and there was a spell when Yeovil could not put a foot on the ball. If it had been Yeovil I could imagine shouts of 'Olé' echoing around the ground with every pass. When we had possession they were closing us down very effectively and when they had the ball Scunthorpe were passing it around in impressive style. I thought that Scunthorpe were easily the best team we have seen here this season and my thoughts about them over-achieving were clearly misplaced. They have obviously held their place in the top two for most of the season very much on merit.

Bartosz Tarachulski got booked and was then involved in another skirmish. Gary Johnson wisely took him off and sent on Rory Fallon. Rory who? I've never heard of this guy, where did he come from? Tony said he had been signed on loan from Swindon and it turned out later that this was only at 3.30 this afternoon. He was tall, if a bit one paced, but was an ideal replacement for Bartosz, although possibly not with as much skill on the floor as Bartosz in retaining possession. With about twenty minutes to go I turned around to Tony and said, 'Normally at this point I am looking at the clock to see if there is enough time for Yeovil to score a winner, but I think tonight it's a question of if we can hold on.' Scunthorpe were very definitely on top and taking the game to Yeovil, but we weren't completely out of it and a Davies cross to Jevons resulted in another miss when it may have been easier for Phil to have scored. Still,

Full stretch for Bartosz and Yeovil to come from behind yet again and defeat Scunthorpe as first take on second.

we can't complain with the 24 goals he has scored so far this season. At least our build-up play was beginning to look better but Scunthorpe were still playing very well and winning all the fifty-fifty balls. Tony commented, 'If we are not careful Scunthorpe are going to get a goal soon,' and I could only agree. We were still making some attacks but usually it was the same story, a good cross to Jevons resulting in mishits or shots wide. However, with twelve minutes to go we won a corner and, when it came across, new signing Fallon put it into the net and the Scunthorpe players were furious. It seemed they felt that Darren Way impeded their goalkeeper who, one way or another, was having a memorable evening! Musselwhite followed the ref all the way to the halfway line and got booked for his efforts.

Unbelievable! After being played off the park we are now 3-2 up. The consensus of opinion was that there was a foul on Musselwhite but this was certainly a case of what goes around comes around, because the free-kick that led to Scunthorpe's equaliser should very definitely not have been awarded.

What a roller-coaster match this was! 1-0 to Yeovil, then 2-1 to Scunthorpe, now 3-2 to Yeovil. Were there any more twists to come? There certainly was, because Chris Weale came out and made a good save from an approaching Scunthorpe forward, and then Arron Davies was drifting in from the left wing around the halfway line. He continued to move diagonally across the field on an impressive run, and we were expecting him to lay it across to an overlapping right winger but, as he made further space to his right, he kept running and then unleashed a fantastic shot. With the goalkeeper rooted on his line in the centre of the goal, the ball went flying into the corner of the goal from close to forty yards. Absolutely unbelievable! That was one of the best goals I have ever seen and from our position you could see it was absolutely intended. He had half the goal to the left of the goalkeeper to aim at and he hit the ball with such power that the goalkeeper had no chance, such was the accuracy of the shot.

Arron Davies has scored too many spectacular goals since joining Yeovil for it to be coincidence. He is a very skilful player with a spectacular shot – witness his long-distance effort at Charlton. By my calculations that was his fifth goal and he only joined us in December, as a midfielder and not as a forward, and most of his appearances have been as a sub! I can't understand how he never got a run in Southampton's first team, as they are not exactly overflowing with talent at the moment! The entire ground was buzzing after the goal. I thought Phil Jevons' first goal against Bristol Rovers was the best goal I was likely to see this year but that effort by Arron has to be the goal of the season. We won't see a better one this year that's for sure!

Our Evertonian, Paul Quayle, had commented before the match had started that he had only been to two matches at Huish Park Stadium. Last year he watched Yeovil beat Wrexham 5-1 and on Saturday it was 4-2 against Bristol Rovers. I shouted down the line to him, 'It looks as if you've got your six goals again Paul!' My post-half-time prediction of 4-2 looked uncannily accurate, although I have to confess ten minutes earlier there didn't seem to be any chance that Yeovil would be 4-2 up; it was far more likely we could be 3-2 down.

To cap the misery for the brave 100 Scunthorpe fans who had travelled so far to see a fantastic match it was now snowing on them at the open visitors end! The game still see-sawed from one end to the other. A Scunthorpe player shot over when it was easier to score and then Arron Davies had another long shot that went narrowly wide.

The crowd was singing, the stadium was buzzing, everyone was happy and the ref awarded four minutes of added time, and of course it wouldn't be Yeovil if we didn't want to make it interesting. With about a minute to go, a scramble in the Yeovil goal-mouth resulted in, yes, a third Scunthorpe goal! There were the usual moans at the Yeovil defence for not clearing the ball more effectively and, on this occasion, I think they could be justified. But we held on for the last thirty seconds to record a memorable 4-3 victory!

An amazing result? No, it was just another typical Yeovil match, with seven goals scored and another come-from-behind win! The last home match was 4-2 against Bristol Rovers, the one before that had four goals with a 2-2 draw against Rochdale, and of course throw into that scoring two goals at Charlton, three goals at Rotherham, beating Shrewsbury at home 4-2 with another brace of late goals and scoring five at Cambridge, and you can see why I get irritated that some fans don't always appreciate the real feast of attacking football that we have been treated to at Yeovil for the last three years. It bugs me to hear people moaning about our defensive frailties because if that is part of the price we must pay for our 100 per cent commitment to attack, then I for one think it is a price worth paying.

Swansea did lose at Darlington and so we are five points clear of Scunthorpe, who are still second, with a game in hand. Fantastic, and all power to Gary Johnson's philosophy of attacking football. This could be the evening that really sealed the probability of our going up as champions. And what a great testimony to the quality of League Two football. You couldn't ask for much more than 4-3 when first play second and both teams played their part in a thoroughly enjoyable and entertaining game. As one Scunthorpe fan posted later on the *606* web pages, 'I would never believe we could score three away from home and lose. It could only be at Yeovil.'

Amen to that but Scunthorpe looked a very good, strong and solid team and not without skill. They controlled long periods of play at various stages and certainly did enough to convince me that they are thoroughly deserving of automatic promotion this season but let's hope not as champions!

When I got home I immediately checked the internet and the league table looked great, with Yeovil five points clear with a game in hand. Swansea lost 2-1 at Darlington and Southend scraped home 1-0 against Grimsby. I got to bed at about 1 a.m. after a very long day, but it couldn't have had a better conclusion. With our memorable New Year's Day win at Swansea and tonight's result we are certainly laying down the gauntlet to our promotion rivals in no uncertain fashion and, with three wins in a row, have certainly steadied the ship after our recent blip in form.

Yeovil Town 4 Scunthorpe United 3

Team: Chris Weale, Andy Lindegaard, Terry Skiverton, Scott Guyett, Michael Rose, Kevin Gall, Darren Way, Lee Johnson, Arron Davies, Phil Jevons, Bartosz Tarachulski

Subs: Andrejs Stolcers (45 for Gall), Rory Fallon (70 for Tarachulski), Kevin Amankwaah (79 for Stolcers)

Subs not used: Steve Collis, Paul Terry

Goal-scorers: Bartosz Tarachulski (16), Lee Johnson (47), Rory Fallon (82), Arron Davies (86)

Attendance: 7,598

Position in League after match: 1st

Kicking on at Ninety

Saturday 26 February 2005 – Stowell
Grimsby Town *v.* Yeovil (League Two)

It is my mother's ninetieth birthday party today, which is why I have not gone to Grimsby to watch the game with Wendy's father.

I am determined not to get sucked into the day-to-day management of Casterbridge Tours but, as our former CEO is no longer with the company, it was important to talk to all the managers based at our Sherborne office as I am now their direct superior and this has taken up a lot of my time over the last forty-eight hours. I was at our Sherborne office all morning and was so appalled by what I found when I asked some simple questions regarding the finance department that, by mid afternoon I had done nothing other than write some pretty stringent instructions about changes that needed to be made sooner rather than later. I really should have been helping Sharron prepare for this evening's party.

I switched the radio on about the fifth minute of the match and Yeovil were taking their third corner, which was an encouraging start, and I gathered that Scott Guyett had been injured in the preliminary warm-up and Kevin Amankwaah was playing in his place. Amankwaah had come on at right-back against Scunthorpe on Tuesday and looked quite good. It seemed Yeovil were playing their usual passing game and seemed to be well on top, which was pleasing because Grimsby gave us quite a tough battle before we beat them 2-1 in the home fixture.

Yeovil seemed to be passing the ball around quite nicely and both the commentator and the assistant seemed to be a bit more eloquent than the last match, although the standard of regional commentaries will never match Five Live! They always seem to be behind the pace of the game and one moment the commentator was describing Arron Davies running towards the goal and then belatedly added that he had let another flyer go from twenty-five yards and we were 1-0 up! Arron Davies is really something else because that is goal number six and they all seem to be long-range shots. I listened to the commentary for the rest of the first half and clearly Grimsby were not playing well and their own supporters were displeased. Yeovil seemed to be playing well and at half-time we were still 1-0 up.

I switched off the radio, wrote a quick letter and made a couple of calls, including to my friend Brian. I told him that he had missed a good match by not coming on Tuesday. He agreed and said it was a pity that Grimsby had just equalised! The score had just flashed up on screen as he watched the rugby! Damn!

I wasn't getting a great deal achieved at the office and Sharron had asked me to go to Sainsburys to pick up some bits and pieces for the party tonight. I locked up the building, picked up the radio and got to Sainsbury's with about twenty minutes to go in the second half. It was still 1-1 and the commentator was wondering whether Yeovil could pinch the winner. Rory Fallon came on so maybe he could be a talisman again. There had been a lot of coverage in the press about how he had signed on the afternoon of the match against Scunthorpe, came on as a sub and scored the go-ahead goal within minutes. Well come on, Rory. Can you do it again?

I went into Sainsbury's but decided I would rather listen to the last ten minutes in the car. Grimsby were certainly having their chances. Lindegaard made a mistake and gave away possession, which allowed Parkinson to make a run on the Yeovil goal. He unleashed a shot from some distance to put Grimsby in the lead with just minutes to go. Oh shit! This was an incredible opportunity to have an eight-point lead but it was obviously not to be.

This was not turning out to be a very good day. I had got sucked into the minutiae of our finance department, Yeovil were now losing and I had my mother's ninetieth party this evening, to which I had contributed very little other than designing the invitation cards. I was responsible for the entertainment of thirty-five guests, I hadn't done anything yet and they were going to be arriving in a couple of hours' time.

Amankwaah seems to be prone to making mistakes away from home and gave the ball away to a Grimsby player, who was left with a one on one with Chris Weale and nearly made it three, which would have sewn the game up. Yeovil were pressing in the dying minutes and it seemed that Jevons was clear on goal when he was pulled down inside the penalty area by what the commentator described as virtually a rugby tackle, but the referee let play continue. Apparently Jevons was distraught at the final whistle and trudged off disconsolately, but that eight-point lead that we had a half-time is at least still five points because Scunthorpe lost at Swansea. However, the way the results seem to be going it seems the rest of the pack is beginning to catch us up.

Has this been a good week or a bad week? We have got six points out of nine in the past seven days, which is certainly promotion form at two points a game and, considering two of those matches have been away at Chester and Grimsby, and the other home against high-flying Scunthorpe, I guess I shouldn't feel too disappointed. If we average two points a game for the rest of the season we will go up as champions. However, we have now lost three of our last four away games with defeats at Oxford, Macclesfield and now Grimsby. Macclesfield have been there or thereabouts all season and are a strong team but we should have certainly done better at both Oxford and Grimsby if we are going to be a championship-winning team.

The radio switches straightaway to the Bristol Rovers match and they have lost 2-1 to Macclesfield, which means that Macclesfield are now only five points behind, although we do have a game in hand over them. But then look at our game in hand. It's at Northampton on Tuesday! From memory we lost midweek at Northampton last year and, as far as I am concerned, they are very much a potential bogey team. They have clawed their way into the play-off zone and are certainly not going to be giving anything away at home against Yeovil.

When I got home I checked the league table. Scunthorpe's loss at Swansea put Swansea level with Scunthorpe but now Southend, who won today at Bury, and Macclesfield have joined them as well, so the reality is we have a five-point lead and a game in hand on three of the four joint-second-placed teams. However, we could lose the advantage of that game in hand if we get beaten or indeed only draw at Northampton on Tuesday. And I don't have good feelings about that game! For me, the big downer today was Macclesfield winning to now be only five points behind and not having played a game more. The only thing is, statistically, their run can't go on much longer. They have now won six in a row and surely they can't keep going, can they?

I am a little concerned that there are now four teams within five points of us. My fear is, if we hit a bad patch of form, three of the four within striking distance could overhaul us and send us into the play-offs.

I get home and have a shave, shower and change and then it's over to Milborne Port to help my mother complete dressing and bring her and two friends to our place. By the time I get home some of the guests are beginning to arrive. After forty or fifty minutes of leaving people to mingle and enjoy their drinks, I realise that old people don't mingle. They sit down and stay in the same place! Sharron asked me if I could take care of the evening, which meant: 'I've arranged the food and everything and now it's your responsibility to make the party hum, Michael.' I tell everyone to help themselves to the buffet, so that takes care of another fifty minutes. Sharron and Wendy had bought several bottles of champagne and asked me if I was going to say a few words to toast my mother. Of course I had forgotten to prepare a speech or any comments so decided to wing it and it didn't go too badly.

A ninety-year-old football reporter cuts her cake! My mother with David, Sarah, Sharron and Lisa.

My mother, being my mother, was determined to have the last word, so promptly stood up and corrected several points of my speech, saying that she had a better memory than I did! She thanked everyone for coming and hoped they would enjoy the rest of the evening 'whatever that involved'. Oh my God! That really puts the pressure on because she obviously expects that I've got something arranged as indeed would normally have been the case if I had not got sidetracked at the office.

While Sharron was cutting up and serving the birthday cake I feverishly prepared some quiz questions and divided everyone into five teams for a quiz. Amazingly, despite the wide range of ages from sixteen to over ninety, the quiz went well and was a lot of fun, although it kept some of the older guests around rather later than anticipated as we didn't finish until well after 11 p.m.

At around 1.30 a.m. I went onto the internet to try and find some flights as I have decided I am off to South-East Asia and I'm going to fly into Bangkok. I'm not sure if this is just going to be a holiday or whether I'm going to take some projects to work on. I will probably visit a school in Thailand that is keen for us to use their facilities for sports tours in South-East Asia. I really fancy renting an apartment near a beach and unwinding because my ongoing worries regarding Casterbridge and making David redundant has really worn me out.

I finally got to bed at 4.00 a.m. after another typical weekend day, reviewing the financial situation with Casterbridge, sweating through Yeovil's match, participating in my mother's ninetieth birthday and trying to arrange flights halfway around the world. Ho hum – roll on retirement.

Grimsby Town 2 Yeovil Town 1

Team: Chris Weale, Andy Lindegaard, Terry Skiverton, Kevin Amankwaah, Michael Rose, Kevin Gall, Darren Way, Lee Johnson, Arron Davies, Phil Jevons, Bartosz Tarachulski

Subs: Rory Fallon (61 for Tarachulski), Paul Terry (61 for Gall), Andrejs Stolcers (88 for Rose)

Subs not used: Steve Collis, Adam Lockwood

Goal-scorer: Arron Davies (11)

Attendance: 4,414

Position in League after match: 1st

Thai Takeaways
Tuesday 1 March 2005 – Pattaya, Thailand
Northampton Town *v.* Yeovil (League Two)

As the game was played on 2 March Thai time, that is the day described in this account.

I arrived at Pattaya yesterday evening (Tuesday) after a twelve-hour flight from the UK and a two-hour taxi transfer from Bangkok. In my usual hectic departure I left my wallet behind at home, with credit cards, cash, etc. Fortunately (and unusually) I had some travellers cheques that could easily support me for at least a couple of weeks in Thailand, and I also had an emergency credit card for just this eventuality taped to the inside of my passport cover. That is three trips in a row when I have rushed off and left something behind. I really need to slow down. Wendy drove up to Heathrow and put my wallet on the next flight, which meant I now faced a five-hour, 250-mile return drive to Bangkok to collect my wallet, cash and credit cards! Not so smart Michael! I would have stayed in Bangkok if I hadn't booked my hotel and taxi transfer to Pattaya before arriving.

Pattaya is a beach resort about two hours from Bangkok with a (very!) wide range of entertainment options, but we will come to that later! Pattaya is no more representative of South-East Asia than Las Vegas typifies America, but it is a fun place to stay for a few days while I decide where I'm going to move on to for the rest of my time in Thailand.

As soon as I got up I went down to the internet shop just outside the hotel to check the result of last night's potentially tricky fixture away at Northampton. This, of course, is our game in hand. The game had actually kicked off at 2.45 this morning Thai time and when I went to the League Two page the result was there as a headline, Northampton 1 Yeovil 1, which I initially took to be a very good result until I saw that Northampton had equalised in the eighty-eighth minute! So that is two away matches in a row within the space of four days where we have dropped a total of three points due to our opponents scoring in the last five minutes. That's not very clever guys. Arron Davies had scored Yeovil's goal yet again so he is really on a hot streak, with four goals in four games, and I think that's seven goals since he joined us in mid-December. No wonder Gary Johnson was so keen to get him in the team.

Gary Johnson had made quite a few changes after the Grimsby match as Kevin Amankwaah started for Scott Guyett, Paul Terry was in midfield rather than Kevin Gall and, although Gall is a favourite of mine, I think that Paul Terry was just what a tough match away at Northampton required. Surprisingly Rory Fallon started in preference to Bartosz Tarachulski.

We now have eleven games left, with six at home and five away, and we are six points clear although the danger team, Macclesfield, now have a game in hand. It is not at all inconceivable that they could replace us at the top of the table if they can sustain their current run of form.

I start to have a close look at Macclesfield's fixtures and am somewhat reassured. Their game in hand doesn't get played until 6 April when they are away at Oxford but they have got some very tricky fixtures to come, including Northampton away this Saturday, promotion contenders Swansea and Scunthorpe away, Cheltenham (still on the fringes of the play-offs) away and a home match against Lincoln, still very much in contention. I think that it is inconceivable Macclesfield can make visits to Northampton, Swansea, Scunthorpe, Oxford and Cheltenham without dropping some significant points.

I check Yeovil's remaining fixtures and am pleased to see that only three of our remaining eleven games are against teams that are currently in the top ten of the league. Is that an easy run in or what? Our most difficult games are away at Darlington a week on Saturday and then our final three matches, which are Wycombe at home, Southend away and Lincoln at home. The last two matches might not be quite so tricky if Southend and Lincoln have secured play-off or promotion spots by the time we get to them. Conversely, if they both have to win to clinch promotion or a play-off place they could be extremely dangerous fixtures.

Once I have reviewed the fixture list I am both reassured and pleased about the point we got at Northampton, which put us six points clear. If we had lost and only been five points clear, another team making two wins up on us would go ahead of us, but any team now attempting to overhaul us will need to improve on our performance by more than two wins because at present our goal difference is so superior that it is worth an extra point. Normally I see a draw as two lost points but the more I think about it I see the draw at Northampton as a good result. It also kept one of the play-off-contending teams very much at arms length as they did not make up any ground on us. Consequently it was a somewhat reassured Yeovil fan that went for a late breakfast at around 1 p.m.

After my late breakfast I went for a walk along the beach, which is always good entertainment. Why is it good entertainment? Because on one side of the road there are a mixture of stalls, shops, eating places and shopping malls and a variety of accommodation, ranging from cheap flop houses with rooms available by the hour to modern

Chris Weale frustrates Northampton and shows why he has twice been voted the best goalkeeper in the division.

and impressive four-star hotels. By contrast on the beach side of the busy thoroughfare the sidewalk is lined by a variety of women of all ages offering such delectable come-ons as 'I go with you' (for the night) and 'I want to sleep with you'! During the day there are usually one or two ladies standing every ten or twenty metres and during the evening there is about one every metre! Some of these women look as young as sixteen, some are in their forties, some are very attractive, some are rather haggard and, of course, this being Thailand, some are guys, or the infamous Thai lady boys!

Most of the women are between twenty and thirty and either stand shyly waiting for the *falang* (foreigner) to make the first approach or try and engage the passing (single male) pedestrians in conversation. This adds a completely new dimension to taking a constitutional walk along the promenade! It is all to easy to lose a couple of hours walking up and down the beach checking out the scenery and options from the ever-changing line up of available young ladies!

Pattaya is without doubt the biggest and brashest of the South-East Asian resorts, and has made valiant efforts to rebrand itself as a family resort, but catering for single Western males is still the main activity. At any time in the afternoon there are dozens of single Western males (most in the forty to seventy age bracket) walking up and down the beach and at night the figure is in the hundreds. And the beachfront area is just a fraction of what Pattaya has on offer, with quite literally thousands of go-go and hostess bars! It is both amusing and sad and my attitude is to go with the flow, and not be judgmental on either side. One soon gets used to seeing elderly guys walking around hand in hand with their girlfriends often decades younger. Our operations director, Amanda, was in Thailand recently and dismissively reported her disdain at Thailand being full of dirty old men with their Thai takeaways!

The girls are inevitably very friendly although some are a little sour faced if they have been hanging around for several hours without any business. Pattaya attracts tens of thousands of single male visitors from around the world each month and there is a casual, easy natured and even respectful banter between both parties throughout the day and evening! It is so open and transparent that one cannot take offence.

I had initially planned to be leaving Pattaya around 2.30 p.m. to go to Bangkok airport, about two and a half hours away, and then be back by early-mid evening, but it was almost 3.30 p.m. and I still had not arranged for a taxi to take me to Bangkok. I had the phone number for the taxi driver who took my mother and myself to Bangkok Airport three years ago and I remembered him as a nice and friendly person, so I called him and arranged for him to pick me up at the hotel at 6 p.m. to take me to Bangkok Airport for a return fare of 2,000 baht, which was about £25.

The trip to Bangkok and back was quite uneventful and five hours later Narong dropped me off a couple of blocks from the hotel so that he did not have to drive down the narrow lanes (or 'sois' as they are known in Thailand) between the two one-way roads that dominate Pattaya.

I walked through a couple of the narrow lanes and it was impossible to walk past a bar without shrill voices yelling out 'Hello, you come here' or 'You please come in.' The never-ending crescendo of music from all of the bars made me wonder how any of the Western guys managed to have a half-decent conversation with any of the literally thousands of very attractive bar girls trying to engage their attention and offer their services as the chosen companion for the night or week!

As I had slept late this morning and the adrenaline was still flowing from the return trip to Bangkok, I decided to wander around Pattaya by night. After I walked along the beach, which was now populated shoulder to shoulder with young girls offering their services, I decided it was time to sit down and went to one of the famous go-go bars.

I went to the Classroom on Soi 1, which is named because most of the go-go dancers who were up on stage were dressed, or rather undressed, in schoolgirl-type uniforms. Considering the entertainment was free, the drinks were competitively priced at 50 baht or about 70p for a coke or a beer. The intention is that you sit and watch the dancers and if you would like to chat with one of the girls you tell one of the waitresses, who will advise the dancing girl to come and sit with you. All wear badges on their uniforms indicating their number, but one of the problems of getting older is that it is impossible to read the numbers! The usual drill thereafter is that you sit and chat with the young lady and occasionally buy her a drink. If you want the lady to spend the rest of the evening with you, you normally have to pay a bar 'fine' of between 200-500 baht, which is between £3 and £7 to 'release' her from her job, and another £7 to £15 for her services. Obviously the size of the bar fine drops the later it is in the evening.

However, the music was far too loud to be able to indulge in a sensible conversation with anyone, so after finishing my drink I paid and went on my way down Pattaya's famous Walking Street which is crammed with a variety of bars, restaurants and discos, all competing for the tourists' attention. Most of the bars have girls on the street, waving the price of a beer to entice clients inside, and some of the bars on Pattaya's infamous Walking Street are mega complexes that consist of maybe twenty smaller open bars, each with about fifteen attractive girls sitting on bar stools with another fifteen girls behind the counter. Imagine seven or eight of these complexes in close proximity, with about 3,000 girls all shouting and competing for your attention

Second best use
of a Yeovil scarf?

while each bar plays music at the loudest volume possible and you begin to understand why Pattaya is an interesting place to visit for a few days but not necessarily one
to spend a long, relaxing vacation! When you factor in that many of the larger bar
complexes may offer open-air Thai boxing or a transvestite show, and there are hundreds of streets in Pattaya full of bars, you will get an impression of both the scale of
the noise and attractions offered. Thank God I don't drink but of course I can sit down
and have a soft drink!

I made my way back to the hotel via the beachfront promenade at about 3 a.m. and
on the way I noticed a familiar face. It was Nong, whom I had met when I was last
here with Sarah and Lisa twelve months ago. We had a brief chat and she remembered me well. I explained that *Around the World with Yeovil Town* would be
significantly enhanced with some pictures of a Yeovil scarf draped around a young
Thai's shoulders and she was more than happy to oblige.

I'm telling you, it's a hard life writing a football book!

Northampton Town 1 Yeovil Town 1

Team: Chris Weale, Andy Lindegaard, Terry Skiverton, Kevin Amankwaah, Michael Rose, Paul Terry, Lee Johnson, Darren Way, Phil Jevons, Rory Fallon, Arron Davies

Subs: Kevin Gall (74 for Jevons), Bartosz Tarachulski (83 for Fallon)

Subs not used: Steve Collis, Adam Lockwood, Andrejs Stolcers

Goal-scorer: Arron Davies (31)

Attendance: 5,630

Position in League after match: 1st

Lucky Old Scunthorpe!

Saturday 5 March 2005 – Pattaya, Thailand
Yeovil Town v. Leyton Orient (League Two)

This is my fourth day in Pattaya and I really haven't managed to achieve a great deal so far! Every time I go out I never fail to be amazed by the number of bars and available females of all shapes and sizes from every province of Thailand. It seems there are between ten and fifteen females for every male and there are certainly plenty of males around. I'm not surprised so many (male) expatriates have retired to Thailand!

On Thursday I went over to the nearby suburb of Jomtien to look into the possibility of renting an apartment for a couple of weeks, but I think the probability is that I will stay here for a few more days and then move on to one or two of the smaller islands along the coast towards Cambodia. I think it will be good to get back to more regular hours and fewer distractions!

I woke at 11 a.m. this morning and spent a couple of hours 'stitching' together digital images I had taken in the Himalaya to make some panoramas, and was quite impressed with the results. After grabbing some breakfast I walked along the beach towards the Asia Siam Hotel, which has a very nice coffee shop at the entrance to its grounds.

Part of the object of coming to Thailand was to relax so I decided to pay my 20 baht (30p) and rent a deck chair on the beach and do some reading and I continued with *Blair's Wars*. I stayed on the beach until about 6 p.m. and then wandered down to the Royal Garden Centre for either a late lunch or early dinner!

When I arrived at the Royal Garden Centre I realised that some of the ladies sitting on the seats in the mall weren't there for the shopping, as the direct eye contact that was so often made was a clear invitation! As the majority of visitors were genuine

shoppers, it would be unfortunate and highly embarrassing if someone made a proposal to an attractive young Thai woman who was actually a mother doing some
family shopping!

Every time I see an older Westerner with a young Thai companion I can hear
Amanda's scathing tones describing those dreadful men with their 'Thai takeaways'!
Indeed, whenever I go for breakfast I am invariably the only person eating alone as all
the other males, young or old, inevitably have a young Thai companion with them. I
am not sure whether that's for me, as I value my privacy and independence, and I am
not sure about wanting to commit myself on a daily basis to someone you hardly
know for the duration of your holiday. But plenty of people do and I understand that
the going rate after having met your wannabe companion either at the beach or at a
bar is a daily retainer of about 500-1,000 baht (£6-12) for them to stay with you for
the duration of your holiday as required! Many of the girls are stunningly attractive
and delightful companions.

Mid-evening is obviously peak time on the beach, which is absolutely wall to wall
with people strolling and browsing. In addition to the available women of all ages are
the infamous Thai lady boys. Their gender is normally revealed by a deeper voice and
a largish Adam's Apple. Extremely loud, brash and overly effeminate they are often tall,
willowy, attractive… and very much male as I once discovered when I got to the point
(literally) of no return in Tahiti in 1976! I am far from being the only male to have
escorted an attractive young lady only to subsequently discover she was anything but!

I could hardly include an account of Pattaya without mentioning the famous Thai
massage parlours, which usually have the appearance of a nightclub with large signs
outside. After entering one is normally guided to a row of chairs and tables where
drinks can be served, and you can observe as many as 70 to 100 ladies behind a large
glass partition. All are dressed in long figure-hugging dresses and are either trying to
catch the punters' attention through the window or looking bored at one of the TVs in
their waiting area. Customers advise a steward of the number of the girl who interests
them, he instantly transmits a signal to her from a beeper in his pocket and she will
then emerge from the viewing area and take the punter to a room, where you have a
massage. This comprises of being bathed completely from head to toe and then lying
on an inflatable lilo. The masseur will then use a bubble-bath lotion to make an
incredible amount of lather and then massage your body with her naked body in
every conceivable position. All this takes about sixty minutes for the equivalent of
£10. Following that, you will then be dried and put on a very large bed and given a
very relaxing massage by the young lady, who will invariably ask you whether you
require any additional services!

I first passed through Thailand in 1972 when travelling overland from England to
Australia, and have visited these parlours from time to time whenever I have passed
through Thailand over the last thirty years. The voyeur in me always enjoys looking at
the line-up of attractive ladies but the somewhat commercial and regimented proce-
dure means there are more personalised entertainment options readily available
throughout Pattaya!

I walked along the beach after dinner at the mall and eventually got back to the
safety of my room for a couple of hours of writing, and then it was time to go down
and check on Yeovil's match. I was so immersed in my journal that it was 11.15 p.m.

A Phil Jevons penalty against Leyton Orient kept Yeovil 6 points clear at the top.

or 4.15 p.m. in England, and well into the second half, when I entered the Internet shop outside the hotel.

Yeovil were at home to Leyton Orient, who are not without their own chances of securing a play-off spot, and an away win at Orient was an integral part of our run of seven consecutive league wins, which has been the key period of the season for us so far. Surely after winning 3-2 at Orient less than three months ago we are not going to trip up at home, although I expected Orient to be determined opponents.

When I checked the League Two latest scores it could not have been any better. Scunthorpe (second) were drawing 0-0 at home to Rushden & Diamonds, Macclesfield (third) were losing 1-0 at Northampton, Swansea (fourth) were losing 1-0 at Notts County and Southend (fifth) were losing 2-1 at Chester. Yeovil were leading 1-0 thanks to a Phil Jevons penalty in the sixth minute. If those results stayed the same for the next twenty-five minutes or so, then Yeovil will be eight points clear! That would be absolutely fantastic and I swear to God or any almighty power available that I won't look at another female for a whole week if those results stay the same. I noticed that Wycombe, who are having a hot-and-cold season, were winning 3-2 at Lincoln but, more significantly, that Nathan Tyson (a Stan Collymore look-alike) had scored a hat-trick for Wycombe. I thought he looked a very useful player when I watched Yeovil beat Wycombe 1-0 earlier in the season.

I couldn't believe it. In twenty minutes we could be eight points clear. That would be terrific. Of course, I would like more than the comfort of one goal against Orient because, with our recent record of conceding late goals, we don't want this to turn into a 1-1 draw and only get one point when all the teams behind us are struggling.

I made a posting on the *606* League Two forum site this week, saying I didn't think Macclesfield's run could last much longer and it looks as if I was absolutely right as they were still losing 1-0 at Northampton. However, I wanted the full times to come up with Yeovil winning 1-0 and for none of the other teams in contention to score late goals. I wanted things to stay exactly as they were, with Scunthorpe drawing and Southend, Swansea and Macclesfield all losing. Something's got to give hasn't it? Let's hope it's not Yeovil conceding a late equaliser!

By my calculations it was 4.50 p.m. in England and I obviously missed one of the changes on the ticker tape because it was now Chester 2 Southend 2. Shit! Southend have equalised but it's still only one point and not three. Why aren't these matches coming up as full times? They have to be over by now.

To fill in some time I checked the Yeovil line-up on the Sky website and it was the same back four as played at Northampton on Tuesday with Amankwaah playing instead of either Guyett or Miles, and it looks as though Andy Lindegaard has cemented himself into a regular place at full-back. He is currently keeping Paul Terry out of the defence, which means that if Terry is going to be playing in midfield someone else is having to drop out, and today it was again Kevin Gall. Bartosz Tarachulski had started today, although he came off in the thirty-fifth minute to be replaced by Rory Fallon. I wonder why he went off that early? Hopefully he was not injured as obviously we want Bartosz to be fully involved over the remaining ten games.

Slowly the full-time scores started to come up. I really didn't want a goal in any of those four matches but the chances were at least one of them will have a late goal. I had no sooner finished writing in my notebook 'I want Yeovil to hold on and Scunthorpe not to win, PLEASE!' than the Sky teleprinter announced Scunthorpe 1 Rushden & Diamonds 0. That is absolutely unbelievable! What am I, a part-time clair-voyant? It was the veteran Peter Beagrie, with a goal in the ninetieth minute. I hadn't noticed that Beagrie had been playing much this season and he certainly didn't play when we beat Scunnie 4-3, although I thought he looked good when we played them last year.

The good news was that Macclesfield's defeat at Northampton quickly came up as a full time, as did Swansea's loss at Notts County. What about Yeovil? Come on, get that bloody result up! Chester and Southend was confirmed as a 2-2 draw and there it was, FT against the Yeovil score and we had held on for a 1-0 win. Great! That puts us on thirty-six games and sixty-nine points, Scunthorpe are on thirty-six games and sixty-three points, six points behind, Southend a further two points behind on sixty-one and we are now nine points clear of Macclesfield, although they still have that game away to Oxford in hand.

Swansea are now down to fifth with sixty points and thirty-six games. It will be a shame if they don't go up for two reasons. LeeTrundle is a very talented player who should be playing on a higher stage than League Two and their new stadium looks absolutely fabulous. It would be a shame not to have the opportunity to go there next year. Am I putting the cart before the horse? Maybe, but surely we are going to get promoted. This has been a really good day and we must have every chance of holding on for the championship.

I check next week's fixtures and Yeovil are away at Darlington, which is arguably our toughest match before the final three games. And Scunthorpe? They are at home to Chester so it's not inconceivable that the gap could be down to three points next week but, thereafter we have a reasonable run of what appear to be relatively easy matches.

I go back to my room to continue with my journal but come back out to watch Norwich against Chelsea in one of the bars. I go up and down the Soi to decide which is the preferred location where I want to watch the game, and there is no shortage of options as most bars have the football on. A lot of people would think this is heaven, watching Premiership football in a bar surrounded by a bevy of young ladies all vying for your attention, but I am pleased to report that I made my selection of venue on which bar had the quietest TV viewing area rather than which had the most attractive women! By the time the match was over, with Chelsea the deserved winners, it was past 2 a.m. and as I was beginning to feel a bit peckish I wandered off down the beach to the Subway for a tuna salad sandwich.

Pattaya never fails to amuse me. Anywhere else in the world, if you cannot sleep you can pop out from your hotel for a pizza or a sandwich. Here, if you cannot sleep, you can just pop out to review and select a companion to keep you company for the remainder of the night and ease you off to sleep, and all for less than the cost of a pizza in New York!

Yeovil Town 1 Leyton Orient 0

Team: Chris Weale, Andy Lindegaard, Terry Skiverton, Kevin Amankwaah, Michael Rose, Paul Terry, Darren Way, Lee Johnson, Phil Jevons, Arron Davies, Bartosz Tarachulski

Subs: Rory Fallon (35 for Tarachulski), Kevin Gall (82 for Lindegaard)

Subs not used: Adam Lockwood, Steve Collis, Andrejs Stolcers

Goal-scorer: Phil Jevons (9 penalty)

Attendance: 6,545

Position in League after match: 1st

A Bar Girl's Life

Saturday 12 March 2005 – Ko Samet, Thailand
Darlington v. Yeovil (League Two)

I am writing this on Ko Samet, an island about thirty-five miles west of Pattaya, and I am staying in a more-than-adequate beach bungalow.

Yesterday I took a minibus from Pattaya to the small port at Ban Phe. I christened it the honey bus as it contained one single lady and four middle-aged men, all with young Thai female companions! These girls are not with their companions because of their overpowering looks or colossal intellect, but because the £6-£12 per day they will earn is attractive when waitresses earn £50 a month and manual workers about

Dining on the beach, Ko Samet.

£80 monthly. Inevitably the Western males treat the girls well and the girls, usually from poor rural families, make delightful companions and use some of the funds they earn to support aged parents.

Before I left Pattaya I asked one of the bar girls I had met if I could see the room where she lived and I have to say it was a very humbling experience. Sow's room was one of a series of rooms on the third floor of a residential block that we entered from a busy street near Pattaya's famous Walking Street. Her room was approximately 10ft x 12ft with a toilet and tap area in a curtained-off corner alcove. making it almost an L-shaped room. She had a box supporting a small statue of Buddha and she prepared an offering of two soft drinks and flowers, which she put in front of the Buddha and prayed. She had a small television and a DVD player balanced on a pile of books. Her possessions and cooking utensils were stacked in boxes in the corner of the room next to the cooking alcove. Sow cooks on the floor and there was also a paper-thin mattress that she unravels for sleep. She put a blanket on the floor, which was tiled and used the floor as an ironing board. There was a poster of Charlie Chaplin in *The Tramp* on the wall and she tells me I am the first *falang* (foreigner) to visit her room.

Sow has two parents in a northern province and, like her nine surviving brothers and sisters, she sends money home to support them whenever she can. In reality Sow is living in a cupboard while I own three homes and another ten properties between LPI, Casterbridge Tours and our pension plan. I found this disparity between the lives of the bar girls and the visitors they befriend as equals very difficult to accept. It is strange but when I go to Nepal I can easily ignore the acute poverty everywhere and I never give to the people begging around me, preferring to make contributions to agencies that encourage communities to help themselves. However, my visit to Sow's room was quite different and I was deeply affected by the difference between the worlds that we inhabit. I don't think Sow quite realised how it affected me and, when I commented on the difference between our living standards, kept saying 'My loom is fine,' an indication that most Buddhists readily accept and adapt to their situation and circumstances.

The ferry from Ban Phe to Ko Samet landed at a beautiful bay with deck chairs, stalls and restaurants sitting in the shade of the trees ringing the beach and I found an air-conditioned room with shower and hot water, set in very pleasant landscaped grounds nearby. I spent this morning on the beach under an umbrella, and ended up swimming in the sea for almost two hours. After a late lunch I walked along the coast to explore some of the surrounding bays during the late afternoon. There are bunga-lows and restaurants around every bay, some attractive and others not so, but the island has a nice feel to it. I went to one of the seafood restaurants set up on the beach for dinner and I could see illuminated fishing boats out at sea. It was a beautiful set-ting and I realised it was 10.15 p.m., so it must be 3.15 p.m. in England! I called Tony with my mobile (there is a transmitter located just behind the beach!) and he was at South Cheriton taking his daughter Tess riding. He had not heard any reports of any goals from Darlington on his car radio.

Common consensus is that we need four more wins and eighty-one points to be certain of promotion, and this is one of our trickier challenges. Tony thinks we will be certainties if we win today. I tell him I am at the beach waiting for my seafood din-ner to be delivered and he says he is freezing! I suspect I am the only Yeovil fan following the game from a Thai beachside seafood restaurant! Twenty minutes later, as Tony was probably not yet home from the stables, I called home and reached Sharron. As my battery was low I asked her if she could get the half-times off the internet and I would call her back, but she was obviously at her computer because she could get them immediately. I waited while she found the web page and then read the scores.

'Darlington 1 Yeovil 0.' Shit – but not entirely unexpected. This is the toughest game until the final three matches and we could still pull it back; after all, we were 2-0 down at Cambridge. 'What about the other scores, Sharron?' 'Cheltenham 0 Scunthorpe 1.' Damn! That's not very good as that will narrow the gap to three points. 'Shrewsbury 0 Macclesfield 0.' Good! Let's hope that two really poor results in a row will stop Macclesfield in their tracks. 'Swansea 0 Rochdale 1.' Great – except I would like to see Swansea and their new stadium in League One next year! 'Wycombe 0 Chester 0, Southend 0 Lincoln 0.' Good. Hopefully two home points on their way to being dropped by Southend, and then my phone dies!

With the exception of Scunthorpe those half-times aren't too bad, although the chances of them remaining the same are highly unlikely. Remember what happened last week when I was in Pattaya. So with a dead phone I had no alternative but to return to my excellent seafood dinner before I wandered back to my room and watched a documentary on Ronaldo. I really wanted to curl up and sleep but duty called and I needed to go and check Yeovil's result. I went back to the beach and found an internet shop. I quickly went to the League Two results page. As I scrolled down the page I cov-ered the screen with a sheet of paper so that I could only see the first few letters of the

Still no crowd at Darlington for our third visit in thirteen months and still Yeovil can't win! Kevin Amankwaah and Lee Johnson look bemused, Andy Lindegaard looks angry!

home team and not the result. I got to Darl...i...n...g...t...o...n... (I am at the right place, Michael, so move the paper across damn it) 2. Please let it be Yeovil 3, I prayed, invoking the memories of Cambridge. Y...e...o...v...i...l... (move the paper Michael) 1. Shit! And double shit!! But I expected it really. Let's hope the other results go our way. I remove the paper and quickly check them. Rushden & Diamonds 3 Northampton 2. Great! Scunthorpe 4 Cheltenham 1. Damn! Not so good. And that's a four-goal turn-around on the day to our previously significant goal advantage.

I noticed that with five minutes to go it was Scunthorpe 2 Cheltenham 1, so it could easily have been 2-2, but Scunthorpe yet again scored, on this occasion, two late goals in the eighty-fifth and ninetieth minutes to follow last week's stoppage-time winner.

I continued with the results. Shrewsbury 0 Macclesfield 1. Shit! I didn't want to see that, but the next two were better, with Southend 0 Lincoln 1 and Swansea 2 Rochdale 2, so only one point made up on Yeovil between Southend and Swansea, and not much damage done by our loss, except of course by Scunthorpe and Macclesfield. Wycombe, whom we still have to play, are running into some form though, and beat Chester 4-2.

I check next week's fixtures as always and Southend are at Cheltenham (still in play-off contention) and Macclesfield have a home game against Orient. Neither of these games are gimmies. Scunthorpe have got a very tricky match at Rochdale but surely I can't keep pointing out Scunthorpe's tricky matches and getting it right? Northampton v. Swansea means that one of them is going to drop points and Yeovil are home to Bury. That is clearly the easiest match for any of the contending teams as Bury have no play-off possibilities and are well clear of the relegation zone, so I guess

Scunthorpe will win comfortably and we will slip up at home! Hopefully I'm only joking and I take some comfort from the fact that Macclesfield have a very tough run in and, of our nine games remaining, five of them are at home.

Come on Yeovil, you can do it. Having been top since January, anything other than the championship will be disappointing and the record of a championship-winning season would be a great boost to the marketability of this book!

Darlington 2 Yeovil Town 1

Team: Chris Weale, Andy Lindegaard, Terry Skiverton, Kevin Amankwaah, Michael Rose, Paul Terry, Lee Johnson, Darren Way, Phil Jevons, Rory Fallon, Arron Davies

Subs: Kevin Gall (55 for Rose), Bartosz Tarachulski (62 for Fallon), Andrejs Stolcers (76 for Jevons)

Subs not used: Steve Collis, Adam Lockwood

Goal-scorer: Darren Way (81)

Attendance: 4,121

Position in League after match: 1st

A Bad Day in Phuket
Saturday 19 March 2005 – Phuket, Thailand
Yeovil v. Bury (League Two)

I am on Phuket, the biggest island in Thailand and one that took a major hit from the Boxing Day tsunami. I flew down yesterday from Pattaya after six glorious days on the island of Ko Samet, in truth one of the weeks of my life. I will always have fond memories of beautiful dinners served on low tables set around reclining mattresses on the beach, long swims and exploring the island on a rented motorbike.

My friend Chris Williams called me on my mobile (complete now with a Thai sim card) when I was on Ko Samet and asked if I was coming down to Phuket to visit him and his daughter, and here I am! Before coming to Phuket I booked into a hotel close to Chris's home. Chris and his dogs met me at the airport yesterday and, after checking into my hotel, we spent an enjoyable afternoon at a deserted beach. Tourists have yet to return to Phuket in big numbers, although the tsunami damage was restricted to just a few areas.

I did not go down for breakfast this morning until 9.59. Well, it did say breakfast is available until 10 a.m.! Chris was a Casterbridge tour guide in 1984 and retired to Phuket after eighteen years as a civil servant in Hong Kong with his daughter, and he came around at 11 a.m. We went to beautiful Surin beach, which was hardly affected by the tsunami. Obviously the offshore depth of water and shape of the land were crucial factors because neighbouring Kamala beach, around the headland, saw massive damage and a loss of life that ran into hundreds. I had a long swim while Chris walked his three dogs along the beach, and then joined him for a late lunch of fried prawns.

Chris is a big Newcastle fan and he felt that Yeovil were pretty much certainties to be promoted and should have every chance of going through League One quite quickly and getting to the Championship. Let's hope our Thai pundit has it right! I spent another hour in the sea after lunch but left at 4 p.m., and Chris dropped me off at the hotel. He was going to be busy tomorrow and suggested that I hired a jeep so I was mobile.

After dinner at an Italian restaurant with Chris and his daughter, I decided the cinema was a better option than the three Premiership games on TV this evening, so I followed Chris's instructions, evading the many motorcycles heading towards me on the wrong side of the road, and got to the cinema at the Central Festival Hall just as my intended choice of film was starting, so I took a motorbike taxi to a nearby roadside seafood restaurant for a late snack. Although I was hoping to hang on until half-time I couldn't wait any longer to find out how Yeovil were doing, so I rang home after ordering my meal and spoke with Sarah, who had come home for the weekend from Sussex University. She went to the internet and I directed her to the League Two latest scores which were:

'Bristol Rovers 1 Mansfield 1' – not interested.

'Cambridge 1 Wycombe 1' – I don't want Wycombe staying competitive as we have to play them three matches from the end of the season.

'Cheltenham 0 Southend 1' – Shit. We don't want Southend getting back into the shake up!

'Chester 0 Notts County 0' – not interested in this match.

'Grimsby 0 Darlington 1' – Another fringe team making a late run.

'Kidderminster 0 Rushden & Diamonds 0'.

'Lincoln 2 Shrewsbury 0' – my God! Every team with a shout seems to be doing well today.

'Macclesfield 0 Leyton Orient 0' – well that's better. Maybe Macclesfield will slip up and, just as I think that, the waiter puts a plate of fried prawns in front of me. I've eaten more seafood in Thailand this last week than the rest of my life combined!

'And the next three matches are all 0-0,' says Sarah. 'That's Northampton–Swansea (good), Oxford–Boston, (not bothered) and Rochdale–Scunthorpe.' Go Rochdale! Is this the possibility of a result in our favour?

I am not stupid; the fact that Sarah had said the next three matches are 0-0 meant the only game remaining is Yeovil's and that has a score. Yeovil top against Bury with nothing to play for and no fear of relegation. We must be ahead already. Great!

'And Yeovil 0 Bury 1' continues Sarah!

Oh shit! What is going on? That is just about the worst combination of results I have heard all season and we are losing what should be a banker home win. The nearby party in the restaurant had come to an abrupt end and quiet has descended. Perhaps they realised it was no longer the time for jovialities when they heard the Yeovil

Attractive company in Phuket partly compensates for a disastrous Yeovil result against Bury.

result! I told Sarah to leave the Internet on the page showing the latest League Two scores and I would ring back in twenty minutes or so at half-time.

Two weeks ago in Pattaya, if it had not been for Peter Beagrie's ninetieth-minute winner we would have been eight points clear, but now if we lose and Scunthorpe win handsomely we will be off the top. My God! Is it all going pear-shaped? Come on Yeovil – we must have won at least nine games coming from behind so far this season. Let's turn this around and if Macclesfield or Scunthorpe don't win, it could still be our day.

Twenty minutes later and I am giving up on my Thai mushroom soup, because it's half-time in England. I call and get Sharron, and the only changes are for the worse. Southend are now 2-0 up at Cheltenham (shit), Macclesfield are 1-0 up against Orient (double shit) and Northampton are 2-1 up against Swansea, which indicates the latter stages of the first half at Northampton obviously involved a lot of fun and games. This is not good. Scunthorpe are bound to win 1-0 with a late winner and we will only be on top by goal average. I tell Sharron that was the worse set of scores that I had heard all season and it couldn't be any worse. Sharron is obviously getting soccer savvy because she said, 'Surely it would be worse if Scunthorpe were winning?' Yes Sharron, you are absolutely right, but give them time and I am sure they will eventually take the lead (probably in the ninetieth minute) to stick the knife well and truly into Yeovil's ambitions. This is the nadir of the season so far for me, just as two weeks ago was the high. Surely we are not going to collapse and throw it all away? Come on Gary Johnson; weave your half-time magic!

The motorbike taxi has come back to collect me and I call Sharron just as I am going into the cinema (11.20 p.m. Thai time). I calculate it to be 4.20 p.m. in the UK and about halfway through the second half. Yeovil are still losing 1-0, Scunthorpe are still drawing 0-0 and Southend are still 2-0 up. I sense that this is not going to be our day and ask Sharron to text me the full-time scores, as my phone will be off in the cinema. She asked if she could do this after 6 p.m. UK time and I confirmed that was not a problem. I don't mind when she sends the text as long as Yeovil win!

I buy my ticket and jot in my notes that I have been given a seat in row thirteen. I reckon that Yeovil have no chance now!

Thai cinemas are an absolute joy with very comfortable seats. You can pay a surcharge to use the back row of the cinema, containing small settees or double-seated love seats! What a delightful touch. I suspect that I was the only person in a Thai cinema with my mind partly on events at Huish Park Stadium as I tried to settle down and watch the movie with my fingers crossed that Yeovil would get two goals late in the second half.

When I got back to the hotel, I switched my phone on. Sure enough the music chimes, which tells me there is a message and it was from Sharron. Southend won 3-0, which will give them bags of confidence. Darlington beat Grimsby 1-0, Lincoln beat Shrewsbury 2-0, Macclesfield won 3-1, so they have kept their form and run going, and there at the bottom was 'Y 0 v 1 B'.

The only glimmers of hope were that Scunthorpe didn't pinch a late winner and only drew at Rochdale, and neither Northampton or Swansea capitalised on our loss as they drew 2-2, but our lead of eight points until the final minute two weeks ago is now down to two points. Most worrying is that Macclesfield are only three points behind with a game in hand, although they still have some tough fixtures to come. Automatic promotion, let alone the championship, is no longer looking a certainty with Southend and Macclesfield now well and truly in the mix, as well as Scunthorpe and Swansea., Considering today's form and our last three games (Wycombe at home, Southend away and Lincoln at home), things are not looking so clever all of a sudden.

At least I can console myself that I am one of the more fortunate Yeovil supporters and I could be in a lot worse places than Thailand. My four-star hotel is costing the grand sum of £13 per night, the food is cheap and the company always delightful in this wonderful country. However all things must end and it is home on Wednesday and then this time next week we will all be in South Africa. Yeovil will be hoping for a result at Boston as four points out of fifteen since the Scunthorpe game is not inspiring me with a great deal of confidence.

Yeovil Town 0 Bury 1

Team: Steve Collis, Andy Lindegaard, Terry Skiverton, Kevin Amankwaah, Michael Rose, Arron Davies, Darren Way, Lee Johnson, Paul Terry, Phil Jevons, Bartosz Tarachulski

Subs: Adam Lockwood (23 for Lindegaard), Kevin Gall (44 for Amankwaah), Rory Fallon (73 for Davies)

Subs not used: Chris Weale, Andrejs Stolcers

Attendance: 6,269

Position in League after match: 1st

Away Win on the Veldt

Saturday 26 March 2005 – Madrid – Johannesburg –
Nelspruit (South Africa)
Boston United v. Yeovil (League Two)

Even by this year's standards, the last few days have been pretty hectic, flying from Phuket to Bangkok on Tuesday and continuing to London on Wednesday. On Thursday I finished unpacking and went to Huish Park, where I interviewed Lee Johnson and John Fry, the chairman of Yeovil Town. Yesterday morning I packed and left for South Africa with Sharron and the children for a family holiday! Sharron was concerned about holiday traffic and wanted to leave at noon. I thought this was ridiculous as I consider anything other than arriving at the airport as they are announcing 'last call' to be an unnecessary waste of time! For once I was right and we were in the terminal a good one and a half hours prior to departure.

The cheapest flights Sharron had found involved a four-hour stopover at Madrid, before we took off in a brand new Airbus at about half past midnight this morning. Not surprisingly I was pretty tired and, unusually for me, slept for almost half of the ten-hour flight to Johannesburg.

This was my fourth visit to South Africa, and the highlight of my previous visits had been in 1998 when the whole family had been fortunate enough to meet Nelson Mandela, who shook hands and spoke with all of us. I told the kids not to wash their hands for at least a month! He is an inspiration to everyone and looked every inch a statesman in waiting when he walked out of jail in 1990. No wonder the Nationalist government kept him incarcerated for so long, and what a unifying force he has been for all races in South Africa. However, the test of South Africa's maturity and Mandela's legacy will be if the country can survive his passing, because today no political element wants to upset the applecart out of respect to the father of the nation. South Africa still has plenty of challenges and major problems to address.

In 1998 we divided our time between hiking in the Drakensberg and exploring the Kruger National Park, and the kids all said that wildlife viewing in the Kruger was the best of all our family holidays, which is why we have come back this year.

With Sarah, now twenty, at university, Lisa eighteen and approaching a gap year and David (sixteen) increasingly interested in doing his own thing, this is likely to be one of our last 'family' holidays and we will spend most of our time observing wildlife in the Kruger. The Elsworth family from nearby Charlton Horethorne will also be in the Kruger at the same time (remember Chris and I travelled back from Nepal in October and I did not recognise him!) and I cannot believe Sharron didn't arrange a firm rendezvous before they left. She thinks we may be staying at Lower Sabi camp-site on the same nights!

As we approached Johannesburg, one of the most violent and crime-ridden cities in the world, my thoughts turned to Yeovil. South Africa's test will be the ten years after Mandela dies. Yeovil's test will be at Boston this afternoon and I'm not optimistic.

On Thursday I interviewed Lee Johnson and John Fry. Neither struck me as over confident, as Lee admitted a bad run of form does affect the collective confidence of a team and, although still quite bullish, I initially thought John Fry seemed a little tired and was not assuming we will be promoted – 'The next three matches will tell us a lot.' Three months ago Boston away, Notts County at home and Rushden away would have yielded nine points. Now we are wondering what they will tell us? Lee ended his interview by commenting he had never got a result at Boston with Watford, Brighton or Yeovil. Great! He'll be in a positive state of mind for sure!

Yesterday I called a friend of mine, Alison Smith, who lives in Johannesburg to confirm I still had her correct cellphone number. I did and Ally insisted on coming to the airport for a quick coffee. We had seen her briefly in 1998 when we also met for coffee at the airport and I went for dinner with her family when I first visited South Africa in 1994. Sadly, her attractive fourteen-year-old daughter, with plenty of attitude, who I met at that dinner died less than a year later following a friend's birthday party. The friend's father had given his daughter a hand grenade stripped of explosive material but sadly not of the incendiary device, which went off when the kids were examining it. I ask you, a hand grenade as a gift for a child? Only in South Africa! Alison's daughter received extensive burns and died within twenty-four hours.

Anyway, we were met by a very bouncy and exuberant Alison and we all went for a coffee and chat, although it gave me cause for reflection that it was almost forty years since I had first met Alison in Bournemouth around 1965-66. Sadly, another mutual friend of ours from those days, who now lives in Western Australia, also tragically lost his daughter recently in a freak car accident when being towed after a breakdown, and I had passed Julian's e-mail address on to Alison thinking there was no one better qualified to give him support. It is the ultimate tragedy for the child to die before the parent and sadly this has happened to two of my friends.

I was quite happy to sit and chat but it was past noon, we had a four-hour drive to Nelspruit and Sharron was keen to collect our rental car and get on our way. We picked up our bright red seven-seater Toyota van and made our farewell. After the usual arguments and two laps of the poorly signposted airport road system, we were finally on our way, heading eastwards away from Johannesburg across Gautang, previously known as the Transvaal. The landscape was dotted with some of the largest coal-burning power stations I have ever seen and, after an hour, I rang Tony to find out what time Yeovil and Boston were kicking off.

It was 12.45 p.m. UK time and Tony told me it had been a 12.15 p.m. kick-off and the game had been going for twenty-five minutes. We had played well and taken the lead with a headed goal from Terry Skiverton. Well done Terry. You are due a few based on previous years' exploits. Since then though, Boston were totally dominant and had equalised. Tony said the goal was blatantly offside, but the referee had overruled the flagging linesman. Nevertheless, it was no more than Boston deserved as they had had eight shots to one and our prospects weren't looking good. I told Tony I would call him at half-time and we pulled over at one of the roadside service areas on the N4 that we were following eastwards.

After a tasty veggie burger I called Tony for a half-time report. It was still 1-1 but Tony was even more downbeat as Boston were now 12-2 ahead on the shot count! Tony said Yeovil were unable to string two passes together and were playing 3-4-3 with Kevin Gall, Phil Jevons and new signing from Lincoln Marcus Richardson up front, and they weren't winning any balls in the air or on the ground. Why wasn't Bartosz playing I wondered? I think he is a key player for Yeovil, although I wonder if

Kevin Gall weaves some magic on the wing against Boston.

Gary Johnson has long-term faith in him. I feel he leads the attack so well his should be the first name on the sheet. Amankwaah had gone off injured and was replaced by David Woozley, another transfer-deadline-day signing from Oxford. Apparently Marvin Brown, another short-term contract signing, had also made the bench.

'So who are the back three?' I asked Tony.

'Lockwood, Skiverton and Amankwaah started with Paul Terry, Lee Johnson, Darren Way and Michael Rose in midfield. Amankwaah and Skiverton looked solid enough at the beginning but Michael Rose is having a nightmare.' Tony added that Lee Johnson ('Never won at Boston') was anonymous and Darren Way was busy as usual but not particularly effective. I asked Tony why Woozley had come on for Amankwaah and not Efe Sodje, the former Nigerian international who we have just signed on a two-year contract from Huddersfield. I had thought he looked particularly good against us last year when playing for Huddersfield. Tony had no idea but felt we had to go back to 4-4-2 as 3-4-3 was patently not working. I remembered John Fry saying Gary Johnson was trying to change the way we play in certain situations but I must say I belong to the 'attack and damn the consequences' school of thought or, as the Americans say: 'You dance with the gal you brought.' If 4-4-2 and a commitment to attacking football with two wide midfielders got us to the top, let's stick with it to keep us there.

Apparently most League Two games were played yesterday and Scunthorpe only drew 1-1 at home to Oxford, again courtesy of a last-minute equaliser. Lucky sods, but this time it only netted them one point and not three! Swansea beat Macclesfield 2-0, which confirmed that Macclesfield had some tricky games and a difficult run in, but Southend had a comfortable 3-0 home win. If we draw we will be two points ahead of Scunthorpe and Southend and for once a draw is looking like a good result.

'Tony, I won't call you,' I said. 'Just call me when there is a goal.' That way I can at least rejoice in the fact that we are on holding on for a point as I drive across South Africa, rather than worry whether we are behind! I knew there was excellent mobile phone coverage along the highway but no sooner did I sit in the car and prepare to drive than the phone goes. 'Not good,' says Tony. 'First minute of the second half and Boston have scored an almost exact replica of their first goal but this time the ref didn't allow it because of offside. It's not looking good, Michael.'

'Tony, I would settle for a draw right now. If I could pay £500 for a point, I would. Ring me when there is a goal. I hope I don't hear from you.'

I set off driving eastward across the veldt with its characteristic grassland savannah landscape. Is it my imagination or do the roadside signs and occasional buildings look more prosperous and tidy than on previous visits? Is South Africa on the up? The currency is certainly recovering from its days in the 16-18 rand per pound zone having strengthened to now be around 11 rand to the pound. If I was thirty years younger and starting off again I think I would be prepared to come here and give it a go rather than Australia.

My thoughts are wandering and I am reflecting on my time in Thailand when I realise we must be at least thirty minutes into the second half and Tony hasn't rung. I checked my phone and, yes, the signal is still good. Looks like we could hang on for a point. Great. No sooner do I think that than it rings. I pick up the phone and say, 'Shit, I didn't want to hear from you, Tony.'

A disappointing glance from Sharron. I hadn't even checked who it was calling and I was swearing. My language in front of the kids is a running sore between Sharron and myself but I have always been my natural self rather than something I'm not. Earthy as my language can be, I always eliminate the obscenities and my language is nothing like as bad as in many of the films they happily watch.

'It's okay, Michael. Skiverton scored again. We are 2-1 up. We've turned it around and the second half has been much better. Richardson and Rose went off and have been replaced by Tarachulski and Stolcers.'

What did I say? We should stick to our proven formula of class players and attacking football. I reckon I should be a manager.

'Boston are on the back foot,' Tony continued, 'and we are passing the ball well. We are looking much more solid.'

'Why wasn't Tarachulski on from the beginning?' I asked.

'I don't know. I don't think Gary Johnson reckons he's fit enough at present, so he is bringing him on to make an impact late in the game.'

'It will be huge if we hold on for three points after the home defeat against Bury,' I said. 'Especially as Boston are still challenging for a play-off place.'

'Well it's looking good, Michael. I'll call you at the final whistle.'

I tried to jot down my thoughts in my notebook but Sharron's disapproving frown and comments, reinforced by the kids, persuades me it is not wise to drive and write at the same time, so I pulled over to make my notes and then kept my eye on my watch until after twelve or thirteen minutes the phone rang. Please God it is not to tell me Boston have equalised in injury time!

'2-1, Michael. It was comfortable in the end,' says Tony.

'What did the commentators say?' I asked.

He who leaps highest scoreth the goal! Terry Skiverton heads the first of his brace at Boston.

'Pretty much that Yeovil did a professional job. Did well to withstand Boston when they took the game to Yeovil and ended up as deserved winners.'

Well, I guess to get a result at Boston will make Lee Johnson in particular happy, and that is a massive win for us after losing at home to Bury. We've now got seven games left and four are at home and the next four, Notts County at home (lower half of the table), Rushden away (bottom but two), Mansfield at home and Kidderminster away could yield us twelve points if we can hold some form together.

Tony commented that 4-4-2 in the second half was a lot better than 3-4-3 (so don't tinker Gary!) and he told me that Lincoln had won yesterday (against Scunthorpe) and Wycombe had lost at home to Northampton (finally coming good?). So we are now four points clear of Scunthorpe and Southend and six points clear of Macclesfield and Swansea. We're still in the driving seat!

After the half-time scenario three points was an unexpected bonus and I continued to drive westwards towards Nelspruit, pleased and content as a result of Yeovil's win. If we can follow that up with a win at home against Notts County on Tuesday we will be back in a very strong position – four or more points clear with six games to go. As it is, with seven games left, surely we can average one and a half points per game and get eighty-two points. Would eighty-two get us the championship? No. Automatic promotion? Probably. Today's win was vital if it stops the rot as, before today, we had only secured four out of the last fifteen points. Hopefully today's win will be the start of a strong conclusion to the season.

One of the distinctive features of South Africa is the number of people just walking along the roadside in the middle of nowhere. Coming from where and going to where? Who knows? I guess there are plenty of settlements not signposted but near to the main roads. As the light gets gloomy it is very hazardous as black skins are not particularly distinctive in the dark.

This being Easter weekend there was not a lot of accommodation available and all Sharron had been able to find was a Mercure Hotel at Nelspruit, a medium-sized town to the south of the Kruger Park. Interestingly enough, I thought I had stayed at this hotel eighteen months ago with my 2003 Chairman's Trek group. Sure enough, when we arrived, out of the thousands of hotels in South Africa, Sharron had booked us into one where I had previously stayed!

As it turned out it was just as well I had stayed previously as the hotel was full and had no record of our booking! However, at that very moment Mark, the young assistant manager, came out of his office, recalled my previous visit and our long conversation about the merits of the South African rugby team and hey presto, two rooms materialised. Just as well I was in a congenial mood on my previous visit!

After an excellent buffet dinner, I was ready for a good night's sleep and took pleasure that Yeovil's position was a lot better than I feared might be the case when the day began.

Boston United 1 Yeovil Town 2

Team: Chris Weale, Kevin Amankwaah, Terry Skiverton, Adam Lockwood, Paul Terry, Darren Way, Lee Johnson, Michael Rose, Phil Jevons, Marcus Richardson, Kevin Gall

Subs: David Woozley (44 for Amankwaah), Andrejs Stolcers (58 for Rose), Bartosz Tarachulski (73 for Richardson)

Subs not used: Steve Collis, Marvin Brown

Goal-scorer: Terry Skiverton (10) (82)

Attendance: 3,069

Position in League after match: 1st

Rumbled in the Jungle

Tuesday 29 March 2005 – Nelspruit – Londolozi Private Game Reserve, South Africa
Yeovil v. Notts County (League Two)

After two days in Nelspruit, today we moved on to the famous Londolozi Private Game Reserve in the Sabi Sand Reserve, which is adjacent to the Kruger Park. The private game reserves in South Africa are world famous for their wildlife and standards of hospitality, but one usually pays between £300 and £600 per person per night, which includes two game drives (6 a.m. and 4 p.m.) and three meals. On the promise that we will try and send them some business, Londolozi are providing a complementary stay for Sharron and myself and about £80 per person for Sarah, Lisa and David. Overall, £240 is expensive but a snip against the rack rate of £2,000 a night for the five of us!

Yesterday there was a football team congregating around the hotel pool. They were all young, black and pretty athletic looking. I went to the front of the hotel and saw their team bus, or should I say stretched minibus, and their team name was 'Dangerous Darkies'! Only in South Africa! What a lovely name, although somewhat less than politically correct!

I was chatting to their coach, who used to play in the South African Premiership for Orlando Pirates, and we talked about South African players in England. He said he had played against Lucas Radebe, the impressive and loyal long-serving Leeds central defender, and had inflicted a 4-0 defeat on Lucas when he had been playing for Kaiser Chiefs. He said the Darkies played in Division One and the winners of their league went into the Premiership and the next four into the play-offs.

'Will you be involved in the play-offs?' I asked.

'It will be a challenge,' he said, flashing a big smile.

He was right. When I looked at the league table, avoiding relegation was obviously the priority!

All the rest of the League Two fixtures were yesterday, which was Easter Sunday, and I was able to check the results on the internet last night. Darlington drew 3-3 at Bristol Rovers but, disappointingly, both Southend (2-0 at Cambridge) and Swansea (2-1 at Cheltenham) had away wins. We could have done without that. Scunthorpe were playing in last night's evening game.

After leaving the hotel we drove through White River. The name is clearly a mis-nomer as there was not a white person in sight. Like most South African towns there were hundreds of blacks on the street, looking as if they were not doing a lot. In Asia one wouldn't comment about hordes of people hanging around but, because of this country's apartheid history, it feels wrong and sad. There were a lot of poor and dejected-looking people around as we drove through White River, and with rampant AIDS, corruption and poverty I cannot but help think that this continent is a blight on all of mankind's achievements. And let's not forget South Africa is the most prosperous nation in Africa!

We briefly stopped at a small Afrikaans roadside shopping centre and I called Martin Holley at Lloyds Bank in Yeovil to transfer some funds. He said Scunthorpe had lost 2-0 at Lincoln last night. Great! That makes a win against Notts County tonight absolutely vital. That would put us four points clear of Southend, seven points clear of both Scunthorpe and Swansea, and eight points in front of Macclesfield. That would be a significant mini gap with only six games left. Surely we won't trip up for two home games in a row?

As we drove I worked out that the league table was currently as follows:

	P	Pts	GD
Yeovil	39	72	+22
Southend	40	71	+19
Scunthorpe	40	68	+18
Swansea	40	68	+16
Macclesfield	39	67	+14

We drove on through grasslands approaching the Kruger Park. We passed dozens of people just walking along the road, seemingly miles from anywhere and then turned off onto a bumpy unmade track taking us to the Sabi Sand Reserve. We turned a corner and six young boys spread themselves across the road in front of us doing a tribal dance! Obviously the ploy was to slow the vehicle down to a stop, perform some 'entertainment' and ask for a tip! A laconic comment came from behind: 'How weird is this?' Well, at least David was awake!

We were soon at the entrance to the Sabi Sand Reserve and paid our 60 rand vehicle fee. The guard laughed when I offered him 30 rand and any two of our children. Sarah and Lisa were not amused.

When we arrived at Londolozi, five drinks were waiting as we entered the reception and Sereena, the manager, welcomed us and explained that, to keep this camp as authentic as possible, it was not walled and animals could enter and freely roam. As a result, at night, we had to be escorted between the main building and our lodges by an armed escort. We were served a sumptuous lunch and then given an hour to unpack and relax before coffee and biscuits on the veranda and a 4.30 p.m. departure for our evening game-viewing drive. I used the time to relax by the small teardrop-shaped pool, complete with waterfall and reached by crossing a dry riverbed. I was contemplative and reflected that seven days previously I had been in Thailand.

Our accommodation in the safari camp was outstanding. The décor and fittings of our lodge, complete with indoor and outdoor showers, would have graced a five-star hotel with distinction. The camp had six lodges and could accommodate twelve people. The kids were clearly very impressed with Londolozi as they were laughing continuously and in good spirits. Quite clearly all was positive in the jungle as far as they were concerned!

As we were the only guests, Sereena joined her husband James on our game drive in an open-top Land Rover, converted with three rows of raised seats behind the armed driver and our tracker. Sarah, Lisa and David sat in the rear row of seats for maximum elevation, bumps and therefore thrill effect from the off-road driving! After a pre-drive briefing from James (no standing up, leaning out or sudden movement near animals and watch out for branches and bushes) we were introduced to our tracker, Zac, who sat up front in a special seat over a front wheel.

'This is Zac – we use him as bait.'

As a former tour guide I wondered how many dozens of times he had used that line. And then we were on our way and pretty soon ran into some kudos. It was when James was telling us about always distinguishing the males by the horns that I could not resist quipping 'I guess that's why they call males horny?' I then proceeded to flog the pun to death for the next couple of days, to the disgust of Sharron and the boredom of the kids. Oh well, I guess little things please horny old male minds!

Our drive sometimes followed rough bulldozed tracks but also went off-road through the scrub and bush. We had some excellent viewings approaching some elephants and a pair of rhinos very closely, but the pièce de resistance was finding four lions that were resting and sleeping. The lions did not get spooked by our approaching slow vehicle and looked very content. They had obviously had a good kill over the last twenty-four hours and were now sleeping after feeding. After a stop for the traditional 'sun-downer' drink in the bush, complete with folding table and table cloth

Keep your distance! We survived but Yeovil were not so fortunate against Notts County.

carefully assembled by Zac, we continued for some nocturnal viewing before we returned to the lodge, where two armed guards were waiting to escort us to our rooms to freshen up before dinner was served.

There was no mobile phone coverage but I used our satellite phone to call Tony, who was at the Brewer's Arms with Patrick eating some dinner before going to the match. Tony said this game was absolutely vital and I agreed, because we have a real chance to re-establish some daylight over the other contenders.

We were escorted back to the main building for a meal on the open deck and Sereena and James both joined us for dinner. We had a delightful meal and in the middle of the African bush discovered it was indeed a small world because when James had taken a gap year prior to going to university, he had worked for five months on a dairy farm near Wincanton! So he knew exactly where Yeovil was located and as a sports fan was fully aware of the significance of tonight's match. He wished me luck as he and Sereena wanted to see Londolozi portrayed positively in this book rather than by a disappointed and dispirited writer!

We returned to our rooms and as well as kerosene lanterns lighting all the paths, we discovered a piping hot bath had been run and was awaiting our return. I have stayed at hundreds of hotels, good, bad and ugly, throughout the world in the last thirty years but this was a first. I left the bath for Sharron because I had an urgent priority – to call Tony. I got through on the satellite phone and the tenor of Tony's voice indicated all was not well.

'The good news is we are only 2-0 down. The bad news is it should be 4-0! Chris Weale had twice miscleared directly to a Notts County player who should have scored!'

Surely he has to be joking. Tony can be quick, dry and amusing but in over twenty years I have rarely known him to wind me up with misleading information. I kept losing the signal and having to call back. Tony said there were forty minutes left and all we could do was hope for a turnaround, although there was no indication that was likely.

I told Tony that I would call him back as it was difficult for him to call my satellite phone and I sat down, unable to believe what I had just heard. This game was when we were meant to cement our recovery from a dodgy spell and pull away from our challengers. Notts County were clear of relegation and had no chance of making the play-offs. I thought they would be relatively easy fodder but clearly everyone was going to raise their game against the league leaders. I should have been recording my thoughts but I could not concentrate enough to write constructively, so compensated by having a game of Tetris on my handheld organiser. I got my highest ever score. Big bloody deal!

Back to the veranda and I called Tony to see if we have engineered another Cambridge away-type fight back. The sound of Africa was everywhere – insects, frogs and a variety of animals that I could not identify. I finally got through.

'It just got worse, Michael. 3-0 to Notts County!'

I don't believe this.

'Wait a minute – penalty to Yeovil.'

It wouldn't be Yeovil without a spot of drama along the way. I'm holding on to a weakening signal at about £1 a minute and I heard the crowd cheer.

'Hold on Michael. The ref says it's got to be retaken. The ref is an absolute joke. The worst I've seen all season.'

So the pressure was on Phil Jevons but a second big cheer from the crowd confirmed he kept his head. He has not missed a penalty all season.

'Ten minutes left to turn this around but don't hold your breath. Notts County are fast and quick passing, in fact everything we are not. They are by far the best team I have seen down here all season.'

I sat at the desk inside our lodge rather than tempt the mosquitoes. With their long unbeaten run since January Southend must be favourites to win the league and our penultimate match of the season at Roots Hall could clinch the championship for them. All the benefits of our win at Boston have been undone and our morale and confidence will be worse for not being able to build upon that good away win. Two home defeats at this stage of the season against lowly teams just defies belief. With six games to go Southend, Scunthorpe, Macclesfield and Swansea and ourselves all have a legitimate chance of automatic promotion. It could be the play-offs for Yeovil at this rate.

Sharron was out of the bath. 'Didn't they throw it away at the end of last season?'

'No, it all started going wrong around Christmas. We finished quite strongly, the damage was done between mid-December and early April.'

Sharron was in the four-poster bed, hidden by a mosquito net. I discovered the satellite reception was as good indoors as it was outside so I'd do without the romantic sounds of Africa, thank you very much. What I needed was three late goals but I knew there was as much chance of that happening as finding a snowball in hell. I rang Tony.

Low point of the season. A second home defeat in succession as Marcus Richardson and Yeovil make no impression on Notts County.

'3-1 Michael, just a minute of injury time left. Chris Weale looks as if he has gone to pieces tonight and the hungrier team won. Gary Johnson needs to scrap this approach, it needs a rethink...'

But I lost the signal before Tony could explain what approach needed to be scrapped. I tried to call Tony back but couldn't get a signal.

'Bloody satellite phone never works,' I moaned.

'Michael, you just made three calls with it,' a voice replies from behind the mosquito net.

'Yes but it didn't get the right result, did it? Bloody phone.'

I didn't expect this result and I was still shocked. When we won at Notts County earlier in the season Gary Johnson had said it was an excellent win as they were a good side who would surprise a few teams this season. I didn't realise you meant they would surprise us Gary!

We have been top since 3 January, which is almost three months. Surely we are not going to let it slip now? This late-season run in is turning out to be a death by a thousand cuts. Please don't blow it now Yeovil. We've got just seven of the last twenty-one points, which is pretty miserable at this stage of the season. If we had got three more wins we would have this league well and truly sewn up by now. Jesus! This is not good and if we cannot handle Bury and Notts County then our final two home games against play-off-contending Wycombe and Lincoln don't look at all easy! Furthermore they are sandwiching a visit to championship-challenging and rampant Southend. This is not looking good.

We have to be up at 5.15 a.m. so I decided I would pass up on a late-night bath. It needs more than hot water, soap and a soaking to cleanse me of the fear of impending doom. I have a distinct feeling that the season could be going pear shaped very rapidly and I got into bed thinking that if we were to collapse from a six-point lead and not get automatic promotion I would not fancy our chances in the play-offs. We have not got anything like the results and points we should have achieved from a relatively easy schedule over the last couple of months.

Rushden away on Saturday will tell us a lot. Please don't let our old rivals, who have struggled all season, now kick another hole in the good ship Yeovil. We are already taking on too much water!

Yeovil Town 1 Notts County 3

Team: Chris Weale, Paul Terry, Adam Lockwood, Terry Skiverton, Andy Lindegaard, Kevin Gall, Darren Way, Lee Johnson, Andrejs Stolcers, Phil Jevons, Bartosz Tarachulski

Subs: Marcus Richardson (45 for Tarachulski), Michael Rose (45 for Gall), Marvin Brown (71 for Terry)

Subs not used: Steve Collis, David Woozley

Goal-scorer: Phil Jevons (86 penalty)

Attendance: 7,221

Position in League after match: 1st

Breakdown in the Kruger

Saturday 2 April 2005 – Kruger National Park, South Africa
Rushden & Diamonds v. Yeovil (League Two)

This is our third complete day in the Kruger. After leaving Londolozi we have spent nights at Skukuza, Letaba and last night at Olifants, with its glorious balcony lookout overlooking the river. We watched lions and hippos crossing the river below us.

Our three days have been characterised by a lot of driving but my experience in the Kruger is that if you are prepared to put the hours in you will invariably find wildlife and good viewings wherever you go. Elephants, giraffe and zebras are fairly common, often standing close to the road, and the most common animals by far are the beautiful impala, which are all over the place. Waterbuck, the ugly looking wildebeest, the comical warthogs immortalised by Disney's *The Lion King*, velvet monkeys and baboons are also all fairly common. We have seen lions on two occasions as well as rhinos, water buffalo and crocodiles. Of the big five we are just waiting to see leopard.

Our three wildlife guidebooks are all getting well thumbed as we try to identify and learn the characteristics of the animals we sight, and we are also all appreciating the magnificent birdlife. Sharron and David are particularly adept at distinguishing between the various species of eagles and vultures, as well as identifying many beautifully coloured birds.

Today we were away by 6.15 a.m., our earliest start yet and very impressive when you consider the Bromfields' normal sleeping habits! We continued southwards past a giraffe, when I thought the ride was getting bumpy. I slowed down, looked out and, yes, we had a flat! Shit. We were on a dirt road, miles from anywhere, with some zebra nearby and two elephants about a quarter of a mile away. Kruger Park instructions made it quite clear if you break down you don't get out of your car. You flag down the next car and ask them to take a note to the nearest camp, who will send out a recovery team!

I was all for getting out of the vehicle and changing the tyre but she who must be obeyed was insistent we did not get out. I used my satellite phone to call Satara Camp but the switchboard operator could hardly understand my English and vice versa, but I thought she had our location and she said she would call the breakdown patrol, which I understood was based at Letaba, about thirty miles to the north. I called the breakdown unit direct five times but each time they picked it up their line cut out.

The sun was coming up, the temperature was warming and we could be waiting all day for a rescue that was not coming, so I decided it was best to fix it ourselves. There wasn't a lot of vegetation so there was no likelihood of any hidden animals surprising us, just snakes. As long as someone kept an eye on the animals, David and I could unload the car, find the wrench and jack and change the wheel. David did the bulk of the work and we were making slow but steady progress when a car stopped and a guy got out and offered to help. He made fast work of the whole exercise and was probably the best person in the Kruger Park to pull up, as it turned out he owns a vehicle maintenance company in Johannesburg. I thought he looked rather professional! We offered profuse thanks and we were on our way by 9 a.m. after calling Satara to tell the switchboard lady we had fixed it. I never did work out if she had alerted and sent a recovery team but I suspect not.

We continued south on the S90 and S41 towards Gudzani Dam. We saw our first ostriches, several elephants close to the road and an impressive-looking crocodile close to Gudzani Dam, before heading eastwards to Satara on the N'wanetsi River road, which follows the river. Several elephants and giraffes standing on the road eventually moved off to let us pass! We eventually got to Satara, one of the largest camps in the park, where we stayed eight years ago. After checking in, we made our way to our rondavaals, which are pretty basic but comfortable cottages with air conditioning, shower and WC plus a table, kitchen and sink outdoors on the veranda.

'Well, let's get some breakfast, or is it lunch?' asked Sharron, after checking in and a sardonic drawl from the back seat replied, 'I thought it was dinner, I've been up so long!' (David).

'Yes,' replied Sharron. 'It's certainly been an adventurous day.'

'We're not even halfway through it yet!'

I dozed for a couple of hours after lunch before waking up mid-afternoon. Sharron was keen to go on a drive so I said I would accompany her, and Lisa was keen to come if she could drive, which I thought was a good idea as she has her driving test in the week after returning to England.

Traffic congestion in the Kruger!

Before leaving the camp I called Tony to see if he would be listening to Yeovil at Rushden on the radio, but with no reply I called my ninety-year-old mother and told her how to find the League Two latest scores page on Teletext. I said I would call her around half-time and she should have the scores for Yeovil at Rushden and for the games involving Southend, Scunthorpe, Macclesfield and Swansea.

As Lisa drove out of the camp I was hoping that our old Conference rivals, Rushden, weren't going to screw us this season just as they did four years ago when overhauling us to win the Conference. Since then Rushden have been up to League One, been relegated back to League Two and this season, while Yeovil have been sitting proudly on top of League Two, Rushden have been flirting dangerously with relegation back to the Conference. It would be ironic if Rushden (third from bottom) were now to upset us again just as they frustrated our promotion four years ago.

Lisa enjoyed driving the big seven-seater Toyota around the Nsemani Dam circuit and was very bubbly. We saw a giraffe with its cute calf, two zebras and some buffalo. We watched an elephant strip all the foliage off ground bushes and then use its trunk to feed itself. I think, of all the animals in the Kruger, elephants are my favourite, especially in a herd and with their calves.

We visited a couple of water holes and then I called my mother using the satellite phone. My mother said all the matches were 0-0 but she had missed the Scunthorpe score and had subsequently lost the page when she checked the league table after getting the scores! I was in the middle of the Kruger, on a satellite phone, directing my ninety-year-old mother in England back to Ceefax page 302 and the football index, so she can return to the latest scores page just to see how Scunthorpe were doing! I was getting more and more frustrated but Mum finally found the page again and read out: 'Swansea v. Cambridge 0-0. Rushden v. Yeovil 0-0. Scunthorpe v. Macclesfield 0-0.'

She told me the league table showed Southend top with seventy-four points, Yeovil second with seventy-two points, Scunthorpe and Swansea on sixty-eight and Macclesfield with sixty-seven. That told me Southend played last night and won, so their run is continuing, and Yeovil are off the top after three months, but hopefully only for a day. I said Macclesfield had some tricky away games to negotiate and today's game at Scunthorpe was clearly one of them. If they draw and we can secure a win at Rushden, we would be six points ahead of both Scunthorpe and Macclesfield with five games to go. A win today could be colossal for Yeovil.

My mother said there were thirty minutes left and I told her I would call back after the games were all over and she had time to check the results. As it was, she kept the latest scores page up and tracked the time of all the goals! Not bad for ninety.

Once we were back at our rondavaal in Satara, I called my mother again. I had a very uneasy feeling about this. We couldn't beat Rushden in our last Conference season when they were top and we were second and now we were top in League Two and there was a gulf of twenty-two places between us, so it will be ironic if they do trip us up.

As the phone rang in England I was dreading and fearing the worse. At least Mum would give it to me up front and straight. 'Give me the worse,' I said.

'2-0,' she replied.

'To Yeovil?' I forlornly asked, knowing the answer.

'Rushden I'm afraid, with two late goals.'

Swansea beat Cambridge 3-0 but at least Scunthorpe and Macclesfield only drew 0-0, which in effect means both dropped two points and each only made a point up on us today. Good old Mum had checked the league table.

	Pts
Southend	74
Yeovil	72
Swansea	71
Scunthorpe	69
Macclesfield	68
Lincoln	65
Darlington	64

And Macclesfield have an away game at Oxford this week in hand.

'Thanks, Mum,' I said and hung up.

I knew things were not going well but after winning at Boston last week, who would have thought that the sum total of games at home to Notts County and away to lowly Rushden would be zero points? If Macclesfield get a point at Oxford there will be three teams within three points of us, and one poor result for us and a win for two of them would put us out of an automatic promotion spot. I can't believe it.

We are now off the top on merit after three months, and not just because another team had played on a Friday. How ironic if we collapse and end up in the play-offs. Southend are in outstanding form, Swansea are inconsistent but getting some results and Macclesfield and Scunthorpe are both reasonably solid, although Scunthorpe have only got one point from their two games this week, which is some compensation for our dreadful results.

As I went to bed, after a good dinner in the Satara restaurant, I had to wonder whether Yeovil's dream of the championship had died after three months in the top spot. For sure, Southend must now be the favourites and how disappointing it is to write those words. After failing to take advantage of our easier fixtures the remaining five will certainly pose a considerable challenge, as all our opponents have something to play for and we have no 'easy' fixtures left.

Rushden & Diamonds 2 Yeovil Town 0

Team: Steve Collis, Andy Lindegaard, Terry Skiverton, Efe Sodje, Adam Lockwood, Paul Terry, Lee Johnson, Darren Way, Arron Davies, Marcus Richardson, Phil Jevons

Subs: Bartosz Tarachulski (51 for Richardson), Andrejs Stolcers (60 for Jevons), Kevin Gall (82 for Tarachulski)

Subs not used: Chris Weale, Michael Rose

Attendance: 3,726

Position in League after match: 2nd

Arron Davies, You're a Star!

Saturday 9 April 2005 – Mount Sheba Hotel, South Africa
Yeovil v. Mansfield Town (League Two)

We are staying at the Mount Sheba Hotel at an elevation of 5,600ft in the Northern Drakensberg, about sixty miles east of the Kruger Park. We left the Kruger on Thursday after nine days, much longer than most visitors spend but well worth it as we had some outstanding viewings, including last Sunday when we saw all the 'big five' (rhino, lion, leopard, elephant and water buffalo) on the same day! We ended up with two excellent leopard viewings. Sharron and I also saw two wild dogs, which are rarely sighted, when we went out late one afternoon from Lower Sabi.

However, perhaps the best sighting was Chris and Linda Elsworth from Charlton Horethorne – yes, the same Chris Elsworth who I walked past twice on the

Kathmandu to Doha flight on 31 October! On Wednesday afternoon Sharron and I had gone out from Lower Sabi and soon discovered a lion sitting on the road in front of us! We also saw a rhino and, as we drove away from Mondozi Dam on a dry and dusty track, we passed a car coming towards us and Sharron said 'That was the Elsworths.' I did a quick U-turn, drove like a madman and caught them up as they pulled into the Mondozi viewing area. As Chris got out of his car I wound down the window and said in my most authoritive and formal South African accent, 'Excuse me sir, but if you are going to get back to camp by 6 p.m. you must restrict your stay here to no more than three minutes.'

Chris laughed. 'My God man. First in Doha and now here. I don't believe it!'

We met up when we got back to Lower Sabi and had a very pleasant evening with Chris, Linda, Sharron and Sarah splitting a bottle of wine on our veranda overlooking the Sabi River, and then we enjoyed our final Kruger buffet. This time I managed to avoid mistaking the custard for salad dressing in the subdued lighting and pouring it all over my salad!

The other highlight of the past week was a night's stay at the Sabi Sabi Private Game Reserve, only fifteen miles away from Londolozi where we stayed two weeks ago. They had also offered a complementary and discounted package and really pulled the stops out to impress us. They gave Sharron and myself the President's Lodge, complete with a private pool, but the pièce de resistance was the biggest bathroom I have ever seen. It must have been at least 30ft x 40ft with two WCs, bidet, chaise longue and an incredible double bath. Unbelievable. The President's Lodge normally retails for £600 per person per night!

However, the best feature was our ranger guide Urrike and her tracker, July, named after the month he was born! Urrike was in her mid-twenties and a slight girl who had tremendous love, affection and knowledge of the Bush and its ecology and animal life. Urrike had a degree in Entomology from the University of Pretoria and was South African to the core, having only left the country to visit nearby Swaziland and Botswana, and she was undoubtedly the best ranger I have ever met. July was an outstanding tracker and at night using a spotlight he picked out birds asleep on a branch, scorpions on tree bark and chameleons hidden in the trees as we drove along at 20kmph along bumpy tracks! The highlight of our two drives was spending forty minutes following and moving with five lions across the grassland near our camp.

We left Sabi Sabi yesterday lunchtime and drove to the Mt Sheba Hotel, located fifteen miles from the historic and picturesque gold-mining settlement of Pilgrim's Rest. With the colder temperature and fires in our room, David thought this was more like a country hotel in Devon and commented: 'This doesn't feel like South Africa.'

I woke at 7 a.m. today and got up to do some writing, until we went for a substantial breakfast served in the pavilion by the swimming pool. I was keen to try and get a fair bit of writing done today but it didn't really happen. When we were here eight years ago Sarah and Lisa had their first games of squash and all the kids wanted to play again, so we spent a couple of hours playing each other on the squash court.

I had hoped to get a couple of hours on the internet before today's matches kicked off but hadn't factored in playing squash. It was now after 3 p.m. UK time and Yeovil had kicked off against Mansfield, so I gave Tony a quick call, thinking this would be the last time that I would be monitoring Yeovil from afar. Next week I will be cheering

Two pacey wingers! Kevin Gall and Arron Davies celebrate Arron's spectacular solo opener against Mansfield.

Yeovil on at Kidderminster. I could hear the crowd noise in the background as Tony answered.

'Good news, Michael. 1-0. Goal of the season from Arron Davies, who ran fifty yards and put it in the corner from the edge of the box. It was a great solo goal.'

I've said it before but Arron Davies is top class. He does this far too often for it to be coincidence, and he is clearly going places with or without Yeovil. No wonder Rupert Lowe only wanted him to come to Yeovil on loan until Gary Johnson called in the favour that Rupert owed him for placing Marian Pahars with Southampton!

However, Tony explained it wasn't exactly one-way traffic, as Mansfield had already missed a penalty that Steve Collis, who had replaced Chris Weale after the Notts County defeat, had saved well. Tony said we were playing 4-3-3 with Jevons, Davies and Gall up front. 'Why no Bartosz?' I asked.

'Apparently he is recovering from a knock,' said Tony.

Paul Terry was playing central midfield, with Lee Johnson and Darren Way either side, and the back four was Michael Rose, Efe Sodje, Terry Skiverton and Adam Lockwood who, after an injury plagued season is finally getting a few games. Tony said Sodje looked shaky and it was he who gave away the penalty, but Yeovil were playing far better than in recent games. I asked Tony how Macclesfield did at Oxford in their midweek game in hand. 'They drew,' he replied, which is good because that's two points dropped as far as I'm concerned. Tony closed by saying we should win but we needed to be careful. I said I would call back at half-time.

I went to reception to see if I could use the internet as I wanted to read the BBC and Yeovil websites and check the league table. The receptionist said she was busy using the hotel's only computer with internet access and could I could come back after 6 p.m. (5 p.m. UK time, when the games would be over)? No I can't, I thought.

I explained I was writing a book about one of England's leading football teams (!) and I'd be happy to wait if I could just have a quick ten minutes now to check some information. I knew the hotel records listed us as VIPs (they were providing us all with a complementary stay) and she was happy to acquiesce. Thank you kind lady and, please note kids, if you don't ask, you don't get. Sometimes it pays to be a pushy bastard as long as you are nice with it!

Once on the internet I read with interest that Sodje, who gave away today's penalty, was also at fault for Rushden's first goal last week. Are my hopes concerning him misplaced? Is he past his sell-by date and that's why Huddersfield let him go?

I quickly checked the current League Two table before today's matches, which was as follows:

	P	Pts	GD
Southend	41	74	+21
Yeovil	41	72	+18
Swansea	41	71	+19
Scunthorpe	41	69	+18
Macclesfield	41	69	+14
Lincoln	41	65	+18
Darlington	41	64	+6
Northampton	41	64	+6
Wycombe	41	60	+7
Rochdale	41	57	0
Mansfield	41	56	+5

So Swansea have come back from the dead and Lincoln are well and truly in the shake up, which means they will be really up for it for our last match of the season – indeed Wycombe (H), Southend (A) and Lincoln (H) would not be anyone's choice for last three matches, and Wycombe have the best away record in the league. I hadn't realised that today's opponents Mansfield still had an outside chance of a play-off spot.

I could have wept when I saw that our outstanding goal difference, which was worth an extra point, has disappeared, along with our supremacy in the league. It is now only third best in the league, inferior to Southend and Swansea and equal with Scunthorpe and Lincoln. Just five weeks ago we were within a ninetieth-minute goal by Peter Beagrie of going eight points clear of Scunthorpe in second place! How have things changed so quickly? Defeats against the likes of Bury, Notts County and Rushden have knocked us for six. Today's game is absolutely vital, so let's hope we can build on our 1-0 lead.

I'd been putting it off. The second half was soon to be underway so I checked the half-times. Cambridge 1 Darlington 1, Grimsby 0 Wycombe 0, Lincoln 0 Swansea 0 (so if we win and Swansea lost we could have a four-point lead over Swansea), Northampton 1 Scunthorpe 2 (ugh) and Yeovil 1... oh no!... Mansfield 1. Please, not again!

And why no Southend and Macclesfield? I checked the fixtures and they are playing midweek in a fortnight because Southend were in the LDV final today. The good

A magnificent penalty save by Steve Collis against Mansfield confirms why he won the 'keeper's spot.

news is one of them will drop points when they play each other. The bad news is if we lose or draw today Southend will be in front and have a game in hand. They would then be very heavy favourites to win the title with only four games left. After so long on top, winning the title is important. Sure, it will be great to go up but going up without being champions will be an anticlimax. Having said that, after our recent results perhaps we should be grateful for going up in any shape or form!

I let the kind receptionist have her computer back and went to the lawn outside our room and tried to call Tony. I wanted to tell him to call me when there was a goal. So far, whenever it is 1-1 at half-time and I am in South Africa and I have asked Tony to advise when there was a goal, Yeovil have always won. I know it has only happened once, against Boston, but everyone knows superstition and routine is the most important factor contributing to the right result. Brendon Owen's books on Yeovil will tell you that!

I could not get through but my phone rang and it was Tony calling me back.

'Everything is happening here. When you tried to call me Mansfield took the lead from a penalty but while I was calling you back Yeovil have equalised! The crowd is really getting into it now.'

I could hear that for myself over the phone and I told Tony to call me when there was a goal. The signal was weak and unreliable in our room so I put my phone on a chair on the lawn about twenty feet from our room and, despite the chilly breeze, left the door open so I could hear it ring, or so I thought. About twenty minutes later Sharron, who was reading in bed upstairs, called down, 'Isn't that your phone ringing?' God – my hearing is bad as the phone was on loud ring! I went out and picked it up.

'Michael, I called to tell you Yeovil took the lead but while it was ringing they've scored a fourth. Jevons got the third and Rose the fourth with a free-kick and, wait a minute, Gall is clear through… we must score… saved. This is a crazy game. Yeovil are pressing with virtually four up front.'

'Who scored the second goal, Tony?'

'You know, I can't remember, there's so much going on. I'll call you when it's over.'

Tony called when he got home. 'It was 5-2 Michael. A late goal from Darren Way, who also got the second ,and we are back on top by one point.'

Clearly this was very much the 'old' Yeovil. Take the lead, go behind, come back and score five, and seven goals in total in the game. So, ho hum, things are back to normal with a resounding win against a team that still had some hopes of a play-off place. And, as a bonus, we have reclaimed the top spot, even if by default, as Southend did not play today.

I did some writing for an hour or so and then we went to dinner. Looking around the dining room I counted thirty-nine guests, thirty-seven white and two black. All the serving staff were black. The head waiter was white. I thought that summed South Africa up and one can see it will be a long time if ever before there is a redistribution of wealth in this country.

To date I have reported on thirty-nine of Yeovil's matches from afar and I have watched eleven in person. Now, as the climax of the season approaches, I will be home in the UK for our last four games – Kidderminster away, Wycombe at home, Southend away and Lincoln at home. How is the season going to end? In order of probability it has to be one of the following possibilities:

1. Promoted either second or third.
2. Promoted as champions.
3. Fail in play-offs.
4. Promoted via play-offs

If we don't go up automatically I cannot see us going up via the play-offs. And while we are on predictions, I checked my handheld computer. We have got seventy-five points from forty-two games. I had predicted seventy-six at this stage two months ago but felt we would close out with three wins and a draw at Southend and finish with eighty-six points. If we did we would definitely go up automatically and probably as champions, but I now think ten points from the next four games may be a touch optimistic.

Back in the room at midnight, I planned to write but instead watched the closing play of the rain-delayed third round of the US Masters golf, always one of the world's outstanding sports events year in year out. A consistent Chris DiMarco was three shots ahead of a charging Tiger Woods.

My word. Is it a year since Phil Mickelson won that epic duel with Ernie Els, which I watched in Thailand while a convalescing Sarah and Lisa slept? That was at the beginning of my year working and travelling overseas, and now I am undecided if I am going to extend it for a second year. For the short term I am very much looking forward to being back in the UK for the final four games, after my season-long odyssey that has taken me to fifteen countries. At least I won't be hanging onto a satellite phone trying to follow our matches.

Yes, it has all come down to the final four games that will make or break our season and I will be there to experience all the anguish or elation in person.

Yeovil 5 Mansfield 2

Team: Steve Collis, Adam Lockwood, Terry Skiverton, Efe Sodje, Michael Rose, Paul Terry, Lee Johnson, Darren Way, Kevin Gall, Phil Jevons, Arron Davies

Subs: Andrejs Stolcers (82 for Gall), Marvin Brown (87 for Jevons), Kevin Amankwaah (88 for Lockwood)

Subs not used: Chris Weale, Colin Miles

Goal-scorers: Arron Davies (5), Darren Way (53) (81), Michael Rose (71), Phil Jevons (72)

Attendance: 6,471

Position in League after match: 1st

Stuttering at Kidderminster

Saturday 16 April 2005 – Aggborough
Kidderminster Harriers v. Yeovil (League Two)

I arrived in England today after three weeks in South Africa so I can see Yeovil's last four games in their quest for the championship. David and I spent the last four days at Sun City, about two hours north of Johannesburg, after Sharron, Sarah and Lisa flew home last Monday. We had a good time relaxing around the pool and doing not a great deal other than reading, listening to music and keeping ourselves amused with a tennis ball and frisbee.

As he is tall I managed to get David into the casino, despite his being underage, and we played blackjack together for an hour, which gave him a big buzz. He managed to lose 475 rand (about £43) but to his credit he made it last a lot longer than I did!

We landed at Madrid at 7.45 a.m. this morning after an overnight flight from Johannesburg and I immediately switched my mobile phone on as I had asked Sharron to text me the result of the Southend game, which was played last night. It was fantastic news: Southend 0 Leyton Orient 1! This was Southend's first defeat in fourteen games (and indeed only their third in their last twenty-three League games) and it could not have come at a better time for Yeovil! Instead of reclaiming the top spot as expected, Southend are now one point behind us! If we can win today we will go four points clear, which will put some pressure on Southend's game in hand, at

Macclesfield next Tuesday! Furthermore, we cannot fail to be top tonight unless we lose badly at Kidderminster and Scunthorpe win heavily!

While we are waiting in the terminal to catch our flight to London I thought if we were to lose today and Scunthorpe were to win, there could be four teams within one point of each other, which would make the final three-week run-in very fraught. I checked my notebook where, a few weeks ago, I had scribbled down the remaining fixtures for all the leading teams. It's not going to be easy for Southend because they have to go Macclesfield in a few days, followed by Oxford away, Yeovil at home and Grimsby away. They are capable of winning all those matches but none of them will be easy. I think I can be fairly certain that at 8 a.m. I was the only person at Madrid Airport checking League Two fixtures for the balance of the season!

The flight to Heathrow was uneventful and Sharron and Sarah were waiting to take David home via Brighton (dropping off Sarah at Sussex University) while I picked up my rental hire car and drove to Kidderminster for the game.

My initial impression when driving into Kidderminster was that it was a small town (not so different from Yeovil then!) and that surely our promotion push could not come undone here. However, Kidderminster are one off the bottom of League Two and facing a drop out of the Football League. They need a win here today to stand any chance of catching Rushden up, so we were in for a competitive game, that's for sure.

I entered the tidy and attractive ground, with stands on all four sides, and we weren't going to be wanting for support as about a third of the crowd were probably Yeovil fans. The lady next to me told me that after last week's great win against Mansfield she had no doubt that we were going to win today and was quite certain that promotion was assured. I wish I was as confident!

We lined up in a 4-3-3 formation with Paul Terry playing a holding role in central midfield. Kevin Gall and Arron Davies were playing up as strikers either side of Phil Jevons and Bartosz was on the bench. Not a good move Gary – he's our talisman! For the third successive game, Steve Collis has the nod over Chris Weale, which is a fair reward for his loyalty, patience and ability. The game was very scrappy at the beginning and the only highlight for Yeovil was a Phil Jevons free-kick that went close. This was the first time I had seen Adam Lockwood this season as he has been desperately unlucky with injuries. Bandanna-clad Efe Sodje started in central defence but a few desperate clearances reminded me of the fears I had in South Africa about whether he had been unloaded by Huddersfield because he was past his sell-by date?

As the half went on Kidderminster came more into the game and the game deteriorated into being quite a scrappy affair. The high and wide clearances being made by Terry Skiverton and Efe Sodje weren't the most constructive way of starting our own attacks! Kidderminster were playing four and sometimes five in midfield and their players seemed quite big, strong and powerful. Our three in midfield were being bustled out of it. The most dangerous opportunity came from Kidderminster, who didn't have a forward good enough to get his head on what should have been a very productive cross from the right wing. Kevin Gall wasn't getting into the game at all as a striker, and he is just not effective playing up front with his back to the goal because, when he does get the ball he has to turn before he can start moving with any pace. It is painfully obvious to me that Kevin is far more effective breaking with speed from

A towering leap by bandanna-clad Nigerian international Efe Sodje clears the ball at Kidderminster.
Terry Skiverton and Paul Terry look on.

wide midfield and I am not quite sure why Gary Johnson has been playing him up front as part of a 4-3-3 formation in recent weeks.

There was a big melee when Kidderminster got upset that we took a free-kick when they thought Yeovil should have just passed the ball back to them. Shades of Plymouth! Collis made a good save from a Kidderminster free-kick and then a bit of Arron Davies magic in the fortieth minute resulted in the Kidderminster goalkeeper making a good save. Steve Collis was called into action again on the stroke of half-time, when he had to make a save at the feet of a Kidderminster forward. Gary Johnson was going to have to make some adjustments at half-time, because clearly Yeovil had been bossed for much of the first half.

A half-time announcement told us that Macclesfield were losing at Lincoln but Scunthorpe were winning at home to Cambridge, which was hardly a surprise. I noticed that Kidderminster had only lost two of their last nine games, so perhaps it was not really surprising that we weren't dominating them in the first half, as they have had fewer defeats than us over in recent games!

I called Tony at half-time, which was a reversal of roles. Tony was quite optimistic and didn't have any problems with the 4-3-3 formation, as he had watched the demolition of Mansfield last week.

The second half started and Yeovil were soon on the attack. Kidderminster were not playing as effectively as in the first half, and I was beginning to think there was a chance we could sneak a result. Adam Lockwood was taken off and replaced by Kevin Amankwaah, and he was either making a fourth in midfield or playing as an attacking full-back. Within minutes of coming on Kevin Amankwaah made the difference because, after a strong run on the right wing, his cross was only cleared as far as

Terry Skiverton. He fed the ball through to Arron Davies, who carried it forward a few feet before slotting it neatly in the corner of the goal.

Thirty minutes left and I called Tony to tell him we had taken the lead. It would be great if we can get all three points but I commented to Tony that I didn't want Lincoln beating Macclesfield and coming to Huish Park for the final game with the incentive of converting a late run into an automatic promotion place.

We were now playing much better but we needed another goal to kill Kidderminster off. Good, Bartosz was coming on! I think we are a much better team when Bartosz is on the field and it had to be for Kevin Gall, who had been totally ineffective today. But it wasn't! It was Phil Jevons that was taken off!

Bartosz was instantly involved in holding the ball and then distributing it effectively to his fellow strikers. Finally Kevin Gall came into the game with a run from midfield, which only confirmed that he has to be running at the defence to be effective. Kevin Amankwaah was involved in another threatening attack and there was no doubt that his introduction has been a very significant factor to the changed tempo of this game. Gary Johnson's substitutions do make a difference more often than not and Yeovil were now well on top. Tarachulski was making a significant contribution to the effectiveness of the forward line. He held the ball up well again and set up Arron Davies, who blasted the ball over the crossbar. However, with seven minutes to go, the game was turned on its head. A poor header by Kevin Amankwaah sent the ball looping backwards into the penalty area and it fell to the Kidderminster substitute, Rowle, who volleyed it neatly into the goal. It was 1-1 with just seven minutes to go. What a blow!

No sooner had the game restarted than Kidderminster were on the attack again, and a great header beat Collis, hit the post, rolled back behind the goalkeeper and out into the penalty area to a Kidderminster player, who had an open goal and incredibly managed to lift it over the crossbar! That has to constitute one of the misses of the season anywhere and could cost Kidderminster their league place at the end of this season if failing to take three points today turns out to be decisive.

The game then erupted into a frenzy of action. In truth, the first eighty-two minutes had been pretty undistinguished but, for the last ten minutes, the ball went from end to end at a pretty frenetic pace and it was all I could do to keep my notes up-to-date as chances went begging at both ends. It was amazing, but a game that had been so bereft of clear chances could have resulted in about six goals in the last ten minutes! An Amankwaah run launched a dangerous Yeovil attack and we squandered a chance when we had two on two. Lee Johnson had two excellent chances in the last five minutes, one of which was desperately beaten away by a defender on the line. However, at the other end Kidderminster also looked sure to score on a couple of occasions. It was an exciting end but not very good for my nerves!

Collis made a second marvellous save in the closing minutes to fingertip a Kidderminster header from a corner over the crossbar, and the incredible pace continued into the four minutes of added time! The game was going from end to end and was like a five-a-side match, with the number of chances that were now being created. Eventually we were all rather relieved to settle for a 1-1 draw when, ten minutes ago, it looked as though we had three points in the bag. Shit!

Lincoln won, which wasn't really what we wanted to hear as a draw against Macclesfield would have been much better, and Scunthorpe also won 4-0. By my calculations there are now four teams covered by just four points. Someone is going to lose out and it is not at all inconceivable that it could be Yeovil.

In truth, we didn't play that well today and, although we had every opportunity to get three points, Kidderminster fully deserved a share of the spoils if not an outright victory, which they should have secured in the last ten minutes. Let's hope we can improve on this performance at home to Wycombe next Saturday.

On the way back I listened to Radio 2, and both Luton and Hull secured promotion from League One to the Championship today. How well Hull have done, to go from League Two to the Championship in successive seasons, after languishing in the bottom league for several years. It was only eighteen months ago when we held Hull to a pulsating 0-0 draw at the KC Stadium and, of course, it was my journey from Everest to watch Yeovil play Hull on the penultimate Saturday of last season that triggered this book.

When I got home I was pleased to meet Sarah Marino from New Zealand, who was staying with us for a few days. Wow, has it really been sixteen years since Sarah worked for us? It's gone in a flash. In sixteen years' time I'll probably be dead and Yeovil should be in the Premiership with a new stadium!

Kidderminster Harriers 1 Yeovil Town 1

Team: Steve Collis, Adam Lockwood, Efe Sodje, Terry Skiverton, Michael Rose, Paul Terry, Darren Way, Lee Johnson, Kevin Gall, Phil Jevons, Arron Davies

Subs: Kevin Amankwaah (58 for Lockwood), Bartosz Tarachulski (76 for Jevons), Andrejs Stolcers (87 for Gall)

Subs not used: Chris Weale, Andy Lindegaard

Goal-scorer: Arron Davies (61)

Attendance: 4,014

Position in League after match: 1st

Missed Chances

Saturday 23 April 2005 – Huish Park
Yeovil v. Wycombe Wanderers (League Two)

I tried to catch up with some work in my office at home before going in to Salcombe House at 10.30 a.m. to read the reports that I had commissioned our US and UK concert sales managers to write over the last forty-eight hours with regards to the pros and cons of running our own European music festival. I read their impressive report with interest and then we had a very productive meeting. I enjoy Casterbridge meetings when we are planning something new rather than solving existing problems as I am at my strongest in matters that are entrepreneurial.

Our long-serving American-based US sales director, Peter, a fanatical Liverpudlian who has been with us since 1988, had agreed to come to today's game, but now had second thoughts because he wanted to work out all the bonuses for his sales team. He finally agreed to come, so it was good to see that the chairman's arm twisting can still sometimes be effective! However our American concert tours manager, Ron, begged off to continue work on the festival project. Ron obviously does not subscribe to Patrick's philosophy that the best way to enhance his career prospects is to accompany the chairman to watch Yeovil!

Before the match started Gary Johnson got a big cheer, because it had been announced two days ago that he had signed a new three-year contract and was committing himself to Yeovil, whether we go up or not. I thought the timing was not coincidental and should be very motivating for the players. I was not really surprised that he is staying because where else in England do you hear the manager's name get chanted enthusiastically by the fans every match? 'Hey Gary Johnson, do you love the town?' cascades down from the terraces three or four times a game, encouraging Gary to return the salutations of the crowd, who immediately burst into applause. You never see that happening for Jose Mourinho or Alex Ferguson and I think that must be worth at least another £50,000 per annum minimum on top of his contract as far as self-esteem is concerned. So keep singing guys!

I felt this could be a tricky game because we found it difficult to break down Wycombe earlier in the season and they still have an outside chance of making the play-offs. There were a couple of veterans in the Wycombe team because, at the age of thirty-nine, Steve Claridge, formerly manager of Weymouth is leading their line, and Rob Lee, the former England international, is in midfield.

We didn't start that positively as we looked a bit edgy early on and I'm still not sure about Kevin Amankwaah or Efe Sodje at this stage. We were still playing 4-3-3, with Arron Davies and Kevin Gall up front either side of Phil Jevons, despite it being so unproductive at Kidderminster last week. I much prefer it when we line up 4-4-2.

After twenty minutes Wycombe were well on top and 'Weymouth reject' was being sung every time Steve Claridge went near the ball! Kevin Gall finally got in the game and forced a corner after a typical run, but Terry Skiverton's resulting header was ruled to be an infringement, which gave a free-kick to Wycombe. Phil Jevons didn't really have any support and there was no-one up front capable of holding the ball up while other players get into position.

Someone's had a radio and there was good news – Swansea were already losing 1-0 at Bristol Rovers, which was always going to be a tricky game with the local derby element.

Michael Rose did not look to be his normal reliable self and, after an already shaky start, then gave the ball away twice within five minutes. I seem to remember that Michael Rose wasn't impressive in his first matches back from injury and it seems that when he has a bad game he has an absolutely stinker! Rose gave the ball away yet again and Terry Skiverton was forced to foul to retrieve the situation. That gave Wycombe a free-kick about three or four yards outside our box and a magnificent strike found the top right-hand corner of the goal. There was absolutely nothing that Steve Collis could do about it and it was no more than Wycombe deserved. However, Swansea were still losing and the news goes out that it was Oxford 1 Scunthorpe 0, which softened the blow a bit.

No sooner was the game restarted than we were on the attack. Lee Johnson collected the ball about four yards outside of the penalty area and sent an absolutely unstoppable shot in on the goal, which passed just below the crossbar and found the back of the net. Wycombe had their lead for all of a minute and that was an absolute cracker. We were right in line with Lee as he let rip and the ball was in the back of the net before you could say boo. Yeovil were now playing far more positively and the good news from Bristol was that Rovers were now leading Swansea 2-0.

What's this? The thirtieth minute and Tarachulski was coming on. Great – and it's Michael Rose that is coming off. I applaud that substitution because Rose was having an absolute nightmare and it was undoubtedly best just to get him off the pitch and tell him to forget about this match. Nothing had gone right for poor Michael Rose today and I applaud Gary Johnson for not hesitating and getting him off even though it was still early in the game.

Paul Terry moved out of midfield to full-back, Arron Davies and Kevin Gall dropped back to join Darren Way and Lee Johnson and we were now playing 4-4-2 with Jevons and Tarachulski up front. Good. It won't do a great deal for Michael Rose's confidence but it was the right substitution and we have switched to a much better shape. So half-time comes and we were drawing 1-1, whereas Scunthorpe and Swansea are both losing. A win today would really put us in a good position and allow us to take advantage of Scunthorpe and Swansea's slip-ups.

I go down the front and chat with Peter, Aaron, Patrick and Tony. Peter seems to be thoroughly enjoying the match now he is here. Aaron, also from our US office, enjoys all sports and is familiar with soccer from his time living in London as a political intern at the House of Commons.

When the the second half recommenced Darren Way was soon through and shooting on goal but he scuffed his shot, which just goes past one of the uprights. However, that was a good promising start and Yeovil were playing much better, putting together some flowing moves. I thought we were likely to score soon, but then a great shot from a Wycombe player fully thirty yards out was only just saved by Steve Collis. We had already had three good chances in the first ten minutes of this half and, after fifteen minutes, Phil Jevons was put through but just failed to control the ball as he advanced into the box. Another Yeovil attack ended up with Phil Jevons shooting into the side netting when everyone in the Yeovil College stand were on their feet, thinking it had gone in.

After hitting the woodwork Kevin Gall went off and was replaced by Andy Lindegaard. Phil Jevons seemed to be involved in a lot of our moves. First the goalkeeper dived at his feet and the ball rolled agonisingly past the post! Minutes later Paul Terry found him with a very clever ball and Jevons shot wide. Tony, who had moved up from the front at half-time to join David and myself, said 'This is unbelievable. We have had five chances and could be 6-1 up!'

Paul Terry was involved in a lot of the action as Yeovil continue to press on. Next up was Darren Way, who burst through only to shoot narrowly wide. As I looked at my watch I thought that, as the game progressed, Efe Sodje had looked much better today. There were fifteen minutes left, which could be absolutely crucial for our season. It could be on the line if we don't get three points from this game. We have had six clear-cut chances in the first thirty minutes of the second half. Statistically, that means we should get three more in the next fifteen and hopefully we can put one of those away.

With about twelve minutes left Gary Johnson takes Phil Jevons off and puts Stolcers on. I am not sure if it's ever a good idea to take your top scorer off because, however uninvolved, he can always pull something out of the bag and score. On the other hand, Phil could have scored a hat-trick this half and maybe Gary thinks it is just not going to be his day.

Lindegaard and Stolcers both went close with efforts and chance number nine, by my reckoning, was a Terry Skiverton header. Then Kevin Amankwaah was on the edge of the area, he had the whole goal lined up, he picked his spot and blasted the ball... which was cleared off the line! This was absolutely impossible. We must have had ten chances in the second half and I've rarely seen a team dominate so much without scoring.

With just three extra minutes to be added on, there was a rare Wycombe attack that looked quite dangerous. The ball rolled past Collis and actually glanced the outside of the post. My God! We could have ended up with nothing!

And that's that. When the final whistle blew we had just one point from this match. That was a real disappointment, although it was encouraging how well we played in the second half. We could not have done more without scoring.

We ask someone with a radio about the other results. Scunthorpe drew 0-0 at Grimsby but Southend, who won impressively at Macclesfield on Tuesday to regain the top of the table, lost 2-1 against Oxford (great!) and Swansea lost 2-0 to Bristol Rovers. So, unbelievably, although we dropped two points, one point is enough for us to regain the top of the table with a single goal giving superiority over Southend with both teams on seventy-seven points. Those other games certainly provided a great set of results as far as Yeovil were concerned, so there is some light at the end of the tunnel, or should I say after ninety minutes! However, we have only got five out of the last twelve points, which isn't exactly convincing form for an end-of-season promotion run-in.

So it is all going to come down to next week and I really don't fancy Southend away. If we lose that surely we will lose all chance of being champions and Southend will be the strong favourites. It is so close that we could go from first to fourth next week if we don't get a good result at Southend with Scunthorpe (seventy-six points) just a point behind Yeovil and Southend, while Swansea (seventy-four points) are just three points behind.

Tony drove us back to Sherborne and I worked in the office for a couple of hours, before Sharron came in and we all went out for dinner at the Rajpoot. Normally staid Ron amused us by reporting that the American television adverts for the popular drug Cialis (a successor to Viagra) end with the announcement: 'If your erection lasts for more than eight hours, please consult your physician!' That's what Yeovil have desperately needed over the last few weeks – some staying power!

Yeovil Town 1 Wycombe Wanderers 1

Team: Steve Collis, Paul Terry, Lee Johnson, Michael Rose, Kevin Amankwaah, Terry Skiverton, Efe Sodje, Arron Davies, Darren Way, Phil Jevons, Kevin Gall

Subs: Bartosz Tarachulski (31 for Rose), Andy Lindegaard (72 for Gall), Andrejs Stolcers (75 for Jevons)

Subs not used: Chris Weale, Colin Miles

Goal-scorer: Lee Johnson (25)

Attendance: 7,421

Position in League after match: 1st

Ecstasy at Southend

Saturday 30 April 2005 – Roots Hall
Southend United v. Yeovil (League Two)

So this is the day that could finally make or break Yeovil's season. If Southend were to beat us comfortably and Swansea and Scunthorpe were both able to win at home against Bristol Rovers and Shrewsbury respectively, which is more than likely, it is not inconceivable that Yeovil could go from first to fourth in the bat of an eyelid. And then, if we have to beat Lincoln at home next week just for a chance of automatic promotion, I would not necessarily fancy our chances after our recent run of form.

My spin on this match is that, if we win at Southend, we must be favourites to be champions. If we draw we should be fairly certain of going up automatically, but if we lose the best we can probably hope for is third or possibly the play-offs.

I found out to my horror last weekend, after the match against Wycombe, that today's match was long since sold out and I did not have a ticket. Patrick and I were planning to go together and so last Sunday I rang the chairman, John Fry, and explained that I couldn't be writing a book about Yeovil's season and not have a ticket for what could be the crucial match. I still had a number of players I wanted to interview as well. I got the message on Monday that a ticket would be waiting for me at the ground and that I could come in on Tuesday and Thursday and interview the players that I needed to meet.

When I went in on Tuesday Gary Johnson was in a jovial mood and said he had no problems in me coming in on Tuesday, Wednesday and Thursday and grabbing players as and when I saw them, as long as I didn't spend too long with each one of them. This was a contrast to the previous week when Gary said he would prefer me not to come in and disturb the players with interviews. I think Gary was beginning to feel the pressure after Kidderminster!

I noticed that we obviously have some very cerebral football players at Yeovil because every day either Andrejs Stolcers or Bartosz Tarachulski were playing chess in the restaurant with Stuart Housley. Chess and not Gameboys rule at Yeovil! The players that I spoke to were all quietly confident that they would be able to get a result at Southend, although I think most of the fans are travelling with some trepidation! Over 1,600 Yeovil fans are going to Southend, so the team will have good support and it should be a fantastic occasion.

A very positive note during the week was that, at the annual PFA Awards last Sunday, five Yeovil players were voted into the league select team that was chosen by their peers. This was the clearest indication most of the players playing in League Two think Yeovil is the strongest team. Only Luton, with six selections for the League One team, had more players named in any of the league teams. So congratulations to Chris Weale, Michael Rose, Darren Way, Lee Johnson and Phil Jevons. So much for my pre-season concerns about whether we could be competitive this year with both Darren Way and Lee Johnson in midfield. That has been put to bed once and for all with both making the league select side, and it just goes to show how little I know about football and why Gary Johnson is a successful manager!

For once in my life I wasn't late and I got to the ground about ten minutes before departure time and clambered aboard coach two. I ended up sitting next to a young guy reading *The Sun*. I was hoping to identify some sports publishers from the *Writers & Artists Yearbook* during the journey but, after a while, I started chatting with Andy, who worked at a factory near Ilchester. We talked about Yeovil (of course) and discovered we both had a great passion for popular music. We had both been disappointed not to secure tickets for this year's Glastonbury Festival.

We got on very well, despite our disparity in years, and found out that we would both like to see the back of Tony Blair as quickly as possible, although Andy was a factory worker who intended to vote Conservative and I was a company chairman who would never vote Conservative!

When we arrived at Southend the ground was bathed in sunshine and, while we were waiting for the match, we discussed the likely Yeovil team. We came up with Collis in goal, a back four of Amankwaah, Sodje, Skiverton and Rose, a midfield of Arron Davies, Lee Johnson, Paul Terry and Kevin Gall with Bartosz and Phil Jevons up front. No Darren Way? The reason we omitted him was because I knew he had been sent home sick during the week when I was at the ground, and there was no sign of him warming up, so it was clear that he was not going to play.

Two-thirds of the stand at our end of the ground was full of Yeovil supporters and, about twenty-five minutes before kick-off, I noticed Martin Brooke, David's tutor from Sherborne School, arriving and I gave him a wave. Andy went back to his seat and we wished each other luck. With fifteen minutes to go the ground was pretty much full all around and a great atmosphere was building up.

The teams finally come out with fireworks being let off, and there were two surprising changes to the Yeovil team that we had not anticipated. Despite making the league select team, Michael Rose was on the bench, replaced by Colin Miles at left-back. Interestingly, I had interviewed Colin this week and he had confirmed that his preference was very much to be in the centre of defence rather than at left-back! Andy Lindegaard had replaced Kevin Gall on the right of midfield, which was again ironic because both Steve Thompson and Andy himself confirmed this week that he had finally made one position his speciality, rather than being a utility player who could play anywhere, and that position was right-back! And here he was, playing on the right side of midfield in the most important match of the season for Yeovil! So when push comes to shove it seems that the management and coaching staff still see Andy as the consummate utility player!

I think these were brave changes made by Gary Johnson and I totally applauded them. Michael Rose has been a consistent player all season, but when he has a bad game he has an absolute stinker, and last week he did not look at all impressive. Everybody knows that Colin Miles is as committed a player as there is at the club and I thought it was a good move to have Andy Lindegaard in for Kevin Gall, who has not impressed in our last two matches. I was also really pleased that Bartosz was starting the game. We play so much better when he is on the pitch as he holds the ball up and distributes it well. I am really not a fan of 4-3-3, with three smaller players up front, and I think we are so much more effective with four in midfield and two wide midfielders breaking forward.

The game was finally underway, with a strange-looking Yeovil midfield of Andy Lindegaard, Lee Johnson, Paul Terry and Arron Davies. One would normally have expected to see both Darren Way and Kevin Gall playing, but I had no problems with this line up and didn't think they would let us down. Southend had the best of the opening minutes, being on the attack without ever threatening but, after five minutes, a Yeovil free-kick led to a Skiverton header that went narrowly wide, and the first real chance had been Yeovil's.

Several of the younger fans in front of me seemed to be more concerned with either waving one finger, two fingers or a wanking gesture at the Southend fans while chanting 'Fuck off Southend.' They really are mindless morons. I can't really understand what the point of coming is if they only want to taunt and antagonise the opposing fans!

Paul Terry had started the match particularly well, both in holding up the ball and distributing it from midfield. I called Tony and told him that we were playing well and more than holding our own, and he told me that Scunthorpe were already 1-0 up. He thought our line-up was defensive, with two right-backs playing but, on the other hand, given that Amankwaah likes to go forward and Lindegaard is playing in midfield, one could say that we've got two attacking players on the right side! Paul Terry has been playing at full-back recently, but he was signed as a central midfielder and likes going forward, so I hadn't considered it to be a defensive line-up but I understood why Tony had made the observation. After Tony hung up I told the fans behind me that Scunthorpe were leading 1-0, and they reported that Swansea were also 1-0 up.

By midway through the half we were more than holding our own and the Yeovil fans were singing: 'Top of the league – we're having a laugh.' There was an extensive period of Southend possession but again without being particularly threatening. Bartosz was holding up and distributing the ball well and Kevin Amankwaah was looking dangerous when he broke forward on the right. Bartosz led an attack by running forward with the ball at his feet and put Paul Terry through, who was tackled just as he was pulling

Yeovil-born Andy Lindegaard was recalled for the vital game at Southend.

the trigger. It seemed that our most effective attacks were coming through Bartosz. I don't want to harp on about this but I really think he is the key player for Yeovil. I don't think that I am alone in this assessment either, because the fans clearly adore him and chant his name, somewhat akin to Hugo Rodrigues last season.

We were playing well and I thought the game was shaping up to be similar to Swansea away, tight but quite absorbing, despite there not being too many clear cut chances. All we needed was a goal to set us on our way.

I noted that Kevin Gall and Michael Rose were both warming up and thought it must be really hard for them to miss this match as both of them have been pretty much regulars all through the season. However, they have been dropped on merit because neither played well last week. Well done, Gary Johnson.

Oh no! Bartosz was going off! What was the matter? It couldn't be lack of fitness to take him off after thirty minutes. That was a real blow. Marcus Richardson replaced him, and at least we were keeping our 4-2-2 shape. This is the first time I have seen Marcus. He is a tall striker and, as soon as he came on, he was involved in the action. When Paul Terry set him up he juggled the ball over the goalkeeper and into the net but the referee disallowed the goal for an infringement on the goalkeeper. Well, at least Southend know that he is a threat and he has made his presence felt. I thought we were doing especially well as three of the five Yeovil players who were nominated for the League Two select team weren't on the pitch, which is a fine testimony to the quality of the squad that Gary Johnson has assembled.

The highlight of the first half came with about ten minutes to go, when a beautiful cross from Andy Lindegaard was met on the edge of the goal area by Arron Davies, who sent a powerful header across the goal that was heading for the corner of the net when Flahavan, the Southend goalie, managed to palm it around the post at full stretch. It was a fantastic save and the best move of the match to date.

'Heeeeeey, Gary Johnson, do you love the town?' comes rolling down the terrace and out pops Gary from the dug-out to return the salutation to the fans. The Yeovil fans clearly think Gary walks on water.

It was a good game and we were holding our own but the positive feeling is somewhat diluted when one of the guys behind me tells me Scunthorpe are now 2-0 up! There were only two minutes to go until half-time, so for heaven's sake, Yeovil, don't give up a goal now, I thought. But no sooner had I written that than Southend were awarded a dangerous free-kick on the edge of the Yeovil box in the added-on time. And what's this? Marcus Richardson was going off and Andrejs Stolcers came on. Clearly Richardson had been injured, which was a shame because he had been very much involved in the last fifteen minutes, using his size to give the Southend defenders something to think about. It was bad luck to have had to use two substitutes before half-time.

The Southend free-kick rebounded off the wall for a corner, which was cleared, and we had successfully negotiated the first half. So, 0-0 at half-time, and I thought we had produced a solid performance. However, we did need to win this match to have the chance of the championship in our own hands, as Scunthorpe were certainly not going to lose today.

During the half-time break I pushed along one of the rows in front of me and spent the time chatting to Martin Brooke, who had to teach a Latin class this morning and then came up by train. He wasn't particularly optimistic as far as the second half was concerned as he couldn't see where a goal was likely to come from. His assessment was probably influenced by his disappointing recent visits to Rushden and Kidderminster. However, I thought we were doing ok, although Andy's predictions that this match had draw written all over it might yet turn out to be correct. As I went back to my seat to prepare for the second half I was thinking we really needed to win so we can go into the last weekend of the season in first place. Come on Yeovil!

Now that Efe Sodje is playing in front of us I've got the opportunity to look at him from close quarters and he proceeded to have a very good second half. I thought his positioning and covering were particularly impressive. As the half progressed we were doing well and certainly giving as good as we got, until Terry Skiverton gave the ball away to a Southend player, which immediately set up an attack, but Sodje saved the day. Skiverton is playing well but he always seems to have a tendency to give the ball away to an opponent in a dangerous position once or twice in every game!

An update comes from behind. Scunthorpe are 3-0 up and Swansea have had a man sent off but are still leading Shrewsbury 1-0 at home. I really don't like the fact that Scunthorpe have scored three, because their goal difference is going to be significantly superior to ours if we end up level with them. I'm rapidly doing the calculations. If we get one point today and Scunthorpe get three we will be one point behind them, and goal difference will only be a factor if we draw and they lose next week.

Another Southend attack has a man free on the far post but, with the goal at his mercy, he heads right into Collis's hands. He could, and should, have scored as that was Southend's best chance of the game and a let-off for Yeovil. For the first time in the match I thought that Southend should have taken the lead. When Southend next attacked, Efe Sodje shepherded the forward out toward the wing but he still managed to pass the ball inside and the Southend forward in receipt cut across the edge of the Yeovil penalty area and made space for himself to shoot. The ball went narrowly wide. We have now had two good Southend attacks within five minutes. Let's hope they are not going to get on top.

As the results stood, midway through the second half, with Southend and Yeovil drawing and Scunthorpe and Swansea both winning, two points could be covering all four teams next week and we could be going into the last match of the season with no-one certain of automatic promotion. Amazing!

Kevin Gall came on for Andy Lindegaard rather than Arron Davies, which was a bit of a surprise, and ran virtually the length of the pitch before shooting wide. I think it is good to use Kevin's speed late in the game when the opposing defence are beginning to tire. With less than ten minutes to go, my heart is thumping, Collis distributes the ball well and a Yeovil attack quickly builds up. An Arron Davies long-range shot is deflected and it falls to Phil Jevons, on his left and inside the box, who neatly dispatches it into the back of the Southend net! Goal! Absolutely incredible and it came from nowhere!

Our stand goes completely mad, with everyone jumping up and down, shouting and hugging each other. The guy on my left, who hasn't said a word to me, grabs my hand to shake it. Everyone is excited, laughing, shouting and the noise is amazing. Three sides of the ground are in abject silence but our stand has gone absolutely wild. It was only a couple of minutes ago that the young lad behind me said we've only got to hold on for another ten minutes and I replied that it was in those ten minutes that Andrejs Stolcers scored at Swansea. I'd been thinking this game was very much along the pattern of the Swansea match, but I really didn't expect Phil Jevons to score in the eighty-third minute just like Andrejs did at Swansea.

The fans were singing 'We are top of the league' and 'Yeovil till I die,' and I called Tony. When he answered there was no way either of us could hear the other, so I just held the phone up in the air and I am sure that 'Yeovil till I die' told it's own story. I shouted down the line, not knowing whether he could hear me or not, that, with seven minutes to go we had taken the lead and everyone had gone crazy. I called home as well to tell Sharron and David. I thought I could hear David, but I'm not sure if he could hear me.

Just minutes after Yeovil scored, Southend had a volley go narrowly wide and I'm not convinced that Collis had it covered, but that was their last serious chance and we managed to hold on for the seven minutes of regulation play with the Yeovil fans in fine voice. The noise was amazing and everyone was waiting to see how much time the referee added on. Three minutes! I put my stopwatch on and in fact he added four and a quarter minutes, with the Yeovil fans baying at the ref, whistling, doing anything to get the game finished before eventually it was over!

We had actually won, and chances are we were going to be promoted. Amazing, and we are in the driving seat as far as the championship is concerned. It was incredible and I had tears in my eyes. Everyone was slapping each other on the back, jumping up and down and totally happy about everything.

Gary Johnson, Steve Thompson and all the subs come on the pitch, there were hugs all round and you would think that we had won the cup final. I was trying to work out the permutations as Scunthorpe had certainly won and, the last I heard, Swansea were hanging on as well but it was difficult to concentrate as the noise was deafening. The players were hugging each other on the pitch and Gary Johnson was clenching and pumping his fists he was so excited. The Yeovil players were saluting their fans and the crowd were singing back their praises.

Everyone in the crowd was really excited because I think pretty much all had gone to Southend with some worries after our recent poor form. Although Southend have lost two of their last three matches since they were beaten in the LDV final, they had previously gone fourteen games without defeat and had been the only team to briefly supplant Yeovil at the top of the league since early January. After our recent poor run of results it was a magnificent performance to come to Southend and get a result, and our usually porous defence had an absolutely outstanding game.

While all the excitement was going on I was trying in my head to calculate what the situation was, and it seems to me that, although promotion is not guaranteed, it would take a peculiar combination of results now for us not to go up. If we were to lose next week by two or three goals and Scunthorpe got a draw or win and both Southend and Swansea won well we could end up in the play-offs. However, if we get a point against Lincoln we are up, irrespective of other results, and if we win we are champions! League Two is the only league where the winners are not known, as Luton have already been crowned champions of League One, in the Championship Sunderland are champions and Chelsea only need a point from their remaining four games in the Premiership to be champions.

Of course, if we had had managed just one win from either Kidderminster away, Rushden away, Bury at home and Notts County at home (just to make reference to four recent dismal results!) we would be champions today. Indeed, if we had secured the title previously I would have been in Morocco today leading a Great Walks trek, but I wouldn't have missed this for anything! I have been going to sports events around the world since 1960 and this has to rank as one of the most exciting and emotional of them all.

This was Southend's last home match of the season, which was why their fans were not leaving and all the Southend players were sitting abjectly in the centre of the pitch, waiting for the Yeovil celebrations to tone down so that they can proceed with their end-of-season awards. I had some sympathy for them as this is exactly what happened to us in our final home game against Hull last year, and we had to wait for their fans to stop celebrating that they had clinched promotion before we could have our end-of-season awards.

Eventually their awards ceremony started, but it was obvious the Yeovil fans weren't going to stop singing for a while! After collecting their awards the Southend players did a somewhat desultory lap of the ground and were gracious enough to applaud the Yeovil fans as they came past, and our fans sportingly responded to their gesture.

All of a sudden the chant is going up 'Bring on the Forest'. Obviously Nottingham Forest have not won today, and so have been relegated to League One. Nottingham Forest were European champions in 1979 and 1980 and were playing in the Premiership until recently, and if eight years ago anyone had predicted that Yeovil, in the former ICIS League, would appear on a fixture list with Nottingham Forest in anything other than the FA Cup they would have been certified!

I finally made my way out of the ground and, once I got to a quiet section, rang Tony, who was already over the moon because Southampton had beaten Norwich 4-3 with a goal two minutes from the end! When I told him it was Jevons he said 'That

Jubilation as we depart Southend with one hand on the trophy.

man has really delivered this season and it just shows you should never take your leading goal-scorer off.'

I congratulated John Fry and thanked him for enabling me to get a ticket. I then made my way back to the coach and shook hands with Andy, who was waiting out-side and we chatted about the match. We agreed we are not quite there yet, although if either Scunthorpe or Swansea had failed to win we would be up already, and now we only need one point.

We got in the bus when the driver was ready to go and I quickly took a picture of all the fans cheering. We made our way out through Southend with several Southend fans sportingly clapping our coach as we went past, and the gesture was returned with gratitude from many of those sitting in the coach. Poor old Southend. They have been in this division for fourteen years and they really thought this was their year. I guess they won't be too excited about going into the play-offs, given their two defeats in the LDV final at the Millennium Stadium. It seems as if it's going to be Yeovil, Scunthorpe and one of Swansea and Southend who will go up automatically.

The old timer in the seat in front of us tells us he's been supporting Yeovil since 1950 and has a fashion sense that seemed to have spanned all five decades. He has a shirt and tie covered by a pullover, with a T-shirt on top and a jacket on top of that! I remember seeing him at Hull last season. My voice was hoarse but everyone was in a great mood because hardly anyone had thought that we would be coming away from Southend with such a positive result. We had hoped, but hope doesn't necessarily mean we expect!

I had some sympathy for the Scunthorpe fans, who probably thought they had done enough with a 4-0 win against Bristol Rovers (so much for my pre season pick for League Two) to put themselves in a position to be top of and probably crowned champions next week, only to be denied by a late Yeovil goal, which means that we are still one point ahead of them despite an inferior goal difference. Ah well, Scunthorpe have had plenty of late goals this season that have kept them close to us and, truly, what goes around comes around!

We got home at about 9.30 p.m. and I left Andy in the car park looking for his new girlfriend, who had come to collect him, and I drove to Sherborne to pick up David after a Rock Soc event, and then made my way home with him.

The first thing I did was go to the internet to check the league table, and my calculations were correct. We could still fail to get automatic promotion if we lost at home to Lincoln by two goals, Scunthorpe drew and Swansea and Southend both won 3-0 away, but they do have tricky games. Lincoln have no chance of getting an automatic promotion place and, win, draw or lose at Yeovil, are going to end up either fifth or sixth, so a good performance at Yeovil will not even mean that they have a lesser-ranked team to play in the play-offs. Sky Sports' website says that Yeovil are 'almost guaranteed to be promoted' and the BBC states that we only need one more point.

As I'm feeling pretty tired, I go to bed before midnight, which is early for me. It was absolutely fantastic to be present today and now we really do have one hand on the trophy. Who could have predicted we would be going into the last match of the season with four teams in with a chance for both promotion and the championship? However, there is no doubt we have the inside track.

Roll on next week!

Southend United 0 Yeovil Town 1

Team: Steve Collis, Kevin Amankwaah, Terry Skiverton, Efe Sodje, Colin Miles, Andy Lindegaard, Lee Johnson, Paul Terry, Arron Davies, Bartosz Tarachulski, Phil Jevons

Subs: Marcus Richardson (29 for Tarachulski), Andrejs Stolcers (44 for Richardson), Kevin Gall (73 for Miles)

Subs not used: Chris Weale, Michael Rose

Goal-scorer: Phil Jevons (83)

Attendance: 11,735

Position in League after match: 1st

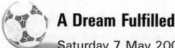

A Dream Fulfilled

Saturday 7 May 2005 – Huish Park
Yeovil v. Lincoln City (League Two)

So here we are, the final day of the season and, amazingly enough, no-one knows which of the four front-running teams is going to be champions, which two are going to be automatically promoted, and which is going to have to go into the play-offs. The position this morning is that Yeovil are one point ahead of Scunthorpe and three points ahead of both Swansea and Southend. Scunthorpe have a better goal difference than us but we have a better goal difference than Swansea and Southend.

The permutations are endless but one thing is certain: if we win, we will be champions. If we draw and Scunthorpe win, then they will be champions. If both Yeovil and Scunthorpe draw then we will be champions and if we draw and Scunthorpe don't win, we will be champions whatever Swansea and Southend do. However, if we lose, Scunthorpe won or drew and Swansea and Southend both win, and we were to lose by two goals and they were both to win by three, then we could actually end up as having to go into the play-offs.

As a former betting man I would have to say it is highly unlikely that a combination of results could occur that would preclude us from being promoted. I calculated the odds of us losing, Scunthorpe drawing or winning and both Swansea and Southend winning as about 50/1. When you take into account the required goal margins in all three games it is closer to 750/1. I am therefore assuming that we will be going up whatever happens today, and I took the liberty of placing a full-page advert in today's Yeovil programme, stating this book would be a unique record of Yeovil's promotion-winning season. I was fairly confident I would not end up with egg on my face, but I did not risk tempting fate by saying championship-winning season! That is just how I run my businesses. I will take managed risks when the balance of probability is in my favour.

For once in my life I was determined not to be late, and had arranged to meet Tony at 1.15 p.m. in Sherborne. We would go to Yeovil together and, just as I was leaving home, Paul Quayle rang and asked me if I was going to the match. 'Yes of course Paul,' I replied.

'Do you know anyone who wants a ticket?' he said.

'Give me five minutes, Paul,' I replied, and I tracked down Patrick in Taunton. He had been disappointed that he hadn't been able to get tickets for Southend or today's match, and when I asked him if he wanted to come he said, 'I'll be in the car within five minutes Michael.'

I rang Paul to say I had found someone for the ticket and we met at Tony's house and drove in together. The sky was blue and indeed Yeovil's conditions for playing football, but in fact when we parked at the Brewer's Arms we realised it was quite windy. As we drove into Yeovil we could hear Brian Laws, the Scunthorpe manager, on the radio talking down Yeovil's prospects and saying we were not in good form. He fully anticipated that, if Scunthorpe won at Shrewsbury, they would claim the championship.

This sounded to me like wishful thinking and I was reminded of Ian Atkins' comments prior to our playing Bristol Rovers here a couple of months ago. You never hear

Party atmosphere for the final game against Lincoln.

Gary Johnson running down opposing teams as he lets our football do his talking, and that's the sort of manager that I prefer to have running my club.

We met Patrick and entered the ground not long after 2 p.m. The ground was already half full, with a fair number of supporters at the Lincoln end, so they had come down in significant numbers. I bumped into Martin Brooke, the Classics teacher from Sherborne and showed him the full-page advertisement that I had placed in the programme. He asked me to put him down for two copies of this book! I also saw Martin Holley from Lloyds TSB Yeovil. He was enthusiastic about the book and apprehensive about today's game!

We discussed the prospects for the match and I told Patrick that one of the omens that was in Yeovil's favour was that every time he and I had attended the last match of the season together and it was against Lincoln we had won! Patrick went for Yeovil 1-0 but I was more optimistic and went for 3-1.

The team was announced, which had Steve Collis in goal, and a back four of Kevin Amankwaah and Colin Miles as full-backs with Efe Sodje and Terry Skiverton as the two central defenders. I had no idea about the shape and Darren Way would not tell me when we spoke on Thursday, but the remaining six were Darren Way, Lee Johnson, Paul Terry, Arron Davies, Kevin Gall and Phil Jevons.

The first goal will be absolutely vital in this match because it could really dent Yeovil's confidence if we have to win to be champions and go a goal behind, whereas if we could get an early goal we could hopefully impose ourselves on the game.

The teams came out to a packed stadium bathed in sunshine and the conditions looked perfect, but the reality was there was a very strong wind swirling around, which wasn't going to make it that easy to play.

When we lined up for the kick-off I was not sure if we were playing 4-4-2 or 4-3-3. Arron Davies and Kevin Gall both lined up on the halfway line and my heart sank as I thought it was 4-3-3 but, as soon as they started playing, Tony said he thought it was 4-4-2!

It was clear for everyone to see that Lincoln were a very big team. Most of their players were 6ft or more and I hoped this wasn't going to be one of those games when we were muscled out of it. Our tallest player was Kevin Amankwaah but, if you put him to one side, I certainly think that if either Terry Skiverton or Colin Miles had been playing in the Lincoln team they would have been among their smaller players!

I told Tony I had been very impressed with Sodje last week at Southend and I really hoped that Kevin Amankwaah would remain steady today and not make any mistakes at the back. Tony was pleased we'd have the wind behind us in the second half and be attacking the favoured Westland end.

Most of the early pressure and good play came from Yeovil and I noted there were six players on the pitch who had played in the Conference for us. After five minutes it was clear that we were playing 4-4-2, with Darren Way on the left side of midfield and Kevin Gall on the right. Arron Davies was up front with Phil Jevons as Bartosz had broken a toe last week at Southend.

Colin Miles brought the ball out of defence and hit a great ball with what I said to Tony had to be 'the best left foot in League Two'. Phil Jevons was playing quite well and, considering he doesn't have a big physical presence, he was managing to hold the ball up well and laid it off to Arron Davies who shot over. Phil has scored twenty-eight goals for us and yet one or two in the row behind were already complaining about him looking lethargic and not moving enough around the pitch! Some people are never satisfied!

A good Kevin Gall run sets up Kevin Amankwaah, who puts in a great cross and certainly the early pressure was all coming from Yeovil. However, not long after that, an innocuous wide ball to the Lincoln number eighteen Derek Asamoah set him clear and we were grateful that his resulting shot was narrowly wide.

In the first ten minutes Kevin Gall was involved in four separate runs down the right-hand side and this, for me, is his position, even though yesterday he told me he preferred playing just off the striker as a forward! Phil Jevons, Colin Miles and Darren Way were involved in a good move that resulted in a corner, then Kevin Gall delivered the ball to Arron Davies who shot narrowly wide. However, Asamoah broke away again and looked a very useful player. The Yeovil defence would need to keep a close watch on him.

Kevin Amankwaah opted to demonstrate his ball-control skills by deciding to dribble the ball out of defence past two Lincoln players rather than getting rid of it quickly. Amankwaah is either a very unorthodox full-back or a very defensive winger. I haven't quite made up my mind which yet!

A great pass from halfway put Darren Way through, and then Kevin Amankwaah set Kevin Gall off on another run. Yeovil's pressure was such that, halfway through the first half, I felt a Yeovil goal would not be long in coming. However, a quick passing

Efe Sodje's status as a Yeovil legend is secured with his two goals against Lincoln which deliver promotion and the League Two championship.

movement from Lincoln showed that our defence was still susceptible to a quick counterattack and a Lincoln player was clear bearing down on our goal. Thankfully, Collis came out very quickly and bravely dived at his feet, smothering the ball. Within seconds the Westland Stand were singing 'There's only one Stevie Collis.' Just like last season, Steve Collis has been rewarded for his patience and is ending the season as our first-choice 'keeper, though this year on merit and not as the result of a Chris Weale injury. Clearly Lincoln were very dangerous on the breakaway and we really needed to get a goal to give us a bit of comfort. I thought Phil Jevons was looking quite sharp. He is not a particularly strong or fast player but his great skill is being able to bury many of the chances that come his way.

Terry Skiverton turned up on the left wing but, when he tried to pass inside to Lee Johnson, he instead gave it away to a Lincoln player. It seems that every match Terry gives two or three balls away and, on this occasion, he left the defence exposed, but Efe Sodje very cleverly broke up the attack. His performances in the last two games have convinced me that he has been an excellent signing.

Yeovil were playing well again and, in the thirty-fourth minute, Phil Jevons was brought down about five yards outside the penalty box. Was this a Lee Johnson special? No, step forward Colin Miles, who rattled the Lincoln crossbar but, it came out rather than went in. A great effort and it's that left foot again!

As we heard that Swansea were leading 1-0 Arron Davies bore down on the Lincoln goal. The ball rolled clear and, although it initially looked as if Phil Jevons had given up on it, his last-ditch effort forced a corner. Arron Davies put in a very good corner that was cleared out towards the left wing where Darren Way picked it up. He hit a hard cross back across the face of the goal towards the far post, and Efe

Sodje came in at some speed, met it on the volley and the ball was in the roof of the net. And two minutes into injury time at the end of the first half. Great!

Seconds later the ref has blown for half-time and we are going in with a 1-0 lead. What a fantastic time to score the goal. That's not going to do much for Lincoln's confidence and Yeovil are really going in on a high. We've got one hand on the championship. We're almost there.

At half-time Tony repeats that he thinks Yeovil have played really nice football considering the conditions and then my phone is ringing. It's Brian the plumber, ringing to ask what the score was and if Yeovil were winning. That's the first time he's done that this season and he told me that Scunthorpe and Southend were still 0-0 and Swansea were 1-0 up. It may well be that even a draw would be enough to make us champions, but hopefully from here we can cement the win and go up in style.

Before any time at all we were underway for the last forty-five minutes of the season, which would hopefully deliver a successful climax to almost a year of hard work, effort and commitment by everyone at the club.

There was a real scramble in front of the Lincoln goal, which went on for at least ten seconds, and there seemed to be at least three occasions when all a Yeovil forward had to do was stick out his foot to put it in the net, but somehow Lincoln survived. Tony commented that was just a foretaste of what was to come: 'We are attacking the home end with the wind at our backs and it's all set up for us to go up as champions and in some style,' he said.

A Darren Way pass went to Phil Jevons, who set up Arron Davies for a run on goal and an impressive shot, which was blocked by the goalkeeper. This just confirmed that this was probably going to be Yeovil's half. We've done very well these last two games after that long, dodgy run from February until Kidderminster. Another goal and I think we will be there.

Two impressive Yeovil attacks went through Kevin Amankwaah, who is playing on the right wing more than right-back and I need to go on record and say that I think Kevin has won me over. I really wasn't sure about him from the very first time I heard his name mentioned on the radio when he made his debut at Macclesfield, but today he was playing like a Trojan. It was another Kevin Amankwaah burst that set up Lee Johnson, who fed the ball through to Darren Way who was brought down in the box. It seemed rather innocuous and most of the crowd were surprised when the ref awarded a penalty. Step up Phil Jevons, who duly dispatches another very stylish penalty to the right of the goalkeeper, who had no chance. We were 2-0 up and that second goal definitely came as a result of a sustained period of Yeovil pressure.

This was the Yeovil of old. We've got our game back and now we can finally say it's for real and we are going to be champions. That was now certain. We were well on top and I thought this could easily end up as 3-0 or 4-0. There was now wave after wave of Yeovil attacks bearing down on the Lincoln goal. Lee Johnson attempted an ambitious scissors kick after the ball was flicked on to him and Terry Skiverton put a great ball through to Kevin Gall, who unleashed Paul Terry for a run on goal.

The news goes around that Grimsby are 1-0 up against Southend. Poor old Southend. They briefly supplanted us at the top but, ever since their LDV final defeat, have hit a dodgy run of form. After having the chance to go top when they hosted us last week it looks as if they will be the team dispatched to the play-offs if they lose to Grimsby and Swansea stay ahead at Bury.

We were really playing well now and the football was flowing. Kevin Gall fed Phil Jevons who set up Arron Davies, and it was only the goalkeeper who kept out the third. A Colin Miles header tested the 'keeper and balls are being sprayed around from the Yeovil midfield using the full width of the pitch. This was truly exhibition-style football. Lincoln were being run ragged by both Kevin Gall and Arron Davies continually bursting through from midfield. Arron Davies went on a memorable run, evaded two tackles and should have scored but his final shot let him down.

A rare Lincoln attack was blocked by Kevin Amankwaah, (he can defend as well!) who retained possession, broke free and set up Kevin Gall, who put in a fantastic cross that was headed behind for a corner. The corner comes in, Sodje leaps high and whips his neck around, and the ball was looping over the goalkeeper and sitting in the back of the net. It's 3-0 and it's all over. We are the champions! Sodje was ecstatic and he ran along the touchline giving high fives to all the Yeovil substitutes.

The crowd was announced as 8,855. We've come a long way since the days in the Conference when we thought a good crowd was 2,500!

Michael Rose was brought on for Colin Miles. It was good that Rose should be part of the day because, for most of the season, he has been a steady performer, but I now wonder if he is one who may not make the transition into League One, even though he has been voted into the League Two select team.

Colin Miles was really excited. He gave Gary Johnson a big hug and pumped his fist at the crowd at least a dozen times. He was so happy and so he should be, He's been with Gary Johnson since he was a junior at Watford and has been a great servant to the club. Andy Lindegaard was brought on for Kevin Gall, who got a rousing reception that he well deserved. He has been a crowd pleaser all season and had a big game today, while Lindegaard was unfortunate not to retain his place after playing well at Southend. Still, it's horses for courses and Kevin Gall had been a continual thorn in Lincoln's defence today However, everyone was pleased to see Andy on the field because he is a local boy and has been with the club for so long. It was only fitting that he should be part of this day.

One more substitution to go and, with ten minutes left, Chris Weale was brought on for Steve Collis in goal. 'Wealey, Wealey, Wealey' echoed around the ground and, again, it was only right that he should be on the pitch today as he has been Yeovil's regular custodian for pretty much all of the last three seasons, and for two years in a row has been voted the outstanding goalkeeper of League Two.

I was very pleased to see Chris Weale on the pitch so he could share in Yeovil's promotion-winning day. Indeed, I had tears in my eyes when I saw Weale being brought on, and I think this was an excellent gesture by the manager. These substitutions confirmed that Gary Johnson's man-management skills are outstanding. No wonder he is worshipped by the fans.

Yeovil were passing the ball around at will now and the chants of 'Olé' came out from the crowd with every completed pass. An announcement is made that the trophy would be presented on completion of the match. The final whistle went and finally the game, the run in and the season was over. Yeovil are champions and heading for League One. Can you believe it? Just two years after we left the Conference!

Apparently it is the Football Association's policy to take the trophy to the ground where the first-placed club were playing at the beginning of the day, but there was a lot of conjecture in the crowd as to whether duplicates had been taken to Bury, Grimsby and Shrewsbury to cover every possibility? That was academic now and the next ten minutes were spent with the Yeovil players congratulating and hugging each other, throwing themselves on the ground, saluting each other, saluting the crowd and hugging Gary Johnson, while a Coca-Cola League Two championship podium was hastily assembled in the middle of the pitch. Efe Sodje was man of the match today for his two goals, and he has been a very, very good signing. He has definitely brought out the best in Terry Skiverton.

We had played in some style, fully deserved our victory and had seized the championship in emphatic style. In truth considering we were six points clear with nine games to go and with a very easy run of fixtures before these last three tricky fixtures against Wycombe, Southend and Lincoln, we should have tied it up much, much earlier, but all's well that ends well. For sheer excitement, the fans and Gary Johnson couldn't have asked for more than to have four teams in the running for the championship on the last day of the season, nor a better resolution than for Yeovil to seal their success with a flowing victory at home. It was a fantastic climax to a great season and of course it hasn't done the prospects for this book any harm either!

In truth, today wasn't quite as exciting as last week because most fans did not go to Southend with a great deal of confidence. To pull off such a victory in an opponent's back yard against a team who could have pretty much tied up the championship for themselves was a fantastic achievement. Furthermore, the tension of the whole match came to a climax with the late goal. That was very exciting and very emotional, and it was last week, when a victory was secured against the odds, that put us into the position to secure the championship today.

After all the players came out in pairs to be announced to the crowd Terry Skiverton was presented with the trophy. The champagne was flowing, the crowd were singing and the players went on another on lap of honour.

In the festivities after the trophy had been presented, the Jolly Green Giant mascot lost his head, which ended up in the crowd and, at the very end, both Phil Jevons and Kevin Gall threw their boots into the crowd so that some lucky fans could keep them as souvenirs. Bartosz was there, with a limp from his broken toe, and his baby son on his shoulders. I really hope he comes back next year because, even though he wasn't playing today, he makes a big difference when he leads the attack.

A soaked Gary Johnson was proudly holding the trophy below us. He has now won an FA Trophy, two championships and missed out on the play-offs by goal difference in his four seasons with Yeovil. Yes, we all said, 'Gary who?' when he was appointed but we have now had one of the most charismatic and successful managers outside of the Premiership. Let's hope we can keep him and I think we have a good chance, because it is clear that he appreciates and enjoys his unique relationship and bond with the fans.

Patrick was so pleased that he was present today. As we walked to the car park he said to me, 'Do you know the last thing I said to Tony yesterday, Michael? It was "God, I wish was able to go to the match tomorrow."' So his wish had come true. And for the second year in succession we walked away together from the last day of the

Champions! Steve Collis, Chris Weale, Darren Way, Paul Terry, Bartosz Tarachukski (part hidden) Andrejs Stolcers, Michael Rose and Kevin Gall celebrate a dream fulfilled!

season victorious against Lincoln, but this year it was a victory that delivered so much more than last year's near miss.

Tony was doubly pleased because it turned out that Southampton stayed alive courtesy of a late equaliser at Crystal Palace, but this was not a day for thinking about the Premiership. It was about a team that, eight years ago, were playing in the ICIS League and who are now about to prepare for playing in League One against the likes of Nottingham Forest.

I got a lift back to Sherborne with Tony and then Paul Quayle dropped me back at our house and, after the heady achievements of the day, I never did get round to doing any work at home in the evening. It was a night for relaxation and reflection after the emotional traumas of the last two Saturdays and, before I went to bed, I thought there could not have been a more exciting or positive conclusion for Yeovil than to secure the championship on the last day of the season.

As I looked back over the season, I thought of the many places where I have followed Yeovil this year – the internet shops in Kathmandu, Buenos Aires and Pattaya, remote parts of Tibet, high mountain camps in Nepal, the flanks of Everest, vibrant nightspots in South-East Asia and South America and from the African Savannah. It's been a hectic and tiring year but one that has been held together, for me, by the pleasure of following my local team and a local team that has come good in a big way and achieved success on a national stage.

We were certainly not as dominant as we were when winning the Conference but it has been the most exciting, memorable and successful season in Yeovil's long history and without a doubt I could not have picked a better year nor a finer conclusion for going 'around the world with Yeovil Town'.

Champions! The ever-positive Patrick (left) and Paul, who followed Yeovil's progress with me in Tibet, celebrate our victory against Lincoln.

Yeovil Town 3 Lincoln City 0

Team: Steve Collis, Kevin Amankwaah, Efe Sodje, Terry Skiverton, Colin Miles, Paul Terry, Darren Way, Lee Johnson, Kevin Gall, Phil Jevons, Arron Davies

Subs: Andy Lindegaard (81 for Gall), Michael Rose (81 for Miles), Chris Weale (84 for Collis)

Subs not used: Adam Lockwood, Andrejs Stolcers

Goal-scorers: Efe Sodje (45) (78), Phil Jevons (54)

Attendance: 8,855

Position in League after match: 1st

Reflections
Thursday 30 June 2005 – Mürren, Switzerland

The heady days of late April and early May have long since passed, and the reality of completing this project dominates my life as pre-season training is getting underway. Over the course of last season I wrote and dictated over 600,000 words (longer than *Lord of the Rings,* as one rejection letter pointed out!) and now I am attempting to package the story into a coherent whole.

When I look back at the journey Yeovil made last year to secure their ambitions in the most dramatic fashion on the final two Saturdays of the season, I am full of admiration for the efforts of everyone involved. Over the season I interviewed Gary Johnson, coach Steve Thompson and virtually every squad member, and I never failed to be impressed by both Gary Johnson's motivational skills and the fact that so many of the squad appeared not just to be mouthing platitudes but had genuinely bought into Gary's dream and vision of what they could and did achieve.

Yeovil clearly have the services of one of the outstanding managers outside of the Premiership and everyone waited with baited breath in June to see if Gary would respond to Derby County's overtures. It did not surprise me that he decided to stay with Yeovil. Successful individuals in any walk of life want to be challenged, taste success and above all be appreciated. So far Yeovil have provided Gary with all these criteria. Contrary to common thought, it is not always about money.

The last three years have seen Yeovil take what I believe are only the first steps of a remarkable journey as they have travelled, via two championships, from the Conference to League One. I have no doubts that over the next two to three years Yeovil will secure a play-off place in League One and that within three to five years we will be watching Championship football at Huish Park Stadium.

Two years ago in the Conference we saw players like Lee Johnson, Darren Way,

Chris Weale, Gavin Williams and Kevin Gall produce outstanding performances way beyond their years and the standard expected from Conference teams. This year the first three were voted into the League Two select team, Gavin Williams was sold to West Ham for £250,000 and Kevin Gall beat Wayne Rooney, Cristiano Ronaldo and Peter Crouch to be voted Player of the FA Cup Fourth Round. Terry Skiverton, Colin Miles, Adam Lockwood and Andy Lindegaard produced performances in the Conference worthy of a higher stage and next year they will be on that stage with Yeovil. Yeovil's Conference-winning squad of 2002/03 was without doubt one of the finest non-league teams in history and their story is far from complete.

There is no reason why Yeovil cannot be playing Championship football within five years, and then Gary Johnson will have the opportunity to really make history and be the first manager to take a club from the Conference to the Premiership. And if that is not the sort of achievement he and his family can dine out on for generations, I don't know what is!

Ten years ago, when we were relegated to the ICIS League, talk of Yeovil in the Premiership when we were playing Bishops Stortford would have been laughed all the way to an institution. Today it is not quite so fanciful, is it? Only two more promotions to go! However getting to the Championship is not a fait accompli. The manager needs ongoing support from a dedicated, ambitious but necessarily pragmatic board and the club needs to be planning now for the future. However, I believe it is a dream that can and will be achieved.

I am not religious and I do not use the words lightly when I say that, at Yeovil, we have been truly blessed with the quality of attacking football laid in front of us in recent years. Anyone watching Gavin Williams in the Conference knew he had every chance of playing international football and he has already made the Welsh squad. Arron Davies will surely wear the red shirt of Wales one day and Lee Johnson, Darren Way, Paul Terry, Colin Miles, Chris Weale and Steve Collis all have the skills and ability to make the transition from Conference to the Championship, a journey spanning four divisions and a tribute to their mentor, Gary Johnson.

When I look back at last year, I realise how fortunate I was in that, although I only saw fifteen games, I watched almost all of our outstanding performances – the mauling of Oxford 6-1, the comebacks to demolish both Shrewsbury and local rivals Bristol Rovers 4-2 and the three outstanding performances against our promotion rivals, winning 2-0 at Swansea on New Year's Day, the tremendous 4-3 victory against Scunthorpe in a real rollercoaster of a match (as were so many) and the absolute pinnacle when we won 1-0 at Southend, which meant the ultimate prize was finally ours for the taking. Make no mistake, if we had not won at Southend, it could have been Yeovil and not Southend consigned to the play-offs.

The games at Swansea and Southend will always be remembered in any history of the club, as indeed we will remember the sporting applause by the home supporters acknowledging our performances against their teams. I think all Yeovil fans will consider the outstanding four teams in the league were the four promoted and were glad that Southend in particular eventually secured the promotion via the play-offs that their season's performance warranted.

We played champagne football against Lincoln to demonstrate that we were probably the best footballing side in the lower two divisions. And that's no hollow statement; after all, Yeovil were England's highest scorers last year, so stand aside Chelsea!

In truth, it if hadn't been for losing our way with totally unexpected defeats at Rushden and Grimsby and at home to Bury and Notts County, together with dropped points at Kidderminster and at home to Wycombe (all this in the latter stages of the season) we could and should have won the league by a country mile and not just three points.

But we won and, in truth, two promotions as champions in three years is great going for any club. I was so pleased that, in three of the key games of the season, Swansea and Southend away and Lincoln at home, our much-maligned defence was magnificent and kept a clean sheet (we will forget the Scunthorpe game!). Indeed, everything was on the line for the last 180 minutes of the season and our defence reigned supreme, so all kudos to Terry Skiverton, Efe Sodje, Colin Miles, Kevin Amankwaah et al.

This is not the time or place to be previewing next season, other than to state I expect to be challenging for a play-off position at worst. Any reader of this book will realise I am disappointed that Bartosz Tarachulski, the very personification of a foot-balling gypsy, will not be with us next season and I think this is a significant loss, as he led the line skillfully and laid the ball off well to both Phil Jevons and the flanks. I suspect much of our season's prospects will revolve around how well we can replace Bartosz with another tall striker.

When I look back at my own year, that this book has also covered, I think I would have done better to have had extended stays in Switzerland, Canada, the US and South-East Asia rather than returning to England so often, partly to keep in close contact with Yeovil and partly because of the problems with our company, which without doubt was the downside of the year for me. I was very impressed by my first visit to South America, and Buenos Aires in particular, and my journey through Nepal and Tibet to the very high flanks of Everest was, even for someone with a lifelong love of travel and who has made a successful career of travel, very much the trip of a lifetime. It was all the more rewarding by travelling with such a congenial group of clients, many of whom will soon be joining me for a reunion in Switzerland.

I am sure that, in August 2004, whatever scenarios Gary Johnson and the Yeovil players thought might evolve over the season, the various possibilities did not include going into the final game of the season being one of four teams who could clinch the championship!

I feel privileged to have had the opportunity to share, enjoy and record Yeovil's remarkable journey from the Conference to League One and I have no doubts that the club's odyssey is far from over. Indeed, I am reminded of the words I overheard from a long-standing Yeovil fan in the Bartlett stand last year: 'I don't know what is going on with Yeovil at present, but it is something very special and I'm going to enjoy it while it lasts.'

Amen to that.

Michael Bromfield
Mürren, Switzerland
30 June 2005

Postscript

Stowell 12 October 2005

Since the above reflections were written at the end of June there has been a dramatic change in the situation at Yeovil with the sudden departure in October of manager Gary Johnson who was appointed manager of nearby Bristol City.

Any reader of this book will have acknowledged three consistent themes running throughout the narrative. Firstly, like most Yeovil supporters, I have the utmost admiration for Gary's talents and what he achieved at Yeovil; secondly the real challenge Yeovil faced in keeping Gary and thirdly my conviction that he could certainly have taken Yeovil to the Championship within three to five years.

So with constant speculation linking Gary with vacancies at a succession of Championship clubs, it was in a way not a surprise that he moved on, although I, like many others, was mistaken in thinking this his close bonds with both the community and fans would count for a lot in persuading Gary to stay with Yeovil.

However, on the other hand his departure was still a major surprise for a number of reasons. Firstly the season had just got underway, secondly it was to a team currently rated lower than Yeovil, thirdly it was to a neighbouring team, which always has the potential for a bit of added aggravation (shades of Harry Redknapp!) and fourthly, and this disappointed many fans, because Gary had indicated that there was little likelihood of a move to Bristol occurring (until an official approach was made). For a man who had spoken so often of 'trust' and 'loyalty' the fact that he had perhaps deflected speculation by giving a truthful but nevertheless misleading impression slightly tarnished his departure.

Why did Gary leave when he still had all to play for with Yeovil?

I am neither privy to his thoughts nor part of the administrative or political structure of the club but I am sure the faltering start to the season did not significantly contribute to his decision. It does now seems clear that Gary had been 'unsettled' and thinking of the possibility of moving on for some time and there was probably more substance to the Coventry and Derby possibilities than was generally appreciated at the time. At Coventry there were factors outside the club that might have curtailed Coventry potential and at Derby there was the ever-thorny problem of the role of a director of football and the associated problems of 'Who's in charge here?'

So why did Gary leave and why to Bristol City?

I think Gary may have felt the Yeovil board of directors lacked ambition and as always there are two sides to this assessment. Clearly and demonstratively the club has won two promotions in three years, has almost tripled its average attendance and has coped with the transition from Conference to League One admirably in most areas. Clearly this could not have been done without a supportive and ambitious board but pragmatic stewardship is also necessary. It is inevitable that managers always want more funds and want success quickly but sometimes it is necessary to consolidate and pause for breath along the way. I am sure both Gary and the board were looking at the same destination but perhaps had differing views on the route and timetable? I know that in my role as chairman in Casterbridge Tours many of our sales personnel think I am unreasonably conservative and cautious and that this may curtail their fast-track growth plans and ambitions. I on the other hand have the long term survival of the company and the next ten years to think about as well as the current year's sales figures and I can look back at twenty years of profits, constant growth and sufficient reserves to always ensure that we have always have a sound foundation for the future. I believe in walking before you run but that does not mean a lack of ambition. I am just careful not to trip up. Who is right? I can understand both sides.

It is clear then, that Gary was wondering about moving on for whatever reasons and I think his doubts about the future with Yeovil were certainly reinforced when early season attendances in League One were lower than the end of season attendances in League Two. Gary was also clearly irritated by a number of fans leaving games early, a point about which I am fully sympathetic. There may sometimes be justifiable reasons in for an early departure but I have never had any time for those who leave early just 'to beat the rush'. As well as disturbing the view of those remaining in this case they have clearly demoralised the manager. Together these two factors must have made Gary wonder whether the club may have already achieved its maximum average attendance in League Two and if there was no further attendance growth this could curtail funds available for additional players. Fans departing early might have made Gary wonder about the long-term commitment of some of Yeovil's support when we were losing or not challenging at the head of the table.

Or were these just convenient pegs to rationalise a wish for a change, an improved salary and a new challenge?

So in retrospect maybe a move to Bristol City shouldn't have been a surprise. Bristol is one of the major cities of England and should have a Premiership team but unlike Wolves, Derby and Coventry the fans are not used to and do not expect Premiership football immediately. Gary has been promised full control of the club from top to bottom and Bristol City is a club and city with all the potential but no immediate expectations. Bristol is of course still in a part of England that he now knows well and requires no major upheaval. Combine this with presumably, a significantly improved salary and his doubts about whether he had taken Yeovil as far as he could and Gary's move looks quite logical. 20/20 vision is a wonderful thing in hindsight!

Time will only tell if it is the right move for Gary. I was as surprised as anyone when Gary left and especially for Bristol City but now I think, given that he was unsettled, that it was perhaps not so surprising. The Bristol City fans are overjoyed to have snared such a successful and charismatic Manager but are notoriously fickle and the club has both financial challenges and a history of dissension at Board level. If he is given time it should work out for Gary but it is far from a certainty and I am convinced he could have made history with Yeovil by taking them from the Conference to the Championship.

It would be churlish for fans to rewrite history and start pointing out Gary's faults and weaknesses. Yes, some aspects of his departure were disappointing but he can always walk in Yeovil with his head held high and owes the club nothing. He delivered big time and we will always be grateful for the fruits of his tenure. Gary Johnson is probably destined to be the most important name associated with Yeovil but this is a book about Yeovil Town FC and not about Gary Johnson. And perhaps Gary's greatest legacy will be that the foundation and momentum he established was strong enough to survive his departure and indeed continue the success that Gary introduced to the club.

Whoever was to succeed Gary Johnson as manager had an impossible act to follow. Gary was popular, charismatic, worshipped and well-loved, and had outstanding media skills. On top of this there was the little matter of his winning three trophies in four years! This was not a legend in the making. Despite his departure he was and still is a legend for all Yeovil fans. However the king is dead, long live the king.

Steve Thompson has been with Yeovil for almost a decade, is a successful coach and was at the side of the master throughout his tenure. As the fans' choice, his was a popular appointment and in his early matches in charge the fans have bent over backwards to encourage him and demonstrate their support. The fans in turn have been comforted with the continuity that he represents with the past four years. If he concentrates on being the first Steve Thompson rather than trying to be the second Gary Johnson, he should do well. Continuity and team spirit is preserved, no significant upheavals or change for changes sake will be made by a new manager putting down markers to show they are in charge. The appointment of Kevin Hodges, the still young former manager of Torquay and Plymouth as assistant manager, could well turn out to be a masterstroke.

The obvious conclusion for many outsiders is that Yeovil will falter without Gary Johnson and Bristol City will tear up the leagues. However, I have a suspicion that the sentiments of the Reflections that I wrote in June are still sound and that the Yeovil story is far from complete. I know John Fry has hopes for a larger stadium and a higher league – and he has overseen two promotions already. He is still ambitious but necessarily pragmatic as well. Chris Weale, Darren Way, Lee Johnson, Phil Jevons, Colin Miles, Kevin Amankwaah, Aaron Davies, Kevin Gall *et al* are still young players and not without considerable ability. That did not change when Gary headed off to Ashton Gate and I still feel confident that within three years we will be in the play-offs.

I, like everyone else, expected this to be the season when Gary Johnson and his still young Yeovil team took their first steps towards attaining their next goal. It is not quite the story we expected but at the time of writing after our less than inspiring start that garnered just two points from our first five games and left us rooted at the foot of the table, we are now eighth after 13 games and two points away from a play-off position. It is still early days but it is worth noting that as I close this postscript we are at the highest position of our 110-year history and that certainly does not give me any grounds for immediate concern!

Indeed, I think most Yeovil fans would have been happy with our current position at the onset of the season. It may be Thomo for Gary but I see no reason for concern – indeed the future is bright, the future is green!

Michael Bromfield
Stowell
12 October 2005

Appendix 1: 2004/05 Fixtures, Results and Goalscorers

August

Sat 7	Bury	A	Lge	1-3	20th	3,171	Caceras 1
Tue 10	Darlington	H	Lge	1-1	18th	5,116	Jevons 1
Sat 14	Boston United	H	Lge	2-0	9th	5,178	Jevons 1, Tarachulski 1
Sat 21	Notts County	A	Lge	2-1	5th	5,024	Jevons 1, Terry 1
Tue 24	Plymouth Argyle	H	CC1	3-2		6,217	Johnson 3
Sat 28	Rushden & Diamonds	H	Lge	3-1	4th	5,088	Johnson 1, Jevons 1, Tarachulski 1
Mon 30	Mansfield Town	A	Lge	1-4	8th	3,826	Skiverton 1

September

Sat 4	Swansea City	H	Lge	1-0	4th	5,826	Williams 1
Sat 11	Cheltenham Town	A	Lge	1-1	5th	3,966	Way 1
Sat 18	Oxford United	H	Lge	6-1	2nd	5,467	Jevons 3, Stolcers 2, Gall 1
Tue 21	Bolton Wanderers	H	CC2	0-2		8,047	
Sat 25	Shrewsbury Town	A	Lge	2-1	1st	4,196	Johnson 1, Tarachulski 1
Tue 28	Torquay United	A	LDV1	3-4		1,610	Caceres 1, Tarachulski 1, Stolcers 1

October

Sat 2	Northampton Town	H	Lge	1-1	1st	5,944	Jevons 1
Fri 8	Rochdale	A	Lge	1-2	3rd	2,402	Jevons 1
Sat 16	Macclesfield Town	H	Lge	1-2	4th	5,313	Way 1
Tue 19	Bristol Rovers	A	Lge	2-2	5th	9,295	Williams 1, Terry 1
Sat 23	Scunthorpe United	A	Lge	0-1	8th	4,470	
Sat 30	Chester City	H	Lge	4-1	5th	5,741	Caceres 1, Jevons 3

November

Sat 6	Wycombe Wanderers	A	Lge	1-0	3rd	5,453	Tarachulski 1
Sat 13	Darlington	A	FAC1	3-3		3,698	Miles 1, Tarachulski 2
Sat 20	Southend United	H	Lge	3-1	3rd	5,839	Guyett 1, Tarachulski 1, Jevons 1
Tue 23	Darlington	H	FAC1	1-0		5,365	Way 1
Sat 30	Lincoln City	A	Lge	1-3	3rd	4,714	Skiverton 1

December

Sat 4	Histon	A	FAC2	3-1		2,564	Johnson 1, Jevons 1, Odubade 1
Tue 7	Kidderminster Harriers	H	Lge	2-1	2nd	4,639	Lindegaard 1, Stolcers 1
Sat 11	Grimsby Town	H	Lge	2-1	2nd	5,733	Johnson 1, Tarachulski 1
Sat 18	Leyton Orient	A	Lge	3-2	2nd	3,867	Terry 1, Tarachulski 1, Davies 1
Sun 26	Cheltenham Town	H	Lge	4-1	2nd	7,320	Terry 1, Gall 1, Jevons 1, Davies 1
Tue 28	Cambridge United	A	Lge	5-3	2nd	3,828	Way 1, Johnson 1, Stolcers 1, Jevons 2

January

Sat 1	Swansea City	A	Lge	2-0	1st	11,225	Stolcers 1, Jevons 1
Mon 3	Shrewsbury Town	H	Lge	4-2	1st	7,250	Terry 1, Way 1, Gall 1, Caceres 1
Sat 8	Rotherham United	A	FAC3	3-0		5,397	Way 1, Stolcers 1, Jevons 1
Sat 15	Oxford United	A	Lge	1-2	1st	6,778	Guyett 1
Sat 22	Cambridge United	H	Lge	2-1	1st	6,204	Terry 1, Jevons 1
Tue 25	Rochdale	H	Lge	2-2	1st	5,180	Johnson 1, Tarachulski 1
Sat 29	Charlton Athletic	A	FAC4	2-3		22,873	Terry 1, Davies 1

February

Sat 5	Macclesfield Town	A	Lge	1-3	1st	2,471	Whitaker (o.g.)
Sat 12	Bristol Rovers	H	Lge	4-2	1st	9,153	Tarachulski 1, Jevons 3
Sat 19	Chester City	A	Lge	2-0	1st	3,072	Davies 1, Jevons 1
Tue 22	Scunthorpe United	H	Lge	4-3	1st	7,598	Johnson 1, Davies 1, Tarachulski 1, Fallon 1
Sat 26	Grimsby Town	A	Lge	1-2	1st	4,414	Davies 1

March

Tue 1	Northampton Town	A	Lge	1-1	1st	5,630	Davies 1
Sat 5	Leyton Orient	H	Lge	1-0	1st	6,545	Jevons 1
Sat 12	Darlington	A	Lge	1-2	1st	4,121	Way 1
Sat 19	Bury	H	Lge	0-1	1st	6,269	
Sat 26	Boston United	A	Lge	2-1	1st	3,069	Skiverton 2
Tue 29	Notts County	H	Lge	1-3	1st	7,221	Jevons 1

April

Sat 2	Rushden & Diamonds	A	Lge	0-2	2nd	3,726	
Sat 9	Mansfield Town	H	Lge	5-2	1st	6,471	Rose 1, Way 2, Davies 1, Jevons 1
Sat 16	Kidderminster Harriers	A	Lge	1-1	1st	4,014	Davies 1
Sat 23	Wycombe Wanderers	H	Lge	1-1	1st	7,421	Johnson 1
Sat 30	Southend United	A	Lge	1-0	1st	11,735	Jevons 1

May

Sat 7	Lincoln City	H	Lge	3-0	1st	8,855	Jevons 1, Sodje 2

Appendix 2: Appearances

Player	League	Cup*	Total
Darren Way	45	7	52
Phil Jevons	45 (1)	6	51 (1)
Lee Johnson	44	7 (1)	51 (1)
Chris Weale	37 (1)	7	44 (1)
Michael Rose	37 (4)	5 (2)	42 (6)
Paul Terry	35 (4)	6 (1)	41 (5)
Terry Skiverton	36 (2)	5	41 (2)
Kevin Gall	30 (14)	6 (2)	36 (16)
Bartosz Tarachulski	27 (15)	7 (1)	34 (16)
Andrejs Stolcers	23 (13)	6 (1)	29 (14)
Andy Lindegaard	19 (10)	4 (1)	23 (11)
Colin Miles	20 (1)	3	23 (1)
Scott Guyett	13 (5)	5	18 (5)
Liam Fontaine	15	3	18
Arron Davies	15 (7)	0 (2)	15 (9)
Gavin Williams	12 (1)	2 (1)	14 (2)
Roy O'Brien	10 (4)	2 (2)	12 (6)
Adrian Caceres	7 (14)	3 (2)	10 (16)
Kevin Amankwaah	10 (5)	0	10 (5)
Steve Collis	7	1	8
Adam Lockwood	6 (4)	1	7 (4)
Efe Sodje	6	0	6
Yemi Odubade	0 (4)	2 (1)	2 (5)
Rory Fallon	2 (4)	0	2 (4)
Stephen Reed	1 (2)	1	2 (2)
Marcus Richardson	2 (2)	0	2 (2)
Nicolas Mirza	0 (3)	1	1 (3)
Simon Weatherstone	0 (6)	0 (1)	0 (7)
Kezie Ibe	0 (3)	0	0 (3)
Marvin Brown	0 (2)	0	0 (2)
David Woozley	0 (1)	0	0 (1)
Steve Thompson	0	0	0
Dale Williams	0	0	0

*Includes the FA Cup, LDV Vans Trophy and Carling Cup
( ) – Substitute appearances

Some observations:

* With 103 starts between them, our two pint-sized midfielders provided continuity starting 89 out of 92 possible League appearances. So much for the author's pre-season concern about whether they were big enough to be combative! Almost identical records – amazing!

* Phil Jevons appeared in every League game. Not only a regular goal scorer but a fit ever present as well! What a great bonus and a great buy!

* Kevin Gall appeared in 44 League games including 14 as a substitute when his pace could be effective.

* Bartosz Tarachulski appeared in 42 of the 46 League games but 15 were as a substitute. Given his goal scoring record, should he have started more?

* In contrast to the consistency in midfield and up front, only two outfield defenders appeared in more than 23 games! Did injuries prevent us from ever establishing a preferred back four?

* Three of our 'prospect' signings Mirza, Odubade and Ibe got just three starts between them and none in the League.

* In contrast to previous years, Adam Lockwood's season never got going with just seven appearances.

Appendix 3: Goalscorers

Player	League	Cup	Total
Phil Jevons	27	2	29
Bartosz Tarachulski	10	3	13
Lee Johnson	7	4	11
Arron Davies	8	1	9
Darren Way	7	2	9
Paul Terry	6	1	7
Andrejs Stolcers	5	2	7
Terry Skiverton	4	0	4
Adrian Caceres	3	1	4
Kevin Gall	3	0	3
Efe Sodje	2	0	2
Gavin Williams	2	0	2
Scott Guyett	2	0	2
Rory Fallon	1	0	1
Andy Lindegaard	1	0	1
Yemi Odubade	0	1	1
Colin Miles	0	1	1

Some observations:

* We were Champions because our two new strikers were an effective strike force and scored 37 League goals between them – at least the author was correct with this prediction!

* And because our midfield scored goals for fun with 33 League goals coming from Johnson, Davies, Way, Terry and Stolcers.

* A special mention to Arron Davies with nine goals from 24 appearances, nine of which were as a substitute. Not bad for a midfielder.

* Kevin Gall's pace made a lot of goals but he still looks short of confidence near the goal with just three strikes from 52 appearances.

* Terry Skiverton chipped in with his usual few goals, but only one goal between Lockwood and Miles.

Appendix 4. End of Month League 2 Tables

31 August 2004

	Team	Pld	W	D	L	F	A	GD	Pts
1	Scunthorpe United	6	4	2	0	13	6	7	14
2	Bristol Rovers	6	4	2	0	9	4	5	14
3	Wycombe Wanderers	6	4	1	1	9	5	4	13
4	Bury	6	3	2	1	14	9	5	11
5	Macclesfield Town	6	3	2	1	10	7	3	11
6	Oxford United	6	3	2	1	5	2	3	11
7	Swansea City	6	3	1	2	5	4	1	10
8	**Yeovil Town**	**6**	**3**	**1**	**2**	**10**	**10**	**0**	**10**
9	Mansfield Town	6	3	0	3	9	7	2	9
10	Leyton Orient	6	2	3	1	8	8	0	9
11	Darlington	6	2	2	2	6	4	2	8
12	Boston United	6	2	2	2	6	6	0	8
13	Rushden & Diamonds	6	2	2	2	5	5	0	8
14	Northampton Town	6	2	2	2	6	7	-1	8
15	Grimsby Town	6	2	1	3	8	6	2	7
16	Cheltenham Town	6	2	1	3	5	7	-2	7
17	Shrewsbury Town	6	2	0	4	5	6	-1	6
18	Cambridge United	6	1	3	2	4	5	-1	6
19	Rochdale	6	2	0	4	7	10	-3	6
20	Notts County	6	1	2	3	5	7	-2	5
21	Southend United	6	1	2	3	4	8	-4	5
22	Kidderminster Harriers	6	1	2	3	2	8	-6	5
23	Lincoln City	6	1	1	4	6	10	-4	4
24	Chester City	6	0	2	4	3	13	-10	2

30 September 2004

	Team	Pld	W	D	L	F	A	GD	Pts
1	**Yeovil Town**	**10**	**6**	**2**	**2**	**20**	**13**	**7**	**20**
2	Scunthorpe United	10	5	4	1	16	9	7	19
3	Swansea City	10	6	1	3	10	5	5	19
4	Wycombe Wanderers	10	5	3	2	13	9	4	18
5	Mansfield Town	10	5	2	3	17	11	6	17
6	Macclesfield Town	10	5	2	3	14	10	4	17
7	Bristol Rovers	10	4	4	2	12	10	2	16
8	Leyton Orient	10	4	4	2	14	13	1	16
9	Oxford United	10	4	4	2	10	10	0	16
10	Boston United	10	3	5	2	12	11	1	14
11	Southend United	10	4	2	4	12	12	0	14
12	Grimsby Town	10	4	1	5	13	10	3	13
13	Northampton Town	10	3	4	3	10	13	-3	13
14	Bury	10	3	3	4	17	16	1	12
15	Rushden & Diamonds	10	3	3	4	7	10	-3	12
16	Darlington	10	2	5	3	8	7	1	11
17	Notts County	10	2	4	4	9	9	0	10
18	Lincoln City	10	2	4	4	10	13	-3	10
19	Cheltenham Town	10	2	4	4	7	10	-3	10
20	Rochdale	10	3	1	6	9	15	-6	10
21	Chester City	10	2	4	4	7	15	-8	10
22	Shrewsbury Town	10	2	3	5	10	12	-2	9
23	Cambridge United	10	1	5	4	7	11	-4	8
24	Kidderminster Harriers	10	2	2	6	4	14	-10	8

31 October 2004

	Team	Pld	W	D	L	F	A	GD	Pts
1	Scunthorpe United	16	8	5	3	26	17	9	29
2	Leyton Orient	16	7	6	3	26	21	5	27
3	Swansea City	15	8	3	4	16	11	5	27
4	**Yeovil Town**	**16**	**7**	**4**	**5**	**29**	**22**	**7**	**25**
5	Bristol Rovers	16	6	7	3	20	15	5	25
6	Macclesfield Town	16	7	3	6	20	19	1	24
7	Southend United	16	7	3	6	23	24	-1	24
8	Mansfield Town	16	6	5	5	23	18	5	23
9	Northampton Town	16	6	5	5	19	18	1	23
10	Bury	16	5	7	4	24	21	3	22
11	Boston United	16	5	7	4	21	19	2	22
12	Darlington	15	5	6	4	17	11	6	21
13	Lincoln City	16	5	6	5	21	20	1	21
14	Rushden & Diamonds	16	5	6	5	15	14	1	21
15	Cheltenham Town	16	5	6	5	14	14	0	21
16	Wycombe Wanderers	16	5	6	5	16	17	-1	21
17	Chester City	16	5	6	5	15	21	-6	21
18	Grimsby Town	16	5	5	6	18	15	3	20
19	Oxford United	16	5	4	7	12	17	-5	19
20	Rochdale	16	5	3	8	17	24	-7	18
21	Notts County	16	4	5	7	17	22	-5	17
22	Shrewsbury Town	16	3	6	7	15	20	-5	15
23	Cambridge United	16	2	7	7	11	17	-6	13
24	Kidderminster Harriers	16	3	3	10	8	26	-18	12

30 November 2004

	Team	Pld	W	D	L	F	A	GD	Pts
1	Scunthorpe United	19	11	5	3	34	18	16	38
2	Swansea City	19	10	3	6	20	17	3	33
3	**Yeovil Town**	**19**	**9**	**4**	**6**	**34**	**26**	**8**	**31**
4	Leyton Orient	19	8	7	4	29	24	5	31
5	Lincoln City	19	8	6	5	30	23	7	30
6	Macclesfield Town	19	9	3	7	23	21	2	30
7	Bury	19	7	7	5	28	23	5	28
8	Southend United	19	8	4	7	29	28	1	28
9	Darlington	19	7	6	6	22	17	5	27
10	Northampton Town	19	7	6	6	24	22	2	27
11	Cheltenham Town	19	7	6	6	17	16	1	27
12	Wycombe Wanderers	19	7	6	6	19	19	0	27
13	Rochdale	19	8	3	8	22	25	-3	27
14	Boston United	19	6	8	5	25	21	4	26
15	Bristol Rovers	19	6	7	6	20	20	0	25
16	Mansfield Town	19	6	6	7	23	20	3	24
17	Grimsby Town	19	6	6	7	21	19	2	24
18	Notts County	19	6	5	8	22	24	-2	23
19	Chester City	19	5	8	6	18	26	-8	23
20	Oxford United	19	6	4	9	15	23	-8	22
21	Rushden & Diamonds	19	5	6	8	17	21	-4	21
22	Shrewsbury Town	19	4	6	9	18	26	-8	18
23	Cambridge United	19	3	7	9	16	22	-6	16
24	Kidderminster Harriers	19	3	3	13	9	34	-25	12

31 December 2004

	Team	Pld	W	D	L	F	A	GD	Pts
1	Scunthorpe United	24	14	7	3	41	21	20	49
2	**Yeovil Town**	**24**	**14**	**4**	**6**	**50**	**34**	**16**	**46**
3	Swansea City	24	14	3	7	33	20	13	45
4	Southend United	24	11	5	8	34	31	3	38
5	Macclesfield Town	24	11	5	8	28	26	2	38
6	Northampton Town	23	10	7	6	32	25	7	37
7	Rochdale	24	10	5	9	30	29	1	35
8	Leyton Orient	24	8	10	6	36	35	1	34
9	Wycombe Wanderers	24	9	7	8	24	24	0	34
10	Darlington	24	9	6	9	28	28	0	33
11	Cheltenham Town	24	8	9	7	22	22	0	33
12	Lincoln City	23	8	8	7	31	26	5	32
13	Boston United	23	8	8	7	31	27	4	32
14	Bristol Rovers	24	7	11	6	26	23	3	32
15	Mansfield Town	23	8	7	8	27	22	5	31
16	Bury	23	7	9	7	31	29	2	30
17	Grimsby Town	24	7	9	8	26	24	2	30
18	Oxford United	24	7	6	11	21	31	-10	27
19	Chester City	24	5	11	8	23	35	-12	26
20	Rushden & Diamonds	24	5	9	10	23	30	-7	24
21	Notts County	23	6	6	11	24	32	-8	24
22	Shrewsbury Town	23	5	7	11	23	31	-8	22
23	Kidderminster Harriers	24	5	3	16	15	44	-29	18
24	Cambridge United	23	3	8	12	22	32	-10	17

31 January 2005

	Team	Pld	W	D	L	F	A	GD	Pts
1	**Yeovil Town**	29	17	5	7	61	41	20	56
2	Swansea City	29	17	4	8	43	26	17	55
3	Scunthorpe United	29	15	8	6	45	28	17	53
4	Southend United	30	14	7	9	43	35	8	49
5	Macclesfield Town	30	14	6	10	40	33	7	48
6	Lincoln City	29	12	9	8	41	31	10	45
7	Northampton Town	28	12	8	8	38	33	5	44
8	Darlington	30	12	8	10	37	33	4	44
9	Rochdale	29	11	9	9	35	32	3	42
10	Leyton Orient	30	10	12	8	43	42	1	42
11	Boston United	29	10	11	8	39	33	6	41
12	Oxford United	30	11	8	11	32	37	-5	41
13	Wycombe Wanderers	29	10	10	9	30	30	0	40
14	Grimsby Town	29	10	9	10	37	33	4	39
15	Bristol Rovers	30	8	14	8	34	32	2	38
16	Cheltenham Town	29	9	11	9	30	30	0	38
17	Mansfield Town	29	9	10	10	31	28	3	37
18	Bury	29	8	11	10	36	35	1	35
19	Notts County	29	8	8	13	28	39	-11	32
20	Chester City	29	6	13	10	25	40	-15	31
21	Rushden & Diamonds	30	6	10	14	26	41	-15	28
22	Shrewsbury Town	29	6	9	14	27	39	-12	27
23	Kidderminster Harriers	30	7	3	20	23	56	-33	24
24	Cambridge United	30	3	11	16	25	42	-17	20

28 February 2005

	Team	Pld	W	D	L	F	A	GD	Pts
1	**Yeovil Town**	**34**	**20**	**5**	**9**	**73**	**51**	**22**	**65**
2	Scunthorpe United	35	17	9	9	53	37	16	60
3	Macclesfield Town	34	18	6	10	49	35	14	60
4	Swansea City	35	18	6	11	48	34	14	60
5	Southend United	35	17	9	9	48	37	11	60
6	Lincoln City	35	15	10	10	50	37	13	55
7	Northampton Town	33	14	10	9	44	38	6	52
8	Darlington	35	14	9	12	42	38	4	51
9	Cheltenham Town	35	13	11	11	38	33	5	50
10	Wycombe Wanderers	35	13	11	11	41	38	3	50
11	Leyton Orient	35	12	13	10	49	49	0	49
12	Mansfield Town	35	12	11	12	37	34	3	47
13	Boston United	34	11	13	10	44	40	4	46
14	Grimsby Town	34	12	10	12	40	38	2	46
15	Rochdale	33	12	10	11	39	39	0	46
16	Oxford United	34	12	8	14	35	44	-9	44
17	Bristol Rovers	35	9	16	10	42	40	2	43
18	Shrewsbury Town	35	10	10	15	41	43	-2	40
19	Notts County	34	10	10	14	33	43	-10	40
20	Bury	35	8	13	14	38	44	-6	37
21	Chester City	35	8	13	14	29	52	-23	37
22	Rushden & Diamonds	35	7	12	16	32	47	-15	33
23	Cambridge United	35	5	12	18	31	48	-17	27
24	Kidderminster Harriers	35	7	5	23	28	65	-37	26

31 March 2005

	Team	Pld	W	D	L	F	A	GD	Pts
1	**Yeovil Town**	**40**	**22**	**6**	**12**	**79**	**59**	**20**	**72**
2	Southend United	40	20	11	9	59	40	19	71
3	Scunthorpe United	40	19	11	10	59	41	18	68
4	Swansea City	40	20	8	12	56	40	16	68
5	Macclesfield Town	39	20	7	12	54	40	14	67
6	Lincoln City	40	18	11	11	61	42	19	65
7	Northampton Town	40	17	12	11	53	45	8	63
8	Darlington	40	17	10	13	49	44	5	61
9	Wycombe Wanderers	40	15	12	13	50	46	4	57
10	Rochdale	40	14	14	12	45	45	0	56
11	Mansfield Town	40	13	14	13	46	43	3	53
12	Cheltenham Town	40	14	11	15	43	45	-2	53
13	Oxford United	39	14	10	15	44	50	-6	52
14	Boston United	40	12	15	13	51	47	4	51
15	Grimsby Town	40	13	12	15	44	46	-2	51
16	Leyton Orient	40	12	15	13	55	59	-4	51
17	Bristol Rovers	40	10	20	10	52	49	3	50
18	Bury	40	11	14	15	46	49	-3	47
19	Notts County	40	12	10	18	41	56	-15	46
20	Chester City	40	10	15	15	38	61	-23	45
21	Shrewsbury Town	40	10	12	18	42	49	-7	42
22	Rushden & Diamonds	40	8	14	18	36	54	-18	38
23	Kidderminster Harriers	40	10	6	24	35	69	-34	36
24	Cambridge United	40	6	14	20	35	54	-19	32

30 April 2005

	Team	Pld	W	D	L	F	A	GD	Pts
1	**Yeovil Town**	45	24	8	13	87	65	22	80
2	Scunthorpe United	45	22	13	10	69	42	27	79
3	Southend United	45	22	11	12	64	45	19	77
4	Swansea City	45	23	8	14	61	43	18	77
5	Lincoln City	45	20	12	13	64	44	20	72
6	Macclesfield Town	45	21	9	15	59	49	10	72
7	Northampton Town	45	19	12	14	59	51	8	69
8	Darlington	45	19	12	14	54	48	6	69
9	Wycombe Wanderers	45	17	14	14	58	51	7	65
10	Rochdale	45	16	17	12	53	47	6	65
11	Mansfield Town	45	15	15	15	55	54	1	60
12	Cheltenham Town	45	16	12	17	50	51	-1	60
13	Leyton Orient	45	15	15	15	63	66	-3	60
14	Oxford United	45	16	11	18	50	62	-12	59
15	Bury	45	14	16	15	54	53	1	58
16	Boston United	45	14	15	16	61	57	4	57
17	Bristol Rovers	45	12	21	12	59	57	2	57
18	Grimsby Town	45	13	16	16	46	50	-4	55
19	Notts County	45	13	12	20	46	62	-16	51
20	Chester City	45	11	16	18	42	69	-27	49
21	Shrewsbury Town	45	11	15	19	48	53	-5	48
22	Rushden & Diamonds	45	10	14	21	42	62	-20	44
23	Cambridge United	45	8	15	22	39	62	-23	39
24	Kidderminster Harriers	45	10	9	26	38	78	-40	39

End of Season League 2 Table, 7 May 2005

	Team	Pld	W	D	L	F	A	GD	Pts
1	**Yeovil Town**	46	25	8	13	90	65	25	83
2	Scunthorpe United	46	22	14	10	69	42	27	80
3	Swansea City	46	24	8	14	62	43	19	80
4	Southend United	46	22	12	12	65	46	19	78
5	Macclesfield Town	46	22	9	15	60	49	11	75
6	Lincoln City	46	20	12	14	64	47	17	72
7	Northampton Town	46	20	12	14	62	51	11	72
8	Darlington	46	20	12	14	57	49	8	72
9	Rochdale	46	16	18	12	54	48	6	66
10	Wycombe Wanderers	46	17	14	15	58	52	6	65
11	Leyton Orient	46	16	15	15	65	67	-2	63
12	Bristol Rovers	46	13	21	12	60	57	3	60
13	Mansfield Town	46	15	15	16	56	56	0	60
14	Cheltenham Town	46	16	12	18	51	54	-3	60
15	Oxford United	46	16	11	19	50	63	-13	59
16	Boston United	46	14	16	16	62	58	4	58
17	Bury	46	14	16	16	54	54	0	58
18	Grimsby Town	46	13	17	16	47	51	-4	56
19	Notts County	46	13	13	20	46	62	-16	52
20	Chester City	46	12	16	18	43	69	-26	52
21	Shrewsbury Town	46	11	16	19	48	53	-5	49
22	Rushden & Diamonds	46	10	14	22	42	63	-21	44
23	Cambridge United	46	8	16	22	39	62	-23	40
24	Kidderminster Harriers	46	10	9	27	38	81	-43	39

If you are interested in purchasing other books published by Tempus, or in case you have difficulty finding any Tempus books in your local bookshop, you can also place orders directly through our website

www.tempus-publishing.com